W9-BGW-601

American Presidents

And First Ladies

Volume III

by

Richard L. McElroy

With Illustrations by Nikhil Patel

Psalm 139

To Joan & Frank —
Good reading &
All Best Wishes —
R. L. McElroy
Psalm 139
6-20-2003

Copyright © 2001 Gillilan Enterprises

All rights reserved.
No part of this book may be reproduced in any form
without the permission of Gillilan Enterprises,
2020 Ninth Street S.W., Canton, Ohio 44706, U.S.A.

Printed in the United States of America.

ISBN   0-9713554-0-1 (Hard Cover Edition)
ISBN   0-9713554-1-X (Soft Cover Edition)

Dedication

This book is dedicated to my lovely wife Pamela. Her patience, understanding, encouragement, interest and constructive eye for criticism made this work possible. A team player since 1967, she continues to be the object of my love and affection.

Acknowledgments

I would like to extend my sincere appreciation to a number of people who contributed to the making of this book: the producers and crew of the Peabody Award winning *American Presidents* series televised on C-SPAN, in particularly Susan Swain, Paul Brown, Brian Lamb and Maura Pierce; historian/authors Roger Bridges, Richard Norton Smith, George Knepper, Gary Brown, Jim Nash, Dr. Jack Fisher, Rob Rupp, H. W. "Skip" Hensel, Judge William Moody, William Armstrong, Karl Harsh, Ken Davison, and Allen Peskin; former students Andrea D'Orazio, Dan Doty, Jennifer Poulton and Kristi Price; staff members Mary Regula, Craig Schermer, Mary Rhodes and Cindy Lazor at the First Ladies Library in Canton, Ohio; Joyce Yut, Rose Anderson, Jennifer Souers, Bud Weber, Jan Whitacre, Amber Zwick, Jo Wilson, Homer Hoffman, Sam Vasbinder, Carol Hayes, Jerry Sandifer, Cindy Sober, Jan Kotila and Rita Zwick, all of the Stark County Historical Society; Gordon Johnroe, Tucker Eskrew and William Griffin of the White House Press Office; the fine staff of the Stark County District Library and the Bellaire, Michigan, Public Library; friends and colleagues Tom Hayes, Dave Burtscher, Jerome Nist, Keith Long, Dawn Campanelli, Keith Gillilan, Carolyn and Jack Hunter, Ohio Governor Bob Taft, George and Thomas Cleveland (grandsons of President Grover Cleveland), Paul Keller, Bill Wyss, Gary Blass, Homer Hoffman, Kurt Topham, Jim Ewing, Ed Hogan, Reverend Bruce Boak, State Senator Scott Oelslager, Frank and Pat Moore, Rachael Knisely and Nikhil Patel. Lastly, but certainly not least, I wish to offer my deepest gratitude to Reverend Douglas Patton of John Knox Presbyterian Church in North Canton who not only put this work to type, but suggested many constructive ideas and took a great deal of time to ensure a good job. Without his help this book would have been an impossibility.

Presidents of the United States

President	Place and Year of Birth		Political Party	Term of Office
1. George Washington	Virginia	1732	Federalist	1789-1797
2. John Adams	Massachusetts	1735	Federalist	1797-1801
3. Thomas Jefferson	Virginia	1743	Dem-Republican	1801-1809
4. James Madison	Virginia	1751	Dem-Republican	1809-1817
5. James Monroe	Virginia	1758	Dem-Republican	1817-1825
6. John Quincy Adams	Massachusetts	1767	Dem-Republican	1825-1829
7. Andrew Jackson	South Carolina	1767	Democrat	1829-1837
8. Martin Van Buren	New York	1782	Democrat	1837-1841
9. William Henry Harrison	Virginia	1773	Whig	1841
10. John Tyler	Virginia	1790	Whig	1841-1845
11. James K. Polk	North Carolina	1767	Democrat	1845-1849
12. Zachary Taylor	Virginia	1784	Whig	1849-1850
13. Millard Fillmore	New York	1800	Whig	1850-1853
14. Franklin Pierce	New Hampshire	1804	Democrat	1853-1857
15. James Buchanan	Pennsylvania	1791	Democrat	1857-1861
16. Abraham Lincoln	Kentucky	1809	Republican	1861-1865
17. Andrew Johnson	North Carolina	1808	Democrat	1865-1869
18. Ulysses S. Grant	Ohio	1822	Republican	1869-1877
19. Rutherford B. Hayes	Ohio	1822	Republican	1877-1881
20. James A. Garfield	Ohio	1831	Republican	1881
21. Chester A. Arthur	Vermont	1829	Republican	1881-1885
22. Grover Cleveland	New Jersey	1837	Democrat	1885-1889
23. Benjamin Harrison	Ohio	1833	Republican	1889-1893
24. Grover Cleveland	New Jersey	1837	Democrat	1893-1897
25. William McKinley	Ohio	1843	Republican	1897-1901
26. Theodore Roosevelt	New York	1858	Republican	1901-1909
27. William Howard Taft	Ohio	1857	Republican	1909-1913
28. Woodrow Wilson	Virginia	1856	Democrat	1913-1921
29. Warren G. Harding	Ohio	1865	Republican	1921-1923
30. Calvin Coolidge	Vermont	1872	Republican	1923-1929
31. Herbert Hoover	Iowa	1874	Republican	1929-1933
32. Franklin D. Roosevelt	New York	1882	Democrat	1933-1945
33. Harry S Truman	Missouri	1884	Democrat	1945-1953
34. Dwight D. Eisenhower	Texas	1890	Republican	1953-1961
35. John F. Kennedy	Massachusetts	1917	Democrat	1961-1963
36. Lyndon B. Johnson	Texas	1908	Democrat	1963-1969
37. Richard M. Nixon	California	1913	Republican	1969-1974
38. Gerald R. Ford	Nebraska	1913	Republican	1974-1977
39. Jimmy Carter	Georgia	1924	Democrat	1977-1981
40. Ronald Reagan	Illinois	1911	Republican	1981-1989
41. George H. W. Bush	Massachusetts	1922	Republican	1989-1993
42. William J. Clinton	Arkansas	1946	Democrat	1993-2001
43. George W. Bush	Connecticut	1946	Republican	2001-

Anecdotes on the Presidents

No Carving For Cal

Gutzon Borglum was a maker of Presidents. He carved four of them into the side of Mt. Rushmore. The great sculptor, however, had a low opinion of the somber, non-talkative Calvin Coolidge. Said Borglum, "If you put a rose in his hand it would wilt."

Contributing in Other Ways

Theodore Roosevelt's request to command troops during World War I was denied by President Wilson. Teddy was too old at the time, but his four sons did serve in the war. Two of them were wounded, and another, Quentin, was killed over the skies of France while on a mission. Theodore Jr., incidentally, died in 1944 during the D-Day invasion in Normandy and was posthumously awarded the Congressional Medal of Honor.

Chester the Patriot

Chester Arthur was probably the first President sworn into office with a *Bible* printed in the United States. Records from the Office of the Clerk of the Supreme Court show that up to Arthur's swearing in, all of the *Bibles* used had been printed in England, most of them published in London or Oxford University. When Arthur was sworn in on September 20, 1881, the *Bible* used was printed in Philadelphia by J.B. Lippincott.

By George, This is Confusing!

In the 1800s it was a popular practice to name sons after the founding father of our nation. In fact, during Grover Cleveland's administration there were eight Congressmen with the given name of George Washington serving in the fifty-third Congress (three of them from Ohio). In addition, 30 states have towns simply named "Washington," and all the states have Washington as part of their names for towns, counties, etc.

Try Elsewhere

Unlike many of his successors, George Washington frowned upon nepotism. He doled out government appointments to those he felt were best qualified. His nephew, Bushrod Washington, a young lawyer, requested a post as federal district attorney for Virginia. Uncle denied the request.

Workaholic

James K. Polk worked so hard as President, he didn't even take time to read newspapers. He gave that job to his wife. Polk rarely took a day off from work, and after two years in office, he traveled no further than three miles from the White House.

Give Me Room!

Being a man of huge proportions, William Howard Taft found it rather inconvenient in accepting Japanese hospitality while he was Secretary of War. In trying to achieve a squatting position at dinner with Japanese officials, a padded stool was provided, less he lay sprawled on the floor. In Kyoto, he could not be transported until some rickshaw men found a double-seater. Everywhere he visited, Taft attracted large gatherings of curious Japanese.

Wrong Profession

President Kennedy was aware that Senator Barry Goldwater might be the Republican candidate for President in 1964, but they still remained friends. Goldwater was also an amateur photographer and once took a snapshot of Kennedy. He sent it to the White House requesting an autograph. Back it came with this inscription: "For Barry Goldwater, whom I urge to follow the career for which he has shown so much talent – photography. From your friend, John Kennedy."

Decision Reversed

When, in 1852, some of Franklin Pierce's political friends approached him on the subject of running for President, he said such an idea was "utterly repugnant to my tastes and wishes." The Democrats at their convention had voted forty-eight times and still could not come up with a nominee. Pierce was nominated on the next ballot as a compromise candidate. He accepted his party's endorsement and was elected by a large majority in the fall.

THE PROFESSOR'S PROMISE

While serving as president of Princeton University, Woodrow Wilson was once questioned by a worried mother who wanted to be certain that Princeton was the best place to send her son. After politely listening to the woman's lengthy comments, Wilson replied, "Madam, we guarantee satisfaction or you will get your son back."

CAUGHT IN THE ACT

Calvin Coolidge had been President just a few days and still resided in a third-floor suite at the Willard Hotel. Very early one morning he saw a burglar going through his clothes. As the young thief lifted Coolidge's wallet and other valuables, the President awoke and said, "I wish you wouldn't do that...I don't mean the watch and chain, only the charm. Read what is engraved on the back of it." The burglar read the engraving and then realized his victim was the President of the United States. Coolidge talked with the young man and learned that he and his college roommate were unable to pay their hotel bill or buy a train ticket back to school. The surprised burglar handed back all of the articles whereupon Coolidge counted out $32, giving it to him and explaining that it was a loan. He then advised the culprit to leave so he would not be arrested by the Secret Service. The man later sent Coolidge the money, repaying him in full.

THE FINAL WORD

A reporter was pestering President Grover Cleveland to make a statement on a major issue of foreign policy. Cleveland listened patiently without saying a word, then finally retorted, "That, sir, is a matter of too great importance to discuss in a five-minute interview – now rapidly drawing to its close."

WIGGLING HIS WAY INTO WASHINGTON

At a White House dinner hosted by President Cleveland, a young European attaché was served a salad which included a worm. He was about to speak in protest when he caught First Lady Frances Cleveland's eye fixed on him in a glaring stare. The attaché decided not to make his predicament an issue and proceeded to eat the salad, worm and all. Mrs. Cleveland smiled and said, "You will go far, young man." Fifteen years that same officer returned to Washington as an ambassador.

DOWN HOME COOKIN!

Before moving into the White House in 1977, Rosalynn Carter was anxious to discover whether the chef there could cook the kind of meals the Carters enjoyed at their home in Georgia. "Yes ma'am," said the chef. "We've been fixing that kind of food for the servants for a long time."

HE ENVIED ROOSTERS

President and Mrs. Coolidge visited a government farm and were taken on separate tours. At the chicken pens Mrs. Coolidge paused to ask the overseer whether the roosters mated more than once a day. "Dozens of times," said the man. "Tell that to the President," requested the First Lady. Coolidge came past the pens a short while later and was told about his wife's inquiry. "Same hen every time?" he asked. "Oh, no, a different one each time," said the overseer. The President nodded and remarked, "Tell *that* to Mrs. Coolidge!"

FANNY'S FAT FANNY FAILS TO FOOL FRANKLIN

Fanny Hurst was a well-known novelist and friend of Franklin D. Roosevelt. She wanted to surprise the President with a change in her appearance, having lost weight while on a diet. She slipped into FDR's White House office unannounced. The President looked up as she entered, then gestured for her to turn around in front of him. When she completed the turn, FDR remarked, "The Hurst may have changed, but it's the same old fanny."

A PRACTICE IN HUMILITY

U.S. Grant was walking on his way to a reception in his honor. It was pouring rain, and Grant offered a stranger the shelter of his umbrella. The stranger was also headed for the reception, but confided he was only going to get a personal glimpse of Grant, having never seen him. He commented, "Between us, I have always thought that Grant was a very much overrated man." Grant replied, "That's my view also."

A Far Distant Choice

In 1845 President Polk appointed James Buchanan as Secretary of State. Ex-President Andrew Jackson made a strong protest. "But you yourself appointed him minister to Russia in your first term," said Polk defensively. "Yes, I did," said Jackson. "It was as far as I could send him out of my sight, and where he could do the least harm. I would have sent him to the North Pole if we had kept a minister there."

If He Had Only Known

During the Revolutionary War an officer in civilian clothes rode past a group of soldiers busily repairing some fortifications near their trenches. Their commander was shouting orders, but made no effort to help his men. The visitor asked why, and the man replied arrogantly, "Sir, I am a corporal!" The stranger apologized, dismounted, and proceeded to help the exhausted soldiers himself. When the job was completed he turned to the officer and said, "Mr. Corporal, next time you have a job like this and not enough men to do it, go to your commander-in-chief and I will come and help you again." Too late, the corporal recognized he was talking to George Washington.

Mighty Sick

In addition to daily enemas, numerous doses of castor oil, and several home remedies, doctors realized they could not save President William Henry Harrison's life. As the patient grew weaker, the doctors bled several pints of blood from him, blistered his right side, and even forced him to drink a cup of crude oil mixed with snakeweed. Harrison was dying from a combination of pneumonia, hepatitis, diarrhea and dehydration. Physicians did their worst, and Harrison, despite coughing violently, insisted interviewing many of the thousands of office seekers who came to the White House.

Not Suited for the Navy

Throughout the Mexican War General Zachary Taylor almost never dressed in his army uniform. He wore a ruffled shirt, a straw hat, and baggy pants. This drew criticism from other high-ranking officers, but Taylor's men loved him for his informality. Once, however, he was to meet with naval officers from a squadron near the mouth of the Rio Grande. The Flag Officer, knowing of Taylor's casual style, dressed in civilian clothes. Taylor, on the other hand, got his uniform out, cleaned it, and polished his boots to properly receive the Navy. The meeting proved somewhat strained and embarrassing to both officers, but the U.S. military enjoyed a good laugh over the incident.

The Party's Over

Chester Arthur opened the White House on New Year's Day in 1883 to greet the public and foreign diplomats as well. While he stood receiving guests he heard a commotion. Shocking news was brought to him that the Minister from the Hawaiian Islands had suddenly dropped dead in a cloakroom. The festivities were ended at once.

Not That Horse, of Course

Early in the Revolutionary War George Washington sent one of his officers into the Virginia countryside to requisition horses from local landowners. Calling at an old country mansion, the officer was met by an elderly widow. "Madam, I have come to claim your horses in the name of the government," he said. "On whose orders?" demanded the woman. "On the orders of George Washington, commander-in-chief of the American army," replied the officer. The old lady smiled and said, "You go back and tell General Washington that his mother says he cannot have her horse."

Morning Glory

Ronald Reagan was accustomed to getting plenty of sleep, even in his days as Governor of California. After he was elected President in 1980, Reagan didn't plan on changing his lifestyle. Stu Spencer informed him that he would have to get up at 7:30 each morning to be briefed by a member of the National Security Council. "Well," said Reagan, "he's going to have a helluva long wait." The briefings were moved to 9:30 A.M.

Breaking Tradition

The first female Chief of Protocol of the White House was appointed by Gerald Ford. His choice was former child star Shirley Temple, who had also served as Ambassador to Ghana. Ford asked her if she wished to be referred to as Madam Ambassador. Shirley replied that Ambassador would be fine, but never Ambassadress, "which sounds more like something a person would be weaving."

Too Much Noise

During the battle of Shiloh in 1862 U.S. Grant was injured when his horse slipped in the mud and fell on him. With a badly swollen ankle, he sat under a tree to sleep. A torrential rain exposed his Union soldiers, but Grant preferred to be with his men along the river bank. But, his pain was so intense he couldn't sleep and sometime after midnight, moved into a log house which was being used as a makeshift hospital. Wounded troops were brought in and surgeons amputated arms and legs of soldiers throughout the night. Their screams of agony prevented Grant from getting any rest. He remarked, "The night was more unendurable than encountering the enemy's fire, and I returned to my tree in the rain."

No Money

Though John F. Kennedy was a millionaire, he was often short of cash, a deficiency which often drew criticism from his father. Kennedy was celebrating his birthday at his Hyannis Port home one day with his family. He stood on the lawn of his home waiting for a helicopter to take him to the airport. He felt his empty pockets, then turned to his father and said, "I don't have a cent." Dad gave him a stack of bills and the President said, "I'll get this back to you, Dad." Joseph Kennedy muttered, "That'll be the day!"

This Man is an Island

Not many U.S. Presidents have islands named after them, but James Madison does. American sailors discovered some uncharted islands in the early 1800s when Commodore David Porter and his crew sailed around Cape Horn into the Pacific Ocean during the War of 1812. Porter named them in honor of our fourth President.

Include Me Out!

In April of 1883 President Arthur took a vacation by train through the south. By the time he had reached Georgia, the President began to feel irritable. In Orlando, Florida, he refused to attend a school picnic which had been organized in his honor. Arthur sat indignantly inside a hot, stuffy railroad car beside the picnic grounds.

Enough Broken Promises

While he was Governor of California, Ronald Reagan opposed the construction of a dam which would have flooded the scenic Round Valley. He claimed it would violate a treaty made long ago with a small Indian tribe. He said, "We've broken too damn many treaties."

Mental Anguish

A couple years after leaving the White House, John Quincy Adams wrote in his diary, "No one knows, and few conceive, the agony of mind that I suffered from the time that I was made by circumstances, and not by my volition, a candidate for the Presidency till I was dismissed from that station by failure of my re-election. They were feelings to be suppressed; and they were suppressed." But Adams returned to politics when, in 1830, he was elected to the House of Representatives, serving seventeen years.

Cover Up

Though John F. Kennedy appeared to be quite healthy, just the opposite was true. He was constantly plagued by chronic back problems, resulting from a serious injury during World War II. His alleged sun tan was no sun tan either. Kennedy suffered from Addison's Disease, a usually fatal dysfunction of the adrenal cortex. Victims of this malady have a noticeable bronzing of the skin. However, the White House issued a story that Kennedy sat under a sun lamp everyday.

Wanted: A Few Good men

Young James A. Garfield knew it would be difficult to be a politician and still remain honest. As a minister of the Disciples of Christ, he tried to convince the church elders that he could keep the faith even in the field of politics. He told them, "I believe that I can enter politics and maintain my integrity, for there is far more need for manly men in politics than in preaching."

DOLLARS DRENCHED

In 1937 President Roosevelt attended the wedding of his son, Franklin Jr., and Ethel du Pont, whose father had spent millions trying to prevent FDR getting elected. The reception was held in the vast du Pont garden and was attended by hundreds of the social elite. A sudden thunderstorm broke over the estate. The President was sitting in his wheelchair under a canopy, gazing at the sight of the thoroughly drenched du Ponts. He gave a hearty laugh and exclaimed, "This is what I call soaking the rich!"

DISEASE RIDDEN?

When Governor James A. Rhodes and President Lyndon Johnson got together in Athens, Ohio, the governor got a bit tongue tied while speaking. They were at Ohio University on May 7, 1964, to celebrate the 160th anniversary of Ohio's oldest college. With the President looking on, Rhodes used the word "heartedly" instead of saying "heartily." His next gaffe caused quite a stir when he intended to say "venerable institution," but it came out "this *venereal* institution."

"Abe-ble" Men

In 1937 the Abraham Lincoln Brigade served with distinction in the Spanish Civil War. More than 3000 American volunteers were recruited by the Communist Party in the states. These men, and a handful of women, sided with rebels against forces assisted by Mussolini and Hitler. Hundreds of the Americans are buried in Spain.

HE HAD HIS FILL

During his youth Millard Fillmore worked as an apprenticed wool carder for a tyrannical boss in Sparta, New York. He walked 100 miles to the shop and stayed for three months. Fillmore was ordered to cut wood and do other hard tasks, and more than once, threatened to fight his master. He ventured home, vowing never to return, and for the next five years worked in a tailor's shop in nearby Newhope.

REBUTTAL TO BUTT

In November of 1909 President Taft visited the Grand Canyon and insisted on riding horseback down the steep Bright Angel trail to the bottom of the canyon. Taft's aide, Archie Butt, tried to dissuade him, feeling his weight would be a handicap to both the horse and rider. Five times Butt advised his determined boss not to go, leading the frustrated Taft to admonish him, "See here, you go to hell. I will do as I damn well please sometimes."

DISPLAY OF DISPLEASURE

Mary Lincoln had a feisty spirit and was known for her unpredictable outbursts years before she became First Lady. According to residents of Springfield, Illinois, she displayed her temper on numerous occasions. It should be pointed out that some of the stories about her were exaggerations fabricated by those who disliked her. Supposedly, Mary once chased her man out of the house with a broom, yelling and screaming at him until he was safely out of danger. A more reliable story claimed she threw a bucket of water on Abe from a second story window while he tried to get in the front door. And several witnesses told of the time Lincoln left home on a Sunday morning to find some peace and quiet at his law office. Mary barged in and began a tirade. The future President took hold of his wife and pushed her out the door onto Jackson Street, shouting, "You make the house intolerable, damn you; get out of here." This was one of the few times Lincoln demonstrated any bad temper in public.

IMPORTANT GUESTS

At his home The Hermitage near Nashville, Andrew Jackson entertained many important guests. Among these were Lafayette and several past and future Presidents, including James Monroe, Martin Van Buren, James K. Polk, Franklin Pierce, and James Buchanan. Two other Americans who served as President were also guests there – Sam Houston (Texas Republic) and seven-year-old Jefferson Davis (Confederacy).

NO KNIGHT THIS NIGHT

Ex-President Ronald Reagan was seventy-eight years old when he visited Queen Elizabeth in London on June 14, 1989. He was there to be knighted. His official title, Knight Grand Cross of the Most Order of Bath, was an honorary one, designated for foreigners. Thus, Reagan remained Mr. President, not Sir Ronald.

Nice Compliment

James Monroe fared well in the eyes of Thomas Jefferson. The third President said you could turn Monroe's soul wrong side outward "and there is not a speck on it." He was even more complimentary of his successor when he spoke of Madison, "…I do not know in the world a man of purer integrity, more dispassionate, disinterested, and devoted to genuine Republicanism."

Growing Old Ungracefully

In November of 1822 Thomas Jefferson experienced a number of setbacks. He fell on the steps of his home and broke his wrist and forearm. Not yet healed, he went riding but was thrown by his horse and sustained multiple severe bruises. He rode again shortly thereafter, and this time, the horse slipped in a river, and its crippled rider got tangled in the reins and nearly drowned. Next came a fever which confined him to bed for three weeks. During this recovery, a flash flood swept away his mill dam, and he had to build it all over again. Jefferson was seventy-nine years old at the time, but lived another three and a half years.

Down And Out

John Kennedy's failure to provide air cover for Cuban freedom fighters when they landed at the Bay of Pigs guaranteed Castro's communist hold of the island-nation. Kennedy was crucified by the press and public, and his popularity reached a new low. During this controversy Kennedy waved at a friendly crowd near the White House and told Paul Fay, "By God, if they think they are going to get me to run for a second time, they're out of their minds. They can have this job when I'm finished…."

Speedy

George Bush liked to play golf in a hurry. Where it might take a foursome four hours to play eighteen holes, Bush and his partners often played in half that time. He called it "speed golf" or "cart polo." As the former President once explained, "We're not good but we're fast!"

Too Generous

The Congressional Medal of Honor is the nation's highest military award and is presented to those Americans who have demonstrated the highest form of valor under fire. Created in 1862 by Congress, President Lincoln presented it to soldiers and sailors of the Union during the Civil War. Lincoln, however, abused the special award when, in 1863, he presented 864 of them to the 27th Maine Infantry. This regiment's enlistment was about to expire, and as an inducement to keep it on active duty during a crucial period, he authorized Medals of Honor for any soldier who volunteered for another tour of duty. But in 1917 a special board removed these names, along with forty-six others, from the Medal of Honor Roll. Among the other forty-six recipients was William F. Cody, better known as "Buffalo Bill."

Special Delivery

Big news sometimes travels along strange routes. In 1844 James K. Polk learned of his election to the Presidency from the postmaster in Nashville, about thirty miles from his home. The postmaster learned of the event when he saw the message penciled on the wrapper of a mail packet from Cincinnati. He quickly rode the distance to inform Polk and become the first person to congratulate him.

Qualified

John Tyler's few months of army service was limited to the state militia – the Virginia Rifles. Though Tyler saw no combat, he did serve long enough to qualify for a veteran's bonus – 160 acres of land in what is now Sioux City, Iowa.

Want an Autograph?

The White House Greetings Office and the Special Assistant for Legislative Affairs send out as many as 1100 signatures on cards each day. At times, more than 60,000 cards a month are sent. The auto pen reproduces the President's signature, while other cards and letters have his signature printed on them. Getting a document or card actually signed by the President personally is a rarity.

Almost an Outrage

In late May of 1981, West German Chancellor Helmut Schmidt visited Ronald Reagan at the White House. After greeting him on the South Lawn, Reagan took Schmidt into the Oval Office. The German leader reached in his pocket and pulled out a small box. He then poured some of the contents onto his wrist and loudly snorted it. Reagan tried to maintain his composure, and after a lengthy meeting told an aide, "My God, I thought this guy was snorting cocaine right in my office." The President's fears were relieved when he was informed that Schmidt was indulging in an old German custom – taking snuff.

Overcoming Fear

How did Theodore Roosevelt overcome fright while living in the Badlands of the Dakota Territory? He explains, "I was afraid at first, ranging from grizzly bears, to "mean" horses and gunfighters; but by acting as if I was not afraid, I gradually ceased to be afraid."

He Gave Everything

During the summer of 1849 James A. Garfield worked various jobs to earn money. He farmed, cut wood, and did carpentry work. Before returning to Chester School he spent his savings on badly needed clothes and paid back his mother. He remarked that when he went back to school in the fall, "I had absolutely only six cents in my pocket. This I threw into the church contribution box on Sunday for luck and started in."

Enough is Enough

While attending college, Jackie Kennedy once said, "Politics is in my blood." Her husband may have had some misgivings about this when he explained, "I see many politicians' wives who are just as vigorous as their husbands. This may be fine for them, but not for me. I spend my days with politicians, not my nights, too. I don't want to come home from the Senate and then have to defend my position to my wife all evening!"

ANDY'S LOVE FOR THE GAME

Andrew Johnson had his critics, but baseball fans owe him a debt of gratitude. He was the first Chief Executive to refer to baseball as the "national game." Johnson liked to play too, often watching or playing in a park behind the White House called the White Lot (where the national Christmas tree is erected each year). In an 1866 game he saw Washington defeat Richmond 102 to 87! Johnson loved the game so much he gave government clerks and the White House employees time off to watch. He had them seated in plush chairs along the first base line and after one game, invited the amateur teams to the White House. In August of 1867 he was the guest of honor at the National Ball Club dinner in Washington. When a new enclosed ballpark was built, fans were charged twenty-five cents admission. Johnson, however, got in free.

OUT-FOXED

In December of 1776 General Cornwallis sent his trunks aboard ship for England with the mistaken belief the Revolutionary War was almost over. Washington had less than 2500 men to the 8000 redcoats. But on Christmas Eve, Washington attacked the enemy at Trenton, and Cornwallis turned his soldiers to the task of cornering and capturing Washington. The British general boasted, "At last we have run down the old fox, and we will bag him in the morning." The "old fox" however, out-foxed Cornwallis, racing behind his main force, circling and defeating three British regiments at Princeton. He would also return to fight another day.

A GOOD PLAGUE?

The summer of 1793 was a rough one for President Washington. Were it not for a yellow fever epidemic, Washington's reputation may have been damaged beyond repair. His rejection of the Treaty of Alliance, and snubbing of French revolutionary Edmond Genet cost him much popularity. Republicans, led by Jefferson and Madison, were so infuriated, said John Adams, that "ten thousand people in the streets of Philadelphia, day after day, threatened to drag Washington out of his house and affect a revolution in the government, or compel it to declare war in favor of French Revolution and against England." But a deadly plague, killing 4,000 of the city's 40,000 inhabitants, dampened any spirits of rebellion.

A GENUINE GENTLEMAN

Former President William Howard Taft was staying in a Chicago hotel in 1918. A friend informed him that his political nemesis, former President Theodore Roosevelt, was also there. Threading him through the dining room amid applause, Taft walked up to Roosevelt and grasped his hand. Teddy was a bit surprised and later remarked, "Wasn't it a gracious thing for him to do?"

TEMPORARY HOUSING

President Calvin Coolidge went for a walk one day with a U.S. Senator from Missouri. On their return to the white-pillared Executive Mansion, the Senator facetiously asked Coolidge, "I wonder who lives here?" "Nobody," replied Coolidge, "They just come and go."

A CHANGE IN THINKING

At one time Herbert Hoover was convinced that honesty and efficiency appealed to all citizens, and guaranteed re-election. But after his bitter defeat by FDR and subsequent years of retirement, he wrote, "I have since learned that efficient government does not interest the people so much as dramatics."

SERIOUS HORSEPLAY

When Harry Truman's artillery battery was attacked by the Germans during World War I, his men scattered and left their positions in the battle of Muese-Argonne. Truman got his panic-stricken men reorganized and led them back to their positions. He discovered that none of his men had been injured, but six horses had been killed.

DWIGHT'S ADVICE

In his inaugural address, Dwight Eisenhower reminded his countrymen that the United States must always be ready to defend liberty. He said, "In the final choice a soldier's pack is not so heavy a burden as a prisoner's chains."

Getting Her Goat

Ronald Reagan and actress Jane Wyman had not been divorced very long when he picked up his daughter Maureen and young son Mike in his station wagon. Mike was carrying a blanket with him, and inside it was a pet goat. Taking the children over to Jane's house, he deposited all three "kids" on her doorstep and sped off back to his ranch. As soon as Jane opened the door the goat dashed into the living room and promptly deposited a load on her white carpet. The goat then spent the night tethered on the front lawn. By early morning the animal had chewed and eaten all of the flowers and shrubs. Jane called her ex-husband and issued an ultimatum which got Ronnie back to her house almost as fast as he left.

Franklin Foiled

He never knew it, but FDR got "taken in" by Russian dictator Joseph Stalin when the two leaders, along with Winston Churchill met at Yalta. You might even say the same thing happened to President Truman when he and Stalin talked at the Potsdam Conference. Some historians point out that Stalin gained the upper hand after meeting with FDR, not so much because of the territorial demands given to the Russians, but actually for another reason. This was not realized until 1946 when *Look Magazine* sent Elliot Roosevelt to the Soviet Union to interview Stalin. During the course of the interview the President's son noticed that Stalin began anticipating his remarks, reacting to questions even before the interpreter had translated any statements. As the interview progressed, Stalin continued to answer questions before Roosevelt finished asking. Young Roosevelt told a joke, and Stalin laughed before the translator concluded his remarks. Then, Elliot Roosevelt discovered all along what no other westerner knew – Stalin understood and spoke English! And at the Yalta meeting, FDR had spoken softly to Churchill numerous times while Stalin sat by, thinking the dictator knew nothing.

A View From The Top

Presidents have had something to say about their position as Chief Executive. Washington remarked at the beginning of his second term that he "felt like a culprit going to the place of his execution." John Adams said that "no man who ever held the office would congratulate a friend on obtaining it." James Buchanan observed, "The Presidency is a distinction far more glorious than the crown of any hereditary monarch in Christendom; but yet, it is a crown of thorns." Grover Cleveland called his second term "a self-inflicted penance for the good of the country." Warren Harding described the office "a hell of a job." And FDR said the Presidency is many things, but above all "a place of moral leadership."

Request Fulfilled

On his deathbed, Chester Arthur urged his son never to enter politics. The former President's request was not honored after he uttered these words on November 18, 1885, for Chester Arthur, Jr. remained an international playboy and lived a life of ease. Only later in life did he settle down to marry, but eventually divorced. He did refrain, however, from the field of politics.

Disappointed

Our thirty-first President, Herbert Hoover, realized that not everyone recognized him. Vacationing with his wife at a small resort in Canada, the former President checked in with a desk clerk at a hotel where he had made reservations. After signing the register the excited clerk asked him if he were related to FBI Director, J. Edgar Hoover. When the ex-President replied he was not, the desk clerk seemed disappointed. A moment later he asked Hoover if he was related to the Hoover family which produced the Hoover vacuum sweeper. Again the former President said, "no." The dejected clerk then commented, "Oh well, no harm done. We do get a kick, though, out of entertaining relatives of real celebrities."

Cussed Cousin

In his inaugural address in 1881, President James A. Garfield condemned the practice of polygamy in the Mormon Church. Garfield believed the only way Utah could become a state was to discontinue the Mormon habit of men having more than one wife. What the President's listeners did not realize was the fact that the founder and former leader of the Mormon Church, Brigham Young, was Garfield's cousin. Young had died in 1877, but the Mormons eventually got the message, and became a state in 1896 after stopping their tradition of multiple marriages.

Genius Jimmy

Lee Iacocca, while he was chairman of the Chrysler Corporation, once asked Jimmy Carter why he decided to run for the Presidency. Carter's response was, "As governor of Georgia, I had visits from some of the other people running for President, and they didn't seem very smart."

Watch Your Step

Political boss and U.S. Senator Roscoe Conkling of New York found it frustrating that the state of Ohio had three consecutive Presidents. One of his sneering remarks alluded to "the smell of the cow yard brought into the White House by Ohio men."

Taking A Stand

John Tyler was a President who understood politics. One of the many controversies he faced was the admission of Texas as a state. Northern abolitionists in Congress opposed adding another slave state to the Union. A newspaper reporter asked Tyler, "Do you want Texas to become part of the United States?" The shrewd Tyler responded, "Half my friends are for it. Half are against it. And I stand with my friends!"

"Larnin Too Spel"

According to a 1986 survey by *The Enquirer* magazine, only forty-five per cent of Americans interviewed could spell President Reagan's name correctly. In Boca Raton, Florida, sixty per cent of the people interviewed flunked. Another poll by the same magazine surveyed 400 children ages eight to ten and showed that fifty-five per cent of them did not want to become President. The reason cited by most of the youngsters was that it was "too much work."

A Hot Time at "Ole Miss"

Many residents living in Mississippi during the Civil War received a "warm" reception from federal troops led by Ulysses S. Grant. When the Union Army took over the University of Mississippi in Oxford, the general turned the campus into a hospital for his wounded soldiers. Before leaving the area, he ordered most of the city burned to the ground.

The Judges Are Judged

Theodore Roosevelt knew he would have difficulty with judges on the Supreme Court in getting them to support his ideas regarding the break up of monopolies and rights for the working people. The President convinced political leaders that he would use his power to see through progressive programs. He once said, "I may not know much law, but I do know that one can put the fear of God in judges."

Groucho's Suggestion

Hollywood celebrities provided a valuable service during World War II when they promoted the sale of war bonds. During a Victory Tour in Washington, D.C., Groucho Marx and First Lady Eleanor Roosevelt sat in a cab waiting for some other movie stars at the airport. Actress Charlotte Greenwood stepped off an airplane in a dress and kicked her leg high into the air. Groucho nudged the First Lady and said, "You can do that too if you make your mind up."

A Good Judge of Character

When President-elect Lincoln visited Columbus, Ohio, a young state senator by the name of James A. Garfield met him. On February 17, 1861, Garfield wrote his wife, "He (Lincoln) has raised a pair of whiskers but, notwithstanding all their beautifying effects, he is distressingly homely. But through all his awkward homeliness, there is a look of transparent, genuine goodness which at once reaches your heart and makes you trust and love him."

Last Order

On his final day in office, President Grover Cleveland in 1897 paused at the White House exit and called an usher. He told William Sinclair to remove the large portrait of himself in the Red Room and store it in the attic. Cleveland said he saw no reason to impose his image on the McKinley administration.

Tall Texan Tale

Lyndon Johnson could "stretch the truth" as well as any politician. Campaigning for Congress, he wasn't shy to mention that one of his ancestors had fought at the battle of the Alamo. A reporter decided to investigate this claim and could find no proof. Later, LBJ, knowing this might become an issue, offered another version: "What I was trying to say was that my ancestor was in a fight at the Alamo – that is, the Alamo Hotel in Eagle Pass, Texas."

"Hot Shot"

In 1774 James Madison drilled with the Orange County, Virginia, militia. He practiced target shooting with a long rifle and must have impressed himself. Madison later boasted that he "should not often miss…the bigness of a man's face at the distance of one hundred yards." By the time the Revolutionary War began, however, Madison had been elected to the Virginia Convention which approved of a substitute soldier in his place.

Forget it!

Criticism of President Ronald Reagan's poor memory was widespread by his second term. At a press conference a reporter said to him, "You said that you would resign if your memory started to go." Reagan laughed, paused, and retorted, "I don't remember saying that."

PRESIDENTIAL PORNOGRAPHY

While attending the World's Fair in Chicago, President Grover Cleveland was captivated by George Watt's painting "Love and Life." Several nude females were depicted and when the fair closed, Watts presented his painting to the White House where the President proudly displayed it. Not all were impressed – particularly many women. The Women's Christian Temperance Union, along with other morally-minded groups thought the work of art was evil and a disgrace. Cleveland gave in, and the masterpiece was removed and carried across the street to the Corcoran Gallery of Art.

PRIVATE CHEF

FDR disliked White House food so much that in 1938 he ordered a small kitchen built on the third floor. He later brought in his mother's cook, Mary Campbell, to run the small kitchen. No doubt this upset "Fluffy" Nesbitt who continued to prepare meals for the rest of the White House.

BEING BLUNT

During a meeting with his advisors, President Reagan discussed economic conditions. One of his aides proposed that a tax be the best way to solve the deficit. Reagan responded, "If that's what you believe, then what in the hell are you doing here?"

NOT-SO-FUNNY

Harry Truman's mother was a confirmed confederate. She even disapproved of her son wearing a blue military uniform. And she did not mellow in her old age. The ninety-four-year-old matriarch was invited to stay at the White House. The President thought he would play a trick on her, explaining that she would be sleeping in the Lincoln bedroom. Mother did not appreciate the gesture, and informed her son that she would sleep on the floor before she would sleep in Lincoln's bed.

LICKING A STRONG MAN

In the autumn of 1859 Abe Lincoln visited the Wisconsin State Fair in Milwaukee. Walking with a group of Republican supporters, he chatted with farmers and visited exhibits. He came to where a strong man was lifting heavy weights. The tall Lincoln flexed his muscles, looked down at the balding, short weightlifter and said, "Why I could lick salt off the top of your head."

SOMETHING FISHY HERE

In their retirement Jimmy and Rosalynn Carter shared gentle rivalries. As fishing companions, Rosalynn often landed six fish to Jimmy's one. The former President noted, "This is not good for the male ego or the marriage. To catch more fish I have to get up earlier and stay later." Carter's mother, Lillian, often told him, "You may be President, but you still haven't learned how to fish."

ENCORE

Julia Ward Howe's verses were put to the music of the 1861 tune "The John Brown Song." Three years later, the "Singing Chaplain," Bishop Charles McCabe, introduced the song in the U.S. Congress before a packed House. President Lincoln was there, too. McCabe gave a stirring rendition, and he observed, "When we came to the chorus the audience sprang to its feet and wept, and began to sing. Mr. Lincoln's voice was heard above the uproar 'Sing it again!'" And so they did, and the nation was blessed with one of its favorite patriotic pieces, "The Battle Hymn of The Republic."

PRIVATE MAN

Within the circle of his family and a few close friends, Woodrow Wilson was an out-going, humorous person. He danced jigs, sang songs, and told corny jokes. He loved the common man in the abstract, but drew back and shrank from actual contact with people, remaining aloof, somber, and formal. No one knew this better than Wilson himself. He once explained, "No man would, on account of my Scottish physiognomy, ever familiarly slap me on the back in a hail-fellow-well-met way. I should hate it."

GUN CONTROL?

Following his trial for shooting four men, including President Reagan, John Hinckley met with his bewildered parents in a mental hospital. When told there was talk of legislating a mandatory death penalty for anyone trying to kill a President, Hinckley revealed, "That wouldn't have stopped me." When asked by his father, "What would have stopped you?," the mentally-disturbed patient stated, "Maybe if I'd had to wait a while to buy a gun. If I had to fill out forms, or get a permit first, or sign in with the police, or anything complicated, I probably wouldn't have done it."

BUILDING A BASE

Ohio newspaperman David R. Locke (alias Petroleum V. Nasby) asked Lincoln if he could defeat Stephen Douglas for the U.S. Senate. Lincoln explained that he would carry Illinois in popular vote, but because of the gerrymandered districts, Douglas would be elected by the state legislature. He told Locke, "You can't overturn a pyramid, but you can undermine it; that's what I've been trying to do."

ROYALTY REJECTED

To escape the rigors of having his privacy constantly interrupted, William McKinley came up with a novel idea. The President discussed the possibility of riding in elegant isolation throughout the nation in his own luxurious private railroad car. When the press learned of this, the cartoonists had a field day, depicting Ohio's Chief Executive traveling in royal extravagance. Not wishing to damage his image as a friendly, out-going fellow, McKinley abandoned the idea.

NO JOKING MATTER

When Lynette "Squeaky" Fromm aimed a .45 caliber Army Colt pistol at Gerald Ford in Sacramento, she was quickly wrestled to the pavement, disarmed, and handcuffed by Secret Service agents. A member of the Charles Manson mass-murder clan, Fromm yelled to her captors, "It didn't go off, fellas." Later, when the pistol was examined, there were four bullets in the gun clip, but none in the firing chamber. Nevertheless, Fromm served a lengthy prison term.

MAKING WAVES WITH THE MARINES

On October 21, 1969, the Nixons held a jazz program at the White House to entertain the Shah of Iran. The President announced to his guests that after the concert there would be dancing to the "best Marine combo in the country." But someone forgot to inform Nixon that, for the first time in many years, the *Navy* band would be playing after the state dinner in the foyer.

NOT OFFENDED

Prior to the 1900 Republican convention, Theodore Roosevelt met with President McKinley to discuss the possibility of serving as a Vice Presidential running mate. Roosevelt told McKinley that he should not be on the ticket with him. Secretary of War Elihu Root, who was standing nearby, added sarcastically, "Of course not – you are not fit for it." The comment by Root must not have been too damaging because Roosevelt appointed him as Secretary of State during his second term. On Roosevelt's forty-sixth birthday, Root sent a message: "You have a very good start in life and your friends have great hopes for you when you grow up."

STILL NOT ENOUGH

When George Washington assumed his duties as our first Chief Executive, he and Martha lived in a house on Cherry Street in New York City. Later they moved into a home on Broadway and Congress provided Washington a yearly salary of $25,000, twenty-one servants (among them seven black slaves), and a coach drawn by six horses. George frequently drew his salary in advance.

NO FRIEND IN PATRICK

In 1789 James Madison was denied a seat in the newly-formed U.S. Senate. The man responsible for this was Patrick Henry, an avid Anti-Federalist who worked furiously to defeat Madison. Instead, the future President had to settle for a seat in the less-prestigious House of Representatives.

Losing with Grace

Martin Van Buren was a good loser. When William Henry Harrison defeated him in the spirited election of 1840, the incumbent Van Buren extended the olive branch. He visited Harrison at his hotel and even offered to vacate the White House early so the President-elect could move in. Van Buren would have attended his successor's inauguration too, but he wasn't invited.

How the Presidents Stack Up

As of 1987, the pages of papers in five different Presidential Libraries stacked up like this: Dwight D. Eisenhower - 16,700,000; John F. Kennedy - 26,100,000; Jimmy Carter - 17,100,000; Lyndon B. Johnson - 27,800,000; and Richard M. Nixon - 42,000,000.

I Am a Sap

Abraham Lincoln had just lost the 1858 Senate race to Stephen Douglas. Mary Lincoln offered her encouragement and predicted great things still to come for her husband. Lincoln told a young reporter, "Mary insists, however, that I am going to be Senator and President of the United States too…Just think of such a sucker as me as President."

Charm in Strange Places

In May of 1754 George Washington and his colonial militia encountered a small detachment of French and Indians at Chestnut Ridge near present-day Pittsburgh. Washington lost a few men but gained a small victory over his foe. In his report to Virginia Governor Dinwiddie, the American officer stated he was "exposed to and received all the enemy's fire…I heard the bullets whistle, and, believe me, there is something charming in the sound."

Political Response

It was charged by his opponents that Martin Van Buren was noncommittal and deceptive on almost every subject. In his autobiography, Van Buren chuckled at this accusation and included one amusing example. When asked if he thought the sun rose in the east, he answered, "I presumed the fact was according to the common impression, but, as I invariably slept until after sunrise, I could not speak from my own knowledge."

No Time for Fun

James K. Polk paid only three visits to people during his first year in the White House; his wife made no visits. They were both too busy working on governmental matters. Sarah and James both felt that receptions and visitations meant lost hours from the duties of the office. In a rare moment of spontaneity, Mrs. Polk once gave permission for a juggler to entertain after a White House dinner. The President was summoned from his desk to watch the event, and reported it "innocent in itself but time unprofitably spent."

Merry Christmas

According to the National Christmas Tree Association of Milwaukee, the first President to set up a Christmas tree in the White House was Franklin Pierce in 1856. Seven decades later, Calvin Coolidge began the tradition of lighting the first Christmas tree on the White House lawn.

Driving the Price Up

President John Kennedy once received a letter from columnist Leonard Lyons, informing him that the current price for a personally-signed Kennedy photograph commanded about sixty-five dollars. Kennedy wrote Lyons:

> Dear Leonard,
> I appreciate your letter about the market on Kennedy signatures. It is hard to believe that the going price is so high now. In order not to depress the market any further, I will not sign this letter.

PLEASE SEND A CLONE

James Buchanan was well liked while serving as ambassador to Russia in the early 1830s. When he visited the Imperial Palace to bid farewell, the Russian Czar asked Buchanan to request President Jackson to "send another minister exactly like himself."

KIDS TO CARTER

Children often see things more clearly than adults. Listed below are some letters sent to President Jimmy Carter by elementary school children, taken from Bill Adler's book *Kids' Letters to President Carter.*

Dear Mr. President
Did you always want to be President or you ever want to be a real person?
> *Victoria L.*

Hi Mr. Pres!
Do you remember me? I was one of the people who waved at you when you came to New York. Remember? I was wearing the brown jacket.
> *Your citizen,*
> *Betsy R.*

Is it lonely to be Pres. of the U.S.A.? Who do you talk to when you have a problem? When I have a problem, I talk to my best friend, Stewart.
p.s. Stewart's phone number is 001-7286. You could call him too.
> *Edward K.*

Does a President have to be smart or just a good talker?
> *Peggy K.*

NO FRIEND OF THE MEDIA

In scorning an antagonistic press, President Jimmy Carter once told reporters at a press conference that "you have my staff outnumbered ten to one." On another occasion he told a roomful of reporters, "I'm not going to say anything terribly important tonight, so you all can put away your crayons."

VISIONARY UMPIRE

As a boy, Harry Truman was usually too busy studying or practicing the piano to take part in neighborhood athletic contests. The main reason, however, that he didn't spend more time playing with his friends was his nearsightedness. Young Harry had to be content with being an umpire once in a while, or filling in as a pinch hitter in an emergency.

SOLDIER-SCHOLAR

When Eisenhower became head of Columbia University in 1948, a friend gave him a book, and the future President replied, "Thanks, I appreciate this very much and I'll try to read it. To tell you the truth, I haven't read a book in nine years."

STALKING HIS PREY

Just five months before moving to Dallas, Texas, assassin Lee Harvey Oswald lived in New Orleans. A television station there interviewed him because of his pro-Castro views. He also visited the public library quite often, where he read books on Marxism and capitalism. One book he checked out was entitled *Portrait of A President* – a book about his victim, John F. Kennedy.

I Am Not a Cow!

Western Pennsylvania in the 1790s was an unsettled and dangerous wilderness. Indians and wild animals made life adventurous but hazardous. James Buchanan, oldest of three brothers and four sisters, was born in a log cabin in Cove Gap. Buchanan's parents fitted all of the children with cow bells when sent out to play, lest they stray too far from home.

Just a Kid

William McKinley was very good at playing marbles and using a bow and arrow as a youth. He was fondest of flying kites, and often his mother's kitchen was cluttered with paper, pots, paste, and string from her son's projects. Though he disliked fishing he enjoyed swimming immensely. He did like pets, but his mother said that he could not have one. McKinley also liked going barefoot and his mother once remarked, "His shoes came off before the snow had left the ground."

Keep it Clean

President Grant did not like to hear dirty stories or off-color jokes. Once, at a White House dinner, the ladies had left the dinner table. Cigars and coffee were then brought in. One of the men said, "As there are no ladies present, I want to tell a story." Before he could begin it, Grant quietly remarked, "But there are gentlemen present." The story was not told.

Pot Luck?

In 1979 former President Richard Nixon bought a four-story Manhattan townhouse for $750,000. He comfortably settled in, but was dismayed one day when he came home and discovered a marijuana cigarette on the steps. Nixon promptly sold the apartment. The buyer was the Syrian government which paid $2,600,000 for it.

WARNING FOR WOODROW

Woodrow Wilson was informed he was too ill to take a long train trip across the nation to gather support for his League of Nations and the peace treaty ending World War I. Family, friends, and doctors told him he would break down before reaching the Rockies. Countered a weak and trembling President, "I don't care if I die the next minute after the treaty is ratified." Though he delayed his trip for three weeks, Wilson undertook his mission, and suffered a crippling stroke in Colorado.

"HUNGRY HOMBRES"

After cruising the Mississippi in 1907 with a group of governors, Theodore Roosevelt decided to visit Louisiana and go out on a bear hunt with some friends. Spending two weeks in the cane brakes, he killed a large black bear. The entire hunting party shot three bears, six deer, a dozen squirrels, one wild turkey, one opossum, a duck, and a wildcat. Roosevelt said they ate everything except the wildcat.

WAS IT GOD OR MAN?

A lot of political deals were made in the 1888 election to make Benjamin Harrison the next President. The Democrats claim of foul play and cheating at the polls actually gave Harrison the victory. Though not personally involved in any wrongdoing, the pious Harrison believed that Almighty God played a major role and proclaimed, "Providence has given us this victory." But Republican National Chairman Matt Quay disagreed, responding, "He ought to know that providence hadn't a damn thing to do with it." Harrison must have realized that Quay was right, for he owed much of his success to party bosses and wasn't even permitted to name his own cabinet.

BOY JOHNNY

Several older national leaders expressed concern about John Kennedy's age. At the 1960 Democratic Convention Lyndon Johnson cried that he "wouldn't be pushed around by a forty-three year old boy." Nevertheless, Kennedy got the nomination, then selected Johnson as his running mate. Even Harry Truman questioned Kennedy's youth and experience, and Dwight Eisenhower referred to JFK as "that boy." But Kennedy reminded his critics by pointing out that he had more experience on Capitol Hill than any other President of the twentieth century. He said he would offer the White House "strength and health and vigor."

A WARNING TO THE ROOKIES

Before leaving office Harry Truman held a welcome breakfast to the newly-elected Democrats to Congress. Truman was bitter because of his party's loss to Dwight Eisenhower. He expressed his dislike for his successor, though he did admire Eisenhower's wife, Mamie. Truman told the freshmen legislators, "Let me tell you something. Some of the newspapers are making snide remarks about Mrs. Eisenhower saying she has a drinking problem. Now it wouldn't surprise me if she did, because look what that poor woman has had to put up with." After referring to Eisenhower as a "son of a bitch," Truman advised to his guests, "But leave his family alone. If I ever hear that one of you attacked the wife or a family member of the President of the United States, I'll personally go into your district and campaign against you."

A SICK MAN

Of all the persons who have tried to shoot a President, John Hinckley was perhaps the most seriously disturbed. His emotional detachment from parents and relatives, his obsession with the movie *"Taxi Driver"* (and its stars Robert DeNiro and Jodie Foster), a severe depression following the murder of Beatles' singer John Lennon, his compulsive lying which fooled even his doctors, an addiction to therapeutic drugs, his hours on end of sitting in a chair holding his cat, and three near successes at suicide convinced most Americans that Hinckley was mentally ill. He was found "not guilty by reason of insanity" for shooting Ronald Reagan, Press Secretary James Brady, and two other men in 1981. His morbid poems and bizarre messages on tape led jurors to commit him to a mental institution. Ironically, Hinckley had no personal ill-feeling toward President Reagan. While living with his parents in Evergreen, Colorado, the twenty-five-year-old loner proudly voted for Reagan in the 1980 election. As election returns came in, Hinckley told his parents, "Maybe there's some hope for this country yet." His parents wrote a book in 1985, and royalties were donated to support research in the field of mental illness.

No Kiss

As best can be surmised, Hannah Simpson Grant never kissed her son, Ulysses. Nor did she visit the White House when her son was President. Hannah adored her children, but never worried unduly about any danger they encountered. When a neighbor rushed in to tell her that her three-year-old son was playing under the hoofs of the horses in the stable, she remarked that the boy could take care of himself.

Shedding Tears of Joy

The Fisk University Jubilee Singers made President Chester Arthur cry. Comprised of a dozen black college students, the group was often denied lodgings in many concert halls and hotels. Arthur was a strong advocate of Negro rights and invited them to the White House. They sang several melodies including the hymn, "Safe in the Arms of Jesus." Deeply touched by their rendition, Arthur was moved to tears. He felt embarrassed and apologized to the singers, explaining he had never before been guilty of such an impulsive display of his feelings.

Carter's Connections

Jimmy Carter's family tree had some wild branches. His great grandfather, Wiley Carter, barely escaped the hangman's noose after he killed a man who took one of his slaves. His grandfather, Littleberry Carter, was shot and killed during a quarrel with a business partner over a homemade merry-go-round. William Carter, Jimmy's great uncle, was killed in an argument over a desk.

Snapped At

Young Theodore Roosevelt was an avid self-taught reader who also conducted experiments in science and natural history at his East Twenty-eighth Street home in New York City. The wealthy Roosevelts had several servants, among them a laundress who threatened to quit. She once asked Theodore's parents, "How can I do the wash with a snapping turtle tied to the sink?"

Shedding Some Light on the Subject

One evening at the White House John Kennedy looked out the window while talking with a military aide. Peering curiously into the distance, he asked the aide, "Why isn't the Jefferson Memorial lit at night?" The aide replied he didn't know, but would find out. He asked several White House personnel, and they responded the same way. He then drove over to the memorial and asked the personnel there. They didn't know either. Next, a phone call was made to the Interior Department but officials there couldn't offer an explanation. The dilemma was soon remedied, and the Jefferson Memorial has been lit at night ever since.

A Joke in Bad Taste

By the time he was seventeen years old, Andrew Jackson had already squandered a modest inheritance. His drinking, gambling, and chasing women left him penniless. He moved from South Carolina to Salisbury, North Carolina, studying law and taking up dancing lessons. The wild youth decided to play a joke, and sent formal invitations to a couple of prostitutes for the dancing school's Christmas ball. Jackson never thought either would show up, and was shocked when both women, a mother and daughter team, appeared at the ball. Townspeople thought the gesture disgraceful. For the first and only time in his life, Jackson publicly apologized for his indiscretion. Reflecting back on his days of reckless behavior, Jackson commented, "I was a raw lad then, but I did my best."

Not Very Complimentary

Jimmy Carter's relationship with the Israelis during his term as President was not on the best of terms. He managed to offend several Jewish leaders with his foreign policy and various remarks. He once welcomed former Prime Minister of Israel, Golda Meir, to the Oval Office by asking whether she got back home to Chicago very often. "Milwaukee," she insisted, naming the midwestern city where she once lived and taught elementary school. Carter then told her that she was the same age as his mother – not a very tactful comment.

CUSSED CUSPIDOR

President Andrew Johnson did not see "eye to eye" with many Republicans in the post-Civil War Congress. A Southern Democrat and former slave holder, Johnson was not willing to extend voting privileges to freed slaves and granted many pardons to Confederate officers imprisoned after the war. Charles Sumner of Massachusetts, one of the Radical Republican leaders in the Senate, visited the White House and urged Johnson to at least compromise on some of his views. The President was a stubborn man and refused Sumner's pleas. Sumner was disgusted and abruptly left, but not before he picked up his hat on the floor. President Johnson, thinking the hat was a spittoon, had spit a wad of chewing tobacco in it! Needless to say, this incident did little improve relations between the two rivals.

LET ME REPHRASE THAT

In the spring of 1877, recently retired President U.S. Grant and his wife Julia went on a worldwide tour. Grant's administration was marked by scandal, and he no doubt was happy in getting away from the burdens of the White House. In England the Grants were entertained with a lavish state dinner at Windsor Castle. Following the dinner they met with Queen Victoria, but the British monarch was somewhat abrupt. She found the Grants pleasant but rather tactless. The queen, a widow since 1861, excused herself, citing her many tiring duties. Julia Grant reportedly remarked, "Yes, I can imagine them. I too have been the wife of a great ruler."

GETTING TOO HEALTHY

In the months following his recovery from a gunshot wound, President Reagan converted an upstairs White House bedroom into an exercise room. Both he and Nancy Reagan devoted themselves to rigorous workouts. A treadmill and a weight machine were installed so the First Family would not have to leave the White House. After a couple of months Reagan increased his chest size, while the biceps in his arms nearly doubled. Before long, he had to buy new suits. First Lady Nancy reminded him, "I'm proud of you but slow down. This is getting expensive!"

A BATTLE WITH PRONOUNS

Shortly before he died of throat cancer in 1885, Grant wrote his doctor, "The fact is I think I am a verb instead of a personal pronoun. A verb is anything that signifies to be, to do, or to suffer. I signify all three."

A GOOD EXCUSE

When Brian Albert, a freshman at Paul D. Schreiber High School in Port Washington, N.Y., missed classes he told his teacher he was "with President Bush." His social studies teacher, Pamela Rothman, believed him and suggested to Bush that he fill out an absence form as an example to parents. A typewritten reply came from the White House, signed by the President, read, "It's OK, he was with me." Bush added a handwritten message, "No make-up (assignment) – Brian learned a lot here!" Brian met the President when his father, sportscaster Marv Albert, interviewed Bush, a former first baseman at Yale. Souvenirs included a photo and a tie clip with the Presidential seal, but no autograph. Said Brian, "I don't collect autographs anymore."

FORGIVENESS

In 1865 President Andrew Johnson had promised to severely punish all rebel leaders, but in fact pardoned nearly all of them. A friend of his, Mrs. Lizinka Ewell, wife of Confederate general Richard Ewell, came to the White House to get her husband out of prison. Johnson listened to Mrs. Ewell's pleas and granted not only a pardon, but ordered all of her husband's confiscated property returned to him. However, he chided Mrs. Ewell for marrying "a wooden-legged traitor."

GETTING AROUND

The first incumbent President to tour the United States was George Washington. For one month, during the autumn of 1789, he journeyed throughout New England. He was accompanied by his secretary, Tobias Lear, an aide-de-camp, six servants, a coach, a luggage wagon, and a total of nine horses. Washington, however, refused to visit Vermont or Rhode Island because they had not yet joined the Union. Eighteen months later he visited all the southern states before returning to his home at Mount Vernon.

CHIEF TO CHIEF

In April of 1861 a delegation of southern Choctaw Indians visited President Lincoln. They were petitioning the federal government for a half million dollars in land claims. Tribal leaders spoke in the hope that Lincoln would grant their request. Everything went fine at the meeting until Lincoln learned that the Indians owned black slaves. Though he would consider their pleas, the President was less sympathetic. A few days later Fort Sumter was fired on by rebel forces, ending any hope of help for the Choctaws.

VOW TO TRY HARDER

President John Kennedy was a man of wit. His live press conferences twice a month became very popular. A female reporter, May Craig, once stood up and asked Kennedy, "Mr. President, do you think you're doing enough for women in the armed services?" Kennedy paused, then answered, "Miss Craig, judging from the tone of your voice, I know I'm not doing enough and I'll try to do better."

ONE THING I WON'T MISS

Though devastated over losing to Ronald Reagan in 1980, incumbent Jimmy Carter noted there were "a few positive things" about losing the race. Carter said Reagan would have to face big problems such as inflation and the Middle East, along with "inheriting Sam Donaldson and a few truculent members of the White House press corps." Reagan soon learned that it was not easy dealing with Donaldson's probing, and sometimes embarrassing, questions.

MUCH ADO ABOUT NOTHING

In 1897 President McKinley was vacationing in Hot Springs, Virginia. He decided he wanted to play a round of golf. Little did he realize the controversy from his fellow Americans, still living under the rigid codes of the Victorian Age. A couple of his advisors suggested playing golf was "too undignified," fearing it would damage the administration. Shock reverberated through the halls of Congress, and the Cabinet even debated the propriety. The *Boston Evening Record* published an article noting there was nothing wrong with a President playing golf as long as he was "shielded from curious onlookers."

QUITE A "TRIP"

While serving as an ambassador to France, Thomas Jefferson fell deeply in love with Maria Cosway who was unhappily married to a painter. Jefferson's wife had died, and the future President was attracted to Maria from the first moment he saw her. In one incident, Jefferson spotted Mrs. Cosway, jumped over a small fountain, tripped, and broke his wrist.

TWO SOUVENIRS

When William McKinley signed the Declaration of War against Spain in April of 1898, he used two pens. With one he wrote "William," then took a second pen and signed "McKinley." He presented both pens to Webb Hayes, soldier and son of our nineteenth President.

THAT'S THE LIMIT!

George Washington had little to say at the 1787 Constitutional Convention, even though he was its leader. Then one member suggested that the Constitution set a limit of 5000 men in the army. Washington could no longer remain silent, declaring, "If that is so, let the Constitution also say that no foreign army should ever invade our country with more than 3000 troops."

DOWN ON THE FARM

James Monroe had fond memories of his childhood, except for the times when he had to pluck geese. Goose-down bedding required stuffing mattresses, pillows and quilts, and goose quills were sharpened and used as pens. But first the geese had to be rounded up three or four times a year to pluck their feathers, a task James and his sister Elizabeth dreaded. The birds jumped, squawked, and bit, and the Monroe children were happy when the down-plucking ordeal was over. So were the geese.

IN THE FLOW

Lincoln had an exceptional capacity to remember both names and faces. This was demonstrated many times. One well-dressed man at the White House stated, "I presume, Mr. President, you have forgotten me." Lincoln's response was quick. "No, your name is Flood," he said. "I saw you last twelve years ago," naming the place and occasion, then cheerfully remarking, "I am glad to see that the *Flood* flows on."

CLOSE CALL

At the age of two Herbert Hoover developed a severe case of croup. Seeing no vital signs, his parents gave him up for dead, placing some pennies over his eyes and pulling a sheet over his face. His uncle, Dr. John Minthorn, rushed over to the house and, arriving in time, revived the child. Hoover contracted several more childhood diseases, but this was his closest brush with death.

TOUGH DECISION

John Tyler vetoed a bill to create a new Bank of the United States and set high tariffs. That same evening an armed mob marched on the White House grounds. Rocks were thrown through the windows and insults were shouted at the new President. Tyler issued guns to his servants and stood firm against the rabble until it dispersed. Later, he vetoed a similar bill, and this touched off more demonstrations. Mobs took to the streets in the capital and a number of other cities. Tyler was burned in effigy, and a smallpox plague sweeping the nation was named in his "honor." Still another similar congressional measure was vetoed. Tyler's cabinet resigned, the Whig Party dumped him, and impeachment resolutions were introduced in the House of Representatives. Tyler rode out the storm during his term as Chief Executive.

LEAVE IT BE!

Lincoln listened patiently to the complaints of men who had voiced their concerns about the Civil War and the economy. After everyone was finished talking, Lincoln left his critics with this parable: "Gentlemen, suppose all the property you were worth was in gold, and you had put it in the hands of Blondin (the famous tightrope walker) to carry across the Niagara River on a rope. Would you shake the cable, or keep shouting to him, 'Blondin, stand up a little straighter – Blondin, stoop a little more – go a little faster – lean a little more to the north – lean a little more to the south'? No, you would hold your breath as well as your tongue and keep your hands off until he was safe over."

DOOMED FUTURE?

Symonds Ryder was one of the leaders in the Disciple of Christ Church. When he learned that one of his ministers, James A. Garfield, was pursing a career in law and politics, he gave harsh criticism to the young man from Ohio. Father Ryder said to a friend about Garfield, "I always thought he'd go to the Devil anyhow, and if he goes to the Capitol, I am sure he will."

FRANKLIN FOOLED

In 1940 FDR invited Italian magician, The Great Giovanni, to a White House dinner party. Following the dinner, Giovanni picked Secretary Henry Morgenthau's pocket, telling the audience that any man who couldn't hold on to his wallet should not be running the Treasury Department. Giovanni next removed a pistol from the holder of a top Secret Service officer. The agent was not amused, and warned the magician he would be shot if he did it again. Roosevelt roared with laughter. Next, Giovanni threw a pack of cards into the air, and the card FDR had chosen stuck to the chandelier. Then, the magician told the President to make certain his watch was on tightly. FDR felt his wrist and discovered his watch was missing. "Hey, give it back," yelled the President. Needless to say, all the guests were greatly impressed.

CLEARED

As Collector of the Port of New York's Custom House, Chester Arthur was the overseer of the largest federal office in the nation, with more than 1000 employees. Money from the workers, and some of the funds collected for violations, ended up in the treasury of the Republican Party. President Grant had appointed Arthur to this post in 1871, but his successor, Rutherford B. Hayes, suspended Arthur seven years later in an effort to end the spoils system. An investigation did uncover some evidence of inefficiency and corruption, but Arthur's personal reputation was not damaged, and three years later he assumed office as the twenty-first President.

REWARD

In August of 1945 Edmund Love of Flint, Michigan, returned from duty in Okinawa and was assigned to the Pentagon. On his way to work one morning, he saw President Harry Truman coming, surrounded by four Secret Service agents. Unpredictably, Love stopped, came to attention, and saluted his Commander-in-Chief. Truman blinked in surprise, telling a Secret Service agent, "Take down the captain's name and address." Love gave the information then asked the agent, "What's this all about?" Truman heard him, turned around and said, "Son, I'd like you to come over for dinner someday. I've been President of the United States for almost five months now. There must be 20,000 members of the armed services stationed in this area and I see some of them every morning when I go for a walk. But you're the first s.o.b. who ever saluted me."

SALT WATER IN HIS VEINS

John Kennedy was born near the Atlantic Ocean. He loved sailing, and family outings on the water were part of his lifelong bond with the sea. As President, he observed, "It is an interesting biological fact that all of us have in our veins the exact same percentage of salt that exists in the ocean, and therefore we have salt in our blood, in our sweat, in our tears. We are tied to the ocean. And when we go back to the sea – whether to sail or to watch it – we are going back from whence we came."

NO RETREAT

To face life's difficulties one often needs to face them squarely. We are reminded of this in an incident which took place during John Kennedy's Presidential campaign of 1960. After a rousing speech in San Antonio to a large, enthusiastic crowd assembled in front of the Alamo, where a handful of Texans held off a large Mexican army, Kennedy wanted to make a quick exit. Turning to Maury Maverick, a local politician, he said, "Maury, let's get out of here. Where's the back door?" Maury replied, "Senator, if there had been a back door at the Alamo, there wouldn't have been any heroes."

HORTICULTURIST

During 1782, Thomas Jefferson kept a calendar diary he called the "Garden Book." In it he recorded the dates of the blooming of each different flower in his Monticello garden. On March 17 a narcissus burst open, followed by a jonquil, hyacinth, ranunculus, iris, nasturtium, tulip, peony, lily, hollyhock, calicanthus, crimson dwarf, and a rose. Jefferson's wife died in early September, and very few entries were made after that.

VERY PATIENT

Few of our Presidents have tried to keep the peace under the difficult and trying circumstances faced by Woodrow Wilson. Even after German U-boats repeatedly sunk U.S. ships, Wilson stated, "We are sincere friends of the German people, and earnestly desire to remain at peace with the government which speaks for them." In maintaining neutrality, Wilson fought off pressure from other European nations to get the U.S. involved. He told his friend and chief advisor, Colonel Edward House, that if France and England "wanted war with us, we would not shrink from it." The astonished House only then realized Wilson's sincerity in remaining neutral.

GET THE STORY STRAIGHT

Grant's illness in 1884 was well publicized. Newspapers reported he was frightfully thin, and losing weight daily due to cancer. Grant told Mark Twain that he stopped by a store and weighed himself on the scales. He told him, "I did not say a word. The scales balanced at 146. Well, I read six newspapers this morning. No two of them have the same figure and no one of them is right."

JOYFUL JOURNEY

In 1850 Lincoln rode in a stage coach bound from Illinois to Washington. Another passenger, a fellow Kentuckian, offered Lincoln some chewing tobacco, but the future President politely refused. Later, this same man offered him a cigar, but Lincoln said no thanks. When the man offered some brandy and a cigar, Lincoln again rejected the offer. The Kentucky man peered at Lincoln and remarked, "My observation, my experience is, among men, that those who have no vice, have damned few virtues." Convinced this man was joking, Lincoln laughed so hard he kicked out the floor of the stage coach and tore out the top of his hat by ramming his hand through it. The two men became friends and arrived in Washington together.

Not Part of the Program

With Ray Conniff directing the choir, singer Carol Feraci performed for the Nixons at the White House. The Presidential family was looking forward to a peaceful evening free of protests against the raging war in Vietnam. But it was not to be. Suddenly, in the middle of her song, Feraci shouted, "Stop bombing human beings, animals, and vegetation."

Applying Pressure

President Kennedy was playing golf at North Palm Beach, Florida, with Chris Dunphy of the Seminole Golf Club. On the first hole, the President made a great shot which landed about three feet from the pin. He glanced over at Dunphy, looking for a conceded "gimme" putt, but Dunphy merely stared at the sky. "You're going to give me this, aren't you?" Kennedy asked. Dunphy shook his head in the negative, explaining to Kennedy, "A putt like this builds character." The President sighed and remarked, "Okay. But let's keep moving. After we finish, I've got an appointment with the Director of Internal Revenue." Replied Dunphy hastily, "The putt's good!"

Follow the Leader

President Theodore Roosevelt played tennis in all sorts of weather. He was playing doubles one day when it began to rain heavily. One of the players said they should stop. The President agreed, and then suggested that conditions were just right for a brisk run. The other three players had no choice but to follow their leader four miles back to the White House. The bedraggled players got a real lesson in physical fitness.

Presidential First

William McKinley declined to ride in an automobile for his second inauguration. He feared the newly-developed horseless carriage might stall in the middle of Pennsylvania Avenue, thus creating considerable embarrassment. Under more private conditions in Canton, Ohio, he went for a spin in a Stanley Steamer, making him the first incumbent Chief Executive to ride in a car.

TAKING A STAND

During the administration of Warren Harding, Senator William Borah, one of the so-called "insurgents" of the Republican Party, was sought as an administration leader. Harding's advisers hoped, in this manner, to keep Borah more or less "in line" with the President's views. The senator listened with interest until Harding finished speaking, then said, "Mr. President, you can get along without me, but I cannot get along without my political views. Thanks just the same."

SWIFT PUNISHMENT

It was a hard life on the frontier. Crime was commonplace; punishment was swift and severe. During the spring and summer of 1751 nineteen-year-old George Washington was surveying lands in Virginia. As the surveying party camped a woman by the name of Mary McDaniel was caught "robing the cloths of Mr. George Washington." She was convicted and sentenced to suffer fifteen lashes upon her bare back.

PROFIT OF DOOM AND GLOOM

Reverend Breckenridge, a Federalist, thundered every Sunday from the pulpit that James Madison was responsible for the War of 1812. The Washington minister also criticized Dolley Madison, declaring that the observation of the Sabbath had been broken by "dinner parties given at the White House." More than once, the fiery preacher wrathfully prophesied to his parishioners, "It is the government that will be punished, and, as with Nineveh of old, it will not be the habitations of the people, but your temples and palaces that will be burned to the ground." These words proved true when English troops set government buildings ablaze.

BUDGED NOT

John Tyler was a strong-minded and stubborn President who failed to get along with Congress, the press, or the Whig Party. He became the first President completely rejected by his own party. But he had no regrets, and voiced, "The barking newspapers and the brawling of demagogues can never drive me from my course. If I am to go into retirement, I will at least take care to do so with a pure and unsullied conscience."

GOING DOWNHILL

William Taft and Helen "Nellie" Herron first met at a sledding party. Taft asked her to ride with him on his bobsled. Years later, he jokingly referred to this encounter and explained, "And Nellie and I have been sliding downhill ever since."

TOUGH GUY

Fist fights between boys in Abilene, Kansas, were of a ferocity almost unbelievable to later generations. Twelve-year-old Dwight Eisenhower took on Wes Merrifield, who was bigger and faster. Witnesses remembered the encounter as a prolonged, sanguine affair. The battle lasted more than two hours, until each boy was too exhausted to swing. Finally, Merrifield gasped, "I can't lick you, Ike." Whereupon young Eisenhower replied through swollen lips, "Well, Wes, I haven't licked you." The fight then ended.

ROUGH AND READY, AND HUMBLE

During the Mexican War Major Jacob Brown built an outpost near Motamoros and named it in honor of his commander General Zachary Taylor, "Old Rough and Ready." Not long after its construction Fort Taylor was attacked by Mexican forces and Brown was killed. Taylor's forces reached the fort and, discovering Brown had been mortally wounded, renamed the Garrison Fort Brown.

HUMAN ZOO

A visitor could not help notice the commotion at the White House while Theodore Roosevelt was President. His children had their pets, and pet projects, scattered all throughout the mansion. Quentin Roosevelt organized his young friends into a group which he called "The White House Gang." When they shot spitballs at a portrait of Andrew Jackson, they were severely scolded by the President. Daughter Ethel used to slide down the White House stairs on a cookie sheet. And guests and family members never knew where they might be stepping on something or in something.

WE LOOK IN THE BOOK

Many of our Presidents have relied upon the Holy Scriptures for guidance and comfort. Among these were Washington, Lincoln, Garfield, McKinley, Wilson, Coolidge, Eisenhower and Carter. John Quincy Adams said, "The first and almost the only Book deserving on universal attention is the *Bible*." And Andrew Jackson advised, "Go to the Scriptures… the joyful promises it contains will be a balsam to your troubles."

A SWEET FELLA

By October of 1813 William Henry Harrison's American Army, made up of volunteers, militia, and some Indians, marched through Michigan in pursuit of Tecumseh and British General Proctor. Crossing over into Canada, his army camped one evening at Drake's Farm. Harrison received a severe tongue-lashing from the mistress of the farm, yelling that the soldiers were thieves and declaring that no honey would be left in the morning. Harrison politely informed her, "I will put a guard over the bees." This was done, but the sentinel permitted the hungry men to indulge. Harrison was a true gentleman, and the next morning ordered his quartermaster to pay for the honey.

WORDS FROM AN OLD-TIMER

When Ronald Reagan was reminded at an American Bar Association meeting that, if re-elected, he would be seventy-six years old upon leaving the White House, the President said, "Well, Andrew Jackson left the White House at the age of seventy-five, and he was still quite vigorous. I know because he told me so." And at the annual Gridiron Club dinner, Reagan noted that the club had been founded in 1885 and told the crowd how disappointed he was "when you didn't invite me the first time."

CAN'T WAIT

President Grant bought his son, Fred, a pocket watch for Christmas. After solemnly swearing the other family members to secrecy, Grant surprised everyone by taking the watch out of his pocket at the dinner table, several days ahead of time, and presenting it to his son. "Why, Lys," said his wife, "you were going to give it to him for a Christmas present." Replied Grant sheepishly, "He doesn't want to wait till Christmas, and neither do I."

A CHANGE OF HEART

No one was more critical of William McKinley than his young, energetic Assistant Secretary of the Navy, Theodore Roosevelt. He felt McKinley lacked courage and should have declared war on Spain after several disputes with that country. The belligerent New Yorker openly sneered, "McKinley has the backbone of a chocolate eclair!" Roosevelt also called him a "white-livered cur" who had "prepared two messages, one for war and one for peace, and doesn't know which one to send in." At a formal state dinner, Roosevelt shook his fist under the nose of Ohio Senator Mark Hanna, McKinley's chief advisor, and yelled, "Damn you! We'll have war for the freedom of Cuba in spite of you and your gutless bunch!" And though his apology was not made public, the fiery Roosevelt later retracted his statement. After McKinley waged a successful war against both Spain and some New York political bosses, Roosevelt told a friend, "I take back my remarks about his backbone."

EMERGENCY SURGERY

It was a strange twist of fate for Dr. Malcolm Perry at Dallas Parkland Hospital. Around one p.m. on Friday, November 22, 1963, he tried to revive John Kennedy by massaging his heart, working on the fatally wounded President for several minutes. Two days later he was again called to the emergency room to open Lee Harvey Oswald's chest and do the same for him. The assassin was shot just an inch below the heart by Jack Ruby, and his wound also was fatal.

HOLDING HIS TONGUE

Rather than deny rumors of infidelity which would just give them more circulation, Congressman James A. Garfield was upset that his political enemies would stoop so low to discredit him. Garfield wrote to a friend, "If I am open to these reports, then no man is safe." But he added that "to turn aside and kick every dog that barks would cost a good deal of precious time."

YOU HEARD IT FROM HARRY

In 1956 the GOP suggested that the Democratic Party be renamed the "Democrat Party." A local NBC newscaster in Kansas City asked former President Harry Truman what he thought of the remark. Truman responded by saying that he thought it was a fine idea, "providing, of course, they let us change the name of their party to 'Publican Party'. You know, in the *Bible* those publicans and big-money boys didn't come off too well."

ROWDY EXIT

Chester Arthur's last White House reception resulted in a huge turnout, with thousands of citizens pushing and shoving. Observed a Washington newspaper reporter, "The crush was so great that the Marine Band was swept from its moorings and could not continue playing because of the pressure of the people. So famous a hero as General Phil Sheridan got in only by being helped through a portico window by two policemen."

A TIP FROM "TIP"

When President Jimmy Carter first invited congressional leaders to a White House breakfast in 1977, only orange juice, coffee and a roll was served to each guest. After another small serving the following week Speaker of the House Thomas "Tip" O'Neill spoke out. "Mr. President, if you're getting me out at eight in the morning, you're getting me out for breakfast. Hell, *Nixon* served us better than this!" Carter took the advice, and from that point on, each congressman was given a full breakfast of eggs, toast, sausage, bacon, grits, and hot cakes.

PICKING UP HIS FEET

When Chester A. Arthur was born on October 5, 1830, his father, a strict Baptist minister, did something very uncharacteristic. He danced! After fathering four daughters, this reserved, no-nonsense man of the cloth, danced for joy, then named the future President after the doctor who gave him birth – Dr. Chester Abell, a cousin of his wife.

SQUEEZE PLAY

There was often a lot of protest wherever Lyndon Johnson went. He was constantly harassed by demonstrators opposed to his Vietnam War policy. At a rally in Hawaii a group of hecklers interrupted his speech. But a team of longshoremen had been brought in to protect the President, and they handled the situation very well. Standing behind the hecklers, the longshoremen grabbed each male protestor by the testicles and gave them a twist. After several of the demonstrators doubled over in misery, the disturbances ended, and Johnson continued his speech.

BOGUS BALLOTS

Political boss Tom Pendergast made sure his candidate for the Senate, Harry S Truman, didn't get out-cheated by his opponents. The Kansas City machine produced about 80,000 ghost votes for Truman. Some people registered thirty times; voters were shown as living in vacant lots or in empty buildings. Thousands of dead people were listed as accredited voters, inspiring a 1934 election day quip that "Now is the time for all good cemeteries to come to the aid of the party." One ward in Kansas City showed absurd proportions when a Pendergast candidate received 19,202 votes to the opponent's twelve. Truman won the 1935 primary and was subsequently elected U.S. Senator.

HERO OR VILLAIN?

For nearly a quarter of a century following his Presidency, John Tyler was dealt with harshly by most historians. Tyler vetoed every important bill, lost support of the Whig Party, and stood firm on the issues of slavery and States' rights. Congress initiated impeachment proceedings against him, but some scholars viewed this courteous, soft-spoken Virginian as a man of exceptional courage and imagination, devoted to principles and establishing himself as a strong Chief Executive even though he assumed office on the death of Harrison. One historian who understood the Presidency, Theodore Roosevelt wryly remarked, "Tyler has been called a mediocre man, but that is unwarranted flattery. He was a politician of monumental littleness!"

A DEMAND NOT MET

In 1863 a woman waited at the White House to see Lincoln. She insisted that her son be promoted to colonel, not as a favor but as a right. The lady stated, "Sir, my grandfather fought at Lexington, my father fought at New Orleans, and my husband was killed at Monterey." Lincoln replied, "I guess, Madam, your family has done enough for the country. It is time to give someone else a chance." She was dismissed and left the office in tears as her request was denied.

JUST A REMINDER

President McKinley once reprimanded his Adjutant General and Army Chief of Staff Henry Corbin. Upon arriving late at a White House dinner, Corbin apologized, saying his watch was slow. The President rebuked him by relating this story: "Lincoln once had an adjutant general who gave the same excuse. 'Well,' said Mr. Lincoln, 'either you must get a new watch or I must get a new adjutant general.'" Corbin got the point, very clearly.

A CHANGE IN PRIORITIES

The Carters were quite accustomed to the hectic schedule of public life. After years as governor of Georgia and then at the White House, Jimmy Carter looked forward to returning to Plains, Georgia, and a somewhat-normal lifestyle. No longer did they have to worry about news broadcasts, election returns, or entertaining heads of state. As the former First Lady explained, "One day we were working in the yard, and we laughed when I commented that it seemed astounding that the most important thing in my life at this moment could be whether or not the brick walk we were building from our house to the street was crooked or straight. And it *was* very important."

TOO WORDY

Vice President John C. Calhoun of South Carolina once wrote President Andrew Jackson a fifty page letter explaining his loyalty and support. Calhoun's stand of tariffs, slavery and the concept of the Union differed greatly from that of his boss. Jackson explained that if a man is innocent, he doesn't need "a fifty page letter to prove it." Later, Calhoun resigned, claiming he was an "oppressed citizen of South Carolina," and that his state was free and independent.

HOSPITALITY PLUS

Once the Hardings moved into the White House in 1921, they opened it to any and all who wished to visit. Florence and Warren welcomed throngs of sightseers who snapped pictures, strolled the walkways and lawn, and leaned against the pillars. The First Lady even pulled up the window shades and waved at the curious faces which pressed against the glass. She said, "It's their White House; let them look in if they want to." Guards were removed from the entrances, and the gates remained open.

WHERE'S MINE?

President John Adams was accused by Anti-Federalists of sending his political cohort Charles C. Pinckney to Europe to procure four mistresses – two for himself and two for Adams. "If this were true," Adams said, "Pinckney has kept them all for himself and cheated me out of my two."

NO HELP WANTED

Only in rare instances did James K. Polk meet with his cabinet. He distrusted his cabinet officials and felt they spent too much time vacationing or attending social functions. In his diary he noted, "I have conducted the government without their aid." Only one other person assisted him – his personal secretary, First Lady Sarah Polk.

ROYAL GEORGE?

George Washington used a coat of arms from his English ancestry: "Exitus acta probat," which has been translated "The end justifies the means," or "At the end of my life my deeds will be approved." You take your pick.

HOW SHOULD WE FEEL?

During James Monroe's term of office the price of a barrel of flour fell from $15 to $4. Though a bargain for consumers, the sharp decrease in farm prices and American manufactured goods brought about hardships. The tremendous influx of foreign products led to unemployment and bankruptcy of businesses at home. Many historians have dubbed this period as the "Era of Good Feeling."

CHANGE OF HEART

Like many politicians, William McKinley viewed politics with a love-hate relationship. In the last year of his first term in the White House he told his secretary, "I would be the happiest man in America if I could go out of office in 1901." However, he actively sought and won a second term.

JUSTIFIED COMPLAINT

President James Garfield lamented, "It will cost me some struggle to keep from despising the office seeker." The twentieth President did not look forward to the constant problem of political appointments, stating that the "intellectual dissipation may cripple me for the remainder of my life." Less than five months after taking his oath, Garfield was gunned down by a disappointed office seeker.

A TALE OF A TAIL

Lincoln insisted on facts when a problem was presented to him. One day a committee visited him voicing a public concern. The case was built up mostly of "probables" and "supposings." Lincoln asked them, "How many legs would a sheep have if you called its tail a leg?" As he expected, they answered, "Five." Lincoln replied, "No it wouldn't; it would have only four. Calling a tail a leg does not make it one."

A LITTLE SELF-CONCEIT

While visiting the midwest, President Woodrow Wilson was the guest speaker at a women's club meeting. The club president gave a lengthy and flattering introduction which Wilson acknowledged thus: "Madam President, Ladies and Gentlemen: Last fall I was much troubled by dizziness. My physicians said it was due to my liver. I know now it was my eminence."

TIRED

President-elect Lincoln was weary from the hundreds of office seekers who besieged him for favors. For five months they invaded his home or met him at the state capital building in Springfield. He told his friend judge David Davis before he took office, "I know it is an awful thing for me to say, but I already wish someone else was here in my place."

WHERE WILL IT END?

Mary Custis Lee was the wife of Robert E. Lee and the only child of Washington Parke Custis (grandson of our first President). Following the Civil War in February of 1869, Mary Lee wrote Andrew Johnson, begging him to have the federal government return the relics taken by Union forces from the Arlington mansion. Though Arlington was General Lee's home, its location and spacious land made it a suitable graveyard for Union soldiers. President Johnson explained that all items would be returned after they had been properly identified. Congress, however, was in no forgiving mood to deliver these cherished items to Robert E. Lee and his wife. Not until 1901, when William McKinley authorized their return, did George Washington's artifacts finally depart to the descendants of the Lee family.

NON-SUPPORT

Campaigning in the Michigan primary in 1980, Republican candidate George Bush and Governor Bill Milliken left a Detroit dinner affair. Amid a crowd of television cameras and microphones, a middle-aged woman approached Bush and cursed him, then shouted, "I wouldn't vote for you if Castro were running!" As she disappeared into the crowd, Milliken asked Bush, "What do you think, George? For or against?" Bush replied, "Undecided. Put her down as a firm undecided." Though he won the Michigan Primary, Bush lost the nomination to Ronald Reagan, but was chosen as the Vice Presidential nominee.

THE SURPRISE PARTY

There was one candidate FDR did not worry about in the 1940 Presidential campaign. Though Wendell Wilkie posed a threat to Roosevelt's bid for a third term, lovely comedienne Gracie Allen did not. Running for President on the Surprise Party ticket, she delighted thousands with her illogical-logic. One of America's most popular and best loved women, she urged Americans to be proud of the national debt because it was the biggest in the world. Gracie stressed the need for more women in politics, reminding admirers that "a woman is much better than a man when it comes to introducing bills in the house." And when asked her opinion of the Neutrality Bill being debated in Congress, Gracie stated, "If we owe it, let's pay it." At a campaign train stop in California, she emerged onto the rear platform with a toy kangaroo holding a baby in its pouch with the slogan "It's In The Bag." She addressed a huge crowd, beginning her speech by saying, "As I look around here and see all those trusting and believing faces shining up at me with love and respect, tears come to my eyes. And do you know why? My girdle is killing me!" For weeks she shook hands and kissed baby girls, explaining, "I won't kiss male babies until they're over twenty-one." Gracie further promised to provide old age to people on pensions, and when asked why there was no Vice Presidential nominee, she explained she did not want any vice on her ticket. Crowds roared with laughter at her campaign slogans such as "Down with common sense, Vote for Gracie," and "Even big politicians don't know what to do. Gracie doesn't know either. But neither do you, so vote for Gracie...." According to her husband and campaign manager George Burns, her expenses totaled about $37.00. Gracie Allen received several thousand write-in votes and explained to the press that, had it not been for Roosevelt and Wilkie, she might have won. And had it not been for Roosevelt, Wilkie might have won too.

A GOOD CATCH

Theodore Roosevelt's African safari was quite successful. By the time he left Africa in March of 1910, he had faced many dangers including poisonous snakes, charging wild animals, epidemics of sleeping sickness, and temperatures of 112 degrees in the shade. But his expedition resulted in bringing back to America more than 11,000 specimens, mostly for the Smithsonian Institution.

NAME SAKE

In 1860 President-elect Lincoln stopped at the State House Rotunda in Columbus to give a brief address to the Ohio General Assembly. Upon leaving, he descended the outside steps where a huge crowd waited for another speech. One young couple surged forward and held their baby up to him. Lincoln raised his hand to quiet the cheering throng, then leaned over and took the child from its father's arms, and kissed it on the forehead. He asked its name and the father replied, "It has no name and we want you to name it." Lincoln answered, "Abraham is too long for such a wee mite of humanity, and we'll call him Abram." The mother took the child back, but explained she would indeed call him Abraham because Abraham "saved his people." As she said this, Lincoln looked up at the sky and remarked, "God knows best."

NUDGES FROM NELLIE

Taft's sleeping habits were often an embarrassment to his wife, especially when he fell asleep at social functions and meetings. The First Lady initially attended White House conferences and seated herself directly behind the President, gently prodding him with her fan whenever he started to doze off. Once, as governor of the Philippines, Taft even fell asleep while a typhoon raged outside their home. Windows shattered, the foundation rocked, and even Taft's chair shook. His wife grumbled, "How could you sleep?" Answered Taft innocently, "Now, Nellie, you know it is just my way. I knew you could handle it." She often referred to him as "Sleeping Beauty," and Taft described his wife as "the council for war."

GETTING TO THE BOTTOM OF THINGS

When Marianne Means interviewed ex-President Truman, she was doing research on a book about First Ladies. Truman opened the conversation: "If you don't say nice things about the Madam, I will spank you." Somewhat surprised, Miss Means protested that her bottom was too large even for a President to spank. Smiling, Truman winked and said, "I've spanked bigger ones than you."

JEALOUS JOHN

John Adams was jealous of military men. As a member of the Continental Congress, he showed little faith at times in George Washington as commander of American forces. In 1777 Washington and his battle-weary soldiers camped in the hills of New Jersey and Adams wrote, "Are we to go on forever this way, maintaining vast armies in idleness, and losing completely the fairest opportunity that ever was offered by destroying an enemy completely in our power?" Unhappy that Washington had not won any smashing victories, Adams was offended by "the superstitious veneration that is sometimes paid to General Washington." He also remarked to a friend, "I, poor creature, worn out with scribbling for my bread and liberty, low in spirits and weak in health, must leave others to wear the laurels which I have sown." But Adams' critics were quick to remind him that while he sat in the safety and comfort of Congress, many others were risking their lives on the battlefield to protect American liberties.

THE WRONG GERALD

The Daughters of the American Revolution gave a dinner in honor of President Gerald Ford. The master of ceremonies for the conservative group in attendance introduced the Chief Executive thus: "Ladies and Gentlemen… the President of the United States, Gerald Smith!" There was a bit more consternation evidenced by the reaction of the audience when it was learned that Gerald Smith was one of America's leading fascists.

FATHERLY ADVICE

John Kennedy was urged by his father to run for the Massachusetts Senate race against the very popular Republican Henry Cabot Lodge. Joe offered this piece of advice to his son: "It takes three things to win in politics. The first is money. The second is money. And the third is money." With Dad's financial help, plus a lot of hard campaigning, John Kennedy won the U.S. Senate seat.

BULLISH ON BILL

President Nixon arrived in Miami Beach to campaign for Republican candidates running for Congress. Addressing a huge crowd on behalf of U.S. Senate candidate Bill Cramer, Nixon stood with Cramer, raised the candidate's hand and told voters, "So be sure when election time rolls around next Tuesday, to vote for my old friend…er…Congressman Bull Cranner!"

Irreplaceable

In 1785 our ambassador to France, Benjamin Franklin, returned home due to ill health. Thomas Jefferson was selected to represent the United States. "You replace Monsieur Franklin," remarked the Comte de Vergennes; to which Jefferson replied quickly, "I *succeed,* Monsieur. No one can replace Benjamin Franklin."

Dead End

John Tyler's two oldest sons also served as his private secretaries in the White House. When Whig President, William Henry Harrison, suddenly died in April of 1841, Tyler filled out the remaining three years and eleven months of the term. The Whigs disowned him, and Tyler became very unpopular. One day Tyler sent his son, Robert, on an errand to procure a special train for him. The railroad superintendent was a faithful Whig, and informed Robert that the railroad was not offering any special rates or accommodations. "What?!" said Robert, "Did you not furnish a special train for the funeral of President Harrison?" "Yes," explained the superintendent calmly, "and if you will only bring your father here in that shape you shall have the best train on the road."

Wrong Gender

It was 1910 and the ladies who ran the Charleston, S.C., Orphanage on Calhoun Street learned they would be visited by a well known Yankee, President William Howard Taft. The superintendent, Miss Emily, and the other women decided to present Taft with a special gift and chose a six year old boy to make the presentation. The boy was selected because of his long, wavy blond hair. Someone found a blue velvet jacket and knickers, and adorned the costume with white lace and white silk stockings. At the appointed time the boy shuffled up to the stage and gave Taft the gift. He had been told to make a few brief remarks. Taft, a man of huge proportions, accepted the gift with a generous smile and said, "What a beautiful little girl!" The other boys in the audience snickered and hooted, and the child shouted at the President, "I ain't no girl, you damned fool!" To the shock and dismay of the women, the youth stalked off the stage, tore his collar away, and stepped on it. That night he persuaded Miss Emily to cut his hair.

PROMISES, PROMISES

Speaking on the steps of the state capitol at Nashville, Tennessee, one evening in October of 1864, Military Governor Andrew Johnson urged a torchlight gathering of Negroes to follow the Union and defend their freedom. He voiced hope that a modern-day Moses might arise to "lead you safely to your Promised Land of freedom and happiness." From the throng came shouts, "You are our Moses!" Amidst wild cheering came another cry, "We want no Moses but you!" The future President responded, "Humble and unworthy as I am, if no better shall be found, I will indeed be your Moses, and lead you through the Red Sea of war and bondage to a fairer future of liberty and peace."

PITY THE OLD MAN

James Buchanan could not wait for his term of office to end. During his last weekend in office Buchanan tried desperately to avoid civil war, preferring to let the burden of decision-making fall on Lincoln. But Buchanan could not control the events about him. His Secretary of War sold weapons from the federal arsenals to confederates, and the treasury was bankrupt, thanks to another secessionist. He met with commissioners from South Carolina, and they vigorously pressed him about his implied promise to surrender Fort Sumter. Nervous and haggard, the indecisive Buchanan yelled at the Southerners, "You don't give me time to consider; you don't give me time to say my prayers. I always say prayers when required to act on any great state affair." The shocked commissioners looked at each other in dismay, and withdrew from the White House.

FAILING TO SEE THE HUMOR

Susan Scanland of Pittsfield, Illinois, was asked her opinion of one of her former borders, Abraham Lincoln. She offered it, but it was not very complimentary: "The laziest man there ever was, good for nothing except to tell stories." She had not forgotten the one time she had prepared a turkey dinner for Lincoln and other friends. No one showed up until much later, when the dinner was cold. Lincoln was down at the drugstore telling jokes and tall tales to a crowd of listeners.

GROOMING THE GROOM

Andrew Jackson had some advice on the subject of marriage. In April of 1833 he cautioned his ward, Andrew J. Hutchings, "… seek a wife who will aid you in your exertions…for you will find it easier to spend two thousand dollars, than to make five hundred. Look at the economy of the mother, and if you find it in *her* you will find it in the daughter."

TIME FOR A CHANGE

The last major renovation of the White House took nearly four years (during the Truman administration). The building was in such a deplorable state that it became a hazard in which to live. All of the replaceable pieces – marble mantles, woodwork, chandeliers, etc. – were numbered and stored away so they could be returned to their proper place during the final phase of reconstruction. A new concrete foundation, twenty-four feet deep, was poured beneath the exterior walls. A heavy steel framework was put up within the structure, and by early 1952, the mansion was completely restored. Total cost of the project was $5,761,000.

AUTO AUDIBLES

In 1914 farmer Harry Truman purchased a three-year-old Stafford touring car for $600. Travel to Independence to see his sweetheart, Bess Wallace, was now more convenient, but at a price. The car stalled many times and had numerous blowouts. One time Truman spent ten minutes cranking the motor, with the handle flying off the crankshaft, spraining his wrist and causing him to bang his head against the radiator. Truman remarked to Bess, "When you have an auto, there is nothing else to cuss about."

A WELCOME TO YOUR HOUSE

President William Henry Harrison was not feeling well. He had delivered a long inaugural speech on a cold, breezy day and would die less than five weeks later. One day a plainly dressed farmer called at the White House, and a servant made the farmer wait in a cold room. After the President visited with this man, he scolded his servant. "Why did you not show this man into the drawing room where it is warm and comfortable?" he asked. The servant replied that the farmer's work clothes might dirty the carpet. Harrison retorted angrily, "Never mind the carpet. That man is one of the people. The carpet, as well as the White House, belong to the people."

Have No Fear of Vampires

William Henry Harrison sent his son to Transylvania. One of several children, William Henry Harrison, Jr., was sent to Lexington, Kentucky, to attend Transylvania College. Father felt it was a fine school, explaining in a letter to his son, "There is no exertion that I would not make and scarcely any sacrifice I would not incur to give you a good education." He also warned him about indulging in "fast living" and drinking. Later, his son died, heavily in debt.

Busy Signal

On the evening of March 5, 1977, President Jimmy Carter hosted a nationwide radio call-in program where citizens could personally talk by phone to him. Reminiscent of FDR's successful Fireside Chats of the 1930s, Carter felt this was a great idea in communicating with the American people. The White House switchboard was inundated with more than nine million callers. But only forty-two were able to get through to the Oval Office.

Confession

Just prior to his execution, Leon Czolgosz asked some guards for a cigar, then informed reporters that he had made up his mind to shoot President McKinley only a couple of days before the assassination. While McKinley visited the Pan-American Exposition in Buffalo, New York, Czolgosz was thwarted by guards and secret service agents four times as he tried to get close to the President. He said murdering McKinley came as a whim because "the ballot was no good." At his trial, it was shown that Czolgosz was a disciple of Emma Goldman, a leading advocate of anarchy which promoted the killing of world leaders and doing away with government.

Trying To Justify Racism

The sneak attack at Pearl Harbor in 1941 aroused intense feelings of hatred and bitterness against the Japanese. A wave of racial prejudice swept the nation. Many Americans were told that the Japanese were nothing but barbarians whose intelligence was only slightly above that of apes. A scientist at the Smithsonian Institution told President Franklin Roosevelt that Japanese skulls were "some 2000 years less developed than our own." In order to overcome this alleged biological inferiority, the President suggested interracial marriages following World War II. Even President Truman, in his diary, remarked that he encouraged the use of atomic weapons because the Japanese were "savages, ruthless, merciless, and fanatic."

Oh, Henry!

Jefferson and Madison had many things in common, among them a dislike for fellow Virginian Patrick Henry. After Henry denounced them both for their views on slavery (they were both against it even though they owned slaves) and religious freedom, he launched a vicious public attack on them. Jefferson wrote to Madison in 1785, "What we have to do I think is devoutly pray for his death." Three years later Henry tried again to ruin Madison politically. Then, in 1792, he sent a letter to Madison suggesting they let bygones be bygones. But Madison, like Jefferson, was unforgiving and never responded to this gesture of reconciliation. To both of them Patrick Henry was an old demagogue who would never change. Perhaps the only other person Madison and Jefferson hated as much was Alexander Hamilton.

A Frank Introduction

In 1932 FDR was campaigning out west. There was a large crowd at the Hollywood Bowl in Los Angeles where the Democratic nominee was scheduled to speak. Will Rogers, the "Cowboy Philosopher" and humorist, introduced Roosevelt to the audience. Rogers called him Franklin and said, "This introduction may not have been flowery, but remember, you are only a candidate. Come back when you are President, and I will do better. I am wasting no oratory on a mere prospect." FDR roared with laughter.

Too Tired

Lincoln once told of a little girl who received some alphabet blocks as a gift. She liked them so much that she played with them at night in her bedroom until she was sleepy. Then, one night, she remembered she had not said her prayers. So she knelt by her bedside and prayed, "Oh Lord, I'm too sleepy to pray, but there are the letters. Spell it out yourself."

Presidential Predictions

The first public opinion poll in the U.S. was conducted in Wilmington, Delaware, on July 24, 1824. It was done to determine voter intentions in the 1824 Presidential election. A random sample of 532 electors was taken and published in the *Harrisburg Pennsylvanian*. It showed a clear lead for Andrew Jackson over John Quincy Adams and two other candidates. Jackson won the poll, and he went on to win the popular vote as well but could not get a majority of electoral votes. The House of Representatives selected Adams amidst cries of a "corrupt bargain" between Adams and Henry Clay. The first nationwide public opinion poll was organized by the *Farm Journal* in the 1912 Presidential race among candidates Woodrow Wilson, Theodore Roosevelt, and incumbent William Howard Taft.

Cheapskate?

Being frugal, devoutly religious, and an "outsider" from Georgia, President Jimmy Carter often had trouble dealing with Senators and Congressmen. This relationship further deteriorated when Carter invited Representatives to a White House breakfast, consisting of rolls and coffee. He then billed the Congress for the meal, at $4.25 a piece.

The Era of Bad Feeling

James Monroe's terms as President, 1817-1825, was called the Era of Good Feeling, but by 1826 the feeling towards Monroe had changed. On two separate occasions the former President asked the U.S. Congress to compensate him for expenses incurred while in public office dating back to 1794. Monroe twice served as ambassador and envoy to France under Presidents Washington and Jefferson. He borrowed money to maintain a lavish lifestyle and went into debt both overseas and at home. In addition to his debts in France, Spain, and England, Monroe also asked to be reimbursed for traveling expenses while Secretary of State and President. He even asked for interest since some of his claims dated back thirty years. Though several members of Congress thought his request was an outrage, with the help of William Henry Harrison and John Quincy Adams, he managed to get a settlement. Monroe was given two payments totaling $60,000 – a hefty sum in 1831. Monroe thought the amount too small. And in spite of this compensation, the fifth President died in poverty.

Dollars Downplayed During Dinner

John Kennedy came from a large family. At dinner time his father Joe led discussions and asked questions about history and current events. He demanded opinions and assessments from his children but there was one topic forbidden at the table – the subject of money. *Fortune* Magazine ran an article years later estimating Joseph Kennedy's fortune at $250,000,000.

"Oops!"

President Ronald Reagan once told some Russian university students that American Indians were not citizens. Reagan may have forgotten that in 1924 Congress passed the Indian Citizenship Act, which declared all Indians born within the territorial limits of the U.S. were full citizens.

A First for Madison

One of the first newspaper cartoon criticizing a President was a political caricature on the subject of James Madison's repeal of the Embargo Act. It appeared in the *Federal Republican* in Washington, D.C., in early 1814. In it, John Wesley Jarvis, better known for his portrait paintings, showed a turtle floating on its back, and its severed head biting Madison's ears.

Ballots Bought by Boss

In the 1896 election, Republican Party boss Mark Hanna left nothing to chance in seeing that his friend, William McKinley, become President. Hanna raised and spent a bankroll of nearly twelve million dollars, and voters turned out in record numbers. An army of Republican election workers transported blacks by the trainload across the Mason-Dixon line. At many voting points, it was noted, "the very graveyards were robbed of the names on their tombstones." And one district out West had 48,000 votes cast, when only 30,000 people were registered. An additional 30,000 voters poured into Indiana and Ohio, many voting twice in one day. McKinley won the popular vote with about seven million, compared to Democratic candidate William Jennings Bryan's six and a half million.

PITCHING PILLS

Shortly before his death, former President Lyndon B. Johnson talked with General Alexander Haig at the LBJ ranch in 1973. Johnson was suffering from heart disease and in the middle of their conversation, Lady Bird brought her husband an assortment of pills and capsules with a glass of water. As Lady Bird retreated to the house, Johnson poured the pills into the palm of his hand then flung them into a nearby shrub. He told Haig, "I'm dying and I want to get it over with."

BIG CHEESE FOR THE BIG CHEESE

Thomas Jefferson was given a huge gift on New Year's Day of 1802. The residents of Cheshire, Massachusetts, gave the President a large chunk of cheese weighing 1235 pounds. Back in July of 1801 Darius Brown began the project by collecting from every milk cow and heifer in the area (with the exception of cows owned by Federalists!). The village blacksmith constructed a monstrous cheese hoop four feet in diameter and eighteen inches high. When the cheese was presented six months later, President Jefferson announced that it was one of the happiest days of his life. He then proceeded to cut off large chunks and served it with bread to all those attending.

A THRILL FROM BILL

In early August of 1993 President Bill Clinton invited a delegation of a Boys Nation group to the White House. Clinton congratulated each young man and posed for pictures. After the event, high schooler Tyler Peterson was asked how he felt. The student explained, "Meeting him, shaking his hand – it was overwhelming. It was better than sex. Of course, I haven't had sex before, but I'm sure this was better."

A THRASHING FOR DASHING

Andrew Johnson was ten years old and should have known better. Serving as an apprentice to a Raleigh, North Carolina, tailor, Johnson was given to John Selby by his widowed mother who could not longer afford to raise the boy. When Andrew and his cousins ran across the yard of John Devereaux, a wealthy citizen, they were caught by Devereaux's coachman, taken back to their shanty, and whipped. The boys had offended some young ladies – by running naked!

COOL AND "CAL"-CU-LATED

Few Chief Executives could match the humor and dry wit of Calvin Coolidge. One morning he invited Congressional leaders to a White House breakfast. Knowing all eyes were fixed on him, the President poured coffee and cream into his saucer instead of his cup. His guests stared, and several Congressmen did the same. Coolidge picked up his saucer, paused, then placed it on the floor for his dog!

REAGAN'S REJECTION

Ronald and Nancy Reagan visited several hotels to appear at each of the inaugural balls in January of 1981. Initially, preparations were made for 42,000 guests, but nearly 60,000 showed up. Thousands were turned away from the main ballrooms in each hotel, with many of them being shunted off into some annex where there was no food or entertainment. Even Neil Reagan had his troubles. At the Shoreham Hotel he told a guard at the ballroom entrance, "I'm the President's brother." The guard told him, "You're the tenth guy that's tried that today."

APPRECIATION FOR WATER

After swimming in the cold Bay of Fundy, FDR was stricken with polio. With resolute courage he fought to regain the use of his lower body through swimming. Though he was wheelchair bound, and forced to wear heavy steel leg braces for the rest of his adult life, Roosevelt found swimming had curative powers. He once explained, "The water put me where I am today, and the water has to bring me back."

ROCK-SOLID SUPPORTER

A West Branch, Iowa, dentist, Dr. William Walker, was an avid rock collector. In the early 1880s, one local boy found his rock collection simply fascinating. The youth was Herbert Hoover who, incidentally, became one of the world's greatest mining engineers. "Many an hour," Dr. Walker recalled, "Herbert spent in my office pouring over specimens while the other children played. And gradually there was born in the boy the determination to win an education. For so often I would have to say 'I don't know' in answer to his questions. That never satisfied him." Forty years later, when Secretary of Commerce Hoover visited West Branch, he called on the elderly doctor and "accidentally" left two fifty dollar bills on the old man's mantelpiece.

THE MAN WHO COULD BE KING

During the Revolutionary War, Colonel Lewis Nicola of the Continental Army sent his commander, George Washington, a letter in behalf of several disgruntled officers. He suggested that Washington, with the help of the military, establish a monarchy and crown himself king. An outraged Washington quickly ordered Colonel Nicola to "banish these thoughts from your mind."

RESTLESS RIOT

Even in death Abraham Lincoln caused a riot. Lincoln's funeral in Philadelphia created bedlam when 300,000 paid their respects on Sunday, April 23, 1865. Pickpockets terrorized the huge crowd while police used billy clubs to keep order. A double line, stretching from Independence Hall for three miles, waited to see the body. Fighting broke out, women screamed and fainted, and some even had their dresses torn off. Clothing littered the square, and it was quite some time before order was restored.

CHIEF LANDSCAPERS

Every President has walked the grounds of the White House property. George Washington personally chose the site, and visited the construction site during his last week in office. Nearly all of his successors have planted flowers or trees. Jefferson had two mounds built on the south lawn as visual barriers for privacy. John Quincy Adams hired a full-time gardener and together they developed extensive plantings. Andrew Johnson had the first fountain installed on the south side in 1867, while Grant built the first one on the north side. And it was Woodrow Wilson's idea to have the Rose Garden.

Too Timid to Tug

As a member of the Constitutional Convention in 1787, James Madison was involved in many debates. Often he would get excited and tend to speak longer than expected. Madison asked a friend to tug at his coattails when the friend thought he got too carried away with his speech. Once, after Madison had debated at the point of exhaustion, he asked his friend, "Why didn't you pull my coattails when you heard me going on like that?" His friend, impressed with Madison's dramatic delivery, responded, "I would rather have laid a finger on lightning!"

Obeying Orders – In Part

John Adams traveled to Europe during the Revolutionary War as our French ambassador. His mission was to secure loans from France and Holland to help finance the war against Great Britain. Crossing the Atlantic Ocean, his ship was attacked by an English battleship. Adams rushed up on deck with a rifle in his hand, ready to fight the enemy. The ship captain asked, "Why are you here, sir? I am commanded to carry you safely to Europe, and I will do it!" He was advised to go below, and did so. But a short time later he emerged again, busily firing away at the British. As a true patriot, Adams was always prepared to risk his life for his country.

What a Way to Lose

In October of 1873 the veterans of the Union Army held a reunion in Toledo, Ohio. Among the honored guests were four "Buckeye" generals – George Custer, William T. Sherman, Phil Sheridan, and President Grant. For three days there were banquets, parades, and speeches. Festivities concluded on a Sunday afternoon where the four leaders met guests at the Toledo Opera House. Grant, dressed in black, stood with the other three men and shook hands with the large crowd. But what began as a stuffy, formal affair turned into a contest among the four men when Sheridan picked up a little girl and kissed her. Custer followed suit. Sherman did likewise, and the three generals jokingly declared that they were all as handsome as the President. Sheridan announced he would kiss the female teenagers, then all four leaders began kissing all of the women present. Some of the ladies who had not been kissed previously reentered the line. A reporter counted the number of babies, girls, and women kissed by these men, and Grant finished a dismal fourth. The final tallies for women kissed were: Custer – 638, Sheridan – 608, Sherman – 571, and Grant – 490. Perhaps this was one battle Grant didn't mind losing.

Gettin' Religion

Abraham Lincoln was not a regular church-goer, nor did he identify with any particular denomination. But midway through his Presidency, he devoted more time to religion. As his wife later recalled, "He first seemed to think about the subject when our boy Willie died, and then more than ever about the time he went to Gettysburg." She also admitted her husband was "never a technical Christian." Thus, Lincoln's religion was profound, but never orthodox or sectarian. It was a gradual, private, and personal process of growth.

A Major Blunder

It was customary for Presidents years ago to have a New Year's reception at the White House for the public. William Howard Taft decided to follow tradition. A little tailor who once did some alterations for Taft's suits joined in the reception line. He patiently waited for more than two hours. The small man finally reached the President to shake his hand. He leaned forward and told Taft, "Don't you remember me, Mr. President? *I made your pants.*" The jovial President boomed, "Of course, of course! Delighted to see you, Major Pants!"

Reorganization

In 1829 President Andrew Jackson felt it was time to light a fire under government workers. Jackson observed that many federal workers, especially those appointed by Jackson's predecessors, had grown lazy, corrupt, and indifferent. The new President remarked, "No man has the right to think that once appointed to public office he can stay there for the rest of his life. If he does, he doesn't do his best work, and the business of the office is handled just to please him." Those opposed to Jackson criticized this program and dubbed it the spoils system. In reality, Jackson dismissed only about eleven per cent of the total number of federal employees, no more than Jefferson had a generation earlier.

I Prefer...

In 1961 the Cold War between Russia and the U.S. seemed to be moving toward a nuclear war. The Soviet dictator Nikita Khrushchev and President John Kennedy agreed to meet in Vienna to discuss troop build-up and armament. Both leaders brought their wives. When it was suggested to Khrushchev that he shake hands with Kennedy, he refused, pointing to the beautiful First Lady and remarking, "I would rather shake hands with her."

Pardon Me!

President Andrew Johnson has been accused of letting Mary Surratt hang for her alleged role in the Lincoln assassination. She owned the boardinghouse in Washington where Booth and the other conspirators met, and despite pleas from many influential people, the execution took place. But it has been shown that Secretary of War Edwin Stanton deliberately withheld the pardon which could have spared Mrs. Surratt's life. Johnson demanded Stanton's resignation and after much difficulty, got it. Removing the Secretary of War was declared illegal by the Radical Republicans and Johnson was impeached.

Things Will Be Different Around Here!

One of Theodore Roosevelt's first problems as President concerned disciplining his son, Quentin. One rainy day Quentin and three of his friends decided to make spit balls and deliberately throw them on the portraits hanging in the White House. It wasn't until evening that the President discovered several paintings covered with spit wads. Immediately he pulled Quentin out of bed and made him remove them. Father also informed his son that it would be a while before he could invite his friends back.

A Nixon Affliction

Not doing well with one of his courses, Richard Nixon met with his professor one day after class. Dr. David Cavers, a Law professor at Duke University, told his student, "You have an affliction common to most writers – intellectual constipation." Though Nixon struggled with some of his courses, he still graduated near the top of his class.

Land Grabber

Perhaps no man was more adept in acquiring land for the U.S. government than William Henry Harrison. By "hook or by crook" Harrison was responsible for annexing hundreds of millions of acres of former Indian-owned lands. Just one example was in 1804 when Harrison conspired with agents and got five Sac chiefs drunk. The general then had them sign a treaty handing over fifty-one million acres for $2200. This single "purchase" included a vast trek which spanned part of what is now Missouri, Indiana, and Wisconsin.

Overstepping His Bounds

Gouverneur Morris bet Alexander Hamilton that he could treat President George Washington informally at a dinner party. Morris slapped Washington on the back and shouted, "Wasn't it so, my old boy?" Washington's only reply was a cold stare. Morris won his wager but later told Hamilton he regretted addressing the first President in such a manner. In his attempt to pierce the protective shield of respect, Morris wanted to demonstrate to friends that he was a close friend. However, Morris, like other Americans, learned that a President of the United States is set apart from all other citizens.

Digging Up Dirt

In the 1840 Presidential Campaign the Democrats did their best to discredit the Whig ticket of William Henry Harrison and John Tyler. They charged that Harrison drank rum and sat on the porch of his log cabin, but this effort backfired. The Democrats then made an allegation that "Tippecanoe" Harrison was too old and that his running mate owned slaves. There was truth to these charges but voters ignored them. In a last desperate measure, Van Buren's supporters produced an Indian squaw who claimed Harrison had fathered her children. When the campaign ended, the Whigs claimed a big victory, winning nineteen of twenty-six states, and proclaiming the "Martin Van was a used-up man."

Roots in Rum

John Adams wrote, "It is no secret that rum was an essential ingredient of the American Revolution." And he was right. Molasses went from the West Indies to Great Britain, then to New England, and New England turned it into rum. The rum then went to Africa for slaves, and most of the slaves went to the Caribbean in exchange for molasses in the 1700s. England wanted both the revenue and exclusive trading rights in this lucrative exchange.

Self-Proclaimed Expert

To say President George Bush enjoyed fishing is like saying kids like candy. On the land, on the sea, or in the air he often practiced his casting. He even could be seen doing it in the White House and aboard *Air Force One*. In April of 1990 Bush and two companions went fishing in the Potomac River. The party first stopped at Bolling Air Force Base where their bass boat was waiting. Prior to their departure, the President demonstrated his passion by casting while talking, while eating breakfast, during a phone conversation, and even while walking to the bathroom. Such practice often pays off. The President caught a couple of large mouth bass and, surprisingly, an eight pound carp. The other two men landed some bass as well, but throughout the rest of the morning Bush reminded his two partners, "Anyone can catch a bass. It takes real skill to land the wily, elusive Potomac carp!"

Wilson Wooes Winter Women

As the U. S. moved closer to war with Germany, Woodrow Wilson grew weary of the anti-war protests going on outside the White House. During the bitter snowy cold of January in 1917, Wilson noticed a group of suffragettes night and day protesting America's support of European allies. The demonstrators were holding a large banner and huddled against a terrible wind. Wilson sent out an aide to invite the women in for tea next to a warm fire. The invitation was declined, and the protests continued.

Small, Indeed!

James Madison was our smallest President – just barely five feet tall and weighing about one hundred pounds. Political enemies and a hostile press seldom failed to mention this, and even those close to Madison were aware of his physique. One day a visitor came to see him for the first time. The White House was crowded, and the President's secretary said to the guest, "The President can't be seen." "My God!" the visitor exclaimed, "Is he *that* small?"

COOLIDGE'S NEAR COLLAPSE

In 1923 a study was made of the interior of the White House. When Calvin Coolidge read the report of the weakened condition of the building, he asked the engineers and architects, "If it is as bad as you say, why doesn't it fall down?" Extensive repairs were made three years later under the direction of U. S. Grant III, grandson of the eighteenth President.

NO COMPARISON

Harry Truman may have initially underestimated his job as Chief Executive. In early June of 1945, less than three months after he had been President, Truman wrote his wife back home in Missouri, "It won't be long until I can sit back and study the whole picture and tell 'em what is to be done in each department. When things come to that stage, there'll be no more to this job than there was to running Jackson County and not any more worry."

MIXED MESSAGE?

In February of 1847 General Zachary Taylor confronted Santa Anna's Mexican forces near Buena Vista. The enemy strength numbered nearly 20,000 compared to Taylor's army of 5,000. Santa Anna sent Taylor a note demanding he surrender. Being the southern gentleman, the general responded, "In reply to your note of this date summoning me to surrender my forces at discretion, I beg leave to say that I decline acceding to your request." Taylor then added abruptly, "Tell Santa Anna to go to hell." Cannons boomed and a slaughter ensued. When the smoke had cleared, the American casualties totaled less than 700 while the enemy lost 3500 men.

FRUSTRATED PROFESSOR

Woodrow Wilson found teaching at Bryn Mawr College, an all-girls institution, not very challenging. He said his students suffered from a "painful absenteeism of mind." He then took a position at Wesleyan University, but felt the male students there were even less prepared. Finally, in the fall of 1890, he joined the faculty at Princeton where he found great success.

NO MAGICIAN'S TRICK

President Eisenhower used a simple piece of string to explain his idea of leadership. There were leaders, he explained, "who just pushed," and when he pushed the string it got tangled up in a pile. Eisenhower then showed that there are other leaders who get out in front and pull. He pulled on the string and moved it forward in a straight line with a definite direction.

FORCED FEEDING

Grant's army was marching through Kentucky and Tennessee. It was cold and rainy, and the Union Army needed food, shelter, and clothing. Getting these basic necessities in a hostile environment often meant pillaging surrounding towns, though Grant usually disapproved of such practice. When his units began plundering homes and farms, Grant attempted to control the pillaging. Riding back from Paducah, Kentucky, the general met a woman who complained about a young lieutenant who had taken some food. Grant patiently listened to the enraged woman, and a couple of hours later ordered all of his troops to report to dress parade, where this order was read:

"Lieutenant Wickfield of the Fourth Indiana having this day eaten everything in Mrs. Selvidge's house but one pumpkin pie; he is hereby ordered to return with an escort of one hundred Calvary and eat that pie."
U. S. Grant, General Commanding

THOU SHALT NOT SMOKE

Jimmy and Rosalynn Carter have never smoked, and constantly preached about the habit and danger of cigarettes. As the former President explained in a book, "Our children have certainly heard their share from us. We have always felt a little self-righteous about keeping after them so much because we never smoked, but they have rarely listened anyway."

Not-So-Fond Memories

William Howard Taft described his term as President in this way: "The President cannot make the corn to grow, he cannot make business good, although when these things occur, political parties do claim some credit for the good things that have happened." He further lamented, "I have come to the conclusion that the major part of the work of a President is to increase the gate receipts of expositions and fairs and bring tourists to town."

Talk About Bureaucracy

The U. S. Department of Agriculture was founded in 1862 while Lincoln was President. At that time nearly forty per cent of Americans were farmers. The USDA had only *nine* employees, and they did their job quite effectively even though the Civil War created much demand for food. When Bill Clinton became President more than 130 years later, less than two per cent of the population consisted of farmers. Yet the USDA had grown to monstrous proportions. By 1993 there were more than 110,000 employees in the Department of Agriculture, consisting of forty-two agencies and 11,000 field offices, some of which were not within fifty miles of a farm. The department had a budget of nine billion dollars and critics claimed much of the money was wasted. Bill Clinton pledged to reduce government bureaucracy and felt the Department of Agriculture was a target for reform.

Where There's Smokestacks, There's Fire

William Henry Harrison had a beautiful 2800 acre estate at North Bend on the Ohio River near Cincinnati (this was also the boyhood home of his grandson Benjamin, who also became President). In 1858 the original Harrison home burned to the ground after a steamboat pilot steered too close to the river bank to give passengers a good look. Sparks flew from the vessel's double black stacks, setting the estate ablaze.

Good Manners

Though Lincoln lived a hard life, he was taught by his parents to be considerate and friendly. Toward the end of the War of 1812, when Lincoln was only six years old and living near Elizabethtown, Kentucky, he recalled an incident: "I had been fishing one day, and caught a little fish which I was taking home. I met a soldier in the road, and having been told at home that we must be good to soldiers, I gave him my fish."

A Solution Untried

Talk of a civil war was the main concern of the delegates who met at the 1860 Democratic Convention. Southerner Andrew Johnson pleaded for unity, but the party was hopelessly split. Johnson condemned abolitionist states like Massachusetts and slave-holding South Carolina. To the displeasure of both the northern and southern delegates, he announced, "I would chain Massachusetts and South Carolina together, and I would transport them to some island in the Arctic Ocean, the colder the better, till they cool off and come to their senses." His remarks received an "icy" response.

Indirect Question

U. S. Grant was a shy man. Even his proposal of marriage would indicate so. While on a carriage ride with Julia Dent, they came to a flooded bridge, and Julia cried, "I'm going to cling to you no matter what happens." Once safely across, Grant turned to his companion and asked, "How would you like to cling to me for the rest of your life?" She accepted.

Hard to Please

As a final friendly gesture, outgoing President Grover Cleveland redecorated part of the White House for William and Ida McKinley. He added touches to the Blue Room and had the large square bedroom painted yellow. Mrs. McKinley hated yellow and upon seeing the bedroom, abruptly turned and left the room. She demanded it be repainted in pink before entering it again.

Money and Menus

According to carefully kept records, the Tafts served food to an average of 2610 individuals each month at the White House. With so much entertaining, President Taft ordered a breakdown of food costs every three months. Taft himself was a voracious eater and weighed as much as 355 pounds.

Devoted and Demoted

In addition to his Scottish terrier, Fala, FDR and Eleanor Roosevelt also owned a police dog by the name of Major. The Roosevelts discovered that Major was very protective; in fact maybe too protective. At White House functions he had the habit of grabbing visitors by the arm. He also partook of a senator's leg one day and bit the hand of a tourist who reached through the iron gate to pet him. Though the President loved having him around, the First Lady gave Major away.

Freeze in a Breeze

Though James Madison did not actually fight in the Revolutionary War, he did suffer a wound of sorts. He and James Monroe once debated the merits of the Constitution on the portico of a Lutheran church in Culpepper, Virginia. A brisk winter wind was so cold that Madison suffered frostbite in his ear. He later pointed to the discolored and deformed blemish, referring to it as "the honorable scars…borne from the battlefield."

He Couldn't Help It

Though impeached by the House of Representatives, Andrew Johnson was found innocent when he was tried before the Senate. He returned to Tennessee to rebuild his eastern hill-country political machine. In 1874, just six years after leaving the Presidency amid turmoil and disgrace, he was elected to the U. S. Senate. He managed to combine his Democratic support with that of Republicans, who were promised he would not attack the Grant administration. But Johnson's Republican supporters should have known better. In his first speech in the Senate, he denounced President Grant's violations of federalism and the corruption then in existence.

V.P. Guidelines

President Lyndon Johnson knew what to look for in a running mate, having served as John Kennedy's Vice President for more than two years. In 1964 Johnson asked his former Senate colleague, Hubert H. Humphrey, to serve as second-in-command. He summoned Humphrey to the White House and explained, "This is like a marriage with no choice of divorce. I need complete and unswerving loyalty…. You most likely won't like the job after you've gotten it. Seldom do a President and Vice President get along." LBJ then added, "You keep out of the news. The news belongs to the President."

Tainted Star?

Lyndon B. Johnson was the first member of Congress to go into uniform during World War II. To say Johnson used his political influence to get special treatment is an understatement. Following an easy basic training, Johnson was instantly commissioned a Lieutenant Commander in the Navy, a rank that a career officer might have spent years obtaining. Bored with a stateside desk job in Navy Command, Johnson convinced President Roosevelt to give him a more exciting assignment overseas. The young Texan reported to General Douglas MacArthur as a special aide. One day while flying on a reconnaissance mission over New Guinea, his plane was attacked and shot at by a Japanese fighter plane. For merely being a passenger, LBJ received the nation's third highest decoration for bravery – the Silver Star. MacArthur pinned the medal on Johnson, and he wore it on his lapel years later when he became President. LBJ spent just seven months in the Navy before returning to his congressional seat, but he often reminded people of his gallantry during combat. Toward the end of his Presidency, however, Johnson confessed, "MacArthur pinned a medal on me for heroism. It looks good on my chest, but it's a good thing they couldn't see what that flight did to my pants!"

Breaking His Promise

In early March of 1900 President McKinley was the main guest at the banquet of the Ohio Society of New York City. Stepping up to the podium, the President remarked, "It is proper that I should say that the managing Board of the Ohio Society has kept the promise made to me some months ago, that I would *not* be expected or required to speak at this banquet; and because of that promise I have made some preparation!" After the crowd's laughter and hearty applause, McKinley gave a lengthy speech about the economy and foreign relations.

A "Rocky" Trip

As a young man, Theodore Roosevelt was in Germany with his family. As they readied to leave for Switzerland, it was discovered that T.R.'s trunk was so filled with rock specimens he had collected that he had discarded some of his clothes. His mother thought it better to leave some stones, but as fast as she threw them out of the trunk, the young naturalist picked them up and stuffed them into his pockets.

No Sweat

Ronald Reagan admitted he was not a hard-working Chief Executive. His frequent lengthy vacations and leisurely work habits led him to remark that he had been at work in the Oval Office "burning the midday oil." In his campaign of 1980 he said, "Show me an executive who works long overtime hours and I'll show you a bad executive." On another occasion he told an audience that after he's gone they'll put a plaque on his *chair* in the Cabinet Room: "Ronald Reagan slept here."

Physical Attributes

The most George Washington ever weighed was about 210 pounds, but his height of 6'3" is suspect. After Washington's death, Dr. James Craik measured his corpse and reported it to be 6'3¼". The physician measured the body from *head to toe*, instead of from head to heel. Washington himself said that he was only six-feet-tall.

Disturbing the Peace

A large chandelier once hung in the White House. Supposedly its tinkling disturbed Theodore Roosevelt, so he banished it to the Capitol to keep the Vice President awake. Years later, this chandelier was moved back to the Treaty Room of the White House at the request of Jacqueline Kennedy.

JESTING WITH THE ARMY

In 1899 President McKinley invited an army officer to the White House to discuss affairs on the island of Cuba which gained its independence as a result of the U.S. defeating the Spanish forces there. Amazed at the President's knowledge of international events, and aware of his busy work schedule, the officer commented, "You do a great deal of work over here." The President replied with a touch of sarcasm, "Oh no! We don't work any over here. We just sit around."

CHANGING THE TITLE

Newspaperman Leonard Lyons recalled driving past a big billboard with President Truman. Both men noticed that the Broadway musical *Gentlemen Prefer Blondes* was advertised. The President, thinking of his wife, remarked, *"Real gentlemen prefer gray."*

SOWING SEEDS FOR THE FUTURE

After months of campaigning in Illinois and debating Stephen Douglas, Abe Lincoln lost the 1858 Senate race in a close election. Lincoln believed his career in politics was over and wrote to his friend Dr. Anson Henry, "I am glad I made the late race… and though I now sink out of view, and shall be forgotten, I believe I have made some marks which will tell for the cause of civil liberty long after I am gone."

LEARNING THE BARE FACTS

The big four leaders of the Western world decided to have a summit meeting to discuss economic and political problems. Giscard of France, Schmidt of West Germany, Callaghan of Great Britain, and President Jimmy Carter agreed to meet in January of 1979 in a warm climate. The meeting took place on the French Caribbean island of Guadeloupe. To their surprise and delight the four leaders took the opportunity to investigate the vacationers on the nudist beach below their open-air thatched-roof hut where they met. Unfortunately for Callaghan, he sat with his back to the beach.

FINANCIAL HELP

Though born in extreme poverty, Andrew Johnson proved quite successful in business. His salaries earned as an elected official were supplemented by the money he made in real estate, farming, railroads, and a couple of flour mills he owned near his homestead in Greenville, South Carolina.

A WARM WELCOME

Though Martin Van Buren and Henry Clay were political adversaries, they enjoyed a private friendship. The somber Van Buren was amused by Clay's joking whenever the two had dinner at the White House. One day the White House laundry caught fire and was spreading fast. Citizens, including Clay, rushed in to put out the flames. Crossing the entrance, Clay met the President, who explained that everything was under control. Clay put his hand on Van Buren's shoulder and remarked, "We want you out of the White House, Mr. Van Buren, but we don't want you *burnt* out." Van Buren laughed and thanked the Senator for his "humane feeling."

TAYLOR TEMPTED

Zachary Taylor's nickname "Old Rough and Ready" was well suited. His habits and comments could be brusque and crude at times. James Buchanan once brought a group of young ladies to meet the President at a White House reception. Taylor was impressed by Buchanan's selections and remarked, "You always pick out the prettiest ladies." Buchanan responded, "Why, Mr. President, I know your taste and mine agree in that respect." Taylor made the ladies blush when he loudly said, "Yes, but I have been so long among Indians and Mexicans I hardly know how to behave myself, surrounded by so many beautiful women!"

NICE TO MICE

Rodents were a problem in the White House throughout much of the 1800s. Numerous attempts to poison and exterminate them were not very successful. Certainly Andrew Johnson did not do much to remedy the problem of rats and mice. One evening he watched mice play in his upstairs bedroom and the next night laid out some white flour and water so the tiny critters could "get their fill." He explained to one of his secretaries that the "little fellows" had given him "their confidence," and he continued to feed them.

MOVING UP IN THE WORLD

Retired General Douglas MacArthur was a guest of John F. Kennedy at the White House one afternoon. Following their meeting, MacArthur met with inquisitive reporters outside and told them that JFK had been a fine naval officer, and that he admired the young President's courageous acts as a PT boat commander. Then MacArthur added, "Judging from the luncheon he served me today, he's living higher now."

WHO CARES?

Retired President Calvin Coolidge wrote Congressman Sol Bloom this response in December of 1929:
"Dear Mr. Bloom, The *Congressional Record* comes to my office and I wish to thank you for your kindness in sending it to me. I had done nothing about getting it because, since I left Washington, I have not cared to know what was going on in the Congress, but your kindness is none the less greatly appreciated."

EISENHOWER HITS MCKINLEY?

April 16, 1953, marked the Opening Day game between the Washington Senators and the New York Yankees. There to throw out the first pitch was the new President, Dwight D. Eisenhower. "Ike" had played baseball at West Point (he played football as well) and was considered a good ballplayer. No doubt some fans expected to see him throw a fast ball for a strike, but the President was rusty, having not played in forty-some years. He wound up and let loose a wild pitch, striking a nearby umpire. Ironically, the umpire's name was William McKinley!

THE OLD FASHION WAY

Just prior to his resignation over the Watergate crisis, President Richard Nixon told his Chief of Staff Alexander Haig, "You know, Al, you soldiers have the best way of dealing with a situation like this. You just leave a man alone in a room with a loaded pistol."

I SAID "NO!"

William McKinley had just been elected President for a second time in 1900. By May of the following year several prominent Republicans came out in favor of him seeking a third term. The President, a bit irritated, issued a statement, "I will say now, once for all, expressing a long settled conviction, that I not only am not and will not be a candidate for a third term, but would not accept a nomination for it if it were tendered me."

THE MISERIES OF WAR

Malaria, typhoid, and pneumonia took a heavy toll of soldiers during the Civil War. Brigadier General James Garfield's regiment, the 42nd Ohio Volunteer Infantry, was no exception. He dreaded facing the fathers and mothers of his dead "boys" back home in northeast Ohio. He commented in a letter, "This fighting with disease is infinitely more horrible than battle…. This is the price of saving the Union. My God, what a costly sacrifice." Garfield was also upset upon learning that captured Confederate officers were sent to Camp Chase in Columbus and allowed to wear sidearms and be attended by slaves.

A GOING-AWAY PRESENT

On Jimmy Carter's last day in office, Max Cleland presented him with a plaque inscribed with these words of Thomas Jefferson: "I have the consolation to reflect that during my administration not a drop of blood of a single citizen was shed by the sword of war." Though Carter failed to be re-elected, his four years as President was marked by great strides in world peace.

FIGHTING WORDS

Theodore Roosevelt's hand-picked successor, William Howard Taft, did not live up to Roosevelt's standards as President. By 1912 Roosevelt decided to oppose Taft and the split in Republican ranks guaranteed Woodrow Wilson's election. Roosevelt referred to Taft as "a flubdub, a puzzlewit, a floppy-souled creature, and a man with brains of about three guinea-pig power." The gentleman Taft remained as silent as long as he could, finally labeling Roosevelt as a "maniac" who presented "a great danger to the nation."

PRESIDENT ORDERS LINDBERGH *NOT* TO FLY

Charles A. Lindbergh became one of America's biggest heroes when he flew non-stop from New York to Paris in 1927. Flying in the "Spirit of St. Louis," Lindbergh's trip took thirty-three and a half hours. Lindbergh wanted to fly back home to American, but Calvin Coolidge ordered the pilot and plane to return by ship. They did, and Lindbergh was first greeted in Washington, D.C., where the President presented him with the Distinguished Flying Cross.

TRAINING SESSION

Even though George Bush served as Vice President for eight years, he did receive some valuable on-the-job training. For a brief time, the Vice President actually served as President. On July 15, 1985, Ronald Reagan signed a document transferring the power of the Presidency to Bush. Reagan underwent surgery to remove a two-inch cancerous growth in his intestines. While Reagan was under anesthesia, Bush served as acting President for a couple hours.

IT COULD HAVE BEEN WORSE

In the spring of 1781 George Washington was busy fighting the British. As he feared, a British warship sailed the Potomac and landed at Mt. Vernon. His cousin, Lund, was in charge of the estate and had promised a fight if redcoats ever came near. Discretion may be the better part of valor, and rather than resist, Lund offered the enemy officers refreshments, gave them ample provisions, and stood by as twenty slaves were stolen. When George learned of the incident, he exploded in anger, remarking he would rather have seen the mansion destroyed. But two and a half years later when he returned, he may have changed his mind. Mt. Vernon was not only completely intact, but remodeled and improved.

LAYING DOWN THE LAW

Quentin Roosevelt was constantly reminded that some of his horseplay at the White House had to be restricted. His father told him that the flower beds on the White House grounds should not be used as a practice area for little boys on stilts. Quentin complained loudly, "I don't see what good it does me for you to be President. You can't do anything here! I wish I was back home!"

WHO'S THE BOSS?

William Henry Harrison was summoned to the White House in 1812 by President James Madison. Harrison had recently defeated the British near Detroit and was to consult with the President on the strategy of the war. After the conference Harrison was ordered to return to his post. Later that evening, however, Dolley Madison announced that the young hero would be attending a party she was conducting. The President laughed and said, "General Harrison should be thirty or forty miles on his way west by now." But the First Lady explained, "I laid my command on him and he is too gallant a man to disobey me. We shall soon see whose orders he obeys." Harrison showed up as the special guest.

FRENCH FUSE BOX FIASCO

In January of 1951 Dwight Eisenhower was appointed as Commander of SHAPE (Supreme Headquarters Allied Powers in Europe). He and Mamie were given an apartment at the Hotel Trianon but the French were economical on the heat. When Mamie plugged in an American electric heater, it blew out every fuse in the hotel. The French press made a big deal of the incident, but Mamie insisted on a smaller, more comfortable residence. Finally, the French government gave the Eisenhowers a warmer villa ten miles west of Paris.

REWARD FOR A SLAVE

Richard Stanhope was aptly rewarded for his services as George Washington's master-servant. Because of his devotion, this black man received both his freedom and 400 acres of land in Champaign County, Ohio, after the first President died. Stanhope was with Washington everyday for more than thirty years, and died in 1862 at the age of 114.

WAITING FOR RACHEL

Andrew Jackson refused to believe his wife Rachel had died. For two days after her death on December 22, 1828, he ordered doctors to bleed the body in an effort to revive her. He also ordered the table on which she was laid out be covered with blankets so when she woke up she would not be uncomfortable.

I'll Try Anything

Several of our Chief Executives were poor businessmen. Perhaps that is one reason they got involved in politics. Truman, Grant, and Lincoln were among those who "tossed in the towel" in regard to private enterprise. Another one was Franklin Roosevelt. Among his business flops were: owning a business selling a coffee substitute, marketing bottled warm spring water for consumption, organizing a blimp service, manufacturing a machine to issue postage stamps with a sanitized back, operating three automated stores in New York City dispensing consumer articles, and serving as the director of three companies speculating and investing German marks (which later became totally worthless). FDR also quit a law partnership which was only moderately successful.

Limitations

William McKinley knew his strengths and weaknesses. One thing he wanted to avoid in both his campaigns for President was debating his opponent William Jennings Bryan. A consummate orator, Bryan stumped the nation in 1896 and 1900 talking to millions of people. McKinley just stayed at home in Canton, Ohio, where he conducted his "front porch campaign" and gave brief talks. Bryan was a theatrical success, but the former Congressman from Ohio won both elections. McKinley told his advisor and financier, Mark Hanna, "I might just as well put up a trapeze on my front lawn and compete with some professional athlete. I have to think when I speak."

More is not Better

In demonstrating his stamina, it has been pointed out that Richard Nixon visited all fifty states during the 1960 Presidential campaign. But it should also be noted that John Kennedy visited forty-four states, and made stops in 237 cities, whereas Nixon only reached 170.

What a Story!

In the autumn of 1940 Franklin Roosevelt was confined to bed with a severe cold. The *Washington Post* committed a classic typographical error in a headline when it announced, "FDR IN BED WITH COED." The newspaper soon got a call from the President. FDR said, "This is Franklin Roosevelt. I'd like 100 copies of that first edition of the *Post*. I want to send it to all of my friends!"

Nixon Exits

Ohioan William Saxbe was a man known for his bluntness. Saxbe served as Attorney General during the final days of the Nixon administration as the Watergate scandal brought increasing pressure on Nixon to resign or face impeachment. Nixon expected Saxbe, the fourth Attorney General in Nixon's administration, to "bail him out," but Saxbe had a reputation for honesty. At one of the President's last cabinet meetings, Saxbe recalls an incident where Nixon "was talking about next month and next year. Already the wolves were at the door. You could hear them…he was talking about these plans and everybody sat there looking down their noses, real serious. I said, 'Mr. President, we shouldn't be talking about next year. Let's talk about next week.' He shut up, turned around and walked out of the Cabinet Room. Within a week he was gone…."

A Promise Kept

Andrew Jackson had no children of his own, and his wife had died before he took his oath of office. He did, however, promise his niece that someday he would put her in the White House as First Lady. Jackson's niece was Sarah Childress Polk, wife of the man Jackson helped to become the eleventh U.S. President.

Behind Every Man…

Before going on its first-ever tour away from Washington, D.C., the U.S. Marine Band had to get permission from President Benjamin Harrison. Director John Philip Sousa knew the best way to go about this. "My years in Washington had taught me," he explained, "that if you wish to see the President, see his wife first. So I asked Mrs. Harrison. She liked the idea of a tour, and promised to speak to the President about it." Harrison saw Sousa the next day and commented with a smile, "I have thought it over, and I believe the country would rather hear you, than see me, so you have my permission to go."

Tyler Ignored

In the first and only time in our history, a Vice Presidential race was decided by the U.S. Senate. In the 1836 Presidential race John Tyler's name was on the ballot for Vice President in five southern states. Having failed to win a majority of popular and electoral votes like the other running mates, the Senate chose Richard Johnson to serve as second in command to Martin Van Buren. The Senators met on February 8, 1837. Four years later Tyler ran again as the Whig second fiddle and won.

Ignored or Disobeyed?

President Richard Nixon did not play tennis, and he felt the tennis court on the White House grounds marred the simplicity and elegance of the South Lawn. He ordered it removed – a decision which made several aides unhappy. When he brought the subject up at meetings, his staff promised to look into the matter. After a few months, he mentioned it again, and his staff resolved to investigate. Eventually, Nixon realized the only way to get rid of the tennis court was to rent a bulldozer and tear it up himself. Years later, in 1990, Nixon remarked, "President Bush can thank my staff for not carrying out my order!"

Self Assured

In September of 1918, Harry Truman wrote his wife that she need not fear for his safety. As an artillery captain, Truman saw plenty of action in France during World War I. He explained to Bess in a letter, "Please don't worry about me because no German shell is made that can hit me. One exploded within fifteen feet of me and I didn't get a scratch, so you see I have them beaten there."

Un-American

Few Presidents promoted the idea of Americanism more than Theodore Roosevelt. He once hired a tutor for his son, Kermit. The tutor was Walter Hinchman, a Harvard graduate in his early twenties. Hinchman arrived one July evening in 1902 bearing a broken thumb. "What's the matter with your thumb?" asked the President. Hinchman explained he had broken it in a cricket game. "Serves you right for playing such a game," responded Roosevelt, grinning as he said it.

Just Watch This!

Not many Americans could watch Harry Truman on television. In the mid-1940s there were only 10,000 sets in the U.S. By 1950, however, there where 10,000,000 households with televisions, and by 1960 there were more than 44,000,000 households with TV. The Kennedy-Nixon debates that year attracted a huge audience, and historians agree that television helped elect Kennedy as President. Television changed forever the way Presidential campaigns were conducted.

A View from the Top

Franklin D. Roosevelt once explained to his son, James, "You can't be a great President without being a great politician. You can't do anything until you get in a position where you can do it. You make as few and as small compromises as you must on your way to the top. You don't want to be compromised by your compromises."

Presidential Support

James Amos, a young black man, was an assistant butler in the White House in the early 1900s. Amos and his father were friends of Theodore Roosevelt. More than once Amos paddled the young Roosevelt boys for mischief and the President always backed him up. One evening the table in the state dining room was set for important guests. T.R.'s daughter, Ethel, examined the brilliantly set table, going from place to place, eating almonds and bon-bons. Amos suggested she go somewhere else, but the little girl was slow to obey. He then took her by the arm firmly and led her toward the door. Ethel yelled, "I'm a young lady. I'm going to tell my father." Shortly, Amos received a message to come to the President. Ethel was there as well when Roosevelt asked, "Now then, what is it this scoundrel did to you?" Ethel gave the details of the incident without exaggeration. After listening to all the facts, the President replied, "James, you did right."

Misunderstanding

In 1968 the GOP made a Nixon commercial for television. The Vietnam War was at its height, and one scene showed a U.S. soldier who had painted LOVE on the front of his helmet. Complaints began pouring in criticizing the Republicans for running a commercial that was unpatriotic, contradictory, and in poor taste. The GOP public relations committee met to discuss whether the advertisement should be removed. A top Nixon-for-President advisor received a letter, thanking the party for including a picture of her son and explained how proud and excited she was. It was signed, "Mrs. William Love."

Put Away Your Spears

William Henry Harrison hated confrontation and political bickering. He indicated he was content to let Congress run the country and would go to almost any extreme to avoid conflict. Just after his inauguration he told Senator Thomas Hart Benton, "I beg you not to be harpooning me in the Senate; if you dislike anything in my administration, put it into Clay or Webster, but don't harpoon me." Harrison, however, lived only one month as President, thus avoiding any showdown.

Evidence Destroyed – We Think!

In June of 1962 Pierre Salinger was sent to Moscow by President Kennedy to meet with Nikita Kruschev. After two days, Salinger returned to the White House with a gift from the Soviet premiere – 250 Havana Cuban cigars. JFK enjoyed cigars, but he asked Salinger, "Do you realize what a scandal this would be if people found out?" Realizing that accepting a gift from enemy Cuba might damage his reputation, Kennedy ordered the cigars turned over to U.S. Customs officials, where they were destroyed – probably very slowly, one at a time!

He Wouldn't Win a Bee

Harry Truman was not an exceptional speller and usually kept a pocket dictionary with him. One time, Louis Gerson, professor of political science at the University of Connecticut, asked Truman to autograph a copy of his memoirs. The President spelled "professor" his usual way – "proffessor." Gerson pointed out, "But Mr. President, that's a misspelling." Truman grinned and said, "Oh, never mind. It'll make the book more valuable."

No Change of Scenery

At the end of his second term, an exhausted FDR said, "I want to go home to Hyde Park. I want to take care of my trees…. I want to make the farm pay. I want to finish my little house on the hill. I want to write history." The threat of war, however, helped change his mind, and the President ran for two more terms.

Blame His Parents!

Dwight Eisenhower was only in office a couple of weeks when he grew tired of autographing pictures and signing various letters and documents. One day, his Vice President, Richard Nixon, was summoned to the Oval Office. When Nixon entered, Eisenhower looked up from his desk and complained, "Dammit, Dick. I wish my name weren't so long!"

Off to the Auction

Like many of his fellow planters in the Virginia Tidewater area, John Tyler was land-rich and cash-poor. Most of the money he earned from his salaries in public office and his private law practice went into his plantation and additional farm. He was so desperate for funds in 1827 that he sold a favorite house slave, Ann Eliza, so he could move to Washington. Tyler tried to sell her to friends but, finding no buyers, instructed that she be put in a wagon and sent to Hubbards' auction block in Richmond. It should be understood, however, that the future President's treatment of slaves was uniformly kind and considerate.

No Hard Feelings

In 1790 James Madison sold Thomas Jefferson a horse for twenty-five English pounds. The animal had hardly been saddled and ridden before it became sick and died. Both men were embarrassed. Jefferson, then Secretary of State, listened to Madison's suggestion that a mutual friend decide on a fair settlement. Jefferson, however, insisted on paying for the dead horse. He sent Madison a check for $92.25, which was $12.00 more than the agreed price. Along with the check he sent a note remarking that the horse's "disorders was of the instant, and might have happened years as well as when it did…." Such incidents turned men against each other, but this particular friendship of historical proportions was maintained.

Quick Cure for Homesickness

When he was eleven years old, Franklin Pierce of Hillsboro, New Hampshire, was sent to an academy in Hancock, fourteen miles away. Just after Frank entered the school, he got homesick and walked back home. His father promptly put him in a wagon and took him back, but only *half way*, leaving him on the roadside and never saying a word. Frank got caught in a torrential rainstorm and trudged the seven miles back to the academy. He finished the term and later attended several other schools in different towns.

You Just Can't Win

President Lyndon Johnson had a reputation of making unexpected visits to his staff members. One day he strode into the office of Malcolm Kilduff, assistant White House press secretary. Glancing at Kilduff's desk top which was clear of any paper, LBJ remarked, "I hope your mind isn't as empty as your desk." For the next few days Kilduff piled papers atop his desk and scattered them in expectation of another visit by the President. When it came, Johnson took one look at the desk and said, "It's evident you can't keep up with your work!"

Born to Get Votes?

Martin Van Buren was literally born "at the polls." His birthplace in Kinderhook, New York, was a tavern owned by his father. This building was where local citizens cast their ballots on Election Day. The youthful Van Buren spent considerable time listening to politics discussed by his father's patrons.

A Minority President

When John F. Kennedy defeated Richard Nixon in 1960, he won the closest Presidential race in the twentieth century. What many people did not realize is that Kennedy DID NOT win a majority of the popular vote. Nearly 69,000,000 voted, with Kennedy getting 49.72% compared to Nixon's 49.55%.

AN INSIDE LOOK

Isaac, one of Jefferson's house servants, provided some insight into the life of the retired President. Jefferson sometimes had as many as twenty books spread open on the floor and often conversed with guests in French and *English*. He kept three fiddles, playing in the afternoon and evening. While riding a horse or taking a walk, Jefferson could be heard singing.

A SORE SUBJECT

Horseback riding for James Madison was not always easy. He was constantly "pained" by hemorrhoid attacks. In late spring and summer, Madison would ride the rough local Virginia roads over 100 miles to sit in the mineral waters at Berkley Springs near the Maryland border. Once at ease after several days, he then returned to his home at Montpelier.

PRESIDENTIAL PULL

The most famous Presidential campaign railroad car was the "Ferdinand Magellan." Built in 1928 by the Pullman Company, it was custom built for our Chief Executives. Nearly eighty-four feet long, it was heavily reinforced with steel and thick glass for security. FDR put the car to good use, traveling more than 50,000 miles. During his whistle-stop campaign in 1948, Harry Truman traveled over 21,000 miles. Eisenhower rode it for 1000 miles, and Ronald Reagan put in 200 miles. The car now rests in Miami, Florida and is open to the public.

THE PRICE IS RIGHT

Early in the twentieth century, Presidential candidates began seeking endorsements from sports heroes. When baseball great Ty Cobb signed up with Democrat James Cox in 1920, the Republicans, whose candidate was Warren G. Harding, approached Babe Ruth. "Hell no, I'm a Democrat," Ruth replied. He then paused and asked, "How much are they offering?" Ruth was told he would be given $4000 to make an appearance with Harding, and he readily agreed. Conflicting schedules, however, prevented the two from getting together. In 1928, Ruth endorsed the Democratic candidate Al Smith.

MY BROTHER'S KEEPER?

On Friday, June 25, 1993, President Bill Clinton received a strange phone call. It was from Henry Ritzenthaler, Clinton's newly discovered half brother. The men, who had never met, didn't have much to talk about. White House staffers no longer greeted each other, "Hey, brother!" For the next few days it was, "Hey, half brother!"

BEN BOXED IN

Republicans were determined that Benjamin Harrison must oust incumbent Grover Cleveland in the 1888 election. Harrison won an extremely close race, and as a result, the new President found himself bound to fulfill hundreds of campaign promises made by Republican Party leaders. Harrison complained, "I could not name my own Cabinet! They had sold out every place to pay the election expenses."

SIMILAR CIRCUMSTANCES

Historians point out the striking similarities regarding the so-called Lincoln-Kennedy "connection." The circumstances involving their Vice Presidents, place of assassination, and other oddities are well documented. Overlooked perhaps are the strange coincidences surrounding Garfield and McKinley. Both of these Presidents were born in northeast Ohio, taught school, served in the Civil War, and were U.S. Congressmen. Garfield and McKinley were both elected in round-numbered years (1880 and 1900 respectively). Both married Ohio-born women, and both were killed by men who were Ohio residents at one time. Garfield and McKinley each lost two children due to disease, and both Presidents died in September. Each was shot twice, with one of the bullets inflicting only superficial wounds. In both cases the lethal bullet could not be located, and perhaps the number eight played an unlucky role – Garfield died eighty days after he was shot, McKinley died eight days later. Both men were delivered to their place of rest by train, and their bodies were removed by train. And in each case, their wound was not necessarily fatal. Lack of proper equipment, unsanitary practices by perplexed physicians, and a general lack of medical knowledge precipitated their death. Both Garfield and McKinley and their wives are buried together under domed monuments in Ohio. And their assassins were very similar in looks and physical makeup.

General Quarters

As Washington's rag-tag, beleaguered army set up winter quarters at Valley Forge, the Commander-in-Chief was offered a comfortable residence in the mansion of John Potts. Deborah Howes, Potts' daughter-in-law, greeted Washington at the doorway. "A thousand thanks, Madam," said the general, "but until my men have their shelters built, I'll live in my tent. I should be no warmer then they."

Granting Grace

While he was serving as Governor of Ohio, William McKinley's friends and supporters urged him to reconsider appointing a fellow Republican who had deserted him for Democrats. They argued that this individual had been a traitor and that he was not entitled to hold office. McKinley listened patiently, then flashed his smile and announced, "Gentlemen, you seem to forget that I am a Methodist and believe in the doctrine of falling from grace." The man was appointed.

Influenced by Mom

Frank Pierce's reputation as an alcoholic was well established. Though he gave up drinking four years before his death, the damage done to his body was so advanced, alcoholism still killed him. The fourteenth President, however, can't be totally blamed, for his mother was a heavy drinker as well. Anna Kendrick Pierce married a Revolutionary War officer and moved into a house in Hillsborough, New Hampshire. The home was attached to a tavern. Anna's thirst for alcohol is well documented in family letters, and she once shocked a Sunday church congregation when she wore a dress so short that her ankles showed. Despite her drinking habits, her son Frank reminded his brother-in-law, "She was a most affectionate and tender mother, strong in many points and weak in some…."

Unlucky Duo

George Washington's army suffered only two casualties when it defeated the Hessians at Trenton, New Jersey, in 1776. One of the soldiers wounded was Captain William Washington (a distant cousin). The other was James Monroe. Both men survived, but Monroe was shot in the chest. Blood gushed from his wound and soaked his uniform. He would have bled to death but a doctor took his index finger and plugged up the wound. A surgeon later treated the wound but never found the bullet.

Misinterpreted

On at least two occasions Jimmy Carter discovered his words to foreign audiences weren't interpreted correctly – or at all. While he was President, Carter flew to Warsaw to strengthen the alliance between the Polish and American people. At the airport in Warsaw he made a brief speech to a welcoming party and during the talk alluded to understanding and appreciating the Polish commitment to the love of freedom. Hours later Carter learned he was quoted by the interpreter as saying he knew and understood "your commitment to free love." Then in 1981, the ex-President was asked to make a commencement address to a graduating class in Osaka, Japan. He wanted to use some humor so he included a joke. The crowd responded with loud, uproarious laughter. Following his talk, Carter asked his interpreter why his audience laughed so hard, but the interpreter didn't answer. Carter pressed him on the issue and finally the interpreter confessed that he simply told the audience, "President Carter just told a funny story and all of you must laugh."

My Hero

In 1862 James A. Garfield was leading his troops through Kentucky. He was surprised and elated to have some important dispatches delivered to him by one of his biggest heroes – none other than Christopher "Kit" Carson. The legendary scout and mountain man, himself a Union officer, had been surrounded and shot at by rebels before locating Garfield. Carson was in Kentucky probably at the request of his friend General John C. Fremont. After a brief but pleasant visit, Carson rode back. Later that same year he returned to the West to command soldiers to fight against Indians and Confederate forces.

Hands Off!

George Washington never shook hands with guests while he was President. He politely bowed to each person in the receiving line, keeping one hand on the hilt of his sword and the other behind his back. John Adams met visitors in a similar manner, but Thomas Jefferson broke tradition and "pumped the flesh."

No Home Repairs Needed

By 1898 the White House elevator wasn't working very well. It was an antique and ran from water pressure of a tank on the roof. Its ascent was often slow and noisy when it worked, but it was a luxury to overweight politicians who otherwise would have to climb the stairs to see President McKinley. When the elevator broke down, which was often, Congressmen complained to the White House staff. McKinley told the staff, "Let them complain. It's too easy for them to get up here the way it is."

Polk Gets Poked

In a January 12, 1848, speech to his fellow Congressmen, Abraham Lincoln had some rather uncomplimentary things to say about President James K. Polk. Lincoln, a Whig Representative, accused the Democrat President of "unnecessarily and unconstitutionally" starting the Mexican War. He ended his harsh attack by declaring that Polk "knows not where he is. He is a bewildered, confused, and miserably perplexed man. God grant he may be able to show there is something about the conscience, more painful than all his mental perplexity." Many Americans felt such criticism too severe, and Lincoln was not re-elected to Congress.

A Prayer and A President

New York Congressman Stephen Van Rensselaer was a religious man who was usually decisive and firm in his political deliberations. But in 1825 his hesitation and indecision led to a moment of prayer, and the result was a choosing of a U.S. President. In the 1824 election none of the four main candidates could muster a majority of the electoral votes. Henry Clay, William Crawford, John Quincy Adams, and Andrew Jackson represented various interests and sections of the country, but neither gained a victory in the race for the White House. That left it up to the House of Representatives to select a President. Congress took its time in voting, and by February a tie existed between Adams and Jackson. Van Rensselaer would cast the deciding vote. Under great pressure, he took his seat and bowed his head in prayer. He noticed something on the floor beside him – it was a discarded ballot, trampled but already marked. He picked it up and cast *that* ballot. John Quincy Adams was declared the winner, amid protests that Henry Clay made a bargain so Jackson would not win. Later, Adams named Clay his Secretary of State, convincing critics that a "corrupt bargain" had been made. But a Congressman from New York had a lot to do with the outcome.

Murderer's Oath

Jubilant throngs throughout the North celebrated Lee's surrender to Grant, ending the Civil War. A large crowd gathered outside the White House to serenade President Lincoln and hopefully hear a few brief remarks. Lincoln appeared that evening and gave a short speech next to a kerosene lamp held by his secretary. Among the many listeners below the portico where Lincoln spoke was John Wilkes Booth. After the talk Booth turned to one of his accomplices and remarked, "That is the last speech he will ever make."

A Nasal Passage

U.S. Grant's disdain for President Andrew Johnson became clear when he announced he would refuse to ride in a carriage with the outgoing Johnson on Inauguration Day. At noon on Johnson's last day, the seventeenth President finished his work at the White House. Completing his tasks, Johnson made his final rounds to shake hands with the staff and his Cabinet. He turned to his Secretary of the Navy, Gideon Welles, and said with a smile of relief, "I can already smell the sweet mountain air of Tennessee." Johnson then assembled his staff and told them before departing, "God bless you all."

A Look for the Good Book

Grant's term ended on Sunday, March 4, 1877, but inaugural ceremonies would not be held until the following day. Rather than have the nation without a President for an entire day, Grant suggested that Rutherford B. Hayes take his oath of office in a private ceremony. During an evening dinner party at the White House, Chief Justice Morrison Waite slipped into the mansion with the necessary documents and swore in Hayes. Only one thing was forgotten – there was no *Bible,* and none could be found. This event took place in the Red Room, and Hayes became the nineteenth President.

No Fears for Francis

Perhaps President Cleveland had some concerns about his young bride, Francis, who was just twenty-one years old. He explained, "I want her to be happy and to possess all she can reasonably desire, but I should feel very much afflicted if she lets many notions in her head." Pausing a moment, he then added, "I think she is pretty level-headed."

A Black White House

A portion of Millard Fillmore's two years and 237 days in office were spent under dark shadows. For a month after President Zachary Taylor's death, the White House, its furniture, mirrors, and chandeliers were draped in funeral black. Henry Clay died in the summer of 1852, and the Executive Mansion was again draped in mourning. Then in October of that same year black silk and crepe was put up again when Daniel Webster died.

Problems, Problems

William Henry Harrison was not only sick during his one month as Chief Executive, he was sick and tired of seeing hordes of office seekers waiting for Presidential appointments. Adding "fuel to the fire" was the ongoing dispute between Secretary of State Henry Clay and Senator Daniel Webster. Of the battle between these two statesmen, Harrison remarked, "They will drive me mad!"

Timid Tyler

Criticism of President John Tyler reached a new level. Burned in effigy in several cities, death threats were also made. One day an unmarked package turned up in the entrance hall of the White House. The household staff gathered around the box, afraid to touch it. Tyler was summoned and, fearing it was a bomb, called his doorman Martin Renehan to dispose of it. Renehan ran to the kitchen and returned with a meat clever. The hall was cleared, and the box was lifted onto a table. Tyler jumped through a door and with other staff members hid behind a marble column. "Martin, Martin, aren't you afraid?" asked the President. Renehan replied, "No sir; it's better for me to die than that the President should be killed by such a devil of a machine. My death is nothing compared with your Excellency's." The Irishman chopped furiously as the onlookers cringed. The wooden box fell apart only to reveal a miniature iron stove. The President and his staff crept back into the hall. Tyler was embarrassed, and emphatically instructed Renehan not to say a word of the incident, explaining, "If you do, they'll have me caricatured." The public never learned of it, and Tyler was spared further criticism.

Bad Back Comeback

William T. Crump worked for nearly ten years as a servant at the White House. One day in 1881 he permanently injured his back while lifting the mortally wounded President, James A. Garfield, into bed. After Garfield's death, Crump was rudely dismissed by President Arthur. Retiring to the seashore in Virginia, Crump became the owner of a successful hotel and restaurant. He named the restaurant after Garfield.

One Isn't Enough!

In 1792 there were three Presidential homes under construction in three different cities. In order to keep the headquarters of the federal government and the President's mansion in their cities, both Philadelphia and New York began construction, competing against the newly-planned Federal City, later called Washington, D.C. (though President George Washington and the Congress preferred the District of Columbia). Though the buildings in New York and Philadelphia were nearly half completed, stone blocks and bricks began to take shape for the White House located on farmland above the Potomac River.

Earliest Visitor

Contrary to popular belief, George Washington DID attend a ceremony at the White House. Following John Adams' inauguration in March of 1797 in Philadelphia, the former President and his wife made their way to Mount Vernon. The carriage stopped along the banks of the Potomac where the new Federal City was under construction. The White House had been partially built, and the Washingtons stopped to gaze at the construction site of outer walls and empty window sockets. Crowds there noticed the fancy coach and stood on the walls of the house for a glimpse. Architect James Hoban ordered a sixteen-gun salute fired. Amidst wild cheering George Washington departed, never to visit there again.

SUMMONING STRENGTH

Franklin D. Roosevelt's last inauguration was also the briefest. Held at the White House, the affair lasted less than ten minutes. Roosevelt nearly collapsed, suffering from arteriosclerosis and heart disease. While he rested in the Green Room, the First Lady entertained 250 luncheon guests. The President said to his son, James, "I can't stand this unless you get me a stiff drink – and you better make it straight." After several minutes he joined his guests, who were shocked at his haggard appearance. One of them, the widow of Woodrow Wilson, commented, "He looks exactly as my husband did when he went into his decline." Secretary of Labor Francis Perkins chided Edith Wilson, "Don't say that to another soul. He has a great and terrible job to do, and he's got to do it even if it kills him." Roosevelt died eleven weeks later.

FROM BOOKS TO BATTLE

In 1850 Rutherford B. Hayes opened a law office in Cincinnati. Business was not good. Having so few clients and being poor, Hayes slept in his law office to save what little money he had. With so much spare time, he joined the Literary Club. In 1861 this group formed a militia company to fight in the Civil War. Hayes was elected captain and was later appointed a major. He retired from the war as a general, having seen a great deal of action.

SEEING THE LIGHT

In 1854 Benjamin Harrison had his first court case. A single candle stood on a table in the darkened courtroom where the Indiana lawyer held his notes. He vainly shifted the candle back and forth to get more light, but finally threw the notes away. It was at this point that Harrison realized he could think clearly and speak quite well without personal notes, and he won the case!

MAINTAINING HIS IMAGE

Just three hours before he was shot, John Kennedy spoke at a breakfast in Fort Worth, Texas. He was presented a wide brimmed cowboy hat, and the 2500 guests assumed he would wear it. But Kennedy was not about to alter his tailored eastern look. He disdained wearing "funny hats" and had remarked to friends on several occasions that he did not wish to be remembered in photographs like the one of Calvin Coolidge wearing an Indian headdress. So he told his guest, "Come to Washington Monday, and I'll put it on in the White House for you."

HOME-MADE SNOW

Andy Jackson found little use for the fancy cotton candy balls the French chef had prepared for a Christmas dinner at the White House. Instead of eating them, he armed each of his two grandchildren with a batch and initiated an all-out "snowball" fight.

A SON AND A GUN

When he was a youngster, Jimmy Carter used to go hunting with his father. One day he shot his first quail. In the next instant an excited Jimmy went running to locate his prize. His father caught up with him, examined the bird and asked, "Jimmy, where's your gun?" Young Carter didn't know, and the two of them spent half the day looking for it before it was found. Jimmy learned a lesson in keeping one's composure, and his dad, to Jimmy's credit, never told the story to anyone.

LOCKS OF LUCK

Following John Adams' inauguration, George and Martha Washington attended a private retirement party in their honor. During the reception Mrs. Oliver Wolcott congratulated Martha and asked if she could have a memento of the First Family. Her request was granted: Mrs. Washington took out a pair of scissors and cut a large lock of hair from her husband's head, then with a big smile, cut off a lock of her own and gave it to Mrs. Wolcott as a gift.

STOP! THIEF!

While First Lady Helen Taft was recovering from a stroke, the President brought her flowers he picked from the White House garden. The first time he picked some the gardener mistook him for a thief and began yelling. Thereafter, whenever Taft brought his wife a bouquet of flowers, he told her, "I stole these for you." Eventually she regained her health but curtailed her activities as First Lady.

BY THE SKIN OF HIS NOSE

Undersecretary of the Navy Franklin D. Roosevelt was a sports enthusiast. In Washington he organized games with friends and recruits from the British embassy. He tried to teach baseball to Ronald Lindsay, a skilled cricket player. FDR's young son Jimmy and some friends told Lindsay he had to slide headfirst into each base, and the first time he did so he skinned his face. The kids roared with laughter, but Papa Roosevelt was furious with them. Lindsay, who later became England's ambassador to the U.S., simply dismissed it as a foolish prank.

MINOR MATTERS

In his first Presidential years Franklin Pierce met *each day* with his cabinet in dispensing patronage. Together these men read recommendations, discussed qualifications and debated political consequences. In addition, Pierce gave undivided attention to small matters, investigating and tracking down petty complaints and trying to soothe wounded egos. The problem was that, while Pierce had a happy White House staff, he also demonstrated an inability to resolve major problems. As domestic and foreign crises mounted, the Chief Executive proved weak and ineffective.

THIS OLD HOUSE

Former President John Quincy Adams was nearly eighty-years-old. With cane in hand he took a slow walk down the street in Boston. Suddenly, a friend slapped him on the shoulder and asked, "Well, how's John Quincy Adams this morning?" The old man turned slowly, smiled and commented, "Fine sir, just grand. But this old tenement that John Quincy lives in is not so good. The underpinning is about to fall away. The thatch is all gone off the roof, and the windows are so dim that John Quincy can hardly see out anymore. As a matter of fact, it wouldn't surprise me if before the winter's over he had to move out. But as for John Quincy Adams, he never was better…never better."

LOW SELF ESTEEM

In 1821 some political leaders approached general Andrew Jackson to run for President. Jackson patiently listened to the group which claimed to speak in behalf of even more powerful backers. Jackson surprised his supporters when he sternly told them, "Do they think I am such a damn fool? No sir! I know what I am fit for. I can command a body of men in a rough way – but I am not fit to be President." A few years later, however, "Old Hickory" changed his mind.

WHAT TO DO?

Former Chief Executive James Monroe in 1828 warned future Presidents to "abstain, after retirement, from becoming partisans in subsequent elections to that office." And Grover Cleveland advised, "The best thing to do with ex-Presidents is to leave them alone to make an honest living like other people."

STONEWALL INTERVENES

William McKinley risked his life in delivering food and coffee to wounded comrades on the battlefield at Antietam on September 17, 1862. Several times he loaded his wagon under Confederate gunfire to feed the wounded and exhausted troops. According to one rebel soldier from Georgia, one of Stonewall Jackson's sharpshooters took aim at the young sergeant. Jackson ordered, "Stop, don't shoot. I have watched that youth for hours. He is too brave to be killed."

WORN OUT

Former President Theodore Roosevelt was getting up in years, but he longed to explore the vast jungles of Brazil. When a reporter asked why he was embarking on such a dangerous journey into the Amazon, T.R. replied, "It's my last chance to be a boy." The trip took its toll, and Roosevelt nearly died there. In fact, he never really recovered.

NAME THAT WOMAN!

President Richard Nixon held a press conference on March sixteenth – which happened to be his wife's birthday. Several members of the media, aware of this special day, were quite surprised when a reporter asked Nixon, "Who is the woman you admire most?" The President, perhaps unaware of the date, responded, "Mrs. Charles DeGaulle."

We Take No Chances

In June of 1993 President Bill Clinton visited some offices on Capitol Hill to meet with some members of Congress. When he asked for a cup of decaffeinated coffee, a Secret Service agent insisted on going back to the White House for fresh coffee poured from an untainted pot.

Veep Vanquished

Lyndon Johnson was a man of purpose and didn't like to waste time. At a White House meeting he informed his exuberant Vice President, Hubert H. Humphrey, that he was allowed only five minutes to speak. "Five minutes by the clock, Hubert, and then the hook comes out! Do you understand what I'm saying?" Humphrey nodded and began his fast-paced presentation while Johnson studied his watch. When the time was up, the President thrust Humphrey, still talking, out of the room and shut the door in his face. This incident took place while four rows of congressmen, several cabinet members, and assorted aides watched.

Good for "Country"

George Bush was the first President to attend the Country Music Awards ceremony. On October 2, 1991, he and the First Lady went to the Grand Ole Opry in Nashville to help recognize the nation's top country-western singers. Near the end of the show singer Reba McEntire sang "For My Broken Heart," then called her "good buddy" George Bush up to the stage. She then said, "I can call you that, can't I?" Bush boomed, "Yes!" Both he and Barbara planted several kisses on Reba. Then the President gave a touching speech on the importance of country music.

Hog Heap at Ham House

On February 19, 2000, George W. Bush was campaigning in Greenville, South Carolina. He finished eating breakfast at Tommy's Country Ham House and a protester, wearing a pig's mask, drove a pickup truck loaded with dried manure to the restaurant and blocked Bush's campaign bus. He abandoned the truck and yelled, "Meat is murder! Pork is death!" The man was a member of PETA (People for the Ethical Treatment of Animals). As police dragged him away, Bush was being interviewed by a television crew outside. Under somewhat smelly conditions he remarked, "I sure am glad I had my bacon for breakfast!"

Sermon "on the Mount"

James Garfield often rode long distances by horseback to preach. The advent of the Civil War may have disrupted the nation, but it did not prevent the young minister from spreading the gospel, even though he was an officer in the Union Army. He conducted services in several churches for his troops. While his regiment was stationed in Alabama, he preached in a small church in Mooresville, a village about six miles south of Decatur. A plaque commemorates the event. And during his congressional years he gave sermons to eager congregations.

False Alarm

When Gerald Ford was five years old he developed a high fever and severe stomach ache. His parents rushed him to Butterworth Hospital in Grand Rapids, Michigan, where doctors diagnosed his problem as an inflamed appendicitis. The boy was quickly operated on, but after surgery it was discovered that his appendix was not infected. Ford's parents were furious, but nothing could be done.

Bitter...to the End

George Washington sent his former military aide James Monroe to France to help reconcile differences between the two nations. But Monroe proved to be a poor diplomat, and soon disagreed with Washington's views on neutrality. At one large affair Monroe refused to drink to a toast proposed in Washington's honor. After hearing of this Washington ordered Monroe home. Relations between the U.S. and France worsened to the point where war almost took place. The first President's opinion of Monroe was a low one, and even on the day before he died, Washington was angry that Monroe had been elected Governor of Virginia.

Dressed to Kill

Though the Civil War raged on in 1863, nothing stopped the flow of office-seekers crowding the White House to see President Lincoln. Even those granted positions were not always happy. One day a young man from Ohio, who had just been appointed to a consulate in South America, came to Lincoln to complain. He came dressed as a dandy, wearing an expensive suit. In a gloomy mood, he remarked, "Mr. President, I can't say I'm so very glad of this appointment after all. Why, I hear they have bugs down there that are liable to eat me up inside of a week." Lincoln responded, "Well, young man, if they do, they'll leave behind a mighty good suit of clothes."

A New Substitution

The Dallas Cowboys were a football powerhouse throughout the 1970s. Nevertheless, coach Tom Landry was constantly seeking to improve his team. In 1976 he interrupted a quarterback strategy session and announced to Roger Staubach and Danny White, "Fellas, we've just picked up another quarterback for the Cowboys and I'd like you to meet him." While the two quarterbacks looked surprised and puzzled, Landry stepped out into the hall and brought in President Gerald Ford, who stood in the doorway grinning and holding a football. White and Staubach nearly fell out of their chairs.

Safe Hideout

John Tyler was somewhat of a renegade. A slave-holder from Virginia, he was nominated by the Whigs as Vice President to balance the ticket with William Henry Harrison in 1840. Harrison died after one month, but Tyler's cabinet resigned, and many of his proposals met defeat in Congress. Even the Whigs refused to support him. When he left the White House in March of 1845, he sought privacy in his mansion on the James River, Sherwood Forest. When asked why he had named his estate after the English woods of Robin Hood fame, the ex-President smiled and replied, "Because it's a good place for an outlaw."

Putting On (H)airs

Though little Grace Bedell of Westfield, New York, is credited with Lincoln's decision to grow a beard, the Republican nominee had also been urged by others to sprout whiskers. On October 12, 1860, three days before he received the letter from Grace, Lincoln was notified by a group of supporters, calling themselves "True Republicans," and advised that their candidate could improve his image and appearance in photographs "provided you would cultivate whiskers and wear standing collars." By late November the President-elect had grown a beard.

BROKE AND HAPPY

During World War II a Hollywood firm offered Supreme Allied Commander Dwight Eisenhower a huge financial inducement for rights to do a film biography. His wife Mamie wrote that she felt he ought to accept the money. But "Ike" replied he could never consider such a deal, writing, "We don't need it anyway – it's fun to be poor!"

HAPPY BIRTHDAY

George Washington's birthday was February 22, 1732, but Washington's family *Bible* records the event as February 11. When Washington was born, the colonies followed the Julian calendar. Twenty years later when America adopted the Gregorian calendar, the old Julian calendar was eleven days off. All dates prior to 1752 were moved eleven days ahead, making our first President's birthday fall on the twenty-second. Today, the official celebration of his birthday takes place on the third Monday in February. Ironically, the third Monday in February will never fall on the twenty-second.

A SON FOR A SHIELD

During his "Good Neighbor" tour to South America, FDR was scheduled to ride in a parade with Uruguay president Gabriel Terra. FDR told his son, James, that the foreign president looked a bit nervous. Asked why, Terra confessed this was his first parade since he had been shot and wounded in another parade months earlier. FDR laughed it off and then reassured him by suggesting, "I'll let my little boy Jimmie ride in the jump seat directly in front of you so you'll be shielded." Terra thought this was a great idea, and though Jimmie was a bit scared he didn't protest. FDR often teased his son about this incident and the possibility of being shot. With a twinkle in his eye, the President laughed and explained, "Better the President's son than the President!"

ZACK BROUGHT BACK

Zachary Taylor died of cholera (and probably food poisoning) in July of 1850. But 141 years later Clara Rising wrote a historical novel, suggesting Taylor was poisoned by political enemies. Following the advice of forensic experts, she secured permission from several of Taylor's descendants to exhume the body and have it examined for arsenic poisoning. A team of specialists went to Louisville, Kentucky, and dug up "Old Rough and Ready." After careful investigation of Taylor's well-preserved, unembalmed body, doctors were able to prove what most historians believed all along – that Taylor died of natural causes. Rising, however, received a great deal of publicity for her book.

YOU HAVE ME CONFUSED

In mid-July of 1991 President Bush and his wife visited Europe. They stopped in England where they were guests of Prime Minister John Major and Queen Elizabeth. There, the Bushes attended a reception held in their honor at Buckingham Palace. While shaking hands in a reception line, an elderly woman met Bush and remarked, "Good to see you, Jeffrey." Bush told her, "I'm the President of the United States." The woman replied, "Well good for you, Jeffrey!"

FATHER KNOWS BEST

To preserve the dignity of his office President Washington solicited advice from many sources as to how often he should receive callers, who should be invited, and how often political and social functions should be conducted. The "Father of Our Country" enjoyed almost no privacy with little time left for work and even less for his family. After several weeks of discussion he finally took a space in a New York newspaper to announce his calling hours: people simply paying their respects should limit themselves to Tuesday and Friday afternoons between two and three o'clock, while those on business should come anytime except Sunday, when he wanted to see no one. Receptions would be held for men only, but Martha would preside on Friday evenings at another party where both men and women could attend. At this less formal affair the President would wear neither his sword or hat.

AMERICANS BEWARE

The concerns President Andrew Jackson expressed in his farewell address to the American people apply even today. Jackson predicted "unless you become more watchful and check this spirit of monopoly and thirst for exclusive privileges, you will in the end find that the most important powers of government, and the control over your dearest wishes, have passed into the hands of the corporations."

ATTEMPTING RECONCILIATION

John Quincy Adams' victory over Andrew Jackson in 1824 created bitter feelings between both men. But the aloof and no-nonsense Adams realized it was politically and social wise to recognize "Old Hickory" for his service to the country as a military leader and politician. Fourteen hundred invitations were sent out to host a large reception on January 8, 1825, marking the anniversary of Jackson's smashing victory over the British at New Orleans in 1815. Nearly a thousand people attended the extravagant gala. Women stood on chairs as Louisa Adams escorted the general during the party. Jackson's wife Rachel, however, was very unhappy. Guests snubbed her, singling her out for her obesity and backwoods manners. Rumors circulated that the divorce from her first husband was illegal, and when she died of heart failure after Andrew's election in 1828, Jackson blamed Washington society and political opponents, including John Quincy Adams, for her death.

CRAZED CASTOFF

It took place during the early months of Richard Nixon's 1974 exile at La Casa Pacifica, his home in San Clemente, California. Though traffic often backed up as curiosity seekers drove by, very few tried to climb the tall iron gate which surrounded the estate. One man, however, did manage to break into the property. Agents captured him and found that he had a set of surgical tools. When questioned, the man explained he was just trying to seek Nixon's permission to castrate himself!

DIVIDE AND CONQUER

Joe and Rose Kennedy needed a larger home for their growing family. They decided to stay in Brookline, Massachusetts, and moved to a big house on Naples Road. Young John and the five other children proved a lot to handle so mom built partitions on the porch to separate the kids. She explained this was for their own good so they wouldn't "knock each other down or gouge each other in the eye with a toy."

NO BUNDLE OF JOY

After their honeymoon the Coolidges returned to Northampton, Vermont. Grace often sat at the bay window in their tiny home waiting for her husband's return from work. One day Calvin came home toting a large leather bag. He told her it contained a wedding gift. Grace thought it was a hat, something her penny-pinching husband might purchase. Calvin upended the bag and emptied out a bundle of loose socks, all of which needed repair. Grace gathered them up and began counting them, whereupon he informed her there was no need to count – there were exactly fifty-two pairs, and he would bring her the rest when she finished mending them. Some gift!

WRONG DIAGNOSIS

On December 20, 1860, President Buchanan was attending a wedding reception in Washington. Hearing a great clamor out in the hallway, the President smiled at a guest and inquired, "Madam, do you suppose the house is on fire?" As it turned out, the news was much worse. The *nation* was on fire – South Carolina had just seceded from the Union, and outright civil war was inevitable.

DELAY OF DELIGHT

The Easter-egg rolling contest was moved from the Capitol to the White House in 1879 when the Hayeses invited youngsters to participate. The event got off to a rollicking start when a poor, ragged boy of fourteen, too old for egg-rolling, snatched a basket of eggs and fled through the gates. The other children ran in pursuit, and the youth was caught by police. The eggs were returned, and the contest continued.

BUSHWHACKED!

Grover Cleveland's contempt for reporters was reinforced on his honeymoon. Traveling to Deer Park in Maryland with his young bride, there was little privacy. Nearly thirty newsmen took residence in a nearby cottage and spied on the couple with binoculars. On walks through the woods, the Clevelands encountered reporters who popped out from behind bushes to ask questions.

ALTERNATE MIRACLE

Farmers in several Texas counties lost their crops due to a severe drought. They appealed to President Jimmy Carter for emergency relief funds, but Carter refused. He decided to fly to Texas to investigate the damage and explain his position. On the day he arrived, there was a torrential downpour. Carter addressed a crowd of Texas farmers and explained, "You asked me for money. I couldn't get you the money. So instead I brought you some rain!"

OLD ABE RESPONDS

In the summer of 1860 Lincoln was campaigning before an unfriendly crowd. Following the end of his speech someone yelled out, "I wouldn't vote for you if you were St. Peter himself!" Lincoln smiled and replied, "My friend, if I were St. Peter, you could not possible vote for me. You would not be in my district!"

NELLIE HAS HER WAY

Nellie Grant was only a teenager but was the talk of Washington society. Her tomboy antics and casual comments offended more than one refined lady. When the President and Mrs. Grant sent their headstrong daughter away to Miss Porter's School in Connecticut, Nellie wrote home vowing to kill herself if forced to remain in such "a dreadful place." Mom and Dad gave in, and the sixteen-year-old returned to the whirling social scene of the White House where she continued to live an exciting life.

SHREWD POLITICIAN

Grover Cleveland enjoyed fishing. He also enjoyed a friendly wager, as long as he won it. The President and two friends once went on a fishing expedition and before they left, agreed that whoever caught the first fish would treat the others to dinner. Cleveland complained that his companions cheated, explaining, "They both had bites but did not pull up the fish." Nevertheless, he did not have to buy dinner. As he told the story later, "I didn't have any bait on my hook!"

GET ME OUT OF HERE!

James Buchanan was simply biding his time as his Presidency neared its end. As the nation edged towards war, he was anxious to hand over the reigns of power to his successor, Abraham Lincoln. On February 24, 1861, Buchanan conducted his last Cabinet meeting. A messenger raced up the White House stairs and handed him a calling card. Buchanan read it, pushed back his chair, stood up and announced, "Gentlemen, Uncle Abe is in the Red Room below. Let us not keep him waiting!"

PUBLIC DISPLAY

In the three month period James Garfield suffered from a gunshot wound, he lost 100 pounds. He died on September 19, 1881, and 70,000 people paid their respects at the Capitol where he lay in state. The embalmer's effort to make the body presentable in the stifling heat proved a failure. Mourners noticed patches of blue on Garfield's withered face, and his mouth was twisted into a cynical smile. Men became sick and several women fainted. Just before noon on September 23, the crowd was cleared, and Lucretia Garfield spent one last hour viewing the body of her husband. Following her vigil she ordered the casket closed, and it remained so.

CARTER COMMENT

Jeff MacNelly was a political cartoonist working for the *Richmond News-Leader*, a newspaper very critical of the Jimmy Carter administration. MacNelly received an invitation to a reception at the White House and gladly accepted. President Carter saw him and joked, "You're not as bad as those editorials, but almost."

MOVIE FAN

Ronald Reagan liked starring in movies – and he enjoyed watching them. In 1983 an economic summit was held in Williamsburg, Virginia, but the President wasn't prepared. Reagan's chief of staff Jim Baker asked his boss why he hadn't opened his briefing book. Reagan replied, "Well, Jim, *The Sound of Music* was on last night."

REGRETS?

Presidents have usually conveyed a love for their position as Chief Executive – that is, publicly. But once in office, or after retiring, they have described their tenure in a different light. Here are some examples:

George Washington, according to Jefferson, said he would "rather be in my grave than in my present situation."

Jefferson described the Presidency as "unceasing drudgery."

John Quincy Adams said, "The four most miserable years of my life were my four years in the Presidency."

Lincoln once remarked, "I wish I had never been born! It is a white elephant on my hands, and hard to manage."

Van Buren described his term as "toilsome and anxious probation."

Harding declared, "This White House is a prison. I can't get away from the men who dog my footsteps. I am in jail!"

Garfield observed, "Four years of this kind of intellectual dissipation may cripple me for the remainder of my life."

Taft exclaimed, "I'll be damned if I am not getting tired of this!"

Coolidge said, "It costs to be President."

HIGH SCHOOL HOOKY

Jimmy Carter was selected as valedictorian of his high school class but never received the honor. During the last week of school, Carter and some friends skipped classes. They were caught and punished, and the future President lost his position as valedictorian. He did, however, get to deliver a speech at the graduation ceremonies.

SEEING RED

As World War II drew to a close, President Truman realized the Russians and the Red Army were undermining the wartime agreements discussed at Yalta. Truman bluntly told Soviet Foreign Minister Molotov that the Russians were breaking all their promises in occupying eastern Europe. According to witnesses, Molotov told Truman, "I have never been talked to like that in my life." Truman shot back, "Carry out your agreements and you won't be talked to like that!"

EQUESTRIAN AFFECTION

In early March of 1863, thirty Confederate soldiers led by Captain John Moesby conducted a daring raid, sneaking behind Union lines near Washington, D.C., and capturing a brigadier general, two captains, thirty men and fifty-eight horses. This episode received a great deal of publicity in both the North and South. President Lincoln found it quite irritating. Trying to find some humor in the incident, Lincoln reportedly said that while he could always promote a new general, but good horses were difficult to find."

KENNEDY COMPETITORS

The Kennedy children learned to be fierce competitors at an early age. More than once when young John was getting ready for a swimming race just for fun, his father Joe would kneel beside the pool and warn, "Come in a winner; second place is no good." In future non-swimming races, John Kennedy remembered this advice.

APPOINTED IMPOSTER

During the 1936 Presidential race FDR got a bit tired aboard his campaign train. Sitting at a picture window, he asked William Simmons, the White House usher, "Bill, how would you like to be President for a while?" Simmons thought it was a joke until FDR moved his wheelchair away from the window, put Simmons in a chair, leaned across him and placed the pince-nez glasses on his nose. The President grinned and added, "Fine, fine. Now take this cigarette holder. That's it. Every time we pass a little town, wave the cigarette holder like this. You be the President. I'm going to take a nap!"

HARRY HUMBLED

Captain Harry Truman was in charge of an artillery unit in France during World War I. At least one of Truman's superiors saw little promise in him. Truman's commanding officer once told him, "It would be a disaster for the country to let you command men."

JESTER JIMMY?

When Georgia Governor Jimmy Carter announced he was running for President, the editor of the *Atlanta Constitution* jokingly ran this headline: "Jimmy Carter Running for What?" The editor further stated, "Governor Jimmy Carter's timing was just right. The state needs a good belly laugh, and Carter obliged by announcing he would run for president." Two years later Carter took his oath as our thirty-ninth Chief Executive.

CLOSE ENCOUNTERS

In 1777 John Adams and his son, John Quincy, set sail across the Atlantic on a dangerous mission to secure aid from France. During the crossing their ship was struck by lightning, killing four crewmen. Afterwards the vessel almost sank when a hurricane tossed it violently. Having braved these dangers, they were later fired upon by British warships but survived and reached France safely.

PRIORITIES

When Dwight Eisenhower married Mamie Doud in 1916, the future general and President explained to her, "Mamie, there's one thing I want you to understand. My country comes first and always will. You come second." It took his wife many years to comprehend the meaning of this statement.

MULTI-PRESIDENT

Millard Fillmore was not just President of the United States. He became the first chancellor of the University of Buffalo, a founder of the Buffalo General Hospital, and first president of the Buffalo Historical Society. Many historians feel he achieved better results as a leader of these institutions than he did as an executive of the federal government.

GETTING IT TOGETHER

James K. Polk did not attend formal school until he was seventeen. He was quite poor and constantly ill, leading a physician to write on his medical record that his patient was "uncouth and uneducated." Despite a late start, Polk graduated as salutatorian from the University of North Carolina in 1818.

A DIRTY MASS

At the outbreak of the Revolutionary War George Washington was disgusted with many of the New England troops. He wrote a relative that the men from Massachusetts "would fight very well (if properly officered) although they are exceeding dirty and nasty people."

SOMETHING IN COMMON

Thomas Jefferson was born and raised in Tidewater, Virginia, and became a farmer there. The same is true for James Madison. Jefferson married a widow; so did Madison. Jefferson was an anti-Federalist who built a mansion and owned slaves. Likewise for Madison. Jefferson was a member of the Virginia House of Delegates and the Continental Congress. So was Madison. Jefferson was Secretary of State under a Virginia President; so was Madison. Jefferson was elected twice as President; so was Madison. Jefferson wrote and edited his own papers on national government which were later published. And the same is so for Madison.

A Unique Gift

On Christmas Day, 1864, Abraham Lincoln sent a note to William Tecumseh Sherman: "Many, many thanks for your Christmas gift…" What was this gift? Lincoln was responding to the general for capturing the city of Savannah, Georgia. Prior to this, Sherman's army seemed to have disappeared. Stretching far ahead of his supply lines, Sherman's 100,000 Union forces lived off the Georgia landscape, eating green corn and taking anything they could carry or consume. Along a sixty-mile wide, 300-mile long path of destruction, parts of Georgia were left in total ruin. The public had no idea what had happened to the Ohio general and his army, and when one politician asked Lincoln if he knew where Sherman was headed, the President responded, "I know the hole he went in at, but I can't tell you what hole he will come out of." After wrecking railroads, burning factories, and capturing rebels and weapons, Sherman sent a telegram which stated, "I beg to present you a Christmas gift – the city of Savannah, with one hundred and fifty heavy guns and plenty of ammunition, also about twenty-five thousand bales of cotton."

Presidential Pay-off

J.H. Bonitz was a White House page boy for President James Buchanan. Bonitz one day witnessed Dan Sickles, an army officer and friend of Buchanan's, murder a man who was having an affair with Sickles' wife. Wanting to protect his friend, Buchanan gave Bonitz a razor, some money, and instructions to get out of town so he would not be able to testify against Sickles. Bonitz returned to his home in North Carolina. As it turned out, Sickles was found innocent by reason of temporary insanity. President Buchanan had used his influence to help obtain a verdict in Sickles's favor, and his seemingly criminal actions were overlooked.

Burnt Offering

Mary Todd Lincoln was not the greatest of cooks, but then her husband was constantly late for dinner while working as an attorney in Springfield, Illinois. More than once Lincoln burst through the front door, sat down at the dinner table with befuddled guests and yelled to Mary, "Bring on the cinders!"

LOOSENING THINGS UP

As a child, FDR once slipped his German-born governess a heavy dose of laxative in her drink. She got quite sick, and the future President's father told him, "You can consider yourself spanked." Years later this same lady was committed to an insane asylum.

BIG MOUTH

In 1920 Franklin Roosevelt spoke before 1500 people in Brooklyn and remarked, that in attempting to get the U.S. ready for war, he had "committed enough illegal acts to put him in jail for 999 years." These words proved an embarrassment to his superiors. As Assistant Naval Secretary, FDR did take some bold steps to mobilize the nation, but his bragging about such deeds drew the wrath of President Wilson. FDR issued a public apology, but his influence with Democratic officials had been tarnished, even though he was a Vice Presidential candidate that year.

ROSE COLORED SPECTACLES

In June of 1930 America was in the throes of depression. Unemployment, bank foreclosures on homes and farms, and tens of thousands of poor standing in soup lines brought protest from all quarters of the country. Receiving a delegation of citizens who came to Washington to seek a program of public relief, President Hoover informed them, "Gentlemen, you are sixty days too late. The depression is over." Hoover may have been the only man in the U.S. who believed it.

THE START OF SOMETHING BIG

After leaving the White House Woodrow Wilson planned to write a book about his eight years as President. He and his wife, Edith Bolling Wilson, lived in a house near the Library of Congress so Wilson could conduct his research more conveniently. But the ex-President was in very poor health, and the only section of his book ever written was the dedication "To E.B.W...." Though Mrs. Wilson never saw the book become a reality, she outlived her husband by forty years. Her last public appearance was at John F. Kennedy's inauguration in 1961. She died on December 28 (her husband's birthday), 1961.

FEMININE FEUD

The competition for the Presidency often extends beyond the candidates. In 1980 Senator Ted Kennedy made another bid for the White House, trying to gain the Democratic nomination and unseat incumbent Jimmy Carter. Kennedy and his beautiful wife, Joan, were having serious marital problems at the time, but Joan agreed to campaign for her estranged husband. In a magazine interview, Joan had this to say in comparing herself to First Lady Rosalynn Carter: "I'm better qualified than Rosalynn. I'm a very sophisticated lady.... And I can make so many more contributions.... Rosalynn doesn't have a master's degree.... It's terrific if Rosalynn Carter wants to sit in on policy meetings, but I have talents and areas of expertise that don't lie in advising my husband...." These remarks created a storm of protest and did nothing to help her husband's cause. In addition, Joan did not possess a master's degree (as she implied), and she was undergoing rehabilitation for alcoholism and seeing a psychiatrist. Divorce soon followed.

DON'T ASK

Reformer Jacob Reis once asked Police Commissioner Theodore Roosevelt if he ever thought about being President. The question angered him, and Roosevelt snapped back, "Don't you dare ask me that!" A brief moment of silence followed. Roosevelt calmed down, then put his hand on Reis's shoulder and explained softly, "I must be wanting to be President. Every young man does. But I won't let myself think of it; I must not, because if I do, I will begin to work for it; I'll be careful, calculating, cautious in word and act, and so – I'll beat myself. See?"

A PRICE TO PAY

Mainly due to the Vietnam War, President Lyndon Johnson's hair turned grayer, and he took on more wrinkles. His daughter, Luci, came in to his room one night, looked at him and remarked, "Your brow looks like it's been plowed." After relating to her some of the latest bad news about the war, he concluded, "What we need is some hard and deep praying."

CONSULTATION OR CONFUSION?

For days after he was felled by an assassin's bullet, President Garfield was surrounded by a mob of puzzled doctors who poked their fingers and dirty instruments into his back to locate the bullet. Physicians and nurses cluttered up the White House sick room. Garfield's friend, Dr. Boynton, was also summoned. He too examined the wound with his fingers and exclaimed to the patient, "My God, General! You ought to have surgical advice." Garfield sarcastically quipped, "There are about forty of them in the adjoining room. Go and consult with them." The bullet was never found, and Garfield died from infection.

A COSTLY AFFAIR

Attending James K. Polk's inaugural celebration proved costly for at least one individual. Commodore Elliot attended inaugural festivities at the White House where he became the target of a pickpocket. Deprived of his wallet, Elliot lost several Presidential mementos which were in it. Included were a letter from Andrew Jackson and a lock of his hair, a letter from Dolley Madison and a lock of her husband's hair. There were two other inaugural balls held at different locations that evening, but the commodore ended up making a bad choice.

CHOOSING NOT TO CHOOSE

James Buchanan has gone down in history as one of our least effective Chief Executives. In his effort to please bickering factions in the pre-Civil War era, Buchanan advocated compromise at all costs and thus "fueled the flames" which led to the Great Rebellion. He once told some Congressmen, "If I know myself, I am a politician neither of the West nor the East, of the North nor the South. I therefore shall forever avoid any expressions the direct tendency of which must be to create sectional jealousies, and at length disunion…."

BULLSEYE

Theodore Roosevelt wasn't a bad shot. Previous to his national prominence in politics, Roosevelt was a rancher and hunter in South Dakota. Once while hunting in the Badlands, he killed two black-tailed deer with a single rifle shot – at over 400 yards! The bullet had broken the back of each animal.

ER, YOU KNOW WHAT I MEANT

It was March 4, 1837, and Martin Van Buren had just been sworn in as President. At the White House he received the Diplomatic Corps, the host of foreign dignitaries including ambassadors and their families. Van Buren repeatedly referred to them as the "Democratic Corps," and it wasn't until a few minutes later that an aide informed the Democratic President that he had committed a slip of the tongue.

FISH BE DAMNED!

In June of 1955 President Eisenhower took off on a vacation to do some fishing at Lake Parmachenee in Maine. Late one afternoon, Ike and an elderly guide went out to catch some fish. In a very short time the President hooked and netted a three-pound landlocked salmon and a good-size trout. "Is fishing always this good?" he asked the guide. "Well…no," came the candid reply. "They stocked the lake for your coming and put wire over the outlet." The President showed a flash of anger and ordered, "Take me back. I don't want to fish in a prison!" Nor did Ike go fishing the next day until the blockading wire was removed.

A RIGHT TO FIGHT

As a second term assemblyman from New York's twenty-first district, Theodore Roosevelt advocated many reforms, thus incurring the wrath of the political bosses. At the state legislature in Albany he boldly and openly attacked the public abuses which had been festering for years. One evening he was leaving a hotel lobby, walking towards the restaurant. A group of rowdies, possibly inspired by political enemies and under the influence of too much liquor, made several sneering remarks at young Roosevelt. One man by the name of "Stubby" Collins was a professional boxer, and intentionally bumped into T.R. and yelled at him for being in his way. Hired to "do in" the state congressman, "Stubby" swung at Roosevelt, but had his punch blocked. In the next instant, the pugilist was knocked to the floor. With the scuffle ended, Teddy walked from the room, remarking to the rest of his tormentors that he had not enjoyed himself "more in a year."

UNDER A MICROSCOPE

No Presidential candidate's background was more thoroughly investigated than Gerald R. Ford. Following his nomination for Vice President by Richard Nixon, the FBI began a massive, intense probe. More than 350 special agents from thirty-three FBI field offices interviewed more than 1000 people. The bureau's report consisted of 1700 pages. Among the interviews was a former high school football player in Grand Rapids, Michigan. More than forty years before, during a game between Ford's alma mater (South High) and Union High, Ford had tackled an opponent after the whistle had blown and, as a result, had been ejected from the game. The agents asked this man if Ford had been a "dirty" player. In addition, the IRS dug deep into Ford's tax returns, while several other agencies conducted their own investigations. Thus, when Ford came before Congress to be confirmed, there was practically nothing the lawmakers did not know. The Senate approved his confirmation ninety-two to three; the House followed suit with a vote of 387 to thirty-five.

AVAILABILITY

On occasion, John Kennedy liked to sneak away from the White House to a movie theater. Once, while attending a film in Washington, D.C., JFK spotted his Secretary of Agriculture Orville Freeman and his wife sitting in front of him. At the end of the film the President tapped Freeman on the shoulder and asked, "Haven't the leaders of the New Frontier got anything better to do with their time than spend it going to the movies?" With wit and humor, Freeman responded, "I wanted to be immediately available on a moment's notice if the President wanted me." Both men roared with laughter.

A GOOD WORD

In 1896, Theodore Roosevelt urged William Howard Taft to tell President William McKinley "what a good fellow I am." Taft went to the White House in Teddy's behalf, and a short time later Roosevelt was appointed Assistant Secretary of the Navy.

A BUNDLE OF BONES

In March of 1797 newly-elected Vice President Thomas Jefferson made ready to move from Monticello to Philadelphia. He forbid his servants to pack luxurious articles. Jefferson was determined to appear as a simple, studious Virginia farmer who considered himself no better than the average American citizen. One article he insisted on packing were the bones of a mastodon which a Kickapoo Indian chief had given him. The Indian had sent a message to Jefferson with the two words, "What is?" The Vice President-elect sent a note of thanks and explanation to the chief. And after arriving in the nation's capital, he placed the mammoth in a museum founded by Benjamin Franklin.

FREE SERVICES

Rumors persisted during the Civil War that Lincoln demanded gold instead of greenbacks for his pay, and that he invested his money in Wall Street to gain a fortune on his $25,000 yearly salary. The truth is, however, that the sixteenth President often failed to draw on his money at all. The U.S. Treasurer, F. E. Spinner, testified that Lincoln was in the habit of leaving his salary at the Treasury without picking it up. In one case, all of his pay remained for eleven months. When Spinner urged him to at least collect his salary and the due interest, Lincoln replied that, "For the good of the country, let it remain. The Treasury needs it more than I do."

WILD TIME IN THE WILDS

In 1826 Andrew Johnson, his mother, stepfather and a friend left their homes in Raleigh, North Carolina, and headed for Tennessee. They were very poor, and all of the family belongings were packed into a two-wheeled cart pulled by a blind pony. The trip was a difficult one. While camping one night a mountain lion emerged from the woods and knocked a skillet off their fire, destroying dinner. Several days later at another site a bear wandered into their camp. Supplies were nearly extinct when the party reached eastern Tennessee and found some food and lodging.

ADVICE FROM GRANDPA

George Washington offered some words of wisdom to a step granddaughter just before her wedding. He told her not to expect to bathe "in an ocean of love.... Love is a mighty pretty-thing, but, like all other delicious things, it is cloying," and added, "love is too dainty a food to live on *alone*," and that it "ought not to be considered further than as a necessary ingredient for that matrimonial *happiness* which results from a combination of causes."

CAROLINE'S DILEMMA

John Kennedy's young daughter, Caroline, had quite a few pets at the White House, but only a couple survived. One of her hamsters drowned in the President's bathtub. Several hamster babies were eaten by the father. Then the mother hamster killed the father and died. Previously, Caroline's pet canary, Robin, died and was buried in the Rose Garden. Another pet, Tom Kitten, also died.

MAKING IT PERFECTLY CLEAR

Right after the Nixons moved into the White House in 1969, they entertained hundreds of their campaign workers in the East Room. First Lady Pat Nixon announced that from now on the Executive Mansion would be open to the little people, proclaiming, "We're going to invite our friends here and not all those big shots." The President quickly interrupted and quipped, "Of course, *all* our friends are big shots."

DOING HIS DUTY

In 1784 the King of Spain sent, upon request, two jackasses to George Washington so he could breed them in America. One died en route across the ocean, and the surviving one was named Royal Gift. Washington advertised that his jackass was available for stud service. The Spanish animal proved very successful in fathering many offspring. This led its master to remark, "He never fails."

LET ME GO!

When James Madison became gravely ill in June of 1836, relatives and well-meaning friends suggested that drugs might prolong his life until July 4, so he could die on Independence Day as had Adams, Jefferson, and Monroe. The former President rejected this idea as absurd; he died on June 28.

CHANGING A LETTER

Joseph Kennedy was a multimillionaire whose efforts to make his son President succeeded. Ex-President Truman was not fond of the Kennedys. Truman was asked if he was worried about John F. Kennedy being a Catholic and taking orders from the Pope. Truman responded, "It's not the Pope I'm worried about, it's the pop."

THINKING OF YOU

Just a few months before he died, Andrew Jackson in 1844 wrote a letter to Sarah Polk. Mrs. Polk received it just prior to the Democratic Convention, and he had written her that "I will put you in the White House if it costs me my life." Jackson kept his promise and worked hard to get the convention to nominate James K. Polk. In fact, the last letter Jackson ever wrote was to President Polk in 1845.

A CLOSER LOOK

William McKinley smoked cigars regularly and chewed tobacco as well, but not in public. Deeply religious, amiable, stoic, and sometimes reserved at social functions, McKinley was perceived by many people as a rather cold and distant personality. Furthermore, he was very patient, and could listen at length to others complain or babble. Mild-mannered and quietly effective, McKinley was aptly described by his Secretary of War Elihu Root: "He had a way of handling men so that they thought his ideas were their own.... He was a man of great power because he was absolutely indifferent to credit. His great desire was to 'get it done!' He cared nothing about the credit, but McKinley *always had his way*."

KNOW THYSELF

John Adams knew James Madison perhaps better than Madison knew himself. In early 1800 Madison attended his last meeting in the House of Representatives. The forty-six-year-old Virginian looked forward to a life of retirement on his plantation. He would still hold two higher offices – Secretary of State and President. Adams wrote his wife, "Mr. Madison is to retire.... It Seems the Mode of becoming great is to retire. Madison I Suppose after a Retirement of a few years is to be President or V.P.... It is marvelous how political Plants grow in the Shade."

Brokenhearted Broadcaster Bounces Back

In 1933 Ronald Reagan's girl friend, Margaret Cleaver, announced she was marrying someone else. To help overcome his sorrows, Reagan purchased his first car, a small two-seater Nash convertible. The dashing man-about-town drove his auto in and around Des Moines, Iowa, with the top down even during the cold and rain. Making $75 a week as a radio announcer, "Dutch" Reagan was already making a name for himself as he dated many pretty young ladies throughout the region.

Life on the Run

When it was suggested to the Hardings that Vice President Calvin Coolidge and his wife accept a wealthy widow's mansion for their home, Mrs. Harding intervened and nixed the idea. She angrily voiced, "Do you think I am going to have those Coolidges living in a house like that? A hotel apartment is plenty good enough for them." Under pressure, Congress refused the donation, and the Vice President remained without a permanent residence for more than forty years.

I Retract That Statement

People who study Presidents are aware of Mark Hanna's comment about Theodore Roosevelt, referring to him as that "damned cowboy" in the White House. Hanna, McKinley's advisor, cabinet member, and a U.S. Senator, did little to hide his dislike for McKinley's successor. Roosevelt explained, "Hanna treats me like a boy. He calls me 'Teddy.'" Both men stubbornly agreed to talk with one another, and after several meals and meetings, Roosevelt won him over. Hanna confessed, "He's a pretty good cuss, after all!"

Out of Touch

While serving as President for eight years, Dwight Eisenhower was removed from the everyday use of conveniences. Servants and aides did just about everything for him. When he left office in 1961, Eisenhower did not know how to dial a telephone, and did not even have a driver's license. As a private citizen it took some time to learn such tasks.

A Show of Strength

Chester A. Arthur was a quartermaster general in New York during the Civil War. After fortifying the harbor at New York City, and providing supplies and equipment for New York regiments, Arthur one day found his authority challenged by another officer. Billy Wilson and his troops ransacked parts of the city because his men lacked food. When Arthur learned of these outrages, he summoned Wilson to his office and ordered him and his men to stop the looting. Wilson replied, "Neither you nor the Governor has nothing to do with me. I'm a colonel in the U.S. Army, and you've got no right to order me." The soft-spoken quartermaster responded, "You are not a colonel, and you won't be until you raised your regiment to its quota of men and receive your commission. Countered Wilson, "Well, I've got my shoulder straps and as long as I wear 'em I don't want no orders from any of you fellas." Arthur jumped forward, ripped off the soldier's officer straps, and placed him under arrest.

Digging Up Dirt

On May 8, 1953, Bob Hope spoke at the White House Correspondents Dinner. President Eisenhower was there, and Hope made certain everyone was informed of Ike's golfing adventures. The comedian kidded the President about all the divots on the White House lawn. He also alluded to all the divots Eisenhower created while tearing up the course at Augusta, Georgia. Hope concluded, "I guess that's what the Republicans meant when they said they'd break up the Solid South."

All Thumbs

On election day in 1944 FDR showed up to vote at the Hyde Park polling place. He told the board of election officials his occupation was "tree grower," and was introduced for the first time to a voting machine. but inside the curtained booth FDR had some difficulty. Suddenly his voice boomed through the curtain, "The goddamned thing won't work!" Poll workers yelled instructions to him, and the President finally figured it out. Later one of the Presidents explained he only said, "The *damned* thing won't work." FDR defeated Republican Thomas Dewey handily; his electoral college margin was 432 to 99.

LEADERSHIP QUALITIES

Even as a child FDR showed signs of leadership. He was constantly bossing other children, so much so that his mother scolded him, remarking, "My son, don't give the orders all of the time. Let the other boy give them sometimes." Little Franklin responded, "Mummie, if I didn't give the orders, nothing would happen." In addition, Franklin hated to lose, and his mother threatened never to play with him until he learned to accept defeat.

A SURPRISED IKE

In 1960 White House reporters held a farewell dinner for President Eisenhower in Augusta, Georgia. Ann Chamberlin of *Time* magazine, one of the few women correspondents, was in attendance. As a liberal-thinking lady for her day, her relationship with the President had never been on the best of terms. Following the main course, cigars were passed around the dinner table, and Ann took one. The President looked somewhat surprised as she lit up and started puffing. Eisenhower's jaw dropped open, and although he said nothing, he was clearly offended. Ann ignored his stony silence and finished her smoke.

TEMPER, TEMPER

As President, George Washington seldom showed his anger. During his first year in office, however, he found it difficult to live within the salary allotted to him by Congress. He personally supervised the spending of every dollar, but found it frustrating. One evening during a formal dinner a servant brought to the table a delicately prepared plate of fish – the first catch of the season. "What fish is this?" he asked. The steward said proudly, "A shad, a very fine catch...." When Washington demanded to know the price, the servant confessed it had cost $3.00. The President's anger erupted; his fists coming down so hard on the dinner table he rattled the coffee cups. "Take it away, sir! It shall never be said that my table sets such an example of luxury and extravagance!" He also complained that tradesmen overcharged him, and protested to his tailor that "your charges are most high" and "you have generally sent many clothes too short and sometimes too tight, for which reason I think it necessary again to mention that I am full six feet high." Washington even rebuked his carpenters as "an idle set of rascals...to make even a chicken coop would employ all them a week."

TRADING JIBES

William Henry Harrison and the Whigs in 1840 accused Martin Van Buren of putting cologne on his whiskers and eating meals served on gold and silver plates. Though these may have been exaggerations, the Whigs promised voters "two dollars a day and roast beef," instead of President Van Buren's policy of "fifty cents a day and French soup." On such flimsy pledges the Whigs carried the election.

BUTTERING UP A HAMMER

U.S. Grant once told of this incident: "When I was a boy my mother one morning found herself without butter for breakfast and sent me to borrow some from a neighbor. I overheard a letter read from the son of a neighbor who was then at West Point, stating that he failed his examination and was coming home. I got the butter, took it home and, without waiting for breakfast, ran to the office of the Congressman for our district. 'Mr. Hammer,' I said, 'will you appoint me to West Point? Congressman Hammer replied, 'No, Davis is there, and has three years to serve.' 'But suppose he should fail – will you send me?' Mr. Hammer laughed. 'If he don't go through, it is no use for you to try, Uly' 'Promise me you will give me the chance, Mr. Hammer, anyhow.' Mr. Hammer promised. The next day the defeated lad came home, and the Congressman, laughing at my sharpness, gave me the appointment." Grant concluded, "Now it was my mother's being without butter that made me general and President."

GETTING A "THOROUGH" UNDERSTANDING

When Theodore Roosevelt was a young boy, his father one day said to him, "Theodore, do you know what a thoroughbred is? Well, I'll show you. See those two dogs? Well, this one" – and he picked up an ugly-looking, low-bred pup and gave him a gentle shaking, causing yelps and barks to fill the air – "this one is not a thoroughbred." Then he picked up a fine-looking pup and shook him hard, not a sound coming forth. "There," said father, "that's your thoroughbred, my boy, and whatever happens, it won't squeal!"

SLAPPED BY THE SENATE

Thomas Jefferson's popularity dwindled during his last two years in office. One of his last official acts was nominating his former secretary, William Short, as ambassador to Russia. Jefferson was horrified when the Senate voted 31-0 against confirming Short.

SHOWING RESPECT

Except for the pet parrot, no one at Jefferson's Monticello home spoke harshly to the Negro slaves. In fact, the blacks there were never referred to as slaves, but servants. Jefferson saw to it that his servants learned many skills and received schooling. His personal servants included Cesar, Burwell, and Jupiter. Later research has shown that his young black female servant, Sally Hemmings, bore Jefferson's children.

A NICE INTRODUCTION, BUT…

As a young lawyer in Indianapolis, Benjamin Harrison was given a lengthy introduction as the grandson of President William Henry Harrison. Though proud of his ancestry, the 5'6" attorney stood straight up and announced to the Republican gathering, "I want it understood that I am the grandson of nobody. I believe that every man should stand on his own merits."

PUT IN HIS PLACE

Following Zachary Taylor's sudden death, Millard Fillmore became President. One day he and his White House servant, Edward, went shopping for a carriage. After carefully inspecting a second-hand vehicle, the new President asked his servant, "How do you like it, Edward?" His servant replied, "It is a very handsome vehicle." Asked Fillmore, "But do you think it would do for the President of the United States to ride in a second-hand carriage?" With a twinkle in his eye, Edward retorted, "Why, your Excellency, aren't you a second-hand President?" Fillmore laughed heartily and later reported the story to friends.

BUSTED UP

Teaching a dog tricks can have its consequences. Fourteen-year-old Grover Cleveland taught his pooch several tricks: walking on its hind legs, lying on its back to play dead, and rolling over on command. He also taught it to climb a ladder. From a bedroom balcony Cleveland yelled for his dog to climb up to him, and it performed magnificently. But on one occasion his pet missed its footing on the top rung and fell two stories. Grover hurried downstairs where the dog stretched out its pink tongue to lick his master's tear-soaked cheeks. It had two broken legs, and one man in the village advised shooting it. Cleveland made splints and nursed it back to health. After a few weeks of tender, loving care, the dog was back in action.

CURLEY WAS CURTAILED

James Michael Curley was a controversial, flamboyant, and out-spoken mayor of Boston. He guaranteed he could deliver support to make Franklin D. Roosevelt the next President and demanded in return to be named Secretary of the Navy. Roosevelt refused, but considered Curley as the ambassador to Italy. Cardinal O'Connell of Boston and the Vatican did not want a man of such unsavory reputation named to the post. So when Curley showed up at the White House, the President suggested a new post – ambassador to Poland. As Roosevelt explained, "It's a very important position, because the next world war could be fought over the Polish Corridor, and it will take the skill of our ambassador to prevent it." Curley was furious. "Poland?!" he screamed. "That's a job you should give to a Republican, or to someone you want to get rid of!" The President countered by saying, "Poland is one of the most important nations in the world." But Curley disagreed: "If Poland is so goddamn important, Mr. President, why don't you resign your office and go over there yourself!" Whereupon he stormed out of the office. Curley's political enemies were delighted, remarking that had he accepted the post, he would have paved the Polish Corridor.

NEAR FATALITY?

Ronald Reagan wasn't the only President whom John Hinckley tried to shoot. Hinckley was arrested at a Nashville airport for carrying a loaded gun at the same time President Jimmy Carter was there. And, in October of 1980, television footage taken during Carter's visit to Dayton, Ohio, spotted Hinckley in the crowd pressing close to shake Carter's hand. A few months later the mentally-disturbed young man fired his pistol at President Reagan.

INVASION OF PRIVACY

Even trying to live the life of an ex-President is not easy. When the Trumans retired to their Delaware Avenue home in Independence, Missouri, there were repeated attempts by visitors to invade their yard, which was surrounded by a wrought-iron fence. Later, a security system and Secret Service men were provided. Feeling he was relatively safe from tourists wanting mementos, Truman observed, "We are just going to leave that fence there, not because we like it, but it's just the American way to take souvenirs. It was said in the First World War that the French fought for their country, the British fought for freedom of the seas, and the Americans fought for souvenirs."

I'M GOING TOO

James A. Garfield taught in several Ohio school districts, including Blue Rock in southern Muskingum County. He was to be paid $50 for a three-month term. The first day on the job Garfield entered a filthy, dilapidated building with a faulty stove. He was required to dig his own coal, in addition to dealing with unruly students and indifferent parents. Anywhere from six to twenty pupils might show up, some too young to learn the alphabet. One young boy and a girl ran off in mid-term and eloped. Garfield left shortly thereafter.

HAT TRICK

In 1956 Harry Truman received an honorary degree from Oxford University, and a picture of the ex-President in an English cap and gown appeared in newsreels and newspapers throughout the world. After returning home, the Trumans invited Randall Jesse and his family over to the house for ice cream. Mr. Jesse had instructed his four-year-old daughter to carefully address Truman as "Mr. President." As the two families were relaxing in the back yard, the little Jesse girl went over to Truman and said, "Mr. President, you sure looked funny in that king's hat." Mr. Jesse said, "Now, Janet, you mustn't ever say the President looks funny. Presidents just don't look funny." "All right," said Janet, who went back to Truman and said, "Mr. President, you sure looked *silly* in that king's hat." Truman excused himself, went into the house, then emerged in his cap and gown. He then picked Janet up in his arms and told her now she had seen the real thing.

A TRAGEDY FORETOLD

When events have a profound impact upon the minds and hearts of a nation, some people experience a premonition of these events. More than a few well-known personalities, in addition to psychics, had premonitions of President John F. Kennedy's death on November 22, 1963. Four years before the assassination Jean Dixon foretold that a black veil would cover the White House in the third year of a Democrat President. And just five weeks before Kennedy was shot, she named the exact day of his death. Harold Sherman, Dr. Regis Riesenman, Reverend Billy Graham, and Jess Stern also felt an impending doom approaching. Graham felt so strongly that he tried to get Kennedy to cancel his trip to Texas. One woman in Los Angeles on the morning of November 22 tried frantically to reach Governor Edmund Brown so he could warn Kennedy. All of these efforts, of course, failed.

ALMOST ESCAPE-PROOF

The Washington, D.C., prison retaining President Garfield's assassin, Charles Guiteau, was secure in 1881, but it was not escape-proof. Twenty-four years later Harry Houdini showed how quickly its locks could be picked. The cell had heavy bars and a large lock with five tumblers. The magician, though manacled in wrist and leg irons, was out of the cell in two minutes. Before returning to the warden's office, Houdini unlocked all the other cells and switched the inmates. This caused great concern for the prison officials, but they soon realized that Houdini was the greatest escape artist in the world, and no jail could hold him.

LEARNING WAS A BEECH

U.S. Grant's schooling at the village of Georgetown, Ohio, was quite thorough, and no-nonsense to boot. One of his teachers, John White, walked constantly throughout the classroom with a long beech switch, using it frequently. White also made the boys cut and bind these sticks into bundles, which were often used up all in one day. Of this strict education Grant remarked, "They taught me that a noun was the name of a person, place or thing so often that I came to believe it."

BEING BRIEF

President Ford was the commencement speaker at his daughter's graduation from Holton-Arms School in Bethesda, Maryland, in June of 1975. Ford addressed the class by saying, "You might be interested to know that my daughter Susan gave me some advice on this speech. She asked me not to talk too long, not to tell any jokes, not to talk about her, and not to talk about the way things were when I was your age. So, in conclusion…"

HER OLD FLAME

One day President Harry Truman saw his wife on her knees by the fireplace burning a stack of love letters she had received from Harry prior to their marriage. Truman told her she shouldn't do that. Bess replied, "Why not? I've read them." Her husband responded, "Bess, think of history." Countered the First Lady, "I am" – and kept right on burning.

JUST IN CASE

The circular parks which interrupt all of the main streets of Washington, D.C., were designed by Pierre L'Enfant of France. Though this design often annoys tourists and motorists, the French architect originated the idea after witnessing mobs of the French Revolution riot unhindered through the streets of Paris. He planned the city's circles so cannons could be placed in them to block entry to the city from any direction.

JAMES THE PROPHET

President-elect James Garfield wrote his friend Burke Hinsdale, "Our government is a modern Republic; the South was rooted and grounded in feudalism based on slavery; and the destruction of slavery has not yet destroyed the feudalism which it caused. Nothing but time can complete its destruction." Only a hundred years later did Garfield's words seem prophetic.

DEATH WISH

In January of 1893 Rutherford B. Hayes was visiting friends in Cleveland. He became quite ill and was urged to stay in bed. Hayes, however, insisted upon returning to his Fremont, Ohio, home, remarking, "I would rather die at Spiegel Grove than to live anywhere else." His wish was granted, and he died that same month.

REMEMBERED FOR SOMETHING

In 1985 the Millard Fillmore Society awarded its Medal of Mediocrity to the Coca Cola Company for "classic indecisiveness" in changing its product almost as often as Fillmore changed political parties. The thirteenth President at various times in his career was a Democrat, a Republican, a Whig, an Anti-Mason, and a Know-Nothing. Other recipients of the Fillmore Medal have included Billy Carter, Brooke Shields, and pop singer Boy George.

SOOTHING WORDS

On January 28, 1986, the space shuttle "Challenger" and the crew of five men and two women astronauts were killed in a terrific explosion just after leaving the launch pad at the Kennedy Space Center. President Reagan explained to a shocked and grieving nation, "Nothing ends here. We will continue our quest in space…. It is all part of taking a chance and expanding man's horizons. The future doesn't belong to the faint-hearted. It belongs to the brave."

PLAYBOY POLITICIAN?

Not even William Henry Harrison escaped being labeled a "playboy." In 1824 the well-known general had difficulty getting elected to the U.S. Congress. Harrison allegedly seduced the daughter of Dr. Browser, a prominent Cincinnati physician. Though this accusation *may* have been true, Harrison was still elected among four candidates.

ROUGH AND READY

Historians are quick to point out that John Adams and Andrew Jackson ousted hundreds of government employees and replaced them with their own people. Certainly one of the most flagrant examples of the spoils system and nepotism during the nineteenth century was President Zachary Taylor, hero of the Mexican War and nicknamed "Old Rough and Ready." In the Postal Department alone there were 3406 removals during Taylor's first year in office, in addition to hundreds of other clerks and employees in post offices throughout the western states and territories. And this does not include those fired in the other departments.

SWEET FELLAS

George Washington had a "hankerin'" for imported English candied almonds. Jefferson liked exotic French and Swiss chocolates, and Andrew Jackson loved blackberry jam. Teddy Roosevelt preferred candy made with saccharin, and Ronald Reagan liked to munch on licorice-flavored jelly beans.

A NOT-SO-SECRET AGENT

Former actor Ronald Reagan always enjoyed a good laugh. As President, he and comedian Bob Hope often traded friendly jibes. Hope once said, "Ronald Reagan is not a typical politician because he doesn't know how to lie, cheat and steal. He's always had an agent for that!"

ALMOST SCRIPTURE

It had been quite some time since seventeen-year-old James Garfield wrote his mother while he attended the Geauga Seminary near Chester, Ohio. Finally he took the time to send her a note, heading his written correspondence as the "First Epistle of James." Garfield at the time also worked as a janitor at the school.

BILL ON BILL

William Howard Taft had no designs for the Presidency, desiring only an appointment to the U.S. Supreme Court. But William McKinley had other ideas. He wanted Taft as the governor of the Philippines. William gave in to William, and had this to say about McKinley's appeal: "I never came in contact with a more sweetly sympathetic nature, nor one more persuasive in his treatment of men." Taft gave up his eight years as a judge on the circuit court and went to the Philippines, further remarking about the President, "I went under the influence of Mr. McKinley's personality, the influence he had of making people do what they ought to do in the interest of the public service." McKinley promised Taft an appointment to the Supreme Court later, explaining, "If I last, and the opportunity comes, I shall appoint you. Yes, if I am here, you will be here." The President, however, did not live through his second term, and Taft had to wait two decades for his appointment.

His Loss, Ohio's Gain

When the Civil War erupted in April of 1861, Lincoln asked the northern states for 75,000 men. Ohio raised three times its quota, upstaging her rival sister states. This presented many problems in finances and logistics. Rifles and other equipment were sadly lacking, so Governor William Dennison sent State Senator James Garfield on a secret mission to procure arms from the governors of Indiana and Illinois. Garfield was further instructed to convince the other governors to put their troops under the unified command of Ohio's George B. McClellan. It was a grueling trip, and the young senator hardly had time to rest. He lost several pounds and, in a letter to his wife, wrote that he had been able to change his clothes only twice during the entire week. Also during this time, Garfield attempted to become colonel of the Seventh Regiment, but his efforts were thwarted when another man took advantage of his absence. He returned home having achieved his objective, and months later received a commission.

Go with the Vets

Lincoln's friend Joe Gellespie asked what kind of cabinet he would select. The President-elect stated he might choose lawyers he knew on the old Eighth Circuit Court. In this way he might be able to avoid a civil war. Gellespie remarked, "But those old lawyers are all Democrats." Came the reply, "I know it, but I would rather have Democrats I know than Republicans I don't know."

Does this make any Sense?

Journalist-historian Alistair Cooke related this story regarding a comment made about the 1988 Presidential election: "On the night of the election, I was in a supermarket and I overheard a large, plump woman with a foreign accent say to a small wizened woman, 'Why, why, why did you vote for Dukakis?' And the wizened lady said very gravely, 'Because eighty-five percent of the people in prison in the United States were not breast-fed!' Now of all the conceivable reasons of voting for anybody, I guess that's as good as any." George Bush might have a difficult time figuring this out as well.

Jimmy's Jibe

Jimmy Carter's dislike of the media was well-known. He got in a "parting shot" at a farewell dinner given him by the press corps at the White House. The President ended his speech by saying, "I want to thank all of you who made my job so easy and enjoyable and comfortable." He then turned to his wife and remarked, "Thank you, Rosalynn."

Defending "Peachy" on the Prairie

Abe Lincoln was in much demand as an Illinois lawyer. He tried more than 3000 cases and argued about 250 cases before the state supreme court. In early September of 1859, less than a year after his defeat to Stephen Douglas in the U.S. Senate race, he defended a young man named Peachy Quinn Harrison on a murder charge. One of Lincoln's star witnesses was Peter Cartwright, Peachy Harrison's grandfather and the same man Lincoln defeated in the 1846 election to the U.S. House of Representatives. Cartwright was a Methodist minister and had once accused Lincoln of being an atheist. The shrewd Lincoln tried to convince the jury that Peachy was provoked into a fight and that killing the assailant was done in self-defense. After a four day trial in sweltering heat, Harrison was found "not guilty." It was one of the last cases Lincoln tried before his nomination as the Republican candidate for President.

Curious George

American artist Benjamin West liked to tell the story of his conversation with King George III during the Revolutionary War. When the king asked him what George Washington would do if he won the war, West replied that Washington would no doubt return to his farm, like the Roman general Cincinnatus did. King George replied, "If he did that, he would be the greatest man in the world." After serving two terms as President, Washington did just that.

Hot to Cold

Beginning with James Monroe's inauguration in 1821, when it was twenty-eight degrees and snowing, temperatures and weather conditions have been recorded. Ronald Reagan's inaugural ceremonies, however, set records for both the warmest and coldest temperatures. On January 20, 1981, it was fifty-six degrees; four years later it was a bone-chilling ten degrees. During six different inaugurations it snowed lightly, while seven others were accompanied with rain.

"BACK" IN ACTION

John Kennedy was rejected by the army when he failed his physical. During a football practice at Harvard he suffered a back injury. For five months he strengthened his back through vigorous exercises. When he felt confident he could pass his physical exam, he joined the Navy.

CONFUSED

Warren Harding was not exactly a wizard when it came to understanding economics and finances. In 1921 he told a colleague, "I can't make a damn thing out of this tax problem. I listen to one side and they seem right, and then – God! – I talk to the other side and they seem just as right; and here I am where I started. I know somewhere there is a book that will give me the truth, but hell, I couldn't read the book!"

PARTING WORDS

At least two Chief Executives were surprised on their first day in office. When Dwight Eisenhower sat at his desk in the Oval Office for the first time, he noticed one of the drawers was locked. Finding a key, he opened it to find a folder marked "Troubles" left by his predecessor, Harry Truman. And when George Bush sat down at his desk on January 21, 1989, he found a memo pad with a printed inscription "Don't let the turkeys get you down." It was left by Ronald Reagan who had written on it, "I'll miss our Thursday lunches." It was signed "Ron."

ESTABLISHING COMMAND

One day in 1919 President Woodrow Wilson accompanied General John J. Pershing on an inspection tour of an American army camp in France. At one point they strolled by a soldier's neatly packed equipment bundle, and Pershing picked up a folding tent pole, explaining to the President how it worked. He threw it down on top of the soldier's equipment and continued walking. They had just gone a few steps when Wilson stated to Pershing, "I am Commander-in-Chief of the Army and authorized to give you orders, am I not?" Pershing replied, "Certainly, sir." Wilson said, "Then, General, you will replace that tent pole as you found it." With a smile, Pershing knelt down, folded the tent pole, and put it back in its proper place. This was Wilson's way of reminding Pershing that he should respect all individuals, regardless of their rank or authority.

MODEL ROLE

In 1939 a youthful John F. Kennedy was touring Rome with U.S. Diplomat Bernard Baruch and his wife, Irene. Mrs. Baruch was an accomplished artist originally from Poland. She asked JFK if he would pose as a model for an angel floating over Saint Theresa. Kennedy agreed, and the painting eventually found its way to the Vatican where it is displayed today.

SET STRAIGHT

When attorney Abe Lincoln was in Pekin, Illinois, he went to visit his friend, Dave Lowry. Approaching the house, Lincoln noticed some boys playing marbles near the walk. He put his hand on the head of Lowry's boy and remarked, "My boy, you're playing marbles!" The youth looked up and replied, "Any damn fool ought to see that." Lincoln often repeated this story.

GETTING THE MESSAGE STRAIGHT

Warren G. Harding had some doubts whether he should continue campaigning for the Presidency following his 1920 nomination. More than once he wanted to quit and have a replacement named. On one occasion Harding phoned his campaign manager, expressing his desire to resign. His wife, however, would not hear of it. Florence seized the telephone from her husband and shouted that they were "in the race until hell freezes over!"

I CAN'T HELP MYSELF

In the 1890s professor Woodrow Wilson became involved with a wealthy New Jersey divorcee, Mary Hulbert Peck. He went so far as to bring her home for dinner. Not wanting to damage his political career, Ellen Wilson treated Mary as a family friend, rather than feed the gossips. Wilson indicated his relationship with Mary Peck was a "contemptible error… a madness of a few months…" leaving him "stained and unworthy." Nevertheless, Wilson continued to write her even while he was President.

Not Quite What the Doctor Ordered

Considering the thousands of office seekers our first twenty Chief Executives had to deal with each year, it is astonishing they achieved anything beyond trying to please the "hungry hoards." Thus, it was a rare event when a caller came to the White House not wanting an appointment of some kind. During Lincoln's first year in office, Doctor R. Shelton Mackenzie of Philadelphia was one of thirty callers one day. After a brief introduction by a secretary, the doctor asked the President if he could have an autograph. Lincoln inquired, "Will you have it on a card or a sheet of paper?" The jolly physician replied, "If the choice rested with myself, I should prefer to have it at the foot of a commission." Lincoln smiled, shook his head, and wrote a few pleasant lines on paper and signed it.

Taking a Bite out of the Fight

In 1863 during the siege of Vicksburg, U.S. Grant made his headquarters aboard a Mississippi steamboat. Going to bed one evening during the battle, the general took out his false teeth and put them in a wash basin. His orderly came in during the night and emptied the basin into the Mississippi. The teeth went too. Grant was perplexed. He couldn't eat or chew on his cigar. The battle was halted until a dentist was summoned by an emergency call. Grant got his new teeth, and the battle continued, with Vicksburg surrendering on July 3.

Making Room for Royalty

President James Buchanan went to great lengths to please important guests, even if it meant an inconvenience to himself. His niece, Harriet Lane, served as First Lady and together they made the Executive Mansion the center of a brilliant social life. One of the most spectacular events centered around the visit of the Prince of Wales, later King Edward VII of Great Britain. Buchanan had once served as the U.S. ambassador to England and took great pains to entertain his host in a royal fashion. The President was a bit surprised when the prince brought such a large party there was not enough room for sleeping accommodations. Buchanan had to sleep in the White House hallway to provide proper quarters for his guests.

The Hoover Damn

Shortly before he died, Warren Harding read a prepared speech before a large audience in Tacoma, Washington. There was much applause, even though Harding stumbled through much of the text. The speech had been written by his Secretary of Commerce Herbert Hoover. Finishing his address, Harding sat down next to his Commerce Secretary and whispered, "Damn it, Hoover. Why don't you use the same English I do?"

Resolved and Revived

A White House desk, called the *Resolute*, was given to President Rutherford B. Hayes by Queen Victoria. It was made from timbers of the *H.M.S. Resolute*. Every President since then has used it. However, by the time Jimmy Carter had taken office, the desk was moved to the Smithsonian. Carter ordered it returned to the Oval Office, and later had a replica made for the Jimmy Carter Library and Museum. The original desk was later moved to President George Bush's study in the White House.

Tired, Retired, and Expired

James Buchanan was happy to leave office on the day of Lincoln's inauguration, and many Americans were happy as well. Buchanan's policy toward the seceding slave states angered most northerners. While he declared there was "no right of secession," Buchanan also pointed out that the Constitution provided no legal way to prevent it. During the last four months of his term, seven states left the Union, and three of his cabinet members resigned. He refused to use force even when Confederate guns fired on a U.S. vessel. In early March of 1861 Buchanan retreated to his twenty-two acre Pennsylvania estate Wheatland, located near Lancaster. He described his residence as a "beau ideal of a statesman's abode," and praised "the comforts and tranquility of home contrasted with the troubles, perplexities, and difficulties of public life." He wrote a book to justify his compromising domestic policies, but strongly supported Lincoln during the Civil War. Always happy to receive guests, he wrote one friend, "…I hope you may not fail to come this way…I should be delighted with a visit…." James Buchanan died peacefully at his beloved Wheatland on June 1, 1868.

A Change of Subjects

During a White House dinner in February of 1903, Theodore Roosevelt and some important guests were having a discussion on the Cuban Treaty. Suddenly, the President's son, Archie, interrupted with "Father, father, FATHER," louder each time. "What is it, Archie?" exclaimed papa. "Father, doesn't the monkey cage at the zoo smell terrible?" Roosevelt paused and replied, "My recollection is that it does, Archie!"

Physician – Heal Thyself

Thomas Jefferson was ahead of his time. He had himself, his daughter, some nephews and nieces, a few slaves, and a student (Meriwether Lewis), all inoculated for smallpox. There were cries of protest – several adults and friends accused him of trying to murder the children. During an outbreak of the disease in Tidewater, Virginia, the future President felt he could waste no time. Jefferson explained how the Chinese took the top off a smallpox sore, powdered it, put it in a glass tube, then blew it into a person's nostrils. The English and French were less crude, but nevertheless understood the advantage of scratching a small place on a person's arm and rubbing in the smallpox germs. Doctors in the surrounding region held little faith in such treatment, but none of the people Jefferson inoculated died from the disease. And though he was not a licensed physician, Jefferson understood medical practice well enough to perform successful surgeries.

Finding a Career

James Madison was a fine, hard-working student. He finished a four-year curriculum at Princeton in just two and a half years. But this cram course in the classics took its toll, with Madison nearly having a physical breakdown. One of his professors, Dr. Witherspoon, said that Madison never did or said "an improper thing." But Madison could not decide between a career in law or the clergy. The jailing of Baptist preachers by Anglicans in early 1774 infuriated him. In addition he looked down on slavery and felt English taxation policies were unfair. When revolution came, he decided to pursue politics. Venturing to Williamsburg, he urged Virginia delegates to promote religious freedom and speak out against taxation.

Worst Fears Confirmed

In December of 1944 Vice President-elect Harry Truman and a World War I veteran were passing the White House on a daily walk. "Someday soon," the friend said, "you will be walking through the front door of that place." Truman looked up at the white columns and remarked, "I hope not, I hope not, but I think you're right." Within four months FDR, in failing health, was dead, and Truman was the thirty-third President.

Getting Even

George Washington dismissed James Monroe as Minister to France for "incompetence, remissness in duty, and the pursuit of wrong causes." Monroe felt his former commander had wronged him. After his return to the United States, he not only asked for expenses incurred while overseas, he also published a book denouncing Washington. The book did not sell well, and neither of the two suffered much damage in their reputations.

Abandoned Agent

FDR enjoyed a good practical joke. Though wheelchair-bound, he was skilled in losing his Secret Service protection. A couple of times at Warm Springs, Georgia, and at his Hyde Park home, the President would have his bodyguard, Gus Gennerich, climb up on the roof on some pretext, then have a hired hand remove the ladder, stranding the gullible agent.

I Shall Return

The only time George Washington left the country was when he was nineteen years old. Though the United States was not yet a nation, Washington left Virginia and sailed to Barbados. He accompanied his half-brother, Lawrence, who was very ill. Lawrence was also George's guardian and never regained his health. George found the voyage enlightening and educational, but contracted smallpox, which left him marked for life.

I Don't Mean You, Dean

John Kennedy regarded the State Department as ineffective, referring to it as "a bowl of jelly," adding, "They never had any ideas over there; never come up with anything new." JFK's feelings, however, did not extend to his resourceful Secretary of State Dean Rusk.

Quite a Gathering

The largest gathering of past and future Presidents took place in the Capitol in December of 1834. These included ex-President John Quincy Adams, ex-President Andrew Jackson, Vice President Martin Van Buren, Senator John Tyler, Senator James Buchanan, and Representatives Millard Fillmore, James K. Polk, and Franklin Pierce. These men all attended a meeting in the Old House Chamber.

Precious Pebbles

James Buchanan never accepted gifts during his four years as our fifteenth President, and he advised his niece, Harriet Lane, the same. Being a bachelor, Buchanan asked his lovely niece to assume the duties of First Lady. Harriet could not resist one young, wealthy admirer who gave her some pebbles which had been fashioned into a bracelet. Several diamonds were included just to make the gift a bit more expensive. When the President was in a good mood, Harriet asked him if he would object to her receiving a bracelet made of stones. Buchanan had no objections. Harriet Lane enjoyed telling this story, reminding listeners that, "Diamonds are pebbles, you know."

Something's Missing Here

Hollywood's greatest child movie star, Shirley Temple, was invited to the White House by Franklin Roosevelt. The President was disappointed that the six-year-old celebrity never smiled. Even a remark to this effect could not induce her to smile. Years later, she explained why. It seems America's little sweet heart had lost a front tooth and was embarrassed by it.

Bucks from "Buck"

In 1866 former President James Buchanan sent Robert Tyler, son of John Tyler, a check for $1000. Tyler was living in Montgomery, Alabama, and was destitute. Like his Presidential father, Robert was a man of fierce pride and would not accept the money. He promptly sent it back.

Tyler's Tirade

In June of 1822 a young Virginia lawyer by the name of John Tyler had a fight with John Macon outside the New Kent County Courthouse. Macon taunted and insulted the future President. Tyler hit Macon in the face with his fist. A wild brawl ensued, and Macon used his riding whip on Tyler. As they wrestled to the ground, Tyler grabbed the whip and slashed Macon several times, cutting his face.

To the King!

As late as June of 1775 many Americans still did not want war with England. Even though fighting broke out at Lexington and Concord, and heavy casualties incurred at Bunker Hill (Breed's Hill), most Americans were hopeful that a peaceful solution could be found. George Washington, commander of the rebel forces, drank a toast to King George III each evening.

A House of a Different Color

Former President, Millard Fillmore was critical of Lincoln. Throughout the Civil War he lived in Buffalo, New York. It was reported that the day after Lincoln was shot, the city fathers ordered every building in Buffalo display a mourning symbol. Fillmore was taking care of his sick wife and supposedly did not hear about the city ordinance. He awoke the next morning to find his house smeared with black paint.

Dinner for Two

Washington thoroughly enjoyed his long-awaited retirement from politics. A few weeks after leaving the Presidency in 1797, he wrote his secretary Tobias Lear from Mount Vernon, "Unless someone pops in, unexpectedly – Mrs. Washington and myself will do what I believe has not been done within the last twenty years by us – that is set down to dinner by ourselves."

LOOKING FOR TROUBLE

As a rancher in the Badlands of North Dakota, Theodore Roosevelt had many thrilling encounters with man and beast. Once, upon returning to his ranch, he discovered that some thieves had stolen his boat. The robbers must have felt confident they would get away for there was no other boat in the area. Roosevelt and two companions hurriedly built a rude craft and started down the rough waters of the Little Missouri in search of the culprits. After floating 150 miles they spotted a camp. T.R. crept ashore and captured three bandits, along with his boat. For a week he and his friends took their captives to the county seat, which was 200 miles away. The boats stuck in ice jams and almost capsized. Each night a fire was built on the river bank while Roosevelt and his assistants divided the watch as guards. Such examples of determination, daring, and adventure made young Theodore a legend in his own time.

HIRAM'S HAUNTED HOUSE

When Bruno and Dorothy Mallone bought their house in 1960, they had it moved because it was located on property which was owned by the growing Hiram College in northeast Ohio. James Garfield lived in the house for five years, having been a graduate of the school and its president. The Mallones and their daughter, along with many other people, believe their house to be occupied by a friendly poltergeist – namely James A. Garfield. Many incidents continue to happen there which simply defy explanation – faucets being turned on and off, lights blinking, clocks stopping, empty rocking chairs rocking, candlesticks flying across the room, candy being thrown on the floor, and the pump-operated melodeon playing classical music by itself. The Mallones have also been disturbed by strange voices. One of the most bizarre incidents happened when Bruno began working a crossword puzzle and set it down only partially completed on a table. When he returned a few minutes later, the entire puzzle was finished in an old style handwriting. Contacting some college officials, they discovered that the unique handwriting matched that of Garfield. None of the Mallones have ever been injured by these weird happenings, and their house to this day continues to attract curious visitors and experts studying the world of psychic phenomena. Though Garfield left the house in 1861 to fight in the Civil War, it is believed his ghost still remains. Incidentally, the author has visited the house and talked with the Mallones, but nothing out of the ordinary occurred during the visit.

I'M WARNING YOU

After Dwight Eisenhower was elected President in 1952, he announced his Cabinet selections. Among those he named was George M. Humphrey of Ohio. Humphrey served as Secretary of the Treasury for nearly five years, and worked hard to cut government spending. By reducing both spending and taxes, Humphrey reasoned that the federal government would become more efficient. Alarmed at the administration's budget for 1957, he warned Eisenhower, "If we don't [cut spending], over a long period of time, I will predict that you will have a depression that will curl your hair." This would prove almost an impossibility, because Eisenhower was bald!

BOUGHT BY BUSH

President and Barbara Bush went on a European tour in the summer of 1992. In London they were the guests of Queen Elizabeth at a luncheon. On the gift table was a small, decorative silver bowl with three little feet. Bush looked at it and asked what it was. The Queen answered, "I don't know. *You* gave it to *me!*"

REVOLTING BEHAVIOR

When the Revolutionary War broke out in 1775, James Monroe was a student at the College of William and Mary. Inspired by patriotic fever, he helped organize a revolt against the royal governor of Virginia. Along with two dozen other students, Monroe raided the arsenal at the Governor's Palace, seizing 200 muskets and 300 swords. The weapons were given to the Williamsburg militia. Monroe never returned to college, but served in the army and later studied law under Thomas Jefferson.

HARRISON THE HARASSER

In his one month as President, William Henry Harrison's biggest complaint was not his ill health, but the hordes of office-seekers waiting to see him each day. Prior to Harrison's inauguration, former President John Quincy Adams explained, "The greatest beggar and the most troublesome of all the office seekers during my administration was General Harrison."

ORDERS, ORDERS!

Much of George Washington's correspondence concerned instructions to his overseer and manager at Mount Vernon. On April 20, 1794, the President ordered that no more wheat was to be planted because of an embargo. A few months later he okayed plans to build a whiskey still. In early December of that same year he reminded his manager to save some of the Madeira wine for him.

STOIC TO THE END

In December of 1799 George Washington spent five hours in the snow and rain to inspect his Mount Vernon plantation. He returned to his house with a chill and quickly developed a severe cold and an inflamed throat. His faithful servant, Tobias Lear, suggested the general take some medicine. Washington replied, "No, you know I never take anything for a cold. Let it go as it came." Two days later he died.

HELL TO THE CHIEF

Rutherford B. Hayes won the highly disputed election of 1876. Shortly after occupying the White House in March of the following year, Hayes and his family sat down to their dinner. A bullet came crashing through a window, passing through two rooms and lodging in the wall of the White House library. No one was injured and the culprit was never caught, but the Hayes family was quite shaken.

POCKET VETO

After Martin Greenfield was liberated from a Nazi concentration camp at the end of World War II, he emigrated to the Bronx in New York City where he worked as a tailor. His boss was a close friend of President Dwight Eisenhower. In the early 1950s, while making a suit for the President, Greenfield sewed a couple of handwritten notes in the pockets of Eisenhower's suit. The messages criticized Eisenhower in his Middle East policy. A few months later Eisenhower played golf with Greenfield's boss and jokingly told him that there was a foreign policy adviser working at his factory. Though Eisenhower found the incident amusing, Greenfield was told not to put any more notes in the President's pockets.

TRUMAN'S TEMPORARY TRAUMA

President Truman always wore his glasses while swimming. One day while swimming at Key West, Florida, a large wave washed his glasses away and repeated dives by Secret Service agents failed to retrieve them. A while later, however, the observant Truman spied his spectacles washed up on the beach. He scooped them up, put them on, and flashed the Secret Service one of his famous grins.

FRUSTRATED FILLMORE

Once a President retires he has little or no financial worries. But that was not always the case, and Millard Fillmore noted in his retirement, "It is a national disgrace that our Presidents should be cast adrift, and be compelled to keep a corner grocery for subsistence.... We elect a man to the presidency, expect him to be honest, to give up a lucrative profession, perhaps, and after we have done with him we let him go into seclusion and perhaps poverty."

ON GUARD AMERICA!

President Dwight Eisenhower once warned, "We are not concerned merely with protecting territory, our people abroad, even our homes; we are concerned with defending a way of life. This, my friends, we must do by strength, a conciliatory spirit, and understanding, and with the cooperation of our friends in the world. It means that we must also defend that way of life always at home."

IN MY OPINION

Theodore Roosevelt had a low opinion of several Presidents. Of Benjamin Harrison he noted, "Damn the President! He is a cold-blooded, narrow-minded, prejudiced, obstinate, timid old psalm-singing Indianapolis politician." But Teddy had his critics too. Calvin Coolidge remarked about Roosevelt, that he was "always getting himself in hot water by talking before he had to commit himself upon issues not well-defined."

Military Misgivings

George Washington realized that commanding the army during the Revolutionary War was an almost impossible task. Most of the soldiers were ill-equipped, inexperienced, and outnumbered by the British redcoats. He confided in Patrick Henry, "From the day I entered upon the command of the American army(s) I date my fall, and the ruin of my reputation."

Name Change

Federal City was the official name of our nation's capital during John Adams' term as President. Thomas Jefferson, however, changed that. In 1801 President Jefferson sponsored a bill which renamed the city Washington, D.C.

Adams' Declaration of No

Thomas Jefferson did not want to write the Declaration of Independence. He believed that task should go to another member of the First Continental Congress – John Adams. But Adams did not feel qualified, and in his frank and open way, he told Jefferson, "I am obnoxious and unpopular," adding further, "You can write ten times better than I can." Jefferson, however, did an outstanding job and after a few revisions, the document was issued.

Farmers Find Friend in Frank

The Great Depression was in full swing by the time Franklin Roosevelt took office in 1933. Banks were foreclosing on a thousand homes a day, mostly on farmers who lost their land due to falling prices and drought. And only two farmers in 100 had electricity in their homes. With government programs such as the Tennessee Valley Authority and the Agricultural Adjustment Act, the standard living for farmers increased.

Bush – Broiled, Boiled, or Baked?

In early September of 1944 naval pilot George Bush was shot down while flying a bombing mission over the island of Chichi Jima. Two of Bush's crewmen died but the future President bailed out over the Pacific Ocean four miles from the island. The Japanese sent out a patrol boat to capture him, but other pilots strafed the enemy and forced them back. After floating three hours in a rubber raft, Bush was rescued by a submarine, the USS *Finback*. The young pilot was lucky not to have been taken prisoner on Chichi Jima. Japanese commanders there had instructed their men to *eat* American captives, explaining that cannibalizing prisoners would give their men added strength.

Powerful Poke Profits Powers

In the late 1940s John Kennedy was a candidate for Congress, but he always found time to watch the Boston Red Sox play at Fenway Park. His friend Dave Powers (later a special assistant in the White House for Kennedy) often accompanied him to the games. Attending a night game, Kennedy turned to Powers in the first inning as slugger Ted Williams was coming to bat and asked him what the chances were of Williams hitting a home run. "Well," guessed Powers, "I'd say he hits one about every fifteen or so times at bat." Kennedy then bet Powers $10 to $1 that Williams would not hit a homer. Powers, not minding losing a dollar, accepted the wager. On the next pitch, Williams smacked the ball over the right field bullpen and into the bleachers. Powers reached over to Kennedy and waited for his money. He later recalled, "You never saw $10 change hands so slowly."

William's Woes

Even the most mild mannered of men who serve in the White House find the pressure unrelenting. William McKinley once observed, "I have had enough of it, heaven knows! I have had all the honors there is in this place, and have responsibilities enough to kill any man."

Monumental Achievement

The first regimental monument erected in the country was dedicated to the 23rd Ohio Volunteer Infantry, which distinguished itself at the battle of Antietam on September 17, 1862. Erected in Cleveland, Ohio, nearly thirty officers and men posed for a photograph beside it on July 26, 1865, the same day the soldiers were mustered out of the army. Two individuals in the 23rd O.V.I. became President – Brigadier General Rutherford B. Hayes and Major William McKinley.

Billy Greets Bill

On September 5, 1901, President William McKinley strode through the stadium at the Pan-American Exposition in Buffalo, New York. Escorted by General Samuel Welch, he waved to the 50,000 spectators and walked past mounted troops. He then turned towards the stands and at this point the U.S. Marine mascot, Billy Goat Marine, broke ranks and stood right in front of McKinley. The President smiled and acknowledged the goat's welcome. The crowd roared with laughter as McKinley enjoyed the gesture as well.

A Remarkable "Feet"

On the day he left office, March 4, 1845, James K. Polk made one last visit before departing to his home in Tennessee. He stopped at the home of former First Lady Dolley Madison on Lafayette Square. When he got there he found Dolley running barefoot outside, racing with two teen-aged daughters of a friend. Dolley seemed impervious to the discomforts of the cold ground, even though she was seventy-seven years old at the time.

All Aboard!

Even as a young man William Howard Taft was a person of large proportions. One day, the young Ohio lawyer wanted to catch the express train in the small town of Somerville, where it did not usually stop. Taft sent a telegram to the railroad division headquarters: "Will you stop through express at Somerville to take on large party?" The train stopped, as had been requested, and the conductor looked surprised to find only one passenger waiting. "Where's the large party we were to take on?" he asked. Replied Taft with a sheepish smile, "I'm it."

A Taylor Tribute

President Zachary Taylor fondly recalled his friendship with former First Lady Dolley Madison, who died in 1849 at the age of eighty-one. Taylor remarked, "What an extraordinary great lady she was! America will never know another like her.... She will never be forgotten because she was truly our First Lady for half a century."

Gaining the Upper Hand... er Leg

William McKinley was a shrewd lawyer. In one of his more celebrated cases as an attorney in Canton, Ohio, he defended a surgeon who was being sued for malpractice. The opposing lawyer maintained that, due to improper surgical techniques, his client's leg was bowed. When McKinley's turn came up he called the plaintiff to the stand and had him roll up his pant legs, revealing that *both* legs were bowed. The case was dismissed and the bowlegged man walked out of court no doubt a bit "bent out of shape."

Teddy's Good Memory

In April of 1901 Theodore Roosevelt, then Vice President, visited Colorado Springs and took a ride on the newly laid Short Line Railroad to stop at Victor, a small Colorado gold mining town. He was escorted to the Gold Coin Club where a luncheon was held in his honor. There was a long line of greeters, among them an aspiring young news reporter, Lowell Thomas. He shook Roosevelt's hand and was handed a lump of sugar from a bowl on the table. Thomas then went back outside and waited in line again. Thinking the Vice President would not recognize him the second time through, Roosevelt shook his hand again and asked, "Does this mean you'll be voting twice at election time?"

Seeing Things Through

William McKinley's determination to achieve objectives was very apparent even during his childhood. One time when he was eight years old, Will went fishing at Mosquito Creek with two other boys near their Niles, Ohio, home. An hour passed without a nibble, and the two other boys got bored and announced they were going swimming instead. They begged Will to go, but he told them he wasn't leaving until he caught some fish. As his friends frolicked in the creek downstream, McKinley patiently waited. When the other two boys returned a while later, young McKinley's persistence had paid off. He took home a long string of fish dangling from the pole across his shoulder.

I'm Doing You a Favor

As president of Princeton University Woodrow Wilson had the final say in expelling students. One day a student threw a bottle of beer through his office window. Wilson expelled him, and the student eventually took up writing as a career. That student was playwright Eugene O'Neill.

Tattered Throne

In October of 1862 President Lincoln called a cabinet meeting. His Postmaster General, William Dennison of Ohio, noticed the worn leather chair at Lincoln's desk and remarked, "I should think that the Presidential chair should be better furniture than that." To which Lincoln replied, "You think that chair is not good…. There are many people who want to sit in it, and I've often wished some of them had it instead of me."

A Sign Of Things To Come

Two of Franklin Pierce's classmates at Bowdoin College in Maine were Henry Wadsworth Longfellow and Nathaniel Hawthorne. Years later, Hawthorne recollected of Pierce's character and his "fascination of manner," the source of which lay "deep in the kindliness of his nature. Few men possess anything like it." Frank Pierce's charm, amiability, and cordial manners were not enough to make him an effective President during the pre-Civil War period.

Fatherly Advice

William Henry Harrison was President for only one month, and John Tyler was summoned at his Williamsburg home to assume duties as Chief Executive. Tyler explained to his children, "Remember you will be much in the public eye. May you never, as the President's family, do ought which you will regret when you shall be nothing higher than plain John Tyler's family."

The Sporting Life

President Eisenhower tried to get his Vice President, Richard Nixon, interested in several sports. Nixon disliked fishing, but in 1952 Eisenhower tried to teach him how to cast for trout, with disastrous results. After hooking a tree limb the first three times, Nixon hooked Eisenhower's shirt on the fourth try. Nixon later agreed to go golfing with his boss. As partners, they lost because Nixon did so poorly. Eisenhower, who hated to lose at anything, told his Veep after the match, "Look here, you're a young man, you're strong, and you can do a lot better than that." Nixon's golf game did improve after several years, but for exercise he turned to walking and swimming.

Giving a Tong Lashing

James Madison wanted to name Albert Gallatin as his Secretary of State. This presented a problem, since Gallatin's political enemies included several leaders in the Senate. The President gave in, naming Robert Smith, brother of a Maryland Senator, as his cabinet member. It proved to be a poor choice. An incompetent, Smith conspired with the opposition in Congress as the nation moved closer to a second war with England. After three years, Madison finally confronted Smith and denounced him. Reportedly, the quarrel became so heated that Smith struck Madison with his cane. Madison snatched up some tongs from a fireplace. Just as the two were about to tangle, an attendant rushed between them. Smith was not given an opportunity to resign. He was simply fired and Madison named James Monroe as his new Secretary of State. Gallatin, incidentally, had been the Secretary of the Treasury and remained so.

Knowing The Candidate

In the 1856 Presidential election Ulysses Grant voted for James Buchanan, a compromising Democrat. Buchanan defeated "The Pathfinder" John C. Fremont, nominee of the newly-formed Republican Party. A few years later, during a discussion of politics, Grant was queried why he voted for Buchanan. His reply was simply, "I knew Fremont."

Pow-Wow Feast

The Grants entertained lavishly. On June 9, 1870, the President held a large reception for chief Red Cloud and his delegation of Ogallalla warriors. After a tour through the White House, the Indians were treated to a fine dinner with foreign dignitaries, cabinet members and their wives. Delighted and impressed, the Indians expressed themselves as having friendship for U.S. Grant who provided "so much good eat and so much squaw." No doubt Red Cloud lost Grant's admiration six years later when he and chiefs Crazy Horse and Sitting Bull wiped out General George Custer's company of men at the Little Big Horn River.

Time for a Change?

Theodore Roosevelt's favorite battle song was "Dixie." His favorite American tune, however, was "Battle Hymn of the Republic." He felt it should be our national anthem. A combined effort initiated a nationwide movement to gain attention and support. Influential citizens, including newspaper editors, were contacted in the South and West. Roosevelt's plan failed, perhaps for fear of offending American Jews who might object to the word "Christ" in the song's lyrics. FDR also had problems with the song.

Liberal Views

Lincoln was asked about an Illinois law forbidding interracial marriages. He told a newspaper man, "The law means nothing. I shall never marry a negress, but I have no objection to anyone else doing so. If a white man wants to marry a Negro woman, let him do it – if the Negro woman can stand it."

"Deweying" It Differently

Annexing the Philippines proved to be costly to the U.S. at the turn of the century. President McKinley's Cabinet, the Congress, and the American people were divided on the issue. At a cost of 10,000 American lives and nearly 100,000 Filipinos, McKinley's Open Door Policy in the Far East angered several foreign countries. The President once lamented to his friend H. H. Kohlsaat, "If old Dewey had just sailed away when he smashed the Spanish fleet, what a lot of trouble he would have saved us."

Undercover Underwear – Or A Briefs-case

George Bush had just been appointed new chief of the Central Intelligence Agency. He boarded a jet passenger plane and soon discovered that the man sitting next to him was Arizona Congressman Barry Goldwater, Jr. Both men had briefcases and when Goldwater got back to his hotel he opened the briefcase to get his shaving kit. He quickly realized the briefcase wasn't his – it belonged to the CIA chief. It was returned several days later. When he was asked if he had discovered any secrets, Goldwater confessed that the only articles in the briefcase was George Bush's dirty underwear.

JUST ASK ALICE

Concerning FDR's longtime affair with Lucy Mercer Rutherford, his cousin and outspoken socialite Alice Roosevelt Longsworth (daughter of Theodore) actually encouraged the romance. Alice later explained, "It was good for Franklin. He deserved a good time. He was married to Eleanor."

PRESIDENT PROVIDES PIRATES PROSTITUTES

Thomas Jefferson was willing to go to great lengths to settle with the Barbary Coast pirates who were taking our ships on the high seas. The Bey of Tunis sent eleven emissaries to Washington, demanding the United States pay a tribute. Jefferson had no intentions of paying a large bribe, but he did direct Secretary of State James Madison to accommodate them by providing lodgings at the Stelle Hotel. No sooner had the pirates settled in when they complained they had no concubines. Eleven prostitutes were procured from the local madam known as "Georgia the Greek" and put into service. The pirates stayed six weeks.

FLAG–WAVING BEN

Benjamin Harrison was proud to be an American, and he believed others should always show their patriotism. He observed, "I rejoice in nothing more than in this movement, recently so prominently developed, of placing a starry banner above every schoolhouse. I have been charged with too sentimental appreciation of the flag. I will not enter upon any defense. God pity the American citizen who does not love it, who does not see in it the story of our great free institutions, and the hope of the home as well as the nation."

MISCHIEVOUS MEN

Franklin Roosevelt's mother did not approve of her son's drinking of alcoholic beverages, even when he was President. When the King of England visited the Roosevelts at Hyde Park, New York, the President greeted him in the study, looked at some glasses on a table and said, "My mother does not approve of cocktails and thinks you should have a cup of tea." The king thought for a moment then responded, "Neither does my mother." Martinis were served and the two leaders thoroughly enjoyed themselves.

GRANT GOES AROUND

U.S. Grant had some strange habits. Among these was a phobia about retracing his steps, which tended to disturb some of his army staff. Whether riding a horse or walking, if Grant went past a place he was looking for, he would never turn back. Instead, he would just keep walking or riding until he worked his way around again. This idiosyncrasy was also used in battle and interpreted as a refusal to retreat.

SANDY'S SUDDEN SNAPSHOT

In 1975 there were two attempts on President Gerald Ford's life when women fired pistol shots at him on two separate visits to California. Shortly afterwards Ford visited Bowling Green State University. A young woman's flashbulb exploded during his visit and Secret Service men jumped on her and wrestled her to the ground. Her hair and neck had been clawed by angry spectators as she was dragged away. The photographer, Sandy Snyder of Ohio, was naturally quite shaken, but she soon got over it. Ford sent an apology, along with a special bracelet with the Presidential seal on it.

POISONED PEAS PITCHED

In the spring of 1776, Thomas Hickey hatched a plot to kill George Washington. Hickey was a member of Washington's guard and a Tory sympathizer. He sought the help of Phoebe Fraunces, the daughter of a New York City tavern keeper. She was to serve Washington a plate of peas, the general's favorite dish. These peas, however, were poisoned. As the meal was being served Phoebe had a change of heart and whispered to Washington not to eat his peas. The general tossed them out a window. Chickens ate them and fell dead. Hickey was arrested, charged with passing counterfeit money and conspiring to enroll prisoners in a secret Tory army. After an investigation, Hickey was found guilty on these and other charges, then executed.

A Lucky "Break"

While Warren G. Harding was attending grade school in Caledonia, Ohio, in the early 1870s, he and a classmate, John Warwick, were caught "fooling around" at the teacher's desk. Warwick was nearest the teacher when both boys were nabbed. Using a three-foot long hickory stick, the teacher struck Warwick across the shoulder blade. The stick broke to pieces and Harding got away with just a verbal scolding.

Fala Freed From Fatty Food

FDR could not understand why his Scottish terrier Fala was gaining weight. One evening the dog was taken to the hospital with a serious intestinal disorder. The President learned that the White House kitchen staff was feeding him. Roosevelt then issued a stern order: "Not even one crumb will be fed to Fala except by the President." From then on, Fala remained in good health.

Haunted Hallways

The White House isn't the only place where ghosts of Presidents have been seen in the twentieth century. Apparitions of U.S. Grant, John Quincy Adams, and James A. Garfield have been seen walking the halls of Congress at the Capitol. Among those who saw these ghosts were guards on duty there.

Chief Confesses Cheating

It was Franklin Roosevelt's custom each year on the night Congress adjourned to host a poker party at the White House. In 1940, the President, Secretary of the Treasury Henry Morgenthau and two others began their game. The rule was that whoever was ahead at the moment the Speaker of the House called to say that Congress adjourned would be declared the winner. On this particular night, Morgenthau was far ahead when the Speaker called, but FDR pretended the phone call was from someone else and the game continued until midnight, when Roosevelt finally pulled ahead. At this point he whispered to an aide to go into another office and call the study. When the phone rang Roosevelt pretended it was the Speaker and declared himself the winner. The next morning Morgenthau read in the paper that Congress had officially adjourned at 9 p.m. He was so angry that he handed in his resignation. Only when FDR called and explained it was all in good fun did Morgenthau agree to remain in the Cabinet.

Unidentified Flying Objects Bypass Truman

In the summer of 1952 flying saucers were reported over the White House. Radar facilities at both Andrews Air Force base and Washington National Airport picked up seven blips on their radar screens, traveling anywhere between 100 to 7200 mph. President Harry Truman expressed concern but didn't want to make any comments for fear it would upset the public.

Heaven or Hell?

In 1846 Abe Lincoln ran against Peter Cartwright for Congress. Lincoln, running as a Whig, was being harassed by his Democratic opponent. In a self-righteous tone, Cartwright demanded to know where Lincoln was going – to heaven or hell. Lincoln, rose, nodded to his adversary, then looked at the audience and commented, "Brother Cartwright asked me directly where I am going. I desire to reply with equal directness. I am going to Congress." Lincoln won the race and served a single two-year term in the U.S. House of Representatives.

Hoover Not Heard

Former President Herbert Hoover still had a lot of political enemies in 1936 – and that was among his own Republican ranks. Hoover, still hoping he could be nominated, was scheduled to speak and initiate a celebration with supporters waiting on the convention floor. But other candidates thwarted his efforts. As Hoover began his speech the microphone "broke down" and nobody heard him. Then, at the 1940 convention in Philadelphia, he was to speak again. It was a warm June evening and there was no air conditioning. In the room beneath the galleries the radiators had been turned up to full. Someone had also opened the back doors of the hall behind the speaker's platform and facing the Pennsylvania railroad track where every few minutes the rumble of trains drowned out Hoover's speech. Hoover realized his microphone worked but its volume was on low. The delegates, what remained of them, listened in agony. The Taft and Wilkie forces made certain Hoover was not re-nominated.

SAVING TAXPAYERS SOME MONEY

While Gerald Ford was serving in Congress as the Minority Leader he established the reputation as a hard-working, but thrifty, legislator. Two habits which drove his staff up the wall also served as an example for others – he went around the halls of Congress each evening turning out lights (even in the hallways) and he wore his pencils down to little stubs.

A VIEW FROM THE TOP

Calvin Coolidge's philosophy on running the government was a bit unorthodox. He seldom worked past 5:00 P.M. or on weekends. As he explained, "The President shouldn't do too much, and he shouldn't *know* too much. The President can't resign...so I constantly said to my cabinet: 'There are many things you gentlemen must not tell me...if you draw me into your departmental decisions and something goes wrong, I must stay here, and by involving me, you have lowered the faith of the people in their government.'"

DAD'S DOUBLE DELIGHT

Through his Republican political connections, Chester Arthur was appointed as Collector of the New York Customs House where two thirds of the nation's imports entered the country. President Grant made the appointment and Arthur supervised more than 1000 employees and collected millions of dollars in tariffs. This position was also one of the most lucrative – Arthur's salary amounted to $40,000 a year, a very large sum in the mid-1870s. On the day of his appointment, the future twenty-first President was overjoyed, but not necessarily because of his new job. His only daughter was born on that day.

LEAVE NO STONE UNTURNED!

When Lyndon Johnson ran for the Senate for the first time in Texas he gathered together a group of campaign workers one evening and took them to a graveyard. He had them take down the names from the tombstones and entered them onto the voting rolls. Thus, on election night, Johnson could show these names as having voted for him. The group moved down the rows of tombstones copying names until they came to a stone so old and worn it was difficult to read. One man said to Johnson, "This one is hard to read. I'm going to skip it." Johnson replied, "You will not skip it. He's got as much right to vote as anybody in this cemetery."

A General Feeling of Disgust

One of President Chester Arthur's last official acts was signing a bill by which former President U.S. Grant became General on the retired list. This entitled him to full pay for life. Grant, however, was not very happy. He was in poor health and near death from throat cancer, and felt he should have received the commission sooner.

Something Fishy Here

A Congressman once sent a large fish to Herbert Hoover at the White House. The big catch was a present from the state of Maine, and Mrs. Hoover, thinking it would make a great meal, sent it to the kitchen. The President was a well known fisherman and when the Congressman arrived he announced he had sent the fish over so he could be photographed with it and Hoover. By the time the fish was located, its head was missing. The First Lady acted quickly. She summoned Lillian Parks, her seamstress, who sewed back the head. The picture was taken.

Truman's Triumph

After leaving the White House in 1953, Bess and Harry Truman settled in their Independence, Missouri, home. Mrs. Truman had asked her husband several times to mow the lawn. Finally, the former President did – at 11:00 on a Sunday morning as many Baptists and Methodists walked by their house on the way to church. Bess hollered out the window, "Harry! Come in here this minute. You know what those churchgoers are saying!" Truman, of course, planned the whole thing, and never was asked to mow again. Bess hired someone else to do it.

Abe's Attitude

After the death of Ann Rutledge, and following his failed courtship with Mary Owens, a dejected Abraham Lincoln had a gloomy outlook on the idea of marriage. He wrote to a friend in 1837, "I have now come to the conclusion never again to think of marrying; and for this reason I can never be satisfied with anyone who would be blockhead enough to have me." Even on the day of his wedding, while Lincoln was getting dressed and shining his boots, Speed Butler, the son of his landlord, asked him where he was going. Lincoln replied, "To hell, I suppose."

Taylor's Temper

After Zachary Taylor was elected President in 1848, many of the Whig Party leaders thought they could easily control him. After all, Taylor had never held public office before and knew very little about politics. Though a southern slaveholder, Taylor was a staunch unionist and threatened to use force on any state which tried to secede. Taylor resented attempts to be manipulated, in addition to demonstrating a quick fiery temper. One day a group of men, including some Whigs, entered the White House making several demands. The President chased them out of his office, shaking his fist at them as they scampered down the stairs.

Completing a Task

Lincoln was an avid theater-goer, and a genuine expert on the plays of Shakespeare. One reason he enjoyed attending live performances was so he could get away from the politicians and office-seekers who wanted to see him. Sometimes the President would fall asleep at a play. One evening in 1864 he and his wife were attending an opera. Lincoln dozed off. His wife nudged him and asked if he wanted to leave before the ending. Lincoln said, "Oh, no, I want to see it out. It's best when you undertake a job, to finish it."

Winston's Winnings

In 1946 former prime minister Winston Churchill visited the United States as a guest of President Harry Truman. They traveled by train on the *Ferdinand Magellan* (Truman's personal car) to Fulton, Missouri, where Churchill would give his famous "Iron Curtain" speech to warn the free world of Russian communism. During the trip Churchill asked Truman if he liked to play poker. Truman responded, "That's correct, Winston. I've played a lot of poker in my life." Churchill went to change into some comfortable clothes and Truman instructed his Missouri friends that, since he felt Churchill was a great poker player, America's reputation was at stake. He expected every man to do his duty. Soon after the game began, the Americans realized Churchill was a poor player. When the English statesman took a break, Truman said to the others, "Now we see he doesn't know the game well enough, so I want you all to play customer poker. Don't embarrass him. He's our guest. Let him win." Truman and his cronies folded their poker hands which would have won, and Churchill made a few dollars. He happily retired to bed and worked on his speech.

KENNEDY CONFUSED

After attending two of the ten inaugural balls, John Kennedy and his wife retired to their new home at the White House. When they arrived around midnight Kennedy discovered his new staff members were already in bed. The White House was dark and the new President could not find any light switches. He thought of going back to his own house in Georgetown but the Presidential limousine was gone. He was also hungry and couldn't locate anything to eat or drink. Finally, he decided to walk the streets of Washington to the residence of Joseph Alsop, a friend and newspaperman. He stayed until 2:00 a.m.

CLINTON'S CONFESSION?

During the 1992 Presidential campaign, there were many allegations made about Bill Clinton's amorous adventures with other women. Even as President, Clinton was constantly asked if there was any truth in the stories of his extramarital affairs while he was governor of Arkansas. In response to one reporter's question, Clinton answered, "I have nothing else to say. We – we did – if – the – the – I – I – the stories are just as they have been said."

DON'T MESS WITH GEORGE

Though only in his early twenties, George Washington proved himself a capable leader in helping England in the French and Indian War. He may have realized that some soldiers doubted his discipline and leadership due to his youth. By 1757 the colonial colonel had hanged three Virginia militiamen for desertion. Many more were severely punished for other infractions.

THIS IS OUTRAGEOUS!

While serving in the U.S. Senate in 1941, Harry Truman visited Memphis, Tennessee. He stayed at the Peabody Hotel but was not happy with its rates. He wrote a letter to his wife Bess, complaining he had been charged too much for his orange juice, toast, and oatmeal. "I don't mind losing $100 on a horse race or in a poker game with friends," he wrote, "but I do hate to pay $5.54 for breakfast."

EISENHOWER'S ERROR

Dwight D. Eisenhower, reflecting on his days in the Oval Office, said, "As President I made two mistakes, and both of them are on the Supreme Court." He was referring to his two appointments which became disappointments – Earl Warren and William Brennan. Eisenhower felt these men had become too liberal and had overstepped their judicial authority.

GROCERY "BILL"

For several years as a youngster, Bill Clinton was raised by his grandparents. Bill's biological father, William Blythe, had been killed in a car accident and his mother lived in New Orleans where she studied to become a nurse. Grandpa Cassidy ran a grocery store and it was there that Bill developed an interest in politics after listening to customers discuss issues of the day. When Virginia Clinton returned to Arkansas she married William Clinton and young Bill's name was changed from William Jefferson Blythe IV to William Jefferson Clinton.

HE LOST MORE THAN JUST AN ELECTION

In 1800, when John Adams was elected the second President, a new community in New Hampshire decided to name itself in honor of him. A quarter of a century later the town citizens were equally happy when Adam's son, John Quincy Adams, became the sixth President. Being quite independent, and not a devoted follower of party politics, John Quincy angered many New Englanders. When Andrew Jackson defeated Adams in the 1828 election the town's people turned on him. Adams, New Hampshire, changed its name to Jackson in 1829.

WIDOW WHIPS WARREN

Warren Harding loved poker. Once as a U.S. Senator he got stuck in an elevator with Mrs. Louise Cromwell Brooks, a wealthy attractive widow. The two became friends and when Harding became President he and his friends played poker at her home. Harding challenged Mrs. Brooks to a game of poker "just the two of us – winner names the stakes." There is no record of what Harding would have asked for, because he lost. His opponent wanted some White House dishes as her prize. The next day she received a barrel of china stamped with the mark of the Benjamin Harrison administration.

No-Handshake Harrison

President-elect William Henry Harrison had a notice put in the newspapers that there would be no handshaking during or after inaugural ceremonies. Harrison's hand and arm were sore from greeting the public in the days before he took office.

Reagan Rises to the Top

Growing up in Dixon, Illinois, was adventurous for Ronald Reagan. As a young man he and a friend once finished off a bottle of wine. The two took a stroll through town and Reagan climbed on top of a stoplight, a short cement post in the middle of the intersection. As Reagan balanced himself atop the post the police chief drove by in his Model T Ford. He asked Reagan what he was doing up there. "Twinkle, twinkle little star. Who do you think *you* are?" was Reagan's response. The chief took him into custody, fined him one dollar, and released him.

Misdiagnosis

Teddy Roosevelt was a sickly child. Even during his last year at Harvard he failed to receive a clean bill of health. The college physician told TR that his heart, damaged by asthma, was weak and that he should avoid all strenuous activity, including climbing steps. Young Roosevelt told the doctor, "I am going to do all the things you tell me not to do. If I've got to live the rest of my life you have described, I don't care how short it is." As it turned out, Theodore Roosevelt was arguably our most athletic President.

William's Warning

Bill Clinton's biological father was killed in an auto accident before Bill was born. His mother remarried but Clinton's stepfather was an alcoholic and often violent. He watched his mother beaten several times. At age fourteen Bill had had enough of his abusive father. When his stepfather came home in a drunken rage, the future President told him, "Daddy, if you're not able to stand up, I'll help you, but you must stand up to hear what I have to say. Don't ever, ever lay your hand on my mother again."

Bogus Baked Bomb

Though FDR was in poor health in 1944, he still campaigned very hard. In October he rode in an open convertible in a steady downpour in New York City. An estimated five million people turned out and wildly cheered their President. Riding in the back seat, FDR was surrounded by Secret Service agents. Suddenly an object was hurled towards the President and landed at his feet. Agent Griffith leaped over the President and covered the missile with his body. But there was no explosion – it was a bagel! FDR howled with laughter.

Proper Guidance

Thomas Jefferson carefully planned the education of his eleven-year-old daughter, Martha, while they were living in Philadelphia. Hiring a number of tutors, Jefferson suggested this daily schedule: "From 8 to 10 practice music. From 10 to 1, dance one day, draw another. From 3 to 4 read French. From 4 to 5 exercise yourself in music. From 5 till bedtime, read English, write, etc.… Inform me what books you read, what times you learn, and enclose me your best copy of every lesson in drawing." Jefferson was serving in Congress at the time and wasn't able to see his daughter much.

Kennedy Caught

While touring Europe in 1937, John Kennedy and his best friend, Lem Billings, visited Germany. Neither liked what they saw there, sensing many Germans disliked Americans. The two young men likewise felt contempt for Nazi dictator Adolf Hitler. Most German people expected foreign guests to return their salute and say, "Heil, Hitler!" Instead, Kennedy and Billings waved their arms and sarcastically yelled, "Hi ya, Hitler." During a visit to Munich they were drinking beer with a group of Nazi Blackshirts, when an American-educated Nazi told them they could keep a couple of large beer mugs as souvenirs, but to hide them as they left. Showing them a back door, the Nazi youth directed them to sneak out. No sooner had they exited the door when a German waiter stopped them and confiscated their "stolen" mugs. They were further detained and ordered to show their passports. Kennedy and Billings finally left but noticed the Blackshirt troopers roaring with laughter.

MILD CONFESSION

U. S. Grant's Presidency was marked by scandal and corruption on a large scale. The closest Grant ever came to admitting failure was when he stated, "It was my fortune, or misfortune, to be called to the office of Chief Executive without any previous political training. Under such circumstances it is but reasonable to admit errors of judgement must have occurred."

AIN'T GONNA BE NO MORE LARNIN

James Buchanan vetoed a bill to create land grant colleges. He justified this by explaining that America didn't need further education. He even went so far to say that educated people were too hard to handle, and that there were already too many intelligent citizens. After Buchanan left office, Congress introduced the bill again and Lincoln signed it into law.

TAFT TACKLES MOTHER NATURE

On the day of William Howard Taft's inauguration, March 4, 1909, ten inches of snow had fallen prior to the ceremony. Paraders and visitors alike couldn't get to the city. But Taft was determined to see the event through. Six thousand workmen cleared the snow from the inaugural route and thirty thousand marchers and one hundred bands performed in a bitter, freezing wind.

HOMESPUN PHILOSOPHER

In June of 1833 President Andrew Jackson was presented with an honorary doctorate degree from Harvard College, over the strong objections of alumni and political opponents such as former President John Quincy Adams. Adams refused to attend the graduation ceremony, commenting that he did not want to see "my darling Harvard disgrace herself by conferring a doctor's degree upon a barbarian who could hardly spell his own name." The Harvard class president delivered an address in Latin, which Jackson could not understand. When Jackson rose to receive his degree, he told the audience, "I shall have to speak in English, not being able to return your compliment in what appears to be the language of Harvard. All the Latin I know is *E. Pluribus Unum*." This remark was followed with great laughter and applause.

GANDHI GONE

John Kennedy played numerous pranks on his friends, particularly his schoolmate chum Lem Billings. During the times when Billings stayed at the White House, President Kennedy often introduced him to celebrities and dignitaries as Congressman Billings, Senator Billings, or General Billings. This of course made Billings feel quite uncomfortable, but Kennedy took pleasure in watching his friend trying to explain his titles to curious guests. On one occasion, after Billings had met and chatted with Indira Gandhi (daughter of India's prime minister Jawaharal Nehru and later prime minister herself), he began receiving invitations from Madame Gandhi at the Blair House where she was staying. Several times he got messages to come over for tea, lunch, or dinner. Each time Billings went to the Blair House he found Miss Gandhi gone, so he left a note that he would return. A couple days later Billings realized what had happened. Kennedy had conspired with the White House switchboard operators to keep feeding him fictitious requests.

WORRIED WATSON WARNS WARREN

In 1923 Senator Watson of Indiana called on President Warren Harding and begged him not to go on his Alaskan tour. Watson put his hand on Harding's shoulder and spoke frankly: "Warren, I am telling you good-bye for the last time. I know about the condition of your heart, and your general state of health, and I do not believe that you will ever survive the trip." After an exhausting trip of six weeks, amid rumors of scandal and corruption within his administration, Harding collapsed and died in San Francisco.

BATTLE SCARS

Lyndon Johnson was accustomed to shoving people around, even "brow beating" his Vice President, Hubert Humphrey. On occasion he shouted at Humphrey to "get going" on an errand or mission. LBJ literally kicked Humphrey hard in the shins. Humphrey once pulled up his pant leg to show his scars to columnist Robert Allen.

TAFT NOT TICKETED

President Taft was on his way to a baseball game to throw out the Opening Day pitch. His chauffeur, George Robinson, was told to park the car next to the ballpark. A policeman approached and ordered Robinson to move the car, then recognized the President and declined to issue a parking ticket. Taft told Robinson, "Take orders only from the President." Robinson was further instructed not to exceed 20 miles per hour.

CARTER GOES OUT TO SEA

In the late 1940s Jimmy Carter was assigned to the *USS Pomfret*, a new submarine based in the Pacific. The sub surfaced to charge its batteries when a heavy storm suddenly approached. Carter was standing on the bridge as the night watch and a huge wave swept over the vessel, taking him with it. Carter found himself swimming under water completely separated from the sub and no one noticed him missing. Just then another wave hurled him back on top of a gun barrel thirty feet behind where he had been standing. Climbing desperately, Carter managed to scramble back to his post.

WOEFUL WOODROW

Woodrow Wilson's first great love was his first cousin, Harriet Augusta Woodrow. He began writing to her while he was a senior at Princeton in 1878. Only a few of more than 200 love letters remain, but Wilson visited her whenever he could, including trips to Harriet's home in Chillicothe, Ohio. The future President was not very successful with other young women and he wrote Harriet that "not a single one has any special attraction for me." Unfortunately, Harriet did not share the same feelings for her cousin. She explained that she did not love him and besides, it would not be right for first cousins to marry. By 1882 the relationship was over and Harriet later married Edward Weller, an acquaintance of Wilson's.

SENATOR'S SOCK SECLUDED

John Kennedy was quite absent-minded. While he was a senator he had a combination sofa-bed installed in his office so he could take short naps. On one occasion he instructed his secretary, Evelyn Lincoln, to wake him in forty-five minutes. She entered his office, woke him, then went back to her desk to handle phone calls. She recalled, "Before I got seated the buzzer began screaming. I rushed back, and there he was on the edge of the bed with one sock on and the other foot bare. After I got down on my hands and knees and tried to find the missing sock, he got so engrossed in a newspaper that he didn't hear me say 'I found it. Here it is.' I laid it on the bed and went back to work. But again the buzzer. Meanwhile a visitor was walking in, so I didn't get back into his office in a split second. The visitor was a bit shocked when the senator shouted, 'What did you leave for? Where is my sock?'"

HALT, THIEF!

John Quincy Adams frequently went skinny dipping in the Potomac River. Leaving his clothes on the river bank, he was surprised one day when a tramp ventured by and stole his shirt, pants, shoes and money. Not wanting to be seen running naked back to the Executive Mansion, he returned to the water and waited until he saw a small boy fishing. He yelled, "Say, boy. Run to the White House and tell Mrs. Adams to send a suit of clothes to the President. I'll wait for you."

FATHER FILLMORE FLEES

Millard Fillmore invited his 80-year-old father to stay at the White House, but Dad soon took his departure. When friends asked him why he didn't want to stay any longer, his father replied, "No, no. I will go; I don't like it here. It isn't a good place for Millard either. I wish he was at home in Buffalo."

CARTER CUTBACKS CAUSE COLD

In an effort to cut down expenses at the White House, and convince other Americans to conserve on energy, Jimmy Carter addressed the people on national television. Wearing a cardigan sweater, he urged his fellow countrymen to turn their thermostats to 65 degrees during the day and 55 degrees at night. He ordered the same for the White House. First Lady Rosalynn found it so cold she began to wear long underwear and sweaters. She remarked, "My offices were so cold I couldn't concentrate, and my staff was typing with gloves on." She pleaded with her husband to turn the thermostats up but he refused.

Resisting Roosevelt's Reform

After he became the 32nd President, FDR initiated sweeping changes in the midst of the Great Depression. Knowing that many Americans would oppose reform, he complained that changes in the cabinet would be very difficult: "The Treasury and the State Department put together are nothing compared to the Navy. The admirals are really something to cope with – and I should know. To change something in the Navy is like punching a feather bed. You punch it with your right and you punch it with your left until you are finally exhausted, then you find the damn bed just as it was before you started punching." As a former assistant secretary of the Navy, Roosevelt knew what he was saying.

Spare Me!

When former President Dwight D. Eisenhower visited Walter Reed Army Hospital in May of 1965, he arrived in a 1964 Lincoln Continental. His chauffeur parked the car in the basement garage of Towers Apartments in northwest Washington, D.C. When he was ready to leave, it was discovered that the trunk had been broken into and the spare tire stolen.

Terror Tad

Much has been written about Tad Lincoln's mischievous behavior. In Springfield, Illinois, young Tad wreaked havoc in the presence of his father, but was rarely punished, except on occasion by his mother. More than once Tad would ransack his father's law office, pulling books off the shelf and leaving papers scattered. He once kicked over a chessboard at home while Lincoln was concentrating on his next move. Another time Tad smeared black ink all over a white marble counter at the telegraph office, and raced through a reception at the Lincoln home swinging a side of bacon to scatter the formally dressed guests.

That Suits Me

Bill Clinton liked to have his suits tailor made. He was told by his tailor, Martin Greenfield of New York, "There isn't a man in my industry who wouldn't give his right arm to be where I am – but if you don't listen to me and don't wear my clothing right, you can ruin my reputation." President Clinton agreed and promised he would follow the advice.

Franklin Flunks

By August of 1905 Franklin and Eleanor Roosevelt had been in Europe for two months on a delayed honeymoon. When the couple stopped at the Imperial Hotel in Paris, Franklin found a letter waiting for him at the front desk – it was from Columbia Law School. To his dismay he discovered he had failed two courses – Contracts and Pleading & Practice. He cabled home and asked his mother to send his law books to London. The young couple continued on to Scotland, and FDR prepared to study for his exams in the fall.

Judged by Jackson

Andrew Jackson believed the U.S. had acquired Texas when Thomas Jefferson bought the Louisiana Territory in 1803. In 1819, however, Secretary of State John Quincy Adams negotiated a treaty with Spain and Mexico which recognized that Texas was *not* part of our nation. Jackson felt Adams had betrayed the U.S. and referred to him as "that old scamp J.Q. Adams."

We Need Heroes

Lincoln once read a scathing biography of George Washington. But Lincoln agreed with many Americans in believing that Washington deserved the praise and honor given him. He said, "Let us believe as in the days of our youth that Washington was spotless. It makes human nature better to believe that one human being was perfect – that human perfection is possible."

Granting His Wish

Before he died of throat cancer in 1885, U.S. Grant slipped his son a piece of paper indicating where he should be buried. He mentioned three places: Illinois, where he once lived and worked; West Point, his alma mater (this was ruled out because his wife could not be buried with him); and New York, where he lived and "her people befriended me." His native state of Ohio, where he was born and raised, was not named. The Grant Tomb was later constructed on Riverside Drive in New York City.

CARTER CUTS COSTS

In 1977 President Jimmy Carter sought ways to cut wasteful federal spending, so he started at the White House. After a brief investigation, Carter discovered the White House paid $85,000 a year for newspapers and magazine subscriptions. In addition, he learned there were 325 television sets and 220 radios in the Executive Mansion. The President immediately took measures to reduce costs in these areas.

RISING TO THE OCCASION

In 1837, during the last six months of his administration, Andrew Jackson was so ill he left his room only five times. He was recovering from a near fatal "hemorrhage of the lungs." Nevertheless, Jackson managed enough energy to host a state dinner for Mexican general Santa Anna, who at the time was the target of much hatred because of his killing Americans at Goliad and the Alamo. Santa Anna was taken prisoner by Sam Houston at the battle of San Jacinto and sent to Washington, D.C., under an armed escort. He should not have expected such good treatment, but Jackson respected Santa Anna as a military leader and wanted to end hostilities in Texas. The two leaders discussed the handling of American settlers and a boundary dispute. The meeting ended with little decided, but Santa Anna was surprised at the cordiality showed him. He was returned to Veracruz on a U.S. warship, and six years later raised another army to fight Americans during the Mexican War.

ABLE ADAMS

In 1769 Jonathan Ames and his mother were accused of murdering Ames' wife Ruth. Suspicious neighbors contacted authorities and the body of Ruth Ames was exhumed and examined for evidence. Ames and his mother were arrested and confined to a jail in Salem, Massachusetts. Thirty-four-year-old John Adams defended them at the trial. After skillful argument and an impassioned closing of remarks, Adams convinced the jury to return a verdict of not guilty.

BRIEF INSTRUCTIONS

On March 23, 1868, President Andrew Johnson summoned three lawyers to the White House. Johnson's impeachment trial was about to take place, and though he would not appear, he needed representation. The meeting was quite brief. Curtis, Evarts, and Nelson, the three attorneys, shook hands with Johnson. Very calmly, he told them, "Gentlemen, my case is in your hands. I feel sure that you will protect my interests." Johnson then went back to work, and three weeks later he was acquitted by one vote in the Senate.

THE KENNEDY ZOO

Historians like to point out all the pets that occupied the White House when Theodore Roosevelt's children lived there. But the Kennedy clan had quite a few animals as well. Their "zoo" included a Welsh terrier Charlie, a German shepherd Clipper, two pet hamsters (which soon multiplied), three canaries, three parakeets, two deer, and two ponies, Macaroni and Leprechaun. And there were other pets as well.

BURNING PASSION

After James Buchanan died his private papers and letters were discovered in his vault. Among the papers was a packet of old love letters with a note: "Please do not open them." Recent evidence shows Buchanan had an illegitimate child (both the mother and daughter are buried in Canton, Ohio). Buchanan's wishes were respected and the letters destroyed.

A MORNING OF MOURNING

By June 28, 1836, James Madison's decreasing health caught up with him. That morning he was eating breakfast with a niece and showed signs of difficulty in swallowing his food. When asked if anything was wrong, Madison responded, "Nothing more than a change of mind, my dear." He then closed his eyes and died.

A CIGAR BUTT TREASURE

A couple of years after leaving the White House, Calvin Coolidge visited the South. His stop in New Orleans proved that he was still a popular figure with the American people. At the train depot there he was mobbed, and a near riot broke out when the former President tossed his cigar away as part of the crowd scrambled to get it as a souvenir.

Sick or Not?

Those close to Franklin Roosevelt were quite concerned about his health in 1944. In February of that year he was secretly accompanied by his two daughters and personal physician to Bethesda Naval Hospital to have two lesions removed. Suspecting the cysts might be cancerous, a surgeon removed both growths, one from his face above the left eyebrow and another from the back of his head. The lesions proved to be non-cancerous, but FDR's health was very poor in relation to his cardiovascular system.

Is that a Yes or No?

As Secretary of State, John Quincy Adams was concerned that President James Monroe would appoint Andrew Jackson to some foreign post. Adams felt Jackson was reckless and uneducated. When he inquired about the possibility of having Jackson as an ambassador, Monroe agreed and added, "I am afraid he would get us into a quarrel."

Not-so-Silent Cal

Myths persist that Calvin Coolidge did little speaking while serving as President. The fact is that he gave more speeches than any of his 29 predecessors. During his 5½ years the White House he held 520 press conferences, an average of 7.8 per month. FDR, who spoke frequently, averaged 6.9 per month. Historian Sidney Warren said, "During his tenure he probably supplied more wordage to the press than Theodore Roosevelt and Woodrow Wilson combined."

Woodrow Won't Whisper

Woodrow Wilson believed strongly, as did William McKinley, that all politics should be done in public – to hide nothing from the people. Wilson explained, "Government ought to be all outside and no inside. I, for my part, believe there ought to be no place where anything can be done that everybody does not know about.… Secrecy means impropriety."

Some Misgivings, Perhaps

James Buchanan had reservations about accepting the Democratic Party's nomination for President. He told a friend, "I had hoped for the nomination in 1844, again in 1848, and even in 1852, but now I would hesitate to take it. Before many years the abolitionists will bring war upon the land. It may come during the next presidential term." Buchanan's words were prophetic and his four years in office prior to the Civil War proved ineffective. Strong leadership from his successor, Abraham Lincoln, guided the Union through the conflict.

Hard Life at Harvard

John Adams attended Harvard College in the early 1750s. His day began when he arose at 5:30, ate breakfast at 6:00, attended classes from 8:00 to 5:00 PM, then spent time at prayer for a half hour. This was followed by a light supper at 7:00. Then Adams studied until 11:00. And for those students who engaged in pranks, the faculty and administration punished them with fines and floggings.

Try, Try Again

Martin Van Buren was the first of three former Presidents to run on a third party ticket (Fillmore and Teddy Roosevelt were the other two). After serving one term and failing to be re-elected as a Democrat in 1840, Van Buren ran as a Free Soiler in 1848. His running mate was Charles Francis Adams, son of John Quincy Adams.

Presidential Praise

In mid-December of 1966, America lost one of its most beloved sons. The grief felt by the people was expressed by two of its well known leaders. Former President Dwight Eisenhower said this loss "touched a common chord in all humanity…we shall not see his like again." And from the White House, Lyndon Johnson observed that this man's influence "was larger than life, and the treasures he left will endure to entertain and enlighten worlds to come." Eisenhower and Johnson were commenting on the death of Walt Disney.

BUCK'S YOUNG BUCK

President James Buchanan had the youngest Vice President. His running mate, southerner John C. Breckenridge, was only 35 when he was elected (he was 36 by the time he took his oath). Breckenridge ran for the Presidency four years later but lost to Abraham Lincoln.

A PRIVATE TIME

Of all of our Chief Executives who served in the military, James Buchanan of Pennsylvania was the only one who never rose above the rank of private. During the war of 1812 he volunteered for the army to help defend the city of Baltimore under the command of Major Charles Sterret. By 1814 he began serving in the Pennsylvania legislature.

A KING WHO NEVER SERVED

Frank Pierce's running mate was Rufus King. Born in North Carolina and serving as a senator from Alabama, King was elected Vice President in 1852. He was terminally ill with tuberculosis and took his oath of office in Havana, Cuba. King died just five weeks after becoming Vice President. His final days were spent at his home in Cahaba, Alabama, thus never performing any of the duties of his office.

PAYBACK TO "OLD HICKORY"

The U.S. District Court at New Orleans fined Andrew Jackson $1000 for contempt in declaring martial law during his fight against British forces there in 1815. Jackson paid the fine but on January 8, 1844, exactly 29 years after the battle, the U.S. Congress returned Jackson's money, with six percent interest.

TROUBLED TRAIN TRIP

After James A. Garfield's inauguration on March 4, 1881, former President Rutherford B. Hayes was involved in a serious train accident. Just a few miles out of Baltimore his train collided head on with another and Hayes was thrown out of his seat. Two people were killed and twenty others were seriously injured. Hayes was shaken but uninjured.

MARTIN ON THE MOVE

In just a little more than three months, Martin Van Buren held three important offices. On December 20, 1828, he resigned as a U.S. Senator and eleven days later assumed the office of governor of New York. Two months later, he was secretary of state under President Andrew Jackson. Leaving the governorship, he took his new post in late March of the same year.

THE ROYAL TREATMENT

Ambassadors John Adams and Thomas Jefferson met King George III of England on March 17, 1786. This was five years after the Revolutionary War ended and feelings between England and the United States were still tense. Some of those in attendance at the king's ball believed His Royal Majesty snubbed Jefferson. At least Jefferson thought he was snubbed. In any event, the future President referred to the king as a "mulish being."

GETTING TO KNOW YOU

At Yale College in 1970, Bill Clinton and a friend were conversing in the school library. Clinton kept staring down the long reading room at an attractive blond female student. A few minutes later the young lady got up out of her chair and walked over to Clinton and said, "Look, if you're going to keep staring at me and I'm going to keep staring back. I think we should at least know each other. I'm Hillary Rodham. What's your name?"

A COOL RECEPTION?

Illinois Senator McKinley was proud to take two of the greatest Illinois football stars to the White House to meet President Coolidge. The senator explained that his two guests, George Halas and Harold "Red" Grange (both future Hall of Famers) were big stars for the Chicago Bears. Coolidge, always the jokester, shook their hands and dryly remarked, "I've always enjoyed animal acts." The three visitors almost died laughing.

HEY, LOOK AT ME!

Reflecting on his state of health, President Ronald Reagan made this observation: "Since I came to the White House, I got two hearing aids, a colon operation, skin cancer, a prostate operation, and I was shot. The damn thing is I've never felt better in my life."

MOM IS BOSS

While growing up, John Adams observed that "passion," not "reason" ruled in his family. He also remembered that, though his father was a man of high morals and discipline, he believed his mother made the major decisions in the family. He said of her that she "frets, squibs, scolds, rages, and raves until she gets her way."

MCKINLEY'S MAN MADE TO LAST

When William McKinley appointed James Wilson of Iowa as his secretary of agriculture, he had no idea what an enduring legacy Wilson would establish. Wilson was in that post during both of McKinley's terms, both of Theodore Roosevelt's terms, all through Taft's administration, and for three days under President Woodrow Wilson. Thus, James Wilson held the same cabinet position for 16 years and one day.

SECOND TO NONE

Millard Fillmore was the second Vice President to assume office upon the death of a President. He was the second President born in the state of New York and the second one whose father was alive when he was inaugurated. Fillmore was also the second President to remarry.

ONE OF A KIND

Today's *Air Force One* is truly magnificent. The present airplane, a Boeing 747, was completed in 1990 at a cost of $650 million to the taxpayers. It has two kitchens and seven bathrooms. In addition, the plane has 19 televisions, 11 VCRs, and 85 telephones. The airplane travels at a speed over 700 mph and is cared for by 140 specialists of the 89th Airlift Wing of the United States Air Force.

DECLARATION OF DOOM

Before leaving his home of Cincinnati for the White House, William Henry Harrison told a crowd on January 26, 1841, "Gentlemen and fellow citizens.... Perhaps this may be the last time I may have the pleasure of speaking to you on earth or seeing you. I will bid you farewell, if forever, fare thee well." A little more than three months later, Harrison was dead, having served the shortest term as any Chief Executive.

WHEELCHAIRED WILSON WILTS WAITING WOMEN

Congresswoman Clare Booth Luce was a brilliant, attractive editor and playwright. In later years she told about a group of women who were selected to see President Woodrow Wilson in March of 1920. The group was at the White House to urge Wilson not to compromise with the Senate opposition to his League of Nations program. Clare, only seventeen years old at the time, was chosen as the spokesperson. Wilson, who had suffered a near-fatal stroke, was brought out in his wheelchair and sat at a table with a shawl wrapped around him. Clare gave a short speech, ending, "You must go on for the salvation of the world!" Wilson ate his meal while he remained slumped over, never looking at the women or responding to them. First Lady Edith Wilson whispered in her husband's ear to say something. Wilson, with his head still lowered, mumbled, "There is skin on my milk." Clare and her friends left angry and disillusioned.

CRYING FOR HELP

During the Civil War disease took a heavy toll on both the Union and Confederate armies. General U.S. Grant once wired the War Department, "I will not move my army without onions." Grant believed that onions prevented dysentery and other maladies. A short time later his soldiers received three train loads of the vegetable.

And We Don't Mean Teddy Bears

On July 4, 1918, the first group of American doughboys marched through the streets of Paris to defend France against the German invaders. Amidst tremendous ovations, the troops heard the shouts of "Teddy! Teddy! Long live the Teddies!" Among the soldiers marching that day were two sons of the 26th President. Archie and Theodore Roosevelt Jr. gleamed with pride as Parisians showed their love and appreciation for their father.

Self Portrait of a Small Ego

In his autobiography, Calvin Coolidge noted that, "...unless men live right they die. Things are so ordered in the world that those who violate its laws cannot escape the penalty. Nature is inexorable. If men do not follow the truth they cannot live." Furthermore, Coolidge stated, "It is a great advantage to a President, and a major source of safety to the country, for him to know that he is not a great man. When a man begins to feel that he is the only one who can lead this republic, he is guilty of treason to the spirit of our institutions."

"Carrie"d Into The White House

The fact that Warren Harding had a couple of mistresses (and a child to one of them) worried many of Harding's Republican campaign managers. Party leaders realized that such a scandal might doom his chances to be elected President. They saw to it that one of his girl friends, Carrie Phillips, was not around during the 1920 campaign. Carrie and her husband were sent on an expense paid "fact finding" tour to the Orient to investigate the raw silk trade until the election was over.

Last Chance?

After his 1932 election Franklin D. Roosevelt was told by a friend that if he was successful as President, he would go down in history as one of the greatest Chief Executives, but if he failed he would live to be the worse one. This was during the Great Depression in America, and after listening intently to these remarks, FDR responded, "If I fail I shall be the last one."

The Making-Up of a President

During the 1952 campaign Dwight Eisenhower decided to use television to reach the public. While a TV make-up man worked on Eisenhower's face, he remarked, "What a come-down. I used to be a paratrooper with you in France. Now I just smear this stuff on homely mugs. And you used to be a five-star general, but now you're just a politician!" The candidate found this comment amusing and repeated it many times.

Changing of the Guard

Just hours after John Kennedy was assassinated, his brother, Attorney General Robert Kennedy, assumed many duties in preparing for a state funeral. He also called McGeorge Bundy, the slain President's national security advisor, and ordered him to protect JFK's White House papers. Bundy in turn ordered that the combinations to John Kennedy's locked files be changed at once, before Lyndon Johnson's men could look through them.

If Opportunity Knocks...

Reflecting on his tenure in office, Gerald Ford told a newspaper reporter in 1998, "I never thought I would be President. My goal was to be Speaker of the House. But I had the opportunity to serve as President, and I did my best. I believe I made a difference."

A Case of Libel

More than one newspaper editor accused former President Theodore Roosevelt of "pulling strings" in securing military positions for his sons so they wouldn't be near the front lines during World War I. Roosevelt never made any special arrangements and he was furious with those who published such lies. In fact, all four of his sons saw heavy action during the war. Quentin was shot down and killed by a German aviator. Archie and Theodore Jr. were both wounded, and Kermit narrowly escaped death. All of Roosevelt's sons were decorated for bravery, but what many people did not know was that his daughter served as well. Edith Roosevelt Derby worked as a nurse in Paris where her husband was a surgeon. During bombardments in and near the city she served with distinction and courage.

Costly Kennedy Clubs

Because of his back problems, John Kennedy only golfed three times while in office, all during the summer of 1963. Following the death of his wife more than three decades later, 5,000 items belonging to the Kennedys were auctioned off at Sotheby's in New York in April of 1996. Kennedy's golf clubs and bag were estimated worth $800. When the bidding was done, actor Arnold Schwarzenegger, who married Kennedy's niece Maria Shriver, purchased them for $772,500.

Cheap Thrills

When sixth grader George Bush and his brother returned home one day, both boys were in for a shock. They had been visiting the Williams kids across town in Greenwich, Connecticut. George's mother had just received a phone call and was furious, but waited for her husband to come home to let him handle the problem. Prescott Bush was so upset with the news that he took his sons into another room and grabbed a squash racket, threatening to beat them unless they apologized to the Williams family. The Bush brothers marched two miles where they knocked on the door and humbly offered their apology. It seems George had paid the Williams's daughter ten cents to run naked!

Resurrected

Jimmy Carter was baptized at age eleven but became a born-again Christian in 1967, due in part to his evangelist sister Ruth Carter Stapleton. He became more active in church affairs and while he was President taught *Bible* classes at the First Baptist Church in Washington. He and his wife Rosalynn took turns reading the *Bible* to each other in bed.

Wait, Wait, Wait

When President Grover Cleveland proposed to 21-year-old Francis Folsom, she said, "yes," but informed him that she and her mother would tour Europe first. Cleveland was not happy and the ladies spent nine months overseas. Cleveland was irritable and grumpy, and on the day of their arrival, he met Frances when the ship docked in New York City on May 27, 1886.

Buchanan's Baby

James Buchanan was our only bachelor President, but he fathered a child. His daughter, Henrietta, died in 1855 at the age of 41 and is buried next to her Mennonite mother in Canton, Ohio. This may explain why Buchanan's fiancée, Ann Coleman, committed suicide in 1819.

We're Getting Outta Here

James Monroe was the first President inaugurated outdoors during the 19th century. Usually, the President took his oath of office in the House of Representatives, but when U.S. Senators insisted on bringing fancy red chairs to the ceremony, the House refused. Instead of the matter becoming a controversy, it was decided to hold the inauguration outside.

Doing His Job Too Well

In 1937 Richard Nixon, a Duke University Law School graduate, landed a job in his hometown of Whittier, California, with the old law firm of Wingert and Bewley. He was given all the divorce cases, but he cost the firm more fees than he earned because he saw to it that most of the intended divorces ended in reconciliation. He was later switched to a trial lawyer, specializing in estates and federal income taxes.

Not a Complete Ban

Though Rutherford B. Hayes and his wife "Lemonade" Lucy refused to serve alcoholic beverages in the White House, they did occasionally "bend" their principles. They served sherbet inside the frozen skin of an orange which was spiked with rum. Designated "Roman Punch," temperance supporters received a supposedly non-alcoholic, mild version of the dessert. And at times, the President indulged in a few beers with his Civil War comrades. And Lucy even sent gifts of wine to friends who owned wine cellars.

A Big Loss

George Washington Adams, a Boston attorney and son of President John Quincy Adams, lived a reckless life. He had an affair with a servant girl which produced an illegitimate daughter. George also drank heavily and suffered serious mental problems. His gambling debts ran high and in 1828, while on a trip to confront his father in the White House, committed suicide by jumping from a steamboat in the Atlantic. The President and his wife Louisa were understandably in great distress. That same year Adams lost his bid for re-election to Andrew Jackson.

Disgruntled Grant

U.S. Grant found the rigid code of conduct at West Point often displeasing. As a cadet there he had his share of demerits. If a West Pointer got 200 "black marks" during his four years, he was dismissed. Grant once received eight demerits for not attending chapel, and he was put under house arrest and forbidden to leave his room. In September of 1839 he wrote his cousin that such treatment was "not exactly republican."

Decided and Undecided

Benjamin Harrison was certain of at least one thing: he was in love with Caroline Scott, and in 1853 at the age of 20, he married her. But he couldn't decide if he wanted to be an attorney or a minister. Harrison ventured on becoming a lawyer and became a workaholic. He wrote his sister, "…I do the same thing every day…eat three meals…sleep six hours, and read dusty old law books the rest of the time."

Words of Wisdom for Warren

Newspaperman Warren Harding decided to get involved in politics. Ohio political boss and McKinley's campaign chairman, Marcus Hanna, advised Harding, "I suppose you want to be President some day. Every Ohio youngster does. Well, you better keep closer in touch with us fellows in Cleveland and not train exclusively with those damn troublemakers in Cincinnati."

Tough Taft

One criticism Theodore Roosevelt had for President Taft was that he (Taft) was too "soft" on monopolies and did not pursue reforms aggressively. But the fact remains that the Taft administration in its single term initiated twice as many anti-trust suits than the Roosevelt administration did in seven and one-half years.

William's Willpower

William McKinley was a man who fought many political battles. In March of 1882 Congressman McKinley wrote his brother Abner, "The constant struggle all the time is anything but agreeable. In politics it is a little more irritating than other things, but I can stand it."

Like Father, Unlike Son

Ten-year-old Jesse Grant showed up late one morning for a White House breakfast. The President gave his son the standard parental lecture, saying to him, "Jess, how is this? Nine o'clock and you just sit down to breakfast? When I was your age I had to get up, feed four or five horses, cut wood for the family, take breakfast and be off to school by eight o'clock." Jess smiled at his father and replied, "But you did not have such a papa as I have!"

A Rocky Time in Rockport

During Richard Nixon's first week as the vice presidential nominee in 1952, he and his wife Pat campaigned in Rockport, Maine. Journalists and photographers followed them to a lobster plant and asked the couple to pick up a couple lobsters. Mrs. Nixon was nervous and her husband explained there was nothing to fear, explaining that the big ones were slow and lazy. Nixon chose the fattest lobster he could find. Its claws flashed open and went for the candidate's throat. Pat screamed as the crustacean grabbed Nixon's lapel. Cameramen enjoyed the session and everyone laughed while a slightly embarrassed Nixon freed himself.

ADVICE TO A PLAYBOY

James K. Polk often sought Andrew Jackson's advice. Nearly 40 years old and still a bachelor, Polk asked Jackson what he could do to promote his political career which at the time was going nowhere. The former President told Polk, "Stop your philandering! You must settle down as a sober married man." Jackson suggested that his niece Sarah Childress would make an excellent wife, and Polk agreed.

MATURE BEYOND HIS YEARS

Calvin Coolidge Jr. received a letter at the White House addressed to the "First Boy of the Land." The 16-year-old sent a curt reply, telling the writer the title was a mistake, since he had done nothing to deserve it. He explained the First Boy of the Land should "be some boy who had distinguished himself through his own actions." Tragically, four months later Calvin Jr. was dead from an infected blister on his big toe after playing tennis without socks.

A MOTHER'S LOVE

In the fall of 1907 William Howard Taft was en route once again to the Philippines when he learned his mother Louise was deathly ill. He made plans to return from California to be at her bedside but received this letter from his mother: "No Taft, to my knowledge, has yet neglected a public duty for the sake of gratifying a private desire. You promised the Filipinos that you would be present at the opening of their first assembly, and if you should break that promise and neglect your plain duty on my account, it would give me no pleasure." Taft returned from the islands and his mother died on December 9, 1907, while her son was Secretary of War.

NOT IN THE RULES

Vice President Calvin Coolidge was presiding over the Senate one day when a heated dispute erupted between two senators. Tempers continued to flare and one senator told another, "Go straight to hell!" The offended senator stormed down the aisle to protest to Coolidge, who sat quietly reading a book. "Did you hear what he said to me?" Coolidge looked up and remarked, "You know, I have been reading the rule book. You don't have to go."

A LAPSE IN MEMORY

When a 1996 grand jury investigated President Bill Clinton and his involvement in the Whitewater land scandal, he responded 272 times with combined answers of "I don't remember," "I don't recall," and "I don't know." No formal charges were ever issued.

SYMBOLIC SUNFLOWER

Anyone running against FDR often had an uphill battle. During the 1936 Presidential campaign, Republican Alf Landon of Kansas adopted the sunflower as his symbol. Roosevelt told reporters, off the record, that the sunflower was yellow, that it had a black heart, and that it was only good for feeding parrots. Several of Roosevelt's supporters went further and flooded the nation with bumper stickers which proclaimed, "Sunflowers Die in November."

COURTROOM COMPROMISE

A wealthy man in Springfield, Illinois, was pursuing a debt of $2.50 owed him by a man of modest means. The poor man denied the debt and refused to pay. The wealthy man decided to sue and asked Abraham Lincoln if he would represent him in court. Lincoln agreed, informing his client that he would charge a fee of $10.00. Lincoln took the ten dollars from the rich man, stepped over to the poor man and gave him five dollars on the condition that he pay the $2.50 debt. Thus, Lincoln made $5.00 on the case and the poor man, after paying the debt, made $2.50. All three men were satisfied.

BLIND AS A BAT

Harry Truman often mentioned that he had very weak eyes as a boy and couldn't see well enough to hit a baseball. The other boys refused to pick him when choosing teams. He explained, "Since I couldn't see the ball, they gave me a special job." "What was that, Mr. President?" someone always asked. "Umpire!" said Truman.

FOREIGN FOE

Former President Harry Truman and First Lady Lady Bird Johnson went to Greece to attend the funeral of King Paul. After the services they met a Greek prince who told them that his great-great-grandfather had served as an aide to General U.S. Grant in the Civil War. Truman, a southerner from Missouri, winked his eye at Mrs. Johnson (a Texan) and replied, "Young man, as far as this lady and I are concerned, your great-great grandfather was on the wrong side."

DESTINY

After serving eight years as Vice President, Richard Nixon observed, "I don't think that a leader can control to any great extent his destiny. Very seldom can he step in and change the situation if the forces of history are running in another direction. That is why men like [Robert] Taft, Clay, Webster and even Stassen never made it, much as they wanted to be President...."

BIG BOOST FROM A BOOK

If Franklin Pierce was going to be elected President in 1852, he would need some help. His friend and former college classmate, author Nathaniel Hawthorne, agreed to write a campaign biography. But many Northerners despised Pierce for his pro-slavery stance. Among them was Horace Mann, a great Massachusetts educator and founder of Antioch (Ohio) College. Mann was married to Elizabeth Peabody, whose sister was married to Hawthorne. When Mann learned of Hawthorne's intended biography, he announced, "If he makes out Pierce to be a great man or a brave man, it will be the greatest work of fiction he ever wrote." Hawthorne's book *The Life of Franklin Pierce* helped get Pierce into the White House, and the author was rewarded by being appointed U.S. Consul to Great Britain.

NO DOGS ALLOWED

George Washington and Thomas Jefferson both owned dogs, but neither would permit their slaves to raise them. They felt that the dogs owned by slaves would destroy livestock on the plantation. Jefferson further remarked that permitting slaves to do so would be "the most engaging of all follies."

MANY HAPPY RETURNS

Several years before William Henry Harrison ran for President, he sued an Indiana man for slander. Harrison believed his reputation was at stake. The court agreed and ordered Harrison's critic to pay him $8,000. Harrison took the settlement and invested it in land, then sold it. Several months later he gave the man back the $8,000 to show he was not interested in money.

GOING TO THE DOGS?

The Second Seminole War began in 1835 and lasted seven years. In 1837 General Zachary Taylor was sent to Florida to defeat the tribe and force them to move west. One method he employed was using bloodhounds to track down Seminoles. This puzzled several members of Congress, including John Quincy Adams. The former President questioned whether the dogs should qualify for a pension.

SOMEONE TOLD

Prior to attending Miami University, Benjamin Harrison went to a small prep school at Farmer's College in Cincinnati. By 1849 his parents became a bit disillusioned when they learned he had taken up the habit of smoking cigars, a practice he continued for the rest of his life.

A TREE WITH NO BRANCHES

Theodore Roosevelt enjoyed the outdoor life. After retiring to his Oyster Bay home he insisted on doing chores himself. One activity he especially enjoyed was chopping down trees. Several times his wife Edith would have a servant remove trees but the former President was insistent. One day she pointed far off to a tree which needed cut, so T.R. grabbed his trusty axe and got busy. His eyesight was not very good and he caused quite a stir when he chopped down a telephone pole!

That Sinking Feeling

Like Lincoln, James Garfield may also have had a premonition of his death. In January of 1881 the President-elect had a dream in which he, Chester Alan Arthur and his friend Major David Swaim were among passengers on a canal boat. During a terrific storm the packet began to sink. Vice President-elect Arthur was sick and lying on a couch. Swaim and Garfield swam to shore. The two men were naked and Garfield started back in the water to save Arthur and the others, but Swaim held him back as the boat went under. After a long journey in hostile territory the two arrived at a house where a black woman took Garfield into her arms and nursed him back to health. At this point Garfield awoke. Less than six months later he was gunned down by an assassin.

Heroic Effort Not Appreciated by All

General William S. Rosecrans was blamed for the Union defeat at Chickamauga, Georgia, on September 20, 1863. The Confederate forces of Bragg and Longstreet drove the Federals back to Chattanooga. Rosecrans fled his headquarters and ordered a retreat without putting up much of a fight. His chief of staff, James A. Garfield, requested to go back and help General George Thomas whose troops were surrounded and outnumbered. Riding through several miles of hostile territory, Garfield dodged bullets while his escort was killed. He found Thomas' army and for five hours helped to repulse repeated Confederate charges. Union soldiers were so low on ammunition they had to use their bayonets. The army was saved and thus prevented the Confederates from advancing on to Chattanooga. Garfield was summoned north to give a personal account of the disaster. Lincoln, Grant and Secretary of War Edwin Stanton all agreed that Rosecrans be relieved of his command. Though Garfield contends he defended Rosecrans' reputation, critics feel his testimony hastened Rosecrans' removal. Years later, when Garfield's star was on the rise, Rosecrans and his friends discredited Garfield, describing him as a man of "intensely selfish nature, morally without courage, of an impulsive nature, uncontrolled by principle, with a continuous trend in the direction of wrong." Garfield simply ignored such criticism when these allegations were repeated during his 1880 race for the White House.

Stragglers Welcomed

John Tyler died in 1862 and during the Civil War his family evacuated their Virginia mansion Sherwood Forest. The Union forces used it as their headquarters and at the war's end ransacked the home. When Julia Tyler returned she found the home almost beyond repair. One day she saw two Confederate soldiers approaching the house. Alarmed, she called for help. The men were stragglers with tattered uniforms and beards. She told them to stop and that they could not come in, but she would give them some bread and water. They entered the house anyway. The soldiers were her sons, David and John, and she hadn't recognized them.

Obsessed with P

President Harding may have been practicing his skills of alliteration when he announced in a speech, "Progression is not proclamation nor palaver. It is not pretense nor play on prejudice. It is not of personal pronouns, nor perennial pronouncement. It is not the perturbation of a people passion-wrought, nor a promise proposed."

First Lady Finds Out

President Gerald Ford was attending the Indianapolis 500 dinner and noticed the beautiful actress, Loni Anderson, was surrounded by a large group of admirers. Soon after the music began, Ford sent a Secret Service agent to Miss Anderson to see if she would dance with him. Ford and Anderson danced to several tunes. A few weeks later Betty Ford and Loni Anderson were guests on the Merv Griffin Show and Griffin asked Miss Anderson about the incident. The First Lady was somewhat surprised when she learned that the Secret Service had to interrupt the President and prevented him from further dancing with the starlet.

Change Your Tune

Chester Arthur thoroughly enjoyed the pageantry of White House social functions, except for one aspect. He disliked the tune "Hail to the Chief" which was played by the U.S. Marine Band whenever the President made an appearance at formal gatherings. He mentioned this to conductor John Phillip Sousa, who agreed with him. Arthur told him, "In that case, change it." Sousa wrote another tune and titled it "Semper Fidelis," which became on of Sousa's greatest pieces.

SLAUGHTER IN SOUTH CAROLINA

Franklin Roosevelt's victory in 1932 over incumbent Herbert Hoover was a landslide victory. No state gave a greater margin of winning than South Carolina. FDR won 98% of the votes in that state. Hoover received fewer than 2000 votes, and in one county Roosevelt had 3103 votes to Hoover's 5.

KILL THE DIRTY RAT!

In December of 1943 General Dwight Eisenhower visited Italy to inspect his army. He stayed with his friend and fellow officer Beetle Smith at the royal family's hunting lodge a few miles outside of Naples. Ike's dog Telek began barking when it discovered a large rat in the general's bathroom. Ike put on his reading glasses, grabbed his Colt .45 pistol and headed for the bathroom with his military staff close behind. Eisenhower's first shot hit the toilet seat as the sound from his gun boomed a deafening roar off the tiled walls. The rat jumped on a pipe and Ike fired again and missed. A third shot nicked the rat's tail. His fourth shot wounded the rodent. An aide quickly entered the bathroom and beat it to death with a log from the fireplace.

BARNYARD BREW

One day in 1902 Dwight Eisenhower and his brother Edgar found a full bottle of beer on the street in Abilene, Kansas. Instead of drinking it themselves, they took it home to their small farm, found a hen, held her beak open and poured the beer down her throat. The hen got drunk and became a neurotic wreck. It never laid another egg.

FROM ACTION TO INACTION

In December of 1863 General James A. Garfield resigned from the military (at the insistence of President Lincoln) to assume his seat in Congress. The House of Representatives at the time was poorly lit, over heated and uncomfortable. Garfield described the Congress as a "skillfully contrived human slaughter-house." He added, "Any man sitting here, during the evening, can feel his skull and brain going through the slow process of roasting."

RELATIVELY SPEAKING

In July of 1945 President Truman visited Norfolk, Virginia, talking with naval officers and inspecting the U.S. fleet. While aboard the *USS Augusta* he saw a young sailor named Lawrence Truman from Kentucky. It turned out that the sailor was the great-grandson of his grandfather's brother. The President wrote his wife that the boy was "a very nice kid… has eyes just like Margaret's."

NO ONE GOES HUNGRY

It could never be said that the Tylers of Virginia didn't know how to treat their guests. In the years after leaving the White House they entertained lavishly. In 1848 John and Julia held banquets for their relatives and friends. During one visit the hosts were served breakfast twice before sunrise. Then at dawn, champagne was served with a third breakfast.

SOME SUPPORT!

Benjamin Harrison's supporters even admitted that their candidate in 1888 lacked personality. Reserved, austere, and intensely private, Harrison was nicknamed "The Human Iceberg." One Republican leader admitted that Harrison "could charm a crowd of twenty thousand – but he could make them all enemies with a personal handshake."

TRAIN OF THOUGHT

During the late 1820s Martin Van Buren was one of America's most powerful politicians. As the Democratic governor of New York, he helped elect Andrew Jackson as President. In one letter to the President, Van Buren expressed his concern that railroad travel was dangerous, explaining that steam engines went too fast at 15 miles per hour. He wrote that locomotives would set fire to the countryside, kill off the canal system and cause unemployment. After Jackson's second term, his Vice President, none other than Martin Van Buren was elected Chief Executive. By the time Van Buren was in the White House, his views had changed.

FLAG-WAVING BEN

Benjamin Harrison was proud to be an American, and he believed others should always show their patriotism. He observed, "I rejoice in nothing more than in this movement, recently so prominently developed, of placing a starry banner above every schoolhouse. I have been charged with too sentimental appreciation of the flag. I will not enter upon any defense. God pity the American citizen who does not love it, who does not see in it the story of our great free institutions, and the hope of the home as well as the nation."

WINNING AT ALL COSTS

During a 1926 visit to his hometown of Abilene, Kansas, Dwight Eisenhower and his wife Mamie met with friends and family. Ike decided to play poker at Joner Callaghan's house. Hours passed and he received a phone call from an irritated Mamie who told him to get home to his parents' house. Eisenhower replied, "I can't come home now; I'm still behind." Mamie yelled, "You come home this minute!" and slammed the phone down. A few hours later Ike returned, with substantial winnings. What ensued was a shouting match some have called "the battle of Abilene."

BRITISH BURNING

When British general Cornwallis occupied Virginia, he destroyed Thomas Jefferson's estate at Elk Hill. He burned the building, took all the livestock, and confiscated thirty slaves, all of whom died when they were exposed to smallpox in Cornwallis' army. But the situation could have been worse. Even though Monticello was occupied for a day by British captain McCleod, nothing was taken or destroyed there.

INSPIRED B FOR A WHILE

The great concert pianist Paderewski toured America in 1900, playing to sellout audiences in major cities throughout the east and midwest. Mrs. E. C. White, a renowned Missouri piano teacher, took her prized pupil to a concert, then led him backstage to meet Paderewski. The fifteen-year-old boy, though quite nervous, shook hands with Paderewski then sat down to play a minuet. Paderewski was impressed and his words of encouragement inspired the boy to continue playing. The youth rose at 5:00 every morning to practice. Eventually he gave up his dream of being a concert pianist. That boy was Harry Truman.

A "SPOTTY" REPUTATION

Young Congressman Abe Lincoln didn't believe President James K. Polk when he accused Mexicans of shedding "American blood on American soil." War was declared, and Lincoln introduced several "spot resolutions" demanding to know the exact spot in which American soldiers had died. Newspapers considered this effort as unpatriotic and politically motivated and dubbed him "Spotty Lincoln." Many Illinois constituents were very unhappy as well. One town passed its own resolution calling Lincoln "the Benedict Arnold of our district." Opposition to Lincoln was so great that his own party, the Whigs, did not re-nominate him for another congressional term in 1848. His career in public office seemed at an end.

DIRECT OFFERING

On Sunday, May 24, 1846, James K. Polk, his wife and her niece, left the White House to attend the First Presbyterian Church. As they were leaving a young man named Bledsoe approached the President. Emaciated and looking ill, Bledsoe needed help. He had worked years ago with Polk in a Tennessee law office. Polk was sympathetic and gave him $5.00 and further instructing a steward to feed and clothe him, then take him to a hotel. The President promised more help the next day.

DEJECTION TO ELECTION TO REJECTION

Martin Van Buren's wife Hannah died in 1819 at the age of 35. She was buried initially in Albany, New York. During his White House years numerous relatives served as hostess. In 1851 the ex-President proposed marriage to Margaret Sylvester who was 28 years younger than Van Buren. She declined, saying she just wanted to remain friends.

CLEVER CLARK CAUGHT

Harry Truman was not supposed to win the Presidential election of 1948. *Newsweek* conducted a poll, interviewing 50 political journalists, and all picked the Republican candidate Thomas Dewey. All other major pollsters also picked him. Even many Democrats admitted defeat, but Truman kept campaigning at a furious pace. Truman's campaign strategist and special counsel, Clark Clifford, was anxious to see the *Newsweek* results, and on the morning of October 11, sneaked off the Truman campaign train to buy a copy. He opened the magazine to read, "Election Forecast: 50 Political Experts Predict a GOP Sweep." Clifford hid the magazine under his coat, not wanting Truman to see it. He walked past the President, who was seated on a sofa. Truman stopped Clifford and inquired, "What does it say, Clark?" Clifford asked, "What does what say?" Truman asked, "What have you got under your coat?" When Clifford said he had nothing, Truman told him, "Clark, I saw you get off the train just now and I think you went in there to see if they had a newsstand with a copy of *Newsweek*. And I think maybe you have it under your coat." Reluctantly, Clifford handed the magazine to Truman who read the results. The President casually looked up at Clifford and remarked, "Don't worry about that poll, Clark. I know every one of those fifty fellows, and not one of them has enough sense to pound sand into a rathole."

PLEASE DON'T EXPLAIN

President Ronald Reagan had a difficult time responding to a reporter's question about the nation's deficit. Reagan's advisors often broke out in a sweat when their boss had to answer questions without prepared notes, and no doubt they cringed when he told the reporter, "The problem is – the deficit is – or should I say – wait a minute – the spending is roughly 23 to 24 percent. So that it is in – ah, er – it what is increasing, while the revenues are staying proportionately the same and what would be the proper amount they should, that we should be taking from the private sector."

IT SHOULD BE THIS WAY, BY GEORGE!

George Washington was sixteen years old when he penned his "Rules of Civility & Decent Behavior In Company and Conversation." He wrote 110 guidelines, several of them pertaining to table manners. In his own words, Washington made the following suggestions for dinner etiquette: "Number 94 –...blow not your broth at Table but Stay till Cools of its Self; 100 – Cleanse not your teeth with the Table Cloth Napkin Fork or Knife but if Others do it let it be done with a Pick Tooth; 101 – Rinse not your Mouth in the Presence of Others; 103 – In Company of your Betters be not longer in eating than they are lay not your Arm but only your hand upon the table"

"SOUND" MONEY

One day Calvin Coolidge was walking hand-in-hand with his young sons, Calvin and John, down the main street of their hometown of Northampton, Massachusetts. They came to the bank where the Coolidges had their savings. The future President stopped and asked his boys to be very quiet. Pointing to the bank, he asked them, "What do you hear?" The sons listened intently and told their father there was only silence. Coolidge looked at the boys and said, "I just thought you could hear your money at work."

A SECRET NOT FOR LONG

Frank Pierce lied to his wife about his involvement in the 1852 Presidential race. He actively sought the nomination and helped organize the campaign. After his election he admitted to his wife Jane of his participation. She was furious and, following their son's tragic death prior to the inauguration, went into a deep depression, believing God was punishing both of them for her husband's ambition. Jane Pierce stayed away from the inauguration and waited a month before moving to the White House. She made very few public appearances and spent much of her time in seclusion and prayer. She wrote letters to her dead son and even held seances to try and communicate with him. Meanwhile, her husband struggled through one of the most inept administrations in history.

DO NOT DISTURB

Once, while President Coolidge was sitting on his front porch in Northampton, Massachusetts, he was reading a newspaper which was hiding his face. A tour bus drove by slowly. Coolidge took a quick glance, then continued to read with his feet propped up. The tour guide remarked to his passengers that this was not very presidential. Coolidge heard the remark, briefly put down his paper, and yelled, "Democrat!"

FOLLOWING FATHER'S FLIGHT PATH

When George Bush's TBF Avenger was shot down in the Pacific during World War II, he was the youngest pilot in the U.S. Navy. Son George W. wanted to follow in his father's footsteps, without having been shot down. From 1968-73 "Junior" flew an F-102 Delta Dagger jet fighter in the Texas National Guard. Unlike his father, George W. never flew in combat and never left the states. He later lamented, "I regret not having gone to Vietnam."

FINDING SOMETHING TO DO

Ex-President Millard Fillmore didn't think it was proper to resume his law practice after leaving office. As a widower without an income, he struggled financially until he met and married a wealthy widow, Carolyn McIntosh. For managing her money, he received $10,000 a year from her trust. Fillmore set about dedicating himself to many charitable institutions and causes including hospitals, historical societies and numerous organizations such as the local chapter of the Society for the Prevention of Cruelty to Animals.

FESSIN' UP

On September 4, 1976, George W. Bush was stopped by a policeman for driving at a slow, erratic pace near the family's home in Kennebunkport, Maine. Believing honesty to be the best policy, G. W. admitted to drinking five beers and pleaded guilty to a DUI charge. He paid a fine of $150 and lost his Maine driver's license. Twenty-four years later, and just five days before the 2000 Presidential election, a Maine lawyer and leading Democrat gave the story to the media in hopes of winning votes for Bush's opponent Al Gore. Though George W. admitted during the campaign that he had been a heavy drinker in his days of youth, he hadn't mentioned this specific incident. After the story broke, he apologized to the American people, and the strategy appeared to work. He was elected anyway. Incidentally, Bush quit drinking alcoholic beverages in 1986.

A MEMBER OF THE "SWAT" TEAM

As a fourth grader in Texas, George W. Bush wanted to amuse his classmates so one day he showed up at school with a goatee and mustache painted on his face. The principal, John Bizilo, told him he was not at school to clown around. Reaching inside his desk, Bizilo pulled out his paddle and swatted Bush three times. "He yelled bloody murder," Bizilo recalled in July of 2000. "Whoever would think he'd be a candidate for President?"

Facts on the Presidents

For a period of forty years, following the inauguration of Taft and including Franklin Roosevelt, no President attended inaugural balls anywhere. And Jimmy Carter in 1977 attended seven of his inaugural balls, while Ronald Reagan in 1981 attended all nine of them!

When William Howard Taft got sick in the Philippines in 1902, it required six men to put him on a stretcher.

Theodore Roosevelt's horse, Tranquility, was well-named. Accompanying him on his 1909 African safari, the animal on several occasions remained perfectly calm while its rider shot at charging lions and other big game.

As President, Abe Lincoln suspended sentences or granted pardons to nearly 1000 people. This includes both military and civilian cases.

In succeeding Jefferson, James Madison was not exactly jubilant, for he knew something of the monumental problems he was about to face. Reportedly at his inauguration, Madison whispered to a friend that he "would much rather be in bed." A happier Jefferson explained, "I have got the burden off my shoulders, while he has now got his on his."

Rutherford B. Hayes once told James Garfield that becoming governor of Ohio was "the surest road to the Presidency." It worked for Hayes, but Garfield chose to remain in Congress until he was elected President.

Theodore Roosevelt told a Labor Day crowd in 1903, "Far and away the best prize that life offers is the chance to work hard at work worth doing."

Prior to being struck down with polio, FDR was a notorious sleepwalker.

According to Lee Simonson, an autograph expert, there are only three handwritten letters by Lyndon Johnson while President, and only twelve by President Herbert Hoover. If one is lucky enough to have such a handwritten letter, it is probably worth tens of thousands of dollars.

Two of FDR's closest companions during his childhood were Debby, his Welsh pony, and Marksman, his red Irish setter.

Thinking of his failure in getting the United States to join the League of Nations, Woodrow Wilson remarked, "I would rather fail in a cause I knew someday will triumph than win in a cause I knew someday will fail."

"People who value their privileges above their principles soon lose both," voiced Dwight D. Eisenhower.

Quipped John F. Kennedy, "Too often we enjoy the comfort of opinion without the discomfort of thought."

"Eating and sleeping," said Gerald Ford, "are a waste of time."

When asked what he thought about the future, Harry Truman observed, "I have no idea. I'm not a prophet. One thing though, we've got to keep the youth stirred up. We've got to make them enthused about the history of the country and about the future."

In February of 1986, Ronald Reagan told Americans in a televised speech, "Good ideas are America's special genius."

Lincoln wanted to be remembered in this way: "I want it said of me by those who knew me best, that I always plucked a thistle and planted a flower where I thought a flower would grow."

We should all follow Thomas Jefferson's advice: "The most valuable of all talents is that of never using two words when one will do."

The Lyndon B. Johnson Library in Austin, Texas, houses 31 million pages of LBJ documents, contained in 41,000 boxes. Each box bears a small gold replica of the Presidential seal and are stacked behind glass walls extending four stories high.

"Every word that a President says weighs a ton," said Calvin Coolidge. Perhaps this is the reason why "Silent Cal" never spoke much.

Herbert Hoover had his own beatitude when he voiced, "Blessed are the young, for they shall inherit the national debt."

George Washington's dental problems may have stemmed from his habit as a youth of cracking walnuts with his teeth.

Calvin Coolidge liked to fish but didn't have much luck. He once said there were 45,000 trout in one of his favorite fishing spots and added, "I haven't caught them all yet, but I've intimidated them."

Rutherford B. Hayes was a brisk walker, getting up very early every morning to take a stroll. He watched his diet too, restricting himself to just one cup of coffee for breakfast and only a cup of tea for lunch.

Chester Arthur, observing the run-down conditions of the White House, referred to it as a "badly kept barracks."

"Silent" Calvin Coolidge was invited to break ground for the cornerstone of a public building. Having performed this ceremonial duty, he was expected to give a speech. Pointing to the broken earth, Coolidge observed solemnly, "That's a mighty fine fishin' worm," then departed.

During his visit to Niagara Falls in 1901, President McKinley was careful to walk only halfway along the bridge connecting the U.S. with Canada. He simply didn't want to be the first incumbent President to leave the boundaries of the United States.

Shortly after the 1912 election, Woodrow Wilson visited an old aunt he had not seen in years. When Wilson told her he had just been elected President of the United States, the elderly lady, thinking her nephew was joking, said, "Don't be silly!"

Thomas Jefferson, in speaking about the U.S. ambassador to Spain, once remarked, "I haven't heard from him in two years. If I don't hear from him next year, I will write him a letter."

President Andrew Johnson referred to Grant as "a dullard, whose brain could have been compressed within the periphery of a nutshell."

While serving as governor of the Northwest Territory, William Henry Harrison was sitting in his living room holding his infant son John Scott in his lap. An enraged Indian fired a shot at them through the shutters but missed.

Though advanced in years and in poor health, ex-President John Quincy Adams remained in his seat in the House of Representatives for two days and one night, all the while actively engaging in debate during a filibuster. He did not eat for nearly thirty hours.

Zachary Taylor had to shut one eye when reading to avoid double vision.

When William Henry Harrison's casket lay in the White House in 1841, there were twenty-six pall bearers, one representing each state.

When Andrew Jackson left the Presidency, he was nearly broke. He didn't even have enough money for traveling expenses back to Tennessee.

There was only one time period in our history when there were no ex-Presidents. That was during John Adams' term in office. George Washington had died in 1799, part way through Adams' term.

Bill Clinton's all-time favorite movie? The western classic *High Noon* starring Gary Cooper and Grace Kelly. His second favorite film? *Prince of Tides* starring Nick Nolte and Barbara Streisand.

U.S. Grant's father, Jesse, was the first mayor of Georgetown. That's Georgetown, *Ohio*, a small town near Cincinnati.

President Chester A. Arthur once received a complaint that a high-ranking government official was drunk. The always-proper Arthur responded, "No gentleman ever sees another gentleman drunk."

When former President John Quincy Adams visited John Tyler at the White House on July 4, 1841, he and other special guests were treated to turtle soup. The turtle had weighed 300 pounds and was a gift from Key West, Florida.

Ronald Reagan was quite a prankster as a student at Eureka College in Illinois. He once electronically wired the front row pews in the college chapel. Several students got a real "jolt" out of the service.

George Washington won the respect of his soldiers in the Revolutionary War by demanding proper treatment from Congress. A constant shortage of food, supplies, and money made army life at times unbearable. He complained of the amount and quality of their rations, once writing Congress that his men were forced to "eat every kind of horse food except hay."

After a lengthy meeting with British Prime Minister Margaret Thatcher, President Jimmy Carter remarked to an aide that it was "the first time I've given someone forty-five minutes and only managed to speak for five minutes myself."

Had it not been for the Mexican War in 1846, U.S. Grant would have taught mathematics at West Point and perhaps been doomed to relative obscurity. He applied for an assistant professorship and was accepted just as war broke out.

While fishing near West Island in Rhode Island in late September of 1883, President Chester Arthur pulled in a eighty-pound sea bass, the largest one seen by inhabitants in years.

While sliding into a base at a celebrity baseball game in Wrigley Field in 1950, Ronald Reagan broke his right thigh in six places.

Bill Clinton's view of winning extended even to competing while playing games with his family. He once said, "Sometimes I'm ashamed of myself at how much I care if I win or lose."

In the 1980s the White House was stripped of its paint on the exterior walls for the first time. Workers were busy, removing forty-two coats of old paint.

Critics of President Dwight D. Eisenhower often referred to the White House during his administration as the "tomb of the well-known soldier."

When Ronald Reagan married his first wife, actress Jane Wyman, they bought two terriers and named them Scotch and Soda.

Should there be an age limit for the President? Dwight D. Eisenhower thought so. Quipped the 34th Chief Executive when he left office in 1961, "No one should ever sit in this office over 70...and that I know."

LBJ once told an audience, "I wanted to be the President who educated young children...who helped to feed the hungry...who helped the poor find their own way...."

"What I am interested in," said Woodrow Wilson, "is having the government of the United States more concerned about human rights than property rights." And fifty years later Jimmy Carter agreed, saying, "Human rights is the soul of our foreign policy, because human rights is the very soul of our sense of nationhood."

"The trouble with Republicans is that when they get into trouble, they start acting like cannibals." The author of this comment was Richard Nixon.

During Thomas Jefferson's term as President, it would have cost you seventy-five cents to buy a turkey.

Warren Harding had a lot less problem with animals than with people. He had his pet dogs sit on chairs and perform tricks during cabinet meetings.

On April 10, 1899, Theodore Roosevelt voiced, "I wish to preach, not the doctrine of ignoble ease, but the doctrine of the strenuous life."

During the Revolutionary War our ambassador to France was John Adams. He wrote to his wife from Paris, "I must study Politicks and War that my sons may have liberty to study Mathematicks and Philosophy."

For relaxation at the White House, President Chester Arthur and his son strummed the banjo and sang tunes.

On April 30, 1856, President James K. Polk was greatly impressed by a group of twenty-five children who demonstrated their skills in literature, music, and mathematics. All of the young students were from the Perkins Institute, and all were blind, deaf, or both.

William Henry Harrison's funeral procession was two miles long. This was longer than his inaugural pageant which preceded it one month earlier.

John and Abigail Adams lived in the newly-constructed White House only four months before Thomas Jefferson occupied it.

FDR on education: "We cannot afford to overlook any sources of human raw material. Genius flowers in the most unexpected places."

John Tyler was President a bit less than one full term, yet he had all four of his Supreme Court nominations rejected by the Senate.

In 1859 Lincoln visited Dayton, Ohio, and sat for a daguerreotype. Another man came into the studio and began painting a portrait of him. Lincoln told the artist, "Keep on. You may make a good one, but never a pretty one."

Chester A. Arthur told George Bliss of the *New York Herald*, "Well, there doesn't seem anything else for an ex-President to do but go into the country and raise big pumpkins."

William McKinley said, "Half-heartedness never won a battle."

Lincoln often removed his boots because of the large corns and blisters on his feet.

Harry Truman insisted his father was not a failure, adding, "He produced a President of the United States."

William McKinley aptly noted, "Every mother wants her son to become President, but no mother wants her son to become a politician."

Many of our Chief Executives have had mistresses. Even Lyndon B. Johnson once remarked, "Of course, I may go into a strange bedroom now and then. *That* I don't want you to write about, but otherwise you can write everything."

Lincoln once noted a difference between his heritage and posterity: "I am not quite as interested in who my grandfather was as I am in what my grandson will become."

Being the son or daughter of a President also has its disadvantages. Many people have great expectations of a Chief Executive's children. FDR recognized this dilemma and noted, "One of the worst things in the world is being the child of a President. It's a terrible life they lead."

When the populace gets tired and disgusted by Washington politics, we can take a little comfort in the words of Thomas Jefferson who observed: "I tremble for my country when I reflect that God is just."

FDR was born into a privileged class of wealth. Between the ages of two and fourteen, he made eight ocean voyages across the Atlantic to Europe.

At a luncheon one afternoon, ex-President Lyndon Johnson explained to reporters that he was a complex man. Then, tapping his forehead, he said, "Sometimes I don't even know what's going on up there."

President Eisenhower once invited Senator Lyndon Johnson to the White House, asking him not to support a bill which would diminish the power of the Presidency. Before LBJ left, Ike remarked, "Remember Lyndon, you might be the one sitting in this chair someday."

FDR once made this observation: "We all know that books burn – yet we have the greater knowledge that books cannot be killed by fire. No man and no force can abolish memory."

Theodore Roosevelt offered this advice: "Be manly and gentle to those weaker than yourselves. Hold your own and at the same time, do your duty to the weak, and you will come pretty near being noble men and women."

The U.S. first used postage stamps during James K. Polk's administration. This idea was introduced by Polk's Postmaster General, Cave Johnson.

Even as a youngster William McKinley believed he was destined for greatness. He commented, "I have never been in doubt since I was old enough to think intelligently that I would sometime be made President."

While serving in the Navy during World War II, Richard Nixon played high-stakes poker. He left as a lieutenant commander along with a $10,000 kitty from his game earnings.

Much of James Madison's political feelings was based on the belief that "all men having power ought to be mistrusted."

FDR has been credited with inventing the world "chiseler" as a synonym for a swindler or cheater.

As Chief Executive, Gerald Ford demonstrated the grit which he once showed on the college football field. In less than two years he vetoed more than fifty bills, many of which called for increased spending. "I am an old lineman," he said.

Even though Thomas Jefferson strongly disagreed with Federalist Party ideals, he actively organized opposition while still claiming, "If I could not go to heaven but with a party, I would not go there at all."

The Eisenhower family was so poor that little Dwight had to wear his mother's button-top shoes to school.

In 1979 Jimmy Carter's administration was under much criticism. A news woman in Portsmouth, New Hampshire, asked him whether his daughter, Amy, ever bragged about her father being President. Quipped Carter, "No, she probably apologizes."

On his carriage ride back from inaugural ceremonies, William McKinley was told by his predecessor, Grover Cleveland, "I am deeply sorry, Mr. President, to pass on to you a war with Spain. It will come within two years. Nothing can stop it." Cleveland's words proved precise.

The 295,000 words of Grant's *Personal Memoirs* filled 1231 pages in two volumes. Grant was the first President to publish a book, and after his death the book sold 312,000 sets at $9.00 a piece.

Martin Van Buren's nicknames of "Slippery Elm" and "Sweet Sandy Whiskers" were given to him by his political opponents, the Whigs.

Abe Lincoln was related to Daniel Boone. And one genealogist of the 1920s traced antecedents of Lincoln's mother back to William the Conqueror, Charlemagne, and King Tut!

Harry Truman neither liked nor appreciated the paintings of Picasso. Said the thirty-third President after viewing a Picasso work, "Any kid can take an egg and a piece of ham and make more understandable pictures."

THE LONG-LOST

"HARRY"

by

PICASSO

McKinley's last words were, "Oh, dear." This was whispered to Dr. Presley Rixey just moments before he died.

Like most other Presidents, Woodrow Wilson was often asked for his autograph. He usually complied, but once announced, "A man's most authentic autograph is the record of his life."

John Kennedy's last words were, "My God, I'm hit!" He uttered this to his wife just a second or two before another bullet killed him.

Thomas Jefferson referred to Washington, D.C., as an "Indian swamp in the wilderness."

Both Abraham Lincoln and James A. Garfield were born in log cabins. And they were distantly related.

Rutherford B. Hayes said, "I try to be a Christian. Or rather I want to be a Christian and help do Christian work."

Observed Warren G. Harding, "I am a man of limited talents from a small town."

On several occasions George Washington remarked that he would have liked to be a fireman.

FDR gave this piece of advice in regard to speech making: "Be sincere; be brief; be seated."

John Adams stated, "It is not true, in fact, that any people ever existed who love the public better than themselves."

Lincoln observed, "There are few things wholly evil or wholly good. Almost everything, especially of Government policy, is an inseparable compound of the two, so that our best judgment of the preponderance between them is continually demanded."

Theodore Roosevelt once noted: "No people is fully civilized where a distinction is drawn between stealing an office and stealing a purse."

Eisenhower once said, "I am a Republican. But I am not, I hope, a blind Republican who puts party above all else."

James Madison observed, "If men were angels, no government would be necessary."

President George Washington once scolded an aide for introducing him too royally.

Woodrow Wilson used both the Oval Office and his upstairs study as his office. His typewriter was hastily shuttled between the two rooms.

Warren Harding loved to chew tobacco so much so that when he ran out, he tossed a cigarette in his mouth and chewed it up.

In 1934 FDR was presented a small medicine chest. It's donor was a descendant of a British sailor who had taken it when the capital was invaded and burned in 1814.

When Herbert Hoover moved into the White House in 1929, he increased the number of telephones and installed thirteen radios.

Jefferson and Madison used a secret code, consisting of numbers, when writing to each other during their retirement.

Theodore Roosevelt reminded us at the turn of the century, "Wildlife and trees are the property of unborn generations."

FDR once paid Justice Oliver Wendell Holmes a ceremonial visit. Holmes was ninety-one-years-old but still had a sharp mind and quick wit. He described Roosevelt as a man with a second-class mind and a "first-class temperament."

President-elect Richard Nixon offered the ambassadorship to the United Nations to Hubert H. Humphrey, the man whom he had just defeated for the Presidency. Humphrey declined.

As war with Spain appeared imminent in March and April of 1898, the White House received seventy-three death threats on McKinley's life. Security was tightened by the Secret Service.

On December 16, 1988, President Reagan spoke to students at the University of Virginia in Charlottesville. Trying to convince his audience that he understood economic problems,. he remarked, "I got a degree in economics. I didn't deserve it, but I got it."

Richard Nixon's bowling scores in his retirement years averaged 152.

Warren Harding did not have far to go in retrieving errant golf shots on the practice green at the White House. His dog Laddie Boy was taught to bring each ball back.

Fishing can have its hazards. George Bush once showed reporters a scar on the back of his hand. He got it when he was assailed by a six pound blue fish while vacationing in Florida.

A compassionate Lincoln reminded a radical Congress during the midst of the Civil War, "The severest justice may not always be the best policy."

On May 6, 1948, President Truman addressed the National Conference on Family Life and told them, "Children and dogs are as necessary to the welfare of this country as Wall Street and the railroads."

Grover Cleveland observed, "A man is known by the company he keeps, and also by the company from which he is kept out."

Thomas Jefferson summed up life in one brief explanation: "Life is the art of avoiding pain."

In his farewell address, George Washington cautioned his countrymen when he stated, "Guard against the postures of pretended patriotism."

On his deathbed, William McKinley remarked to George Cortelyou, "It's mighty lonesome in here."

In 1962 John Kennedy observed, "It is easier to make the speeches than to make the judgments."

Calvin Coolidge hoped that people didn't expect too much from him. He was quoted as saying that Americans wanted "a solemn ass for President."

John Adams spent more than one-fourth of his term away from Washington. The second Chief Executive felt he could govern just as effectively from his home in Quincy, Massachusetts.

In describing his liberal ideals, Woodrow Wilson declared he was "a progressive with the brakes on."

Reflecting on the dangers of his office, President McKinley revealed to his friend Herman Kohlsaat, "If it were not for Ida, I would prefer to go as Lincoln went." McKinley was shot on September 6, 1901.

Theodore Roosevelt was a man of action and wasn't afraid to make any decision. He once explained, "A council of war never fights."

Thomas Jefferson warned his successors that "great innovations should not be forced on slender majorities."

Lincoln once remarked about the burden of the Presidency: "If to be head of Hell is as hard as what I have to undergo here [at the White House], I could find it in my heart to pity Satan himself."

William McKinley had just died and Theodore Roosevelt was sworn in as President in Buffalo, New York. The new Chief Executive asked a friend, Herman Kohlsaat, to come and see him. When Kohlsaat arrived he saw Roosevelt conferring with a tall, thin college professor whom the President called "Woody." It was Woodrow Wilson, who later would defeat Teddy in the election of 1912.

Woodrow Wilson once described Calvin Coolidge as "no one in particular."

James A. Garfield once observed, "Never let us praise poverty, for a child at least."

While on his death bed, a delirious Andrew Jackson sang *Auld Lang Syne*.

Jefferson observed, "Honesty is the first chapter in the book of wisdom."

Zachary Taylor's hero had been George Washington. Taylor requested that his inaugural oath be solemnized with the same *Bible* which Washington used in his first inauguration. It was sent from New York City and used on March 5, 1849.

William Henry Harrison sired ten children, and he once complained, "My nursery is filling up faster than my treasury."

Martin Van Buren was a widower by the time he entered the White House. With no wife to rule over Washington society, Van Buren at least pleased the ladies, for he was accompanied by his four sons – all of them in their twenties and all eligible bachelors.

President Rutherford B. Hayes was not much of a sports enthusiast, except when it came to croquet. He was a wizard at the game, playing it on the White House lawn.

At John Kennedy's inauguration in 1961, there were eight former or future First Ladies in attendance.

As of 1994 *Air Force One* was equipped with seven bathrooms and eighty-five telephones.

In 1964 there were more than fifty books published on the subject of John F. Kennedy.

As for making decisions and changing laws, William McKinley once told his Secretary of State John Sherman, "...my rule is to make haste slowly."

"Most people are as happy as they make up their minds to be." So said Abraham Lincoln.

On Saturday morning, June 5, 1852, Franklin Pierce took his wife for a carriage ride in Boston. A friend on horseback galloped up to them and blurted out that Pierce, a dark horse candidate, had been nominated for President. Jane Pierce fainted.

In a letter to William McKinley in 1892, ex-President Hayes warned the future Chief Executive, "All appointments hurt. Five friends are made cold or hostile for every appointment; no new friends are made. All patronage is perilous to men of real ability or merit. It aids only those who lack other claims to public support."

When U.S. Grant captured Vicksburg, Mississippi, after a long siege, he bagged 30,000 Confederate prisoners.

Though Martin Van Buren was an aristocratic politician, he was also a man of principle, particularly on the stance against slavery. In 1848 the Free Soil Party chose the Democratic ex-President as their candidate. But his anti-slavery views cost him the support of the southern and border states.

When Andrew Johnson moved into the Executive Mansion in 1865, he removed the bathtub, installed years earlier by Dolley Madison. He said bathtubs were undemocratic!

Thomas Jefferson explained, "The execution of laws is much more important than the making of them."

James A. Garfield once remarked, "I do not care what others say or think of me. But there is one man's opinion which I very much value, and that is the opinion of James Garfield."

Herbert Hoover said, "One who brandishes a pistol must be prepared to shoot."

Dwight D. Eisenhower observed, "Only Americans can hurt America."

William Henry Harrison said, "It is cheaper to feed the Indians than to fight them."

After Millard Fillmore's death, his son burned many of his father's private papers and letters.

Following his daughter's wedding at the White House, U.S. Grant was found crying. He thought his darling Nellie, twenty, was too young to marry.

When Woodrow Wilson's daughter, Julie, was married, she received presents from all over the world. If Julie cried, it may have been due to one of the gifts – a bushel of onions!

British statesman and author John Morley, on his return to London, reported on his observations regarding Theodore Roosevelt: "I saw two tremendous forces of nature while I was gone. One was Niagara Falls, and the other the President of the United States, and I am not sure which is the more wonderful."

Observed Dwight Eisenhower, "When you are in any contest you should work as if there were – to the very last minute – a chance to lose it. This is battle, this is politics, this is anything."

When Luci Johnson was asked by a reporter how she would describe her relationship with her father-President, she hesitated only a moment before answering, "Blood."

Quoted Thomas Jefferson, "Liberty is a boisterous sea. Timid men prefer the calm of despotism."

At the age of sixteen, James A. Garfield in 1848 worked for some of his neighbors, chopping wood for fifty cents a day, cutting grass for fifty cents an acre, and doing many other types of labor.

One of our future Presidents carried a gun with him on the way to school. As a youngster Zach Taylor and his two older brothers walked to school through the Kentucky forest. Robbers, Indians, and wild animals often spelled trouble, and the boys more than once had to defend themselves.

As Chairman of the House Ways and Means Committee, Millard Fillmore was instrumental in getting funds to help Samuel Morse (a fellow New Yorker) develop the telegraph.

As one of the last of the log cabin Presidents, James Garfield referred to his birthplace as a "politically-perfect mansion."

Theodore Roosevelt referred to the Presidency as his "bully pulpit."

John Tyler's cabinet, composed of Whigs who supported Harrison, resigned. The House initiated impeachment, and the Senate rejected his Supreme Court appointments. The Whig Party officially kicked him out, and Tyler was dubbed as "the man without a party." His wife, Julia, retorted, "If he wants a party, I will give him a party."

In 1901 Harry Truman worked as a timekeeper for fifteen cents an hour on the Santa Fe Railroad.

During George Washington's term in office, the population of the U.S. reached four million.

John Adams once whittled a miniature canoe out of pinewood and launched it on the Braintree, Massachusetts, town creek.

Sounding like the former tailor he was, Andrew Johnson stated, "I have no other ambition in life than to mend the breaches in the torn and tattered constitution of my country."

Calvin Coolidge believed that most problems would take care of themselves. His philosophy of leadership (or lack of it) was reflected in his axiom: "If you see ten troubles coming down the road, you can be sure that nine will run into the ditch before they reach you."

After returning from his tour of Central America, Theodore Roosevelt wrote William Howard Taft, "You have proved to be my best friend, for during my absence the country has turned its attention from my teeth to your stomach." Such flattery helped convince Taft to succeed Roosevelt as President, but their friendship soon ended.

When Gerald Ford took his oath following Nixon's resignation, his left hand rested on his son's *Bible* which was held by wife Betty. It was opened to *Proverbs 3:5-6*, "Trust in the Lord with all thine heart, and lean not unto thine own understanding. In all thy ways acknowledge him, and he shall direct thy paths." Ford knew this passage well, for he had used this each night for many years as his bedtime prayer.

Theodore Roosevelt felt the Vice Presidency was as useless as "a fifth wheel to a coach."

Franklin Pierce was very unpopular during the Civil War. Nevertheless, Nathaniel Hawthorne dedicated his book, *Our Old Home*, to the former President. Hawthorne's publisher objected, but Pierce had been a good friend and a college classmate of the author.

John Adams' pen name was Humphrey Ploughjogger, writing an essay on agriculture in 1763 for Boston newspapers.

Following Chief Tecumseh's death, his brother, The Prophet, put a curse on William Henry Harrison.

Warren Harding loved to party, and the Gayety Burlesque in Washington built a special reviewing box so he could watch the shows and not be seen by anyone else in the audience.

In May of 1829 James Monroe became the first President to ride a steamboat, the *SS Savannah.*

Calvin Coolidge liked to stay in bed and have his head rubbed with petroleum jelly.

Genealogists discovered that George Bush is the tenth cousin, once removed, of his Vice President Dan Quayle. Bush is also kin to ten other Presidents, including Pierce, Buchanan, Lincoln, Nixon, and Ford.

In 1892 many Republican leaders were hesitant to endorse Benjamin Harrison for another nomination, feeling he could not be re-elected. Speaker of the House Thomas B. Reed was urged by Harrison supporters to "join the bandwagon." Reed replied, "I never ride in an ice-cart." Though re-nominated, Harrison lost the election to his predecessor Grover Cleveland.

Peter Benchley, the author of *Jaws* and *The Deep*, was a speech writer for Lyndon Johnson for two years. He wrote minor speeches along with numerous jokes for the President, but the material was seldom used. LBJ would remark, "I'm not a funny President."

Though Chester Arthur was a Quartermaster General during the Civil War, he had some misgivings in supporting Lincoln for a second term. The future President wrote his brother in 1864 that "he would not vote at all rather than vote for Lincoln for next President."

As a teacher, James Garfield once told a class, "Gentlemen, I can express my creed of life in one word: 'I believe in *work!* I BELIEVE IN *WORK!*'"

During a warm day in the nation's capital, President Coolidge went to a baseball game to watch the Yankees play the Washington Senators. Babe Ruth walked over to Coolidge, shook his hand, and remarked casually, "Geez, it's hot, ain't it, Prez?"

In 1759 George Washington wrote these instructions to the captains of the Virginia militia regiments: "Discipline is the soul of an army. It makes small numbers formidable; procures success to the weak, and esteem to all."

President Benjamin Harrison particularly enjoyed bowling and playing billiards with a few close friends, but he constantly lost at both. In mid-July of 1889 he discovered a four leaf clover. It brought him no luck as he continued his losing ways.

On election night in 1904 Theodore Roosevelt proclaimed, "Under no circumstances will I be a candidate for or accept another nomination." These words came back to haunt him when he made a bid for a third term on the Bull Moose ticket in 1912.

Observed Andrew Jackson, "One man with courage makes a majority."

In a rare display of ill-temper, President Taft denounced newspaper and magazine editors "as murderers and thieves," and he would, if he had his own way, "condemn them all to hell and eternal damnation."

Commenting on the socialistic programs of the Roosevelt administration, ex-President Hoover told a group of St. Louis Republicans in 1935, "A good many things go around in the dark besides Santa Claus."

Ulysses S. Grant advised, "Keep the church and the state forever separate."

"Fear is the foundation of most governments," observed John Adams.

In 1881, on his first Sunday as President, Chester Arthur worshiped at a Negro church, and returned there on Thanksgiving, too.

Lincoln lost just one wrestling match on the frontier. In 1832 at Beardstown, Illinois, Lincoln's friends wagered money, hats, knives, blankets, and tomahawks. But Lorenzo Thomas bested the future President.

FDR once said to Winston Churchill, "It is fun to be in the same decade with you."

In 1832 James Buchanan served as ambassador to Russia. He negotiated a commercial treaty between the U.S. which remained an agreement for eighty years.

While visiting the Buckeye State, President Kennedy once told a crowd, "There is no city in the United States in which I get a warmer welcome and less votes than Columbus, Ohio."

Said Ronald Reagan, "Washington is the only city where sound travels faster than light."

"When more and more people are thrown out of work unemployment results." So observed the perceptive Calvin Coolidge.

"New ideas can be good or bad, just the same as old ones." – FDR.

John Kennedy once said, "A child miseducated is a child lost."

James A. Garfield observed, "The sanctity of marriage and the family make the cornerstone of our American society and civilization."

John Adams wrote to Thomas Jefferson in 1816, "You and I ought not to die before we have explained ourselves to each other." Within a decade, the two former political enemies had grown in friendship, though they had not met personally in more than twenty years.

When he was a small boy, author Washington Irving received a pat on the head from George Washington. He passed on this ritual to future generations of family and friends.

While serving as governor of California, Ronald Reagan was a guest on David Frost's TV talk show, and remarked, "I wonder what the ten Commandments would be like if Moses had to run them through a hostile legislature."

The first ex-President to go into business was U.S. Grant. Four years after leaving office, he joined a New York banking house founded in his name. Later, a partner cheated him out of a fortune and brought financial ruin to Grant and his family.

In 1899 President William McKinley dismissed the prospect of discovering oil on his farm in Minerva, Ohio, remarking to his press secretary, "I have been so near wealth so many times, Cortelyou, that I don't get excited over these things nowadays."

In 1808 Thomas Jefferson said, "I think one war is enough for the life of one man."

The largest room in the White House is the East Room.

The Red Room, also known as the Music Room, is often used as a parlor by the First Lady.

There are three Oval rooms in the White House.

President Eisenhower once issued a Top Secret directive to order a Mother's Day card.

During the Revolutionary War, George Washington didn't see his home, Mount Vernon, for six years.

Warren G. Harding played ping-pong every morning.

The first furnace in the White House was installed when Franklin Pierce was President.

Lyndon Johnson's most prized school paper was entitled, "I'd Rather Be Momma's Boy."

At a White House dinner a fight broke out when the British and French ambassadors drew swords against each other. No blood was shed, for the President, James Monroe, intervened.

Remarked William Howard Taft's mother, "I find that Willie needs constant watching and correcting. It requires great caution and firmness, but I do believe we cannot love our children too much."

George Bush was sworn into office with two *Bibles*. In addition to the one owned by his family, Bush also borrowed the *Bible* on which George Washington took his first oath. It was loaned to him by the Masonic Hall in New York City where it is kept. Several Presidents have used this *Bible*.

President Herbert Hoover once stood in the Rapidan River in Virginia to fly cast for fish. What was so odd was that he fished in his suit.

Rutherford B. Hayes would sometimes lock himself in a bathroom when there was a lot of commotion in the White House. He did this so he could get some work done.

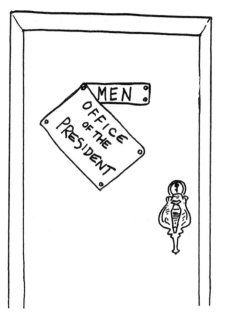

Lyndon Johnson had a Texas barbecue on the White House roof.

Men who chewed tobacco must have felt happy in 1829. That was the year Andrew Jackson installed twenty spittoons in the White House parlors.

Chester Arthur, like William McKinley, always wore a flower in his lapel.

When Lincoln learned that his Secretary of War, Simon Cameron, was running the War Department to make money during the Civil War, he forced Cameron to resign the post. At a cabinet meeting he told the members, including Cameron, "War isn't very fair. Some men get killed; others make a killing."

Of the seventy-seven young men who entered West Point in 1839, only thirty-nine graduated four years later. Among those was U.S. Grant, who ranked in the lower half of the class.

During his two terms, Grover Cleveland vetoed more bills (508) than all the previous Presidents combined. Cleveland said he deserved a monument, "not for anything I have done, but for the foolishness I have put a stop to."

In the early morning of January 18, 1862, just past midnight, John Tyler died. His last words, spoken to his bedside doctor and in the presence of his wife, were, "perhaps it is best."

On occasions when his wife was his bridge partner, Dwight Eisenhower threw his cards down in disgust and left the table. He couldn't understand why she would play a certain card.

Ronald Reagan's nickname, "Dutch," came from his father. John Reagan said his baby son looked "like a fat Dutchman."

Rutherford B. Hayes vetoed the Chinese Immigration Bill, which would have restricted thousands of Orientals from entering the U.S. He announced he would not wound the pride of "a polite and sensitive people."

Benjamin Harrison told listeners at his inauguration in 1889, "The masses of our people are better fed, clothed, and housed than their fathers were…. Not all of our people are happy and prosperous…but on the whole, the opportunities to the individual to secure the comforts of life are better than are found elsewhere."

"How Firm a Foundation" was the favorite hymn of both Presidents Jackson and Theodore Roosevelt. Shortly before he died at the Hermitage, Jackson requested that it be sung at his bedside. Calvin Coolidge observed, "It is only when men begin to worship that they begin to grow."

In May of 1993 President Bill Clinton was interviewed by New York radio host Don Imus. Clinton remarked, "There are always going to be people who want to be President, and some days I'd like to give it to them."

On April 9, 1965, Lyndon Johnson became the first President to see a baseball game in a domed stadium. The Yankees beat the Astros, 2-1, in the first exhibition game played in the Astrodome. Mickey Mantle hit the first indoor home run.

The first American to receive the Nobel Peace Prize was Theodore Roosevelt. Though a proponent of the "Big Stick" policy, TR used force only when he believed it necessary. He donated his Nobel Prize money to charity.

Harry Truman wanted the nation to stage an elaborate funeral for him after he died. He told a friend, "It'll be a damn fine show. I'm just sorry I'm not going to be around to see it."

Winston Churchill said about his encounters with our thirty-second President, "Meeting Franklin is like opening a bottle of champagne."

Facing certain re-election at age 60, George Washington told Thomas Jefferson that his memory was fading.

The Ronald Reagan Presidential Library opened November 4, 1991. It was completed at a staggering cost of $56.8 million.

The White House averages nearly 7000 visitors a day. However, only ten rooms are open to the public. The remaining 122 rooms are off limits.

When the War of 1812 began, President Madison felt a bit unprepared. There were only eight generals in the country, and most of them were politically appointed.

Regarding the Civil War, U.S. Grant once explained, "I would not have the anniversaries of our victories celebrated, nor those of our defeats made fast days and spent in humiliation and prayer; but I would like to see the truthful history written."

James A. Garfield had the largest head of our Chief Executives. His hat size was about 7 5/8 inches, and all of his hats were specially made. Calvin Coolidge had the smallest – his hat size was 7 1/8.

Taft was the first President to own a car.

Benjamin Harrison's first teacher, Harriet Root, felt her young pupil was very bright and determined, but added that the boy was "terribly stubborn about many things."

As a baby in 1790 John Tyler gazed into a night Virginia sky and stretched out his hand to grab the shining moon. At this his mother remarked, "This child is destined to be a President of the United States, his wishes to fly so high."

Though Ronald Reagan saved seventy-seven people from drowning at Lowell Park, Illinois, few people thanked him. One man, however, rewarded the young lifeguard with ten dollars for retrieving his dentures from a river bottom.

At age nine, a mischievous Grover Cleveland wrote in a school report, "If we expect to become great and good men and be respected and esteemed by our friends, we must improve our time when we are young."

To demonstrate his interest in economizing the government, President Herbert Hoover donated the horses in the White House stables to the U.S. Army.

In early February of 1917 Woodrow Wilson vetoed a congressional act excluding all Asians from the country. The previous week he vetoed a bill requiring literacy tests for immigrants, but Congress passed the measure over his veto. Wilson was a true friend of the immigrants.

During the Presidential campaign of 1912, Woodrow Wilson stated, "Whatever may be said against the chewing of tobacco, this at least can be said of it, that it gives a man time to think between sentences."

Voting fraud is nothing new in American politics. In the 1844 election between Polk and Clay, the two candidates combined polled a total of 55,000 in New York City. That's 10,000 more than the number of registered voters in the city then!

Nixon was often uncomfortable when meeting female heads of state. He thought that India's Indira Gandhi was arrogant and anti-American. And when Imelda Marcos of the Philippines entered the White House under a cloud of perfume, Nixon had warned an aide, "Don't leave me alone with that woman."

During the winter of 1777-78 at Valley Forge, George Washington saw 3000 American soldiers die from disease, hunger, and freezing temperatures. Scores of others deserted. More than one-fourth of his army was lost.

During the war against England in June of 1813, the country was virtually leaderless. President Madison was gravely ill, and spent several months of convalescence at his Virginia home.

White House chef Henry Haller worked for five different Presidents, from LBJ to Reagan. In all of that time the only Chief Executive he knew who actually cooked was Gerald Ford, when Ford invited the press to watch him make English muffins.

George Bush's last act as President took place in the White House before leaving to attend Bill Clinton's inauguration. He wrote a letter to his successor, put it in an envelope, and placed it in the desk inside the Oval Office. Neither Bush nor Clinton revealed the note's content.

President Gerald Ford reminded his fellow Americans, "Let us remember our national pride is our most valuable asset."

Theodore Roosevelt observed, "The man who loves other countries as his own stands on a level with the man who loves other women as much as he loves his wife."

Former President Harry Truman and his wife, Bess, refused to allow any Secret Service men in their Independence, Missouri, home.

England's Prime Minister, Margaret Thatcher, once lamented about Ronald Reagan, "Poor dear, there's nothing between his ears."

Part of Theodore Roosevelt's ninety-six-acre home at Sagamore Hill includes the family's pet cemetery.

James Madison wrote that "self-interest is the engine of government."

Would John Kennedy run for governor or the U.S. Senate? In early 1952 he pointed to the Massachusetts State House and told a friend, "I hate to think of myself up in that corner office deciding on a sewer contract." He ran for the Senate and won.

Some people questioned whether Gerald Ford was fit to be President. He left no doubt in people's minds when he announced, "I am disgustingly sane."

On one Christmas Day Theodore Roosevelt watched three of his four sons chase a turkey with hatchets on the south White House lawn.

On December 30, 1877, Rutherford and Lucy Hayes reenacted their wedding as part of their silver anniversary celebration. The same pastor, and most of their friends who attended the ceremony twenty-five years earlier witnessed this event.

In 1844 Abraham Lincoln was practicing law and working on Henry Clay's Presidential campaign. But he found time to write several lengthy poems. His poetry was published in a small book nearly 150 years later.

In the years following his Presidency, Herbert Hoover read and personally answered an average of 40,000 letters a year – for a period covering more than thirty years!

Richard Nixon said there was one rule for a successful politician: "Never let a dollar touch your hand."

Former President Dwight Eisenhower was buried on his grandson's birthday. David Eisenhower was twenty-one.

Everyone in Lyndon Johnson's immediate family had the same initials – LBJ. Even one of his favorite puppies was dubbed "Little Beagle Junior."

Grover Cleveland warned his countrymen, "The Ship of Democracy, which has weathered all storms, may sink through the mutiny of those on board."

In 1798 the U.S. came very close to declaring war on France. Appropriations were made, and President John Adams named a commander-in-chief to lead the American Army. He nominated George Washington. Though retired and in failing health, Washington accepted the position, but war was averted.

Harry Truman was small and frail as a child. He also wore thick expensive glasses, and his mother did not allow him to take part in contact sports or rough activities. The thirty-third President later admitted, "I was kind of a sissy. If there was any danger of getting into a fight, I always ran."

John Adams yearned for the simpler things in life. He once stated, "As much as I converse with sages and heroes, they have very little of my love and admiration. I long for rural and domestic scenes, the warbling of birds and the prattling of my children."

At the age of ten Harry Truman was wheeled in a baby carriage. He had contracted diphtheria, and his mother took special precautions to transport the weakened youth.

During a trip to Vermont in 1791, James Madison and Thomas Jefferson were arrested for riding in a carriage on Sunday, an illegal activity at the time.

Theodore Roosevelt reminded us, "The boy can best become a good man by being a good boy – not a goody-goody boy, but just a plain good boy."

President Gerald Ford dropped by his alma mater, the University of Michigan, to watch football practice. A former lineman, Ford was also known for his notorious golf shots. Center John Vitale told the President he needed to work on his golf game.

After learning he had been elected President, Governor Woodrow Wilson of New Jersey remarked to his wife, "Now we can't go to Rydal" (in England where they had spent several happy summers).

Lincoln, like FDR, was a habitual sleepwalker in the early years of his marriage.

John F. Kennedy probably took more baths than any President. This was largely due to his ailing back which constantly needed soaking in hot water.

James K. Polk's last words were whispered to his wife: "I love you, Sarah, I love you."

In 1851 Millard Fillmore could be heard loudly singing his favorite tune, *Old Folks at Home*, accompanied on the piano by his daughter Mary Abigail.

President Harry Truman invited film star Shirley Temple to his inauguration. She gave the President a pen and piece of paper and requested an autograph. Truman refused, saying, "You should know better than that, Shirley!"

Martin Van Buren observed, "The second, sober thought of the people is seldom wrong, and always efficient."

Dwight D. Eisenhower was bald, and so was his Secretary of Treasury George Humphrey. One day "Ike" remarked to Humphrey, "I see you part your hair the way I do."

One of the horses Grant captured during the Civil War was one owned by Mrs. Jefferson Davis. Grant dubbed his prize "Little Jeff" and rode him while his favorite steed, Cincinnati, rested.

After leaving the White House, an exhausted James K. Polk remarked, "I now retire as a servant and regain my position as a sovereign."

In the 1864 election Lincoln did quite well back in his home township of New Salem, Illinois. He received 208 votes; his opponents got three.

Ex-President John Tyler had to find some faults with Lincoln. The confederate Virginian protested that the sixteenth President offended the English-speaking world with his natural grammar and earthy, homespun speeches.

Our ninth Chief Executive, William Henry Harrison, observed, "All the measures of the Government are directed to the purpose of making the rich richer and the poor poorer."

James Garfield realized the White House was far removed from main street America. He stated, "The President is the last person in the world to know what the people really want and think."

The first two letters Lyndon B. Johnson wrote as President were to Caroline and John Kennedy, Jr., expressing his grief over the death of their father.

The "Church of Presidents" is St. John's Episcopal Church, just across Lafayette Square by the White House.

One month before he left office, President Ronald Reagan was asked by a college student what he would do after he retired. Reagan explained that he would remain active, then added, "In Hollywood, if you don't sing or dance you end up as an after dinner speaker."

Woodrow Wilson was absolutely correct when he announced, "I can predict with absolute certainty that within another generation there will be another world war if the nations of the world do not concert the method by which to prevent it."

Benjamin Harrison was wrong on at least one point when he remarked at a banquet in Detroit on February 22, 1888, "I am a dead statesman, but a living and rejuvenated Republican." Harrison was elected President the following November.

President Herbert Hoover said of his position, "This is not a showman's job. I will not step out of character."

There had been no dancing at the White House for nearly twenty-five years, until Andrew Johnson held a rollicking "Juvenile Soiree" for 400 young members of a dancing academy in December of 1868.

While in Paris during the early years of the American Revolution, John Adams remarked to his son, John Quincy, "The longer I live and the more I see of public men, the more I want to be a private one."

Calvin Coolidge used this analogy to describe the Presidency: "Like the glory of a morning sunrise, it can only be experienced – it cannot be told."

Abraham Lincoln considered George Washington "the mightiest name on earth."

Chester Arthur was an expert fisherman and could cast his trout-fly line accurately up to seventy-eight feet.

At a Union League Club banquet at Delmonico's Restaurant in New York City, Chester Arthur, then Vice President, told friends, "If it were not for the reporters, I would tell you the truth."

When Lyndon Johnson asked a friend for a candid opinion of the image he projected on television, he was told, "It's a cross between Machiavelli and a river boat gambler."

Quipped Eisenhower, "People want peace so much that governments had better get out of their way and let them have it."

In 1947 Ronald Reagan posed for magazine ads promoting Royal Crown Cola.

While serving as governor of Massachusetts, Calvin Coolidge wrote his only book, *Have Faith in Massachusetts*.

Benjamin Harrison refused to campaign outside of Indiana for the office of President.

Grant reduced his philosophy of war to four words: "When in doubt, fight."

Andrew Jackson once remarked, "War is a blessing compared with national degradation."

The practice of shorthand was first used in 1858 when reporters were sent to Illinois to record the Lincoln-Douglas senate debates.

Though he may have been a wealthy land owner, George Washington had to borrow money in order to make the journey to New York for his inauguration.

When James A. Garfield's presidential powers of appointments were challenged by political bosses, he told Whitelaw Reid, "Of course, I deprecate war, but if it is brought to my door the bringer will find me at home."

When his granddaughter was born in 1929, President Hoover commented, "Thank God she doesn't have to be confirmed by the Senate."

Woodrow Wilson said the Presidency is an office where "a man must put on his war paint."

Lincoln did not understand finances very well. But he did know that, during the Civil War in 1863, horses cost the government $125 a piece.

The war in Korea had just ended; another war in Vietnam had already begun. President Eisenhower in June of 1954 told the Joint Chiefs of Staff, "There is no victory except through our imagination."

James Buchanan observed in his last year as Chief Executive, "What is right and what is practicable are two different things."

At the height of his political career, Chester Arthur said to a friend, "Honors to me now are not what they once were."

After leaving the White House, our nineteenth President, Rutherford B. Hayes, remarked he was "heartily tired of this life of bondage, responsibility, and toil."

Frank Pierce knew his limitations. In his inaugural address on March 4, 1853, he told his listeners, "You have summoned me in my weakness; you must sustain me by your strength."

James Polk felt no one with presidential ambitions should be part of the cabinet, saying such a person would be "an unsafe advisor."

Thomas Jefferson wrote in an 1816 letter, "Where the press is free and every man able to read, all is safe."

"Courage is an opportunity which sooner or later is presented to us all," voiced John Kennedy.

Calvin Coolidge revealed a well-known work habit: "I don't work at night. If a man can't finish his job in the daytime, he's not smart."

Woodrow Wilson observed, "A man who never changes his mind is dead."

Upon reflection, Millard Fillmore noted, "Had I been chosen President again, I am certain I could not have lived another year."

How did Franklin Pierce feel about becoming President? He informed friends, "You are looking at the most surprised man that ever lived."

Comparing vocations, Lyndon Johnson remarked, "My White House job pays more than the public school systems, but the tenure is less certain."

James Buchanan advised his niece, White House hostess Harriet Lane, "A long visit to a friend is often a great bore. Never make people twice glad."

Lincoln observed that the press "was the only link or cord which connects the people with the governing power."

The day before resigning from the Presidency, Richard Nixon remarked to his special counsel Fred Buzhardt that many of the people visiting the Oval Office left in tears. Trying to maintain a sense of humor, Nixon added, "It ought to be me that's doing the crying."

As governor and President, Jimmy Carter was always punctual, explaining that being on time "has been almost an obsession." Even during hectic political campaigns, Carter rarely deviated from a set schedule.

James Buchanan spent much of his retirement justifying his conciliatory policies when he wrote a book entitled, *Mr. Buchanan's Administration on the Eve of the Rebellion*. It was not a best seller.

Once as a youngster John Kennedy lost a sailboat race. He explained to his crew (which included brother Ted), "Winning is important but loving sailing is even more important."

One of Grover Cleveland's political friends complained about the twenty-fourth President, "He would rather do something badly for himself than have somebody else do it well."

During the War of 1812 John Tyler became a captain of Virginia volunteers. He resigned, however, and returned to the state legislature after one month because his company had seen no action.

When Millard Fillmore ran for President in 1856 on the Whig/Know-Nothing ticket, he carried only one state – Maryland.

While the Nixon administration was crumbling under the Watergate scandal, son-in-law David Eisenhower cajoled advisors and White House staff people into a Whiffle Ball Home Run Derby, the object being to hit the ball over the fence of the President's tennis courts.

Rutherford and Lucy Hayes liked to retire early. When Hayes felt it was getting near bedtime, he instructed the Marine Band to play *Home, Sweet Home* after dinner, hoping the White House guests would take the hint and leave.

When Martin Van Buren presided over the Senate as Vice President, two loaded pistols lay beside him.

Chester Arthur said the White House looked like "a badly kept barracks." He insisted it be renovated. For three months he slept in the house of John Jones, returning to the mansion in December of 1881.

According to John Kennedy, the most underrated President was James Madison.

James A. Garfield told a group of friends on election night in 1880, "I am proud, yet there is a tone of sadness running through this triumph which I can hardly explain."

The undertaker's fee for embalming the body of Abraham Lincoln totaled $7,459 – a hefty sum in 1865.

Lincoln once observed, "If you look for the bad in people you will sure find it."

Regarding William Howard Taft's huge proportions, it was said he was molded between "two six foot parentheses."

Even wounded men in battle are sometimes forced to fight. In defending Fort Harrison, Indiana, in September of 1813, Zachary Taylor ordered rifles to the "sick and indisposed" to repulse a frenzied Indian attack.

As a star center on the University of Michigan football team, Gerald Ford helped his squad go undefeated three consecutive seasons: 1932, '33, and '34.

In 1840 William Harrison refused to announce his views on any controversial issue. Democrats dubbed him "General Mum."

During the Civil War government officials intercepted mail sent by Confederate spies and sympathizers to Northerners. One dispatch from a known conspirator was addressed to former President Frank Pierce, who opposed Lincoln's ideas on preserving the Union and abolishing slavery. Lincoln read this letter, then had it forwarded to Pierce.

Rutherford B. Hayes believed as a youth he would someday achieve greatness and power, reflecting "but the more I learn, the more I feel my littleness."

During Harding's tainted administration in 1922 the Republicans lost seventy-six seats in the House and eight seats in the Senate, but still maintained a majority in both Houses.

Calvin Coolidge's favorite brand of cigars were Fonseca Corona Fines de Luxe, a twenty-one cent black Havana.

While swimming in Mosquito Creek, young William McKinley nearly drowned. As he went down, he was rescued by Jacob Shealer.

The first National Monument was selected on September 24, 1906, by Theodore Roosevelt. He named Devils Tower in Wyoming, which rises 865 feet above the Belle Fourche River.

In December of 1928 a plot to kill President Hoover by blowing up his train as it traveled from Chile to Argentina was thwarted by Buenos Aires police.

John Tyler was a great uncle of Harry Truman.

In 1784 Andrew Jackson taught school for a term in the Waxhaw region between North and South Carolina. Frustrated, he left to study law.

Theodore Roosevelt once counted more than twenty varieties of birds on the grounds of the White House.

FDR said Presidential aides should have "a passion for anonymity."

In a letter in June of 1829, Franklin Pierce explained, "My doctrine is that almost everything depends on ourselves. We can be satisfied if we will."

In assuming the Presidency on March 4, 1837, Martin Van Buren told a large inaugural crowd, "I tread in the footsteps of illustrious men…. In receiving from the people the sacred trust confined to my illustrious predecessor Andrew Jackson."

James K. Polk worked very hard as Chief Executive, and died just three months after leaving office. In his diary, he noted on January 28, 1847, "In truth, though I occupy a very high position, I am the hardest working man in the country."

Grant's great-grandfather was Captain Noah Grant, killed in battle during the French and Indian War in 1756. His grandfather was also Captain Noah Grant, who served in the Continental Army during the entire American Revolution.

Herbert Hoover played shortstop on the Stanford University baseball team. He was also the equipment manager.

Frank Pierce was a good reader. As an elementary pupil in a brick schoolhouse in Hillsboro, New Hampshire, he spent much of his recess tutoring slow learners.

Little Harry Truman nearly choked to death on a peach pit. His mother saved his life by forcing the seed down his throat with her fingers.

Andrew Johnson was not much of an athlete. His favorite activities were checkers, gardening, and attending the circus.

At Kenyon College in Gambier, Ohio, Rutherford B. Hayes took part in a class revolt, refusing to take his chemistry exam.

James Monroe was among twenty-five firebrand patriots who raided the Royal Governor's Palace in Williamsburg to steal 200 muskets and 300 swords to help arm the militia. He was seventeen years old at the time.

On the subject of Manifest Destiny and expansion, Benjamin Harrison in 1888 commented, "We Americans have no commission from God to police the world."

William Henry Harrison noted, "The newspapers must not be taken too seriously."

In his diary, President Rutherford B. Hayes lamented, "Nothing brings out the lower traits of human nature like office seeking."

As the nation approached the coming of civil war, Millard Fillmore told Congress in December of 1852, "Let us remember that revolutions do not always establish freedom."

Franklin D. Roosevelt was the first incumbent Chief Executive to visit the Soviet Union.

As a youngster Calvin Coolidge earned spare money selling popcorn balls and apples at town meetings in Plymouth, Vermont.

Lincoln said, "No man, whether he be a private citizen or President of the United States, can successfully carry on a controversy with a great newspaper, and escape destruction, unless he owns a newspaper equally great...."

Thomas Jefferson inherited a 1000-acre plantation at the age of fourteen.

On October 10, 1792, the revolutionary National Assembly of France conferred French citizenship upon three Americans: George Washington, Alexander Hamilton, and James Madison.

As the youngest President ever elected up to that time, U.S. Grant told the Inaugural Day crowd on March 4, 1869, "The office has come to me unsought; I commence its duties untrampled."

During Lincoln's first year in office armed soldiers hid in the shrubbery encircling the Executive Mansion. Reserve troops with rifles and bayonets stayed in the basement.

In 1930 former President Calvin Coolidge dedicated a dam on the Gila River in Arizona. It was named in honor of, you guessed it, Calvin Coolidge.

In running for re-election in 1912, President Taft won only two states – Vermont and Utah. Woodrow Wilson won forty and Theodore Roosevelt six.

James Buchanan's assessment of John Quincy Adams was not very complimentary, explaining, "His disposition is as perverse and mulish as that of his father."

What did Calvin Coolidge consider his greatest achievement as President? "Minding my own business," he said.

Commenting on the subject of people seeking political appointments, Thomas Jefferson warned the public, "Whenever a man has cast a longing eye on offices, a rottenness begins in his conduct."

Woodrow Wilson once described Chester Arthur as "a non-entity with side whiskers."

Lieutenant Harry Truman was about to leave for France to fight the Germans in 1918. He informed his worried fiancée, Bess Wallace, not to fret. "Don't worry about me not taking care of myself.... I'm going to use my brains, if I have any, for Uncle Sam's best advantage and I'm going to aim to keep them in good working order, which can't be done by stopping bullets."

Lincoln received many telegrams from crackpots. He referred to these dispatches as "crazygrams."

Benjamin Harrison was the first President with a billion dollar budget appropriated by Congress.

Warren G. Harding once quipped, "When I was a boy I was told that anybody could become President; I'm beginning to believe it."

James Buchanan noted, "There is nothing stable but Heaven and the Constitution."

As Zachary Taylor lay dying at the White House on July 5, 1850, his doctor told him, "You have fought the good fight, but you cannot make a stand."

In a message to Congress in 1929, President Hoover told the members, "If law is upheld only by government officials, then all law is at an end."

James Monroe was a great President, at least in the eyes of John Quincy Adams, who claimed Monroe had built a nation of brick and "left her constructed of marble."

Eisenhower stated in his memoirs, "Anyone who goes into politics becomes public property the day he does so."

U.S. Grant was not beyond playing practical jokes. The President sometimes gave out trick cigars to friends and enemies alike. Once lit, the cigars would explode.

During one particularly busy time at the White House in June of 1993, President Bill Clinton told a *Newsweek* reporter, "It was like hell week around here!"

As a freshman in the U.S. Senate in 1934, Harry Truman confessed, "I'm as ignorant as a fool about everything worth knowing."

Released documents in 1993 have revealed there were at least eight plots to assassinate Cuban leader Fidel Castro during the Kennedy administration. The earliest attempt involved Mafia leaders recruited by the CIA.

By 1782 James Madison had 118 slaves.

Noting Ronald Reagan's boyish nature and youthful image before the television camera, Gerald Ford once quipped, "Reagan has prematurely orange hair."

While attending high school in rural Texas during the 1920s, Lyndon Johnson worked as a shoe shine boy.

President Grover Cleveland was rather unhappy with newspaper reporters. In a speech at Harvard University he remarked, "Oh, those ghouls of the press!"

Under increasing pressure to resign office because of the Watergate scandal, President Richard Nixon felt his legal staff was not only outnumbered, but outmaneuvered by the opposition. A frustrated Nixon lamented, "If we only had some bright young people around! We need some *minds!*"

Calvin Coolidge put it in simple terms when he observed, "When things are going all right, it is a good plan to let them alone."

George Bush wears his watch on his right hand. That's because he is left-handed.

James Madison said he preferred being home rather than attend all the inaugural festivities.

As a youth, Andrew Jackson was teased a lot. His habit of slobbering attracted the attention of other children. Such criticism usually resulted in a fist fight.

Because of his addiction to cigars, Grant was dubbed "Smoky Caesar" by the press.

After meeting President Andrew Johnson, Charles Dickens stated he would pick him out anywhere "as a character of mark."

George B. McClellan kept the Union Army in camp for months, refusing to attack Lee's forces. Having many more men and supplies, Lincoln tried to convince him to take the initiative. He personally asked the general, "How can you be a hero on the field of inaction?"

John Kennedy was the first incumbent President to visit Ireland.

Franklin D. Roosevelt once remarked to Hollywood giant, Orson Welles, "You and I are the two best actors in the world."

While John Tyler played the violin, his wife Julia strummed the guitar.

Herbert Hoover was the first President to have a phone on his desk.

Ronald Reagan served 8000 pounds of jellybeans at his inauguration. He began eating them after he quit smoking.

FDR was the first President to leave the U.S. by air, and the first one to celebrate a birthday aloft. These events took place aboard the *Dixie Clipper* in 1943.

Shortly before his death in January of 1933, Calvin Coolidge looked with bewilderment at the tremendous changes throughout a depression-ridden nation. He quipped, "I feel I no longer fit in with the times."

The Fillmores were a musical family. In just a little more than a year a piano tuner, Jacob Hilbus, made nine calls at the White House. He tuned pianos, organs, and harps at the Executive Mansion for each President from Monroe to Pierce.

What is work like for a President? Grover Cleveland once observed, "When I left my breakfast table and went to my office, it used to seem that a yoke was placed around my neck from which I could not escape."

James and Lucretia Garfield made certain their five children all had music and dancing lessons. The seventeen-year-old son, Hal, was a gifted pianist, and the President often slipped upstairs to hear his oldest son play on the Bradbury upright piano.

FDR had no misgivings about going to war. He voiced, "We would rather die on our feet than live on our knees."

Jefferson reminded his fellow countrymen, "The boisterous sea of liberty is never without a wave."

"The dead do not need us, but forever and forever more we need them," voiced James A. Garfield.

Lyndon Johnson started school when he was four-years-old.

Richard Nixon was keenly aware of his lengthy nose, but never really minded when photographers took his picture. He once mentioned, "The ski nose never hurt Bob Hope."

Gifts of food sent to the White House are never accepted – the food is destroyed.

When the Trumans ate outside the White House on the lawn, Harry would slip bits of food under the table to feed a squirrel.

When the Hardings held a birthday party for their Airedale, Laddie Boy, they invited neighborhood dogs to the White House celebration. The cake consisted of layers of dog biscuits topped with icing.

Thomas Jefferson predicted that "no man will ever bring out of the Presidency the reputation which carries him in."

Theodore Roosevelt explained, "Taft meant well, but he meant well feebly."

When Jefferson attended his inaugural ceremonies on March 4, 1809, he told a friend, "You must tell me how to behave, for it is more than forty years since I have been to a ball." Indeed, it had been four decades since Thomas Jefferson had last danced.

Jefferson's birthplace, *Shadwell*, near Charlottesville, was also the home of his mother. On February 1, 1770, it burnt to the ground. A slave broke the news to him: "Master, the old place is burnt down. Everything's gone." Then he added, with a touch of sincerity, "Not all. We saved your fiddle."

Thomas Jefferson's favorite mounts were The General and Caractacus, which he rode during the Revolutionary War period.

Jefferson's last written words were entered into his account book on June 21, 1826: "Issacs for cheese 4.84."

In 1907 Secretary of War William Howard Taft visited Russia where he met Czar Nicholas II. To Taft's delight, he was presented a huge cake, adorned with Russian and American flags bearing the date of the Mayflower landing.

Regarding Gerald Ford's pardoning of Richard Nixon from all Watergate crimes, Ford told an advisor, "It could easily cost me the next election if I run again. But, damn it, I don't need the polls to tell me whether I'm right or wrong." Ford was right on both counts.

William Howard Taft's mother often reminded people that her infant son laughed continuously.

Theodore Roosevelt was an avid reader. One of the articles he packed on his safari in 1909 was his "Pigskin Library," which contained more than sixty books, stashed in a aluminum case, and wrapped with oil cloth. In the evenings, T.R. and his son, Kermit, would devote time to the classics in the wilds of Africa.

Calvin Coolidge's silence was purposeful. He once explained, "I have noticed that nothing I never said ever did me any harm."

James Earl Carter officially changed his name to Jimmy.

For his service in the Mexican War, Franklin Pierce was nicknamed "Young Hickory of the Granite Hills." But the New Hampshire senator fell far short of the military deeds of "Old Hickory" Andrew Jackson.

Not all Presidents look upon editorial cartoonists with disdain. Abe Lincoln said, "Thomas Nast has been our best recruiting sergeant." Nast's cartoons focused attention on Copperheads and other Northerners who sympathized with the South during the Civil War. Years later, Nast's cartoons broke the corrupt "Boss" Tweed ring in New York City.

Ronald Reagan has had his share of *lipus linguiis*. He once stated that "trees pollute more than humans."

Prior to his fireside chats and radio presentations, FDR called in a Navy medic to spray his throat and treat his sinuses to give him his marvelous baritone voice.

Jimmy Carter's mother, Lillian, joined the Peace Corps at age sixty-eight! The former nurse who advanced racial equality in Georgia died in 1983.

George Bush observed, "The importance of the White House doesn't come from its occupants, but from it's owners – the American people."

William McKinley was the first incumbent to ride in a automobile. Reaching a speed of eighteen miles per hour, the President almost lost his hat and didn't enjoy the ride.

In January of 1994 Bill Clinton visited Boris Yeltsin in Russia. He was treated to a fancy dinner, eating caviar and moose lip!

On April 13, 1883, President Chester Arthur invited the Cleveland Forest Citys to the White House. He told these baseball players, "Good ballplayers make good citizens."

Grover Cleveland didn't think much of physical activity. He once said that "bodily movement is among the dreary and unsatisfactory things of life."

In selecting native tribesmen as guides and porters for his African safari, ex-President Theodore Roosevelt carefully chose his men from several different tribes. In this way they were unable to communicate with each other, thus minimizing the danger of plotting, mutiny, and murder among rival tribesmen and the white hunters.

General Zachary Taylor was so small he needed help each time he mounted his horse.

U.S. Grant once ran a billiard parlor to support his family.

Calvin Coolidge once quipped, "A man who builds a factory builds a temple."

Grover Cleveland observed, "My father used to say that it was wicked to go fishing on Sunday, but he never said anything about draw-poker."

Theodore Roosevelt told an audience, "Let us not pray for a light burden, but a strong back."

In his later years John Adams was reported to have chosen these words for his epitaph: "Here lies John Adams, who was responsible for keeping peace with France in 1800."

In a letter written in 1820, Zachary Taylor offered some advice on the American fighting man: "Better to have a practical, then a theoretical soldier…but when a soldier can combine both, it gives him every advantage."

"The best customer of American industry," said FDR, "is the well-paid worker."

When reporters wanted to know President Reagan's golf score and handicap, White House spokesman Larry Speakes informed them, "It is a state secret."

"Judges are as honest as other men, and not more so." Thus said Thomas Jefferson.

During the year in which he was nominated and elected President (1860), Abraham Lincoln lost nearly forty pounds.

When Theodore Roosevelt toyed with the idea of seeking an unprecedented third term in 1912, his wife, Edith, advised him to "put it out of your mind. You will never be President again." She was right.

Woodrow Wilson referred to all women he liked as "my little girl" – even those older than he.

President Reagan once secured the votes of four Louisiana Democrats by promising to provide a support program for sugar. When a reporter asked one of them if this meant Reagan's vote could be bought, he replied, "No, but it can be rented."

Whenever Millard Fillmore returned home from business trips, he gave his wife books. She had been his teacher, and Fillmore remarked that his wife, Abigail, was a "notable reader."

During the War of 1812, President Madison's tobacco crop sold for three cents a pound. Just two years after the war, he sold his tobacco for fourteen cents a pound.

One of Washington's moral maxims was, "Few men have virtue to withstand the highest bidder."

Jefferson offered this valuable piece of advice: "In matters of principle, stand like a rock; in matters of taste, swim with the current. Give up money, give up fame, give up science, give up the earth itself and all it contains, rather than do an immoral act."

After signing the European peace pact in Helsinki, Finland, in August of 1975, Gerald Ford remarked, "Peace is not a piece of paper."

In a speech on George Washington's birthday in 1866, Andrew Johnson told listeners, "The time has come to take the Constitution down, to unroll it, reread it, and to understand its provisions thoroughly."

FDR once wrote a movie screenplay entitled *"Old Ironsides,"* but could not get any Hollywood studios to buy it.

The first Chief Executive to start the habit of smoking cigarettes was Chester A. Arthur.

The first President younger than fifty-years-old was James K. Polk. He was forty-nine when he entered the White House in 1845.

John Quincy Adams was a habitual "skinny-dipper." He continued to use the Potomac River for this purpose until he was eighty years old.

"Maintaining slavery," observed Jefferson, "was like holding a wolf by the ears – you didn't like it, but you didn't dare let it go."

On the subject of determination, Gerald Ford said, "I'll make hours of sacrifice – whatever efforts are needed. Some people call it plodding."

Woodrow Wilson observed, "We grow great by dreams. All big men are dreamers."

Our first President once wrote, "I hope I shall always possess firmness and virtue enough to maintain what I consider the most enjoyable of all titles, the character of an honest man."

In writing his book, *Profiles in Courage*, John Kennedy remarked, "Being courageous requires no exceptional qualifications, no magic formula, no special combination of time, place, and circumstance. It is an opportunity that sooner or later is presented to us all."

U.S. Grant once remarked, "There never was a time when, in my opinion, some way could not be found to prevent the drawing of the sword."

All four sons of FDR and Eleanor Roosevelt served in World War II. Each one saw action in combat and each was highly decorated.

Travel from the White House to his home near Nashville took Andrew Jackson twenty-five days by carriage.

Lincoln was always quick to remind people that his jokes and stories were not his own. In his unassuming, modest way, he explained, "I remember a good story when I hear it, but I never invented anything original. I am only a retail dealer."

George Washington's most famous racehorse was Magnolia, but it was his trusty Nelson which carried him through much of the Revolutionary War. Another horse, Blueskin, sometimes was used to give Nelson a rest.

Brothers Milton and Dwight Eisenhower not only looked alike, their voices were similar too. Both were practical jokers and during the 1920s each brother called the other man's wife on the phone pretending to be the husband. The wives never caught on.

Jefferson had this to say about college educators: "We should propose that the professors follow no other calling, so that their whole time may be given to their academical functions." Maybe he felt most teachers could do little else!

On November 27, 1920, President Calvin Coolidge remarked, "Civilization and profits go hand in hand."

John Kennedy remarked, "War will exist until that distant day when the conscientious objector enjoys the same reputation and prestige that the warrior does today."

One of James Roosevelt's jobs at the White House prior to joining the U.S. Marines was autographing photos for his father, FDR.

As a young man in southern California, Richard Nixon worked as a bean picker, a swimming pool janitor, and an amusement park barker.

The first incumbent President to attend a minor league baseball game was George Bush. This was in 1990 in Hagerstown, Maryland.

President James Monroe could trust his personal secretary – it was his brother, Joseph.

In 1904 Theodore Roosevelt invited Apache Indian chief Geronimo to ride in the inaugural parade.

Richard Nixon's White House breakfasts were neither time-consuming or elaborate. Each morning the President spent just a few minutes downing his wheat germ, orange juice, and milk.

FDR's favorite number was 100. He used this number on several of his license plates.

Harry Truman believed there were three prerequisites for anyone qualified for high public office: banking, farming, and serving in the military. Truman, of course, served in all three capacities.

At their sister's wedding on April 24, 1954, the three Kennedy brothers stood on the dais behind the bride and groom (Peter Lawford) and sang to the newlyweds. The lyrics were specially written by songster Sammy Cahn.

Lyndon Johnson taped several thousands of hours of conversations while he was President. Many have been released to the public.

The interaction between baseball and the Presidency took firm hold when Grover Cleveland invited Cap Anson's champion Chicago White Stockings to the White House during his first term.

Lyndon Johnson reminded his fellow Americans, "I don't get ulcers. I *give* them."

On both occasions as he was sworn in as President, Harry Truman lowered his head and kissed the *Bible*.

Journalist William Allen White met William McKinley but was not impressed with the Presidential candidate. He wrote that McKinley was "on the whole decent, on the whole dumb," and added, "He walked among men like a bronze statue...determinedly looking for his pedestal."

During Eisenhower's eight years as Chief Executive, his wife Mamie set foot in the Oval Office only four times.

Though World War II had been over for two years, Harry Truman asked Americans to observe meatless Tuesdays and no chicken on Thursday. Truman sought to feed starving Europeans.

Referring to U.S. air supremacy over the Nazis, FDR stated, "Hitler built a fortress around Europe but he forgot to put a roof on it."

Eisenhower was the first incumbent President to visit Paris since Woodrow Wilson.

In the first two years of his administration Abraham Lincoln wrote 230 personal letters. In the next two years he wrote more than 1100.

A high-ranking army officer, guilty of shameful acts in repeated drunken sprees, had his case dismissed by President Andrew Johnson. The Chief Executive remarked, "Any man who fought as he did may get drunk as often as he pleases."

During the Civil War a friend asked former President Millard Fillmore if he would accept a nomination and run against Lincoln. Fillmore wrote in response, "I can assure you in all sincerity that I have no desire ever to occupy that exalted station again, and more especially at a time like this."

Lincoln held high regard for farmers, stating, "Cultivators of the earth are the most valuable citizens." He felt farmers were independent-minded, virtuous, and wedded to the best interests of the state.

Near the end of his second term President Jefferson acknowledged, "A short conference saves a long letter."

In 1776 John Adams acknowledged, "When annual elections end, there slavery begins."

As a member of the Third Congress, James Madison represented a newly-shaped district which included Madison County. It had been carved out of Culpepper County and named in his honor.

Thomas Jefferson's favorite horse was Wildair.

A year after his inauguration George Washington signed a congressional act which provided for a national capital. It was designated as "Grand Columbian Federal City," later referred to as "Federal City" and eventually Washington, District of Columbia.

The oldest Presidential birthplace still standing is "Old House" (formerly "Peacefield") in Quincy, Massachusetts, now called Braintree. Built in 1681, it was the birthplace of John Adams.

James Madison was not just a legislator. He was also an amateur scientist. He was fond of dissecting small animals such as rabbits and squirrels.

In the spring of 1864 General George Meade met with Grant, expressing concern that the Confederate army still had great determination to win the war. Meade observed that the enemy seemed inclined to make a cat fight of the affair, and Grant supposedly answered, "Our cat has the longest tail."

Franklin D. Roosevelt was a moderately heavy smoker. By April of 1944 he had cut down from twenty-five cigarettes a day to five. But years of smoking helped contribute to the President's problems with arteriosclerosis and heart disease.

Martin Van Buren commented to his law partner in 1828, "Is it possible to be anything in this country without being a politician?"

At the battle of Tippecanoe in 1811 William Henry Harrison's horse was shot through the neck. Its rider had bullets pass through the rim of his hat and graze his head. In other military action, Harrison was wounded twice more, including a hip wound at Fort Meigs.

At his first inaugural Eisenhower reminded his countrymen, "…in the final choice, a soldier's pack is not so heavy burden as a prisoner's chains."

Jimmy Carter spent much of his childhood fishing for "stumpknockers" and "redbellies" with black and white youths.

Jefferson observed that, "Pride costs us more than hunger, thirst, and cold."

Warren Harding's last trip in 1923, via train and boat, was dubbed the "Voyage of Understanding."

After leaving the White House, Franklin and Jane Pierce spent two years on the island of Madeirá, Portugal. Jane had tuberculosis, and her husband was an alcoholic.

Martin Van Buren married Hannah Hoes in 1807. She was not only a childhood sweetheart, but a distant cousin.

Rutherford B. Hayes was not even President when he confided in his diary just three months before he was nominated, "In politics I am growing indifferent. I would like it, if I could now return to my planting and books at home." Hayes had served as a three-term Ohio governor but nevertheless actively sought the Presidency.

John Quincy Adams once commented to his wife, Louisa, "I will die the moment I give up public life."

Warren G. Harding supposedly remarked to a group of political friends after his election to the White House, "We're in the Big Leagues now, boys. We're going to play ball." Unfortunately, Harding played ball badly, committing many errors.

Richard Nixon believed one could never really win in politics, stating, "Victory is never total."

Dwight Eisenhower once told a crowd in Peoria, Illinois, "Farming looks mighty easy when your plow is a pencil and you're a thousand miles from a corn field."

As President, Lyndon Johnson declared war on poverty. It was a war many felt Johnson lost. In a magazine interview the ex-President stated, "If I became dictator of the world I'd give all the poor a cottage and birth-control pills – and I'd make damn sure the didn't get one if they didn't take the other."

John Adams must have had some doubts about taking his seat in the Continental Congress. In May of 1770 he wrote his wife, Abigail, that he had "consented to my own ruin, to your ruin, and the ruin of our children. I give you this warning, that you may prepare your mind for your fate."

FDR observed, "A good leader can't get too far ahead of his followers."

In a message to Congress in 1883, Chester A. Arthur declared, "It is not part of our policy to create and maintain a navy able to cope with that of other great powers of the world."

On July 4, 1776, Thomas Jefferson not only signed the Declaration of Independence, he also bought his first thermometer. It read seventy-six degrees.

Harry Truman had the oldest Vice President – Alban Barkley, who was seventy-four years old when he left office. Incidentally, the term "Veep" was first used with Barkley when his ten-year-old grandson used the contraction.

When Martin Van Buren ran for re-election in 1840, he became the only Presidential candidate to seek election without a running mate.

"Our Country Right or Wrong" was the 1852 Democratic campaign slogan for Frank Pierce. It helped elect him as our fourteenth President.

William Howard Taft felt the shadow of Theodore Roosevelt on his administration. A frustrated Taft stated, "There is no use trying to be a William Howard Taft with Roosevelt's ways. Our ways are different."

Lyndon Johnson observed, "Poverty has many roots but the tap root is ignorance."

William Henry Harrison's first few months in the army in 1791 were spent as recruiting officer. American recruits were paid $2.10 a month.

President Harding played a number of musical instruments. On several occasions he practiced with the Marine Band during rehearsals at the White House.

Gerald Ford woke up one Christmas morning to find a *Playboy Magazine* in his gift stocking. He believes his son, Steve, put it there, but wife Betty indicates it could have been her.

As President, Harry Truman said he signed his name an average of 600 times a day.

Dwight Eisenhower is the only U.S. President who does not have a town or city bearing his last name.

When Andrew Johnson purchased Alaska from the Russians in 1867, the press dubbed the acquisition as "Seward's Folly" (after Secretary of State William Seward) and "Johnson's Polar Bear Garden."

In his youth John Adams wanted to be a minister. As he grew older he realized, however, that his independent, out-spoken opinions might generate much controversy. He became a lawyer instead.

Calvin Coolidge had lost much of his hair by the time he was President. But then the origin of the name Calvin means "bald one."

During their twenty-nine years of marriage, Woodrow and Ellen Wilson exchanged more than 1400 love letters.

George Washington got around quite a bit. As commander-in-chief during the Revolutionary War, he established his army headquarters in sixty-five different communities in seven states.

While Richard Nixon was visiting China, one American newsman asked, "How do you like the Great Wall, Mr. President?" Nixon looked at the structure and replied, "I must say the Great Wall is a great wall!"

Calvin Coolidge remarked, "I think the American public wants a solemn ass as President and I think I'll go along with them."

Having only six months of schooling, Lincoln often felt inadequate in spelling and composing sentences. He once told Noah Brooks that punctuation was a matter of feeling rather than education. Lincoln found the semicolon to be "a very useful little chap."

John Kennedy won a Pulitzer Prize for his book *Profiles in Courage*. When the youthful Senator ran for the Presidency in 1960, Eleanor Roosevelt remarked that the young candidate was "more profile than courage."

Jimmy Carter, a confirmed Christian and a minister, was often disturbed by the antics of his flamboyant brother, Billy. The hard-drinking Billy embarrassed the First Family several times. In 1977 he stated the "Christians should be thrown to the lions."

George Washington believed that even more important than scholars, statesmen, or artists, were mothers.

Gerald Ford did not seek the Presidency. "My personal ambition," he said, "had always been to be Speaker of the House, but I never got enough votes...."

Grant held great respect and confidence in his friend, William Tecumseh Sherman. During the Civil War some critics tried to discredit Sherman, but Grant and Lincoln both decided to retain him as a commander of the Union forces. Sherman later remarked, "Grant stood by me when I was crazy, and I stood by him when he was drunk, and now we stand by each other."

Thomas Jefferson warned, "An injured friend is the bitterest of foes."

In 1856 Andrew Johnson pointed out, "Slavery exists. It is black in the South, and white in the North."

The first funeral conducted at the White House was probably in 1807 when a child born to Fanny and Davey, two of President Jefferson's slaves, died. The baby had been born in the basement servant's quarters.

John Quincy Adams' White House guests were often exposed to strong odors. The stables were located near the West Wing, and on summer evenings the smell of manure permeated the State Dining Room.

Presidents Andrew Jackson and James K. Polk, both from Tennessee, were always looking for ways to cut costs. Both men replaced some of the White House staff with slaves from their estate.

In the early 1830s gardening enthusiast Martin Van Buren toured the English countryside, including King William IV's retreat at Windsor Castle. He took extensive notes and when he returned to Washington, Van Buren encouraged landscaping on the White House grounds where he would preside just a few years later.

Andrew Johnson's position on reconstruction made him many enemies. One day, after vetoing a congressional bill, he met with some Senators and asked them, "Did you hear my last speech?" Came a reply, "I hope so!"

Jefferson once noted, "The man who reads nothing at all is better educated than the man who reads nothing but newspapers."

Franklin Pierce observed, "Men are dwarfs; principles alone are abiding."

Just before he died, George Washington told his physician, "Doctor, I die hard, but am not afraid to go."

Lincoln's lunch usually consisted of an apple and a glass of milk. This came several hours after his breakfast of a slice of toast and a cup of coffee.

James Madison's meticulous note taking of the Continental Congress in 1787 was an arduous task. He attended every session for five months, later admitting the ordeal "nearly killed me."

FDR named his Presidential railroad car the *Ferdinand Magellan*.

Theodore Roosevelt reminded us at the turn of the century, "Wildlife and trees are the property of unborn generations."

The residence of the Chief Executive is a busy place. More than one and a half million visitors a year take a public tour of the White House. In addition, official guests at receptions and dinners total more than 50,000 annually.

President Hoover once issued an order that no staff member was to pet his dog, King Tut. The dog was becoming too accustomed to the affection from White House employees and ignored its master when he called.

John Quincy Adams was not one to hand out compliments to people. He went one step further in his criticism of President William Henry Harrison. On Inauguration Day, 1841, Adams described the horse on which Harrison rode as "particularly mean-looking."

Before leaving office, Dwight Eisenhower gave newly-elected President John Kennedy some valuable advice: "There are no easy matters that will come to you as President. If they are easy, they will be settled at a lower level."

Lincoln was constantly prodding General McClellan to move his large army against the outnumbered rebels, but the general found many excuses to delay action. McClellan's forces and supplies were nearly double those of the enemy, and Lincoln compared sending troops to him like "shovelling fleas across a barnyard – only half seem to arrive."

When a reporter asked President George Bush what deficit-reduction proposals he would deliver to the Democrats in Congress, he responded, "It's a very good question, very direct, and I'm not going to answer it."

Tensions in the Middle East were running high in 1984. Following a half-hour lecture by the Lebanese Foreign Minister on the complex realities of his country's political factions, President Reagan remarked, "You know, your nose looks just like Danny Thomas'."

Zachary Taylor's horse, Whitey, was brought to the White House to live with its master. But grazing on the White House grounds proved detrimental to the horse. Souvenir hunters plucked his tail until not a single hair remained.

James Buchanan employed his nephew, Buck Henry, as his personal secretary. The fifteenth President was very strict with the young man. Buchanan ordered him sternly about, admonished him in public, and opened and read his mail. Buck was not even allowed to lock his bedroom door.

Franklin Pierce was the first Chief Executive to have a full time bodyguard. Talk of secession and Civil War made Washington, D.C., a dangerous city. Nevertheless, Pierce often rode his horse, Union, through the streets in the evening, accompanied by a guard.

William Henry Harrison was known as the "Log Cabin-Hard Cider President." One Sunday in March of 1841 he appeared in church wearing a pair of white silk gloves with brightly colored log cabins on them.

Andrew Johnson had a barber's chair installed in his private White House bathroom.

Noted James Madison, "The advancement and diffusion of knowledge is the only guardian of true liberty."

On his two trips to Europe by ship, Woodrow Wilson spent six months away from the White House. No doubt his long absence weakened his political base and undercut his power.

Gerald Ford had the White House swimming pool removed, saying later, "You don't need a pool in the White House to get in deep water."

William McKinley was not much of a football fan. After watching a Yale-Princeton game, he expressed his disappointment and remarked, "It was no game at all. They got into a scrap and kept fighting all the time they should have been playing ball."

In campaigning for the Presidency in 1960, JFK told his elegant, aristocratic and often aloof wife, "I don't think the American people are ready for a woman like you." He was, of course, wrong. Jackie Kennedy campaigned hard for her husband, and added a touch of class to the White House.

Andrew Johnson once announced, "I'll campaign against any man who votes against free education."

George Washington said, "Liberty, when it begins to take root, is a plant of rapid growth."

Dwight Eisenhower observed, "Pessimism never won any battle."

After only a week in office Lincoln was besieged by office-seekers. One stopped him in a carriage and shoved his recommendation papers at the new President. Lincoln frowned and shouted, "No! I won't open shop in the street!"

When Lyndon Johnson boarded *Air Force One*, he wasted little time. After stepping aboard the jet, it was taxiing down the runway within ten seconds.

In 1977 Jimmy Carter ordered the Presidential yacht *Sequoia* be sold. He considered the pleasure boat an "unnecessary thrill."

Andrew Jackson had many friends – and a lot of enemies too. There were more than 200 threats and attempts to kill him.

John Kennedy observed, "If we are strong, our character will speak for itself. If we are weak, words will be of no help."

George Bush often showered with First Dog Millie. It was the only way he could get the pooch clean.

Theodore and Franklin Roosevelt were both noted oologists – people who collect and study bird eggs.

In December of 1990 former President Ronald Reagan told an audience, "Before Christmas I like to curl up at night with a good book – my checkbook. It's the only way I can keep my wife from using it."

Abraham Lincoln entered the Black Hawk War as a captain and came out a private.

Calvin Coolidge noted, "No person was ever honored for what he received. Honor has been the reward for what he gave."

The last book FDR read was *The Punch and Judy Murders* by Carter Dickson. It was left open to page seventy-eight, the beginning of a chapter entitled, "Six Feet of Earth." At 1:15 P.M., on the afternoon of April 12, 1945, the President suffered a cerebral hemorrhage and died a couple of hours later.

In June of 1845 Andrew Jackson wrote his last two letters before his death – both to President James K. Polk.

"The care of human life and happiness…is the first and only legitimate object of good government," said Thomas Jefferson.

At the end of his term, Millard Fillmore remarked that the most exciting thing that happened to him in office was singer Jenny Lind's visit to the White House. The 1850 tour of the "Swedish Nightingale" brought packed houses and standing room only in nearly every city.

In his farewell address George Washington reminded his countrymen to behave themselves, and that national morality demands religious principles.

Jimmy and Rosalynn Carter gave some tips on life after retirement: plan ahead, find meaningful volunteer work, be aware of the pressure of time, and attend college classes.

James Buchanan defined his lifelong philosophy of compromise and conciliation by declaring, "This federal government is nothing but a system of restraints from beginning to end."

John Quincy Adams once said, "My sense of duty shall never yield to the pleasures of party."

Calvin Coolidge once observed, "If you don't say anything you won't be called upon to repeat it."

The ever-philosophical Theodore Roosevelt noted, "Both life and death are part of the Great Adventure."

The first toast made by a President in the White House was purportedly made by John Quincy Adams on September 6, 1825. As the Marine Corps Band played the 'Marseillaise,' Adams proposed a toast in honor of his guest, Lafayette.

In 1938 President FDR told an audience, "If the fires of freedom and civil liberties burn low in other lands, they must burn brighter in our own."

When Ohio sculptor Tom Jones made a bust of Abraham Lincoln in 1860 he asked the President-elect what he thought of the results. Replied Lincoln, "I think it looks very much like the critter." The marble bust stands today just outside the Senate Chamber at the State House in Columbus.

After listening to Enrico Caruso sing, Theodore Roosevelt is reputed to have remarked, "There have been many Presidents, but only one Caruso."

The Adams home in Braintree, Massachusetts was sometimes used as an emergency hospital during the Revolutionary War.

James Madison was an epileptic, and Thomas Jefferson had a slight speech impediment.

As Chief Executive Benjamin Harrison created seventeen national parks.

"The knowledge of words is the gate of scholarship," said Woodrow Wilson.

The first President to kiss the *Bible* after repeating his inaugural oath was the first President, George Washington.

In his inaugural address, John F. Kennedy reminded Americans that "if a free society cannot help the many who are poor, it cannot save the few who are rich."

The first code clerk hired by the federal government worked for President James Monroe and his Secretary of State John Quincy Adams. Among his duties was deciphering secret messages.

U.S. Grant's parents refused to attend the wedding of their son and daughter-in-law Julia Dent of Missouri. The Dents owned several slaves, and the Grants disapproved.

Woodrow Wilson was so distraught over the death of his first wife, Ellen, that he openly expressed a desire to be assassinated so he could join her in heaven. He soon recovered and married widow Edith Galt.

The 600 acres of land donated by the state of Virginia made up part of the District of Columbia. But this wasn't enough, so in 1791 George Washington completed negotiations with nineteen other landowners for more space. Washington, D.C. now contains sixty-nine square miles of land.

In 1948 Congress passed a law that anyone threatening the life of a President by mail was subject to a $1000 fine or five years imprisonment, or both.

The White House has had at least 32 coats of paint on its exterior since it was built in 1800.

Several Presidents have had daughters married in the White House. But only one had a son married there – John Quincy Adams. His son, John, married Mary Hellen there in 1828.

The first woman counselor to a President was Anne L. Armstrong. She was hired by Richard Nixon.

Richard Nixon typified the competitive spirit, and once stated, "I never in my life wanted to be left behind."

In response to a suggestion to run for the Presidency, Zachary Taylor said, "The idea of my becoming President seems too ridiculous to think about."

As he lay very ill on his bed, James Madison looked up at his wife and remarked, "I always talk better lying down."

James Polk dreaded farm work. He thought farm animals were stupid and their smell rotten. Skipping his chores, he hid in the barn to read or work on math problems. Soon, his father apprenticed him out as an assistant cloth maker.

At a White House Christmas party during Andrew Jackson's administration, Vice President Martin Van Buren entertained many children. After losing a game of plate spinning, he was forced to strut around the room, gobbling like a turkey.

Jefferson once quipped, "Science is my passion; politics my duty."

Dwight D. Eisenhower was often bored by GOP "big wigs." Just prior to leaving office, he told some dinner guests at the White House, "They say I'm not a politician but I will say this–I am a better politician than most of those around me."

While he was still eighteen years old Gerald R. Ford, Jr. was nicknamed "Junie."

President Chester Arthur was very concerned about time, so he called for an international meeting to determine standard time zones.

As Lieutenant Governor of Massachusetts, Calvin Coolidge adhered to a creed which hung on a plaque above the fireplace at his Northampton home:

> A wise old owl lived in an oak;
> the more he saw the less he spoke.
> The less he spoke the more he heard;
> why can't we be like that old bird?

Harry and Bess Truman often referred to the Executive Mansion as "The Great White Jail."

Weary of being a college professor at Princeton, Woodrow Wilson once confided to a friend, "I am tired of a merely talking profession. I want to do something." A couple of years later he became governor of New Jersey, and a year after that, President.

On the occasion of a serenade at the White House, Lincoln was called by a crowd to appear and make a few brief remarks. He came to the window with his petite wife and announced, "Here I am, and here is Mrs. Lincoln. That's the long and the short of it."

In 1787 Thomas Jefferson wrote his sister, "I love those most whom I loved first."

James Garfield said, "Poverty is uncomfortable, as I can testify; but nine times out of ten the best thing that can happen to a young man is to be tossed overboard and compelled to sink or swim for himself."

Columnist Franklin P. Jones, referring to frequent gaffes by Gerald Ford, defined Presidential error as "Fordian slip."

George Washington became a major in the Virginia volunteer militia at age nineteen.

James K. Polk was the oldest of ten children born in his family.

When Millard Fillmore was eighteen-years-old he took his small earnings as a tailor's apprentice and bought a dictionary.

As a boy, "Teddy" Roosevelt collected hundreds of specimens – flowers, rocks, insects and small animals. He once put some mice in the ice box, but Mom threw them out. Muttered Roosevelt, "What hurt me is the loss to science."

In 1987 *The Union Register* asked, "So what if Reagan's Cabinet members pass a drug test? Wouldn't you rather see them pass an IQ test?"

Shortly before his death, President Warren Harding announced, "Understanding. That is what the world and the nation most need."

Martin Van Buren once wrote, "To yield to necessity is the real triumph of reason and strength of mind."

John Adams often referred to his wife as "Dearest Friend."

At age twenty-five William Henry Harrison became secretary of the Northwest Territory, appointed by President John Adams in 1798. Two years later he became the first governor of the Indiana Territory.

In 1898 Dwight Eisenhower was seven years old and worked for his uncle, Abraham Lincoln Eisenhower, in Abilene, Kansas. He was paid one penny a day, doing odd jobs and running errands for his veterinarian uncle.

Assuming the Presidency after Garfield's death, Chester A. Arthur said, "My sole ambition is to enjoy the confidence of my countrymen."

In 1941 President Franklin Roosevelt wanted to create a national conservation institute and name it in honor of our twenty-third President, Benjamin Harrison, an avid environmentalist and outdoorsman. World War II broke out, however, and the idea was forgotten.

John Kennedy was quite competitive. A friend once asked him if he ever minded quitting games. "Not as long as I'm winning," he said.

Calvin Coolidge observed, "Few men are lacking in capacity, but they fail because they are lacking in application."

The last note Grant wrote was the day before his death. Dying of throat cancer and unable to speak, Grant noticed his clock chimed only eleven times, even though it was noon. He scribbled an order to his son, "Fix the clock right. It only struck eleven."

While commanding the American Army in 1777, George Washington stated, "Nothing is more agreeable, and ornamental, than good music." And Thomas Jefferson referred to music as "the favorite passion of my soul."

Speaking of music, the polka was first danced at the White House in February of 1845 during a farewell gala for President John Tyler.

Gerald Ford was not much of a music fan. He once stated, "Betty said I can't even *listen* on key."

James Monroe noted, "Peace is the best time for improvement and preparation of every kind; it is in peace that our commerce flourishes most, that taxes are most easily paid, and that the revenue is most productive."

While visiting the Shoshone and Arapaho Indians in 1883, President Chester Arthur accepted an Indian pony. It was sent to the White House in the fall and he gave it to his daughter Nell.

Weary of European royalty and its pompous egos, ex-President Theodore Roosevelt said, "If I ever meet another king, I think I shall bite him!"

Though never in the military, John Adams did more than his share in serving his country. As a member of the Continental Congress during the Revolutionary War, Adams served as chairman of thirty committees and was an active member on several others. In addition, he was a special envoy overseas in procuring aid for the struggling nation.

Herbert Hoover reminded us, "Freedom is the open window through which pours the sunlight of the human spirit and of human dignity. With the preservation of these moral and spiritual qualities will come future greatness."

As the story goes, when John Kennedy first went to Congress as Representative of Massachusetts' Eleventh District, he was mistaken for a page boy as he tried to get past the guards to enter the House Chamber on Capitol Hill.

Lincoln once told some friends, "All that I am, or hope to be, I owe to my angel mother."

In his Inaugural Address Grover Cleveland informed his listeners, "The government you have chosen me to lead is yours."

Warned U.S. Grant, "Too long denial of guaranteed right is sure to lead to revolution – bloody revolution, where suffering must fall upon the innocent as well as the guilty."

Mario Cuomo, governor of New York, once told of a meeting with President Reagan, who confused him with Chrysler executive Lee Iacocca. Said Cuomo, "I guess we (Italians) all look alike."

Thomas Jefferson reminded us, "Eternal vigilance is the price of liberty."

Leading his Union Army through Kentucky and Tennessee in 1862, James A. Garfield became very ill. He suffered so much from camp diarrhea that he lost thirty-five pounds. Worse than this was seeing many of his young volunteers from northeast Ohio succumb to pneumonia, scarlet fever and the like.

The longest sentence in an inaugural address probably goes to our second President, John Adams. His next to the last sentence contained more than seven hundred words.

No man whose name ends in *a, i, o,* or *u,* has ever been elected President. Only three have been President whose names ended in *e,* and just two Chief Executive's last names ended in *y.* These facts may demonstrate the point that few men of ethnic or foreign background can hope to occupy the White House.

According to published records, the book of Psalms has been used more than any other book of Biblical passages selected by Presidents for their inaugural oaths. The *Bible* was opened to Psalms on at least nine occasions, with Proverbs being used five separate times.

William Howard Taft weighed more than George Washington and Andrew Jackson combined.

Dwight Eisenhower sat for a Norman Rockwell painting in 1952. A cover portrait was used for the *Saturday Evening Post,* but the Presidential candidate didn't care much for it. Eisenhower remarked, however, that he believed the illustration brought him three million votes.

During Hoover's administration fifty revolutions took place in Latin America, and the U.S. did not intervene in any of them.

On one August Sunday morning in 1991 George Bush attended church services in Kennebunkport, Maine. One man in the congregation began praying aloud for peace. It got to be a bit excessive. The man was removed, and a judge fined him one hundred dollars for disrupting the church service.

During a trip through New England in 1867, President Andrew Johnson stopped at Yale to address some students. In his speech he told them that his one regret was his failure to choose the right profession – he should have been a schoolteacher. Johnson was the only U.S. President who never attended school.

U.S. Grant's moment of glory in the Mexican War came when his regiment accompanied Winfield Scott's army into Mexico City in 1847. Along with a small party of men, he dragged a cannon into a church belfry and fired with devastating effect on Mexicans defending a city gate. Not long after this, Grant retired from the army to earn more money for his family, but he failed at several business ventures.

Presidents traditionally throw out the first baseball when the major leagues begin play in April. But Warren G. Harding "threw a curve" when he failed to throw out the ball at an Opening Day game for the Washington Senators. The President refused because he had a sore arm.

Teddy bears became cherished toys after the turn of the century, but this was not the only toy inspired by Theodore "Teddy" Roosevelt. One toy company found success when it produced a whistle, depicting a large set of gleaming teeth, which fit over the mouth. It was called "Teddy's Teeth."

In his autobiography, Calvin Coolidge thought people in high office "are always surrounded by worshipers. They are constantly, and for the most part sincerely, assured of their greatness." He further cautioned they live in an artificial atmosphere "of adulation and exaltation which sooner or later impairs their judgment."

Benjamin Harrison was the first incumbent President to attend a major league baseball game. On June 2, 1892, he watched two National League teams, Washington and Cincinnati, play an eleven inning contest. The Reds beat Washington 7-4.

Andrew Jackson used opium. Doctors prescribed the medicine to ease the ex-President's pain and discomfort. Suffering from tuberculosis, chronic diarrhea, blindness, and infection, "Old Hickory" died in 1845.

A television newscaster made this announcement: "Mrs. Julie Nixon Eisenhower has decided not to visit a clinic for the mentally retarded in Dubuque, Iowa. Instead she will visit her parents, President and Mrs. Nixon, at their oceanside villa in San Clemente, California."

Following a promotion during the Civil War, Benjamin Harrison wrote his wife, "If my ambition is to soar anymore after I come home, you will have to give it wings." Apparently Caroline Harrison did just that. Her husband not only served as U.S. Senator, but was elected as our twenty-third President in 1888.

James Madison once asked, "What spectacle can be more edifying or more seasonable than that of liberty and learning, each leaning on the other for their mutual and surest support?" These words are carved in marble at the entrance of the Madison Annex of the Library of Congress.

President Taft's White House breakfast often consisted of a dozen eggs, eight pancakes, a pound of bacon, and several glasses of juice.

Two years before he died, James K. Polk wrongly predicted that "no President of the United States of either party will ever again be re-elected."

Though he wrote an autobiography, Martin Van Buren never once mentioned his wife, Hannah.

Grant's soldiers spared at least one city in the South. After capturing Port Gibson, Mississippi, the general remarked that it was "too beautiful to burn."

Lyndon Johnson was once introduced by the Governor of Michigan, who sang high praises to the President. In a rare display of humility, Johnson began his speech by saying, "I wish my mother and father might have been here to hear that introduction. My father would have enjoyed it, and my mother would have believed it."

When John F. Kennedy's top advisor and close friend, Ted Sorenson, was asked if it were he who wrote the famous line "Ask not what your country can do for you," Sorenson replied, "Ask not."

Debates in early Congress centered around the design of coins. Federalists wanted to place President Washington's likeness on a coin. With Washington's popularity so great, the proposal seemed a certainty. But James Madison spearheaded the opposition, and instead an emblem of liberty was substituted.

Theodore Roosevelt informs us that giraffes don't graze. They eat from trees, meaning they browse. He observed this while hunting big game in Africa, and he shot several giraffes for museums back in the U.S.

After a tumultuous four years as Chief Executive, William Howard Taft remarked in 1912, "I hope that somebody, sometime, will recognize the agony of spirit that I have undergone."

By 1790 George Washington had just one tooth, a lower left bicuspid.

Martin Van Buren achieved many milestones as an elected official. Though he was one of America's most powerful politicians, his happiest years were spent as a farmer at his retirement home at Lindenwald near Kinderhook, New York. Nothing could compare to working the land as "a farmer in my native town."

It was Lyndon B. Johnson's final moment in office, January 20, 1969. Richard Nixon was sworn in as the new President. He handed LBJ a blanket to ward off the chill. Nixon asked him how he felt, and the ex-President replied, "This is the happiest day of my life."

Television interviewer Barbara Walters described Richard Nixon as "most appealing and rather sexy."

As John Adams readied to move his administration from Philadelphia to new facilities in the District of Columbia, the number of federal clerks and officers totaled 126.

In July of 1986 ex-President Nixon was in Moscow on a private visit. Consoling some American losers in the Goodwill games being held there, he told them, "I've won and lost a few myself."

Martin Van Buren once bet $40,000 that he would win the Presidency, and won the wager!

Woodrow Wilson, son of a Presbyterian minister, once observed, "The secular year begins with a hangover and ends with overindulgence. The church year begins with hope and ends with fulfillment."

"There is no truth existing which I fear, as would wish unknown to the whole world." – Thomas Jefferson.

Lincoln left us with this piece of advice: "Nearly all men can stand adversity, but if you want to test a man's character, give him power."

Said Harry Truman, "Everybody has the right to express what he thinks. That, of course, lets the crackpot in. But if you cannot tell a crackpot when you see one, then you *ought* to be taken in."

Following Richard Nixon's resignation, Gerald Ford reassured his countrymen, "I believe that truth is the glue that holds government together, and not only government but civilization itself."

James Madison must have felt a bit relieved when his old political nemesis, John Adams, remarked, "…even with his thousand faults and blunders Madison's Administration has acquired more glory and established more union than all three predecessors, Washington, Adams, and Jefferson."

Abraham Lincoln said, "Quarrel not at all. No man resolved to make the most of himself can spare time for personal contention. Better give your path to a dog than be bitten by him."

President Theodore Roosevelt is responsible for setting aside no fewer than 230 million acres for national parks and sanctuaries.

Following FDR's death on April 12, 1945, Dr. Ross McIntire, the President's personal physician, received a cable from the State Department. It was a secret message from Russian dictator Joseph Stalin, requesting an autopsy on FDR because he suspected he had been poisoned. The doctor decided it wasn't even worth a response, except to say thank you.

Lincoln was familiar with sorrow, having lost two sons by the time he had been President. His comforting words remind us: "Sorrow comes to all…. Perfect relief is not possible, except with time. You can not now realize that you will ever feel better…and yet…You are sure to be happy again."

The first incumbent President to visit Western Indians on their own soil was Chester Arthur. In 1883 Arthur parleyed with Chief Washokie of the Shoshones, and did some fishing at Yellowstone National Park as well. The next President to pay the tribes a visit came two decades later when Theodore Roosevelt traveled west.

As he was leaving his home in Indianapolis, President-elect Benjamin Harrison addressed a large crowd from the back of a train. In a farewell speech he voiced, "The moment of decision is one of isolation."

William McKinley lay in bed for eight days after being shot by an assassin. The President sensed the end was near when, just a few hours before his death, he called the doctors to his bedside and announced, "It is useless, gentlemen. I think we ought to have prayer."

For the first few years the law firm of Lincoln and Herndon kept no books. Fees were evenly divided between the two. No receipts or bookkeeping entries were recorded.

Theodore Roosevelt once announced that there was "no greater issue than that of conservation."

When he was eleven and twelve years old, Abe Lincoln would come home from a church meeting, climb a stump, and repeat the day's sermon word for word.

In March of 1963 John Kennedy visited Arlington National Cemetery. He walked up a grassy slope and told his wife, "I could stay up here forever." It was on this same slope that Kennedy was buried after he was shot.

In poetic wisdom, Thomas Jefferson declared, "If a nation expects to be ignorant and free, it expects what never was and never will be."

Though *"The Star-Spangled Banner"* did not become an official song until 1931, President Woodrow Wilson designated it as the anthem of the U.S. military in 1916.

Andrew Johnson's daughter, Martha, married a relative of Abraham Lincoln's.

Of the first forty-two Presidents, eighteen of them have been of Irish ancestry.

Visitors to the nation's capital in 1827, while walking along Pennsylvania Avenue, could not help but notice the street was bordered with scraggly poplar trees, planted under the direction of Thomas Jefferson. It might be said Jefferson was a real "poplar" fellow.

Many references have been made to U.S. Grant's shyness. As a general in the field he always pinned the flaps of his tent securely when he took a bath. While other generals stood in a tub and had fellow officers rinse them down with a bucket of water, Grant preferred this ritual by himself.

President Benjamin Harrison used a rowing machine to get his exercise.

Martin Van Buren used gold spoons when he ate dinners at the White House.

Franklin D. Roosevelt's favorite sport was sailing.

Former President George Bush had two sons running for governor in 1994. George W. won in Texas and Jeb lost in Florida but eventually won four years later. And, of course, George W. was later elected President.

William Henry Harrison and his wife Anna had ten children.

In 1860 President-elect Abraham Lincoln wrote, "I regret the necessity of saying I have no daughter." The Lincolns had four sons.

Grant once read the lengthy novel *Ben Hur* in one thirty-hour sitting. Its author, Lew Wallace, was one of Grant's best generals in the Civil War, and was later sent to Turkey as the U.S. ambassador.

Prior to his death in 1826, Thomas Jefferson had debts amounting to $107,000, a staggering sum in those days. In an effort to pay his creditors, he set up a lottery to sell Monticello. There were no buyers, however, and his plans to raise the money were discontinued.

After his nomination to Congress in 1862, Brigadier General James Garfield faced a decision whether to continue serving in the Civil War or assume his seat in the House. He wrote, "I shall try the rough sea if the bullets will let me."

"America did not invent human rights. In a very real sense, it is the other way around. Human rights invented America." So said Jimmy Carter.

In 1848 Chester Arthur finished college and taught at a district school in Schaghticoke, New York. He received eighteen dollars a month.

George Washington remarked, "My temper leads me to peace and harmony with all men."

Former House Speaker "Tip" O'Neill had this to say about John F. Kennedy's terms in Congress: "I've never seen a Congressman get so much press while doing so little work."

Warren G. Harding once sold insurance.

Following Germany's defeat in World War I, President Woodrow Wilson went to the Paris Peace Conference via a converted German liner, renamed the *George Washington*. Previous to Wilson's trip the same ship took Harry Truman and hundreds of other "Yanks" over to France.

Harry Truman once told his wife about dying, "When my time comes, I want to go out like a light and not create a lot of business for hospitals, nurses, and doctors."

Though "Texas" was Theodore Roosevelt's favorite horse (and the one he rode in the Spanish-American War), "Pickle," "Diamond," and "Bleistein" were his riding horses back at Sagamore Hill.

James Madison's father had eighty-five books on his Virginia plantation, and by age eleven James had read them all.

After tens of thousands had died fighting the Civil War, Abraham Lincoln said that winning a war depended upon being able "to face the arithmetic."

Theodore Roosevelt gained forty pounds his first term as President.

When his son, Quentin, was shot down and killed in the skies over France in July of 1918, Theodore Roosevelt remarked, "I feel as though I was a hundred years old and had never been young."

Said Woodrow Wilson, "If we do not carry faith into politics, then politics takes the place of faith – and that is the end of justice, freedom, and charity."

Nineteen Presidents were sons of farmers.

Abraham Lincoln was a bit concerned with his son Robert, who failed fifteen subjects on his Harvard College entrance exam.

John Quincy Adams once quipped, "To believe all men honest would be folly. To believe no man is honest is something worse."

Harry Truman's first political job was that of a census taker in his home state of Missouri.

President Coolidge sometimes sat in his office with his feet in the wastepaper basket!

In April of 2001, the White House lawn got a new look. George W. Bush had a ball diamond built — to play whiffle ball.

Thomas Jefferson was the first American to introduce central heating for buildings.

President Franklin Pierce spent his first night in the White House sleeping on the floor. His bedroom was not yet finished.

Thomas Jefferson believed in "equal rights for all…special privileges for none."

William Henry Harrison dreaded that his body would be stolen from the grave after he died. He was actually buried in five different coffins – each inside the other.

Woodrow Wilson observed, "America lives in the heart of every man everywhere who wishes to find a region where he will be free to work out his destiny as he chooses."

Asked by a reporter why he didn't want to be President for another term, Calvin Coolidge remarked, "It's not too good a job. There's no room for advancement."

William Howard Taft was the first American President to see a Rose Bowl game.

In a 1912 speech to workingmen, Woodrow Wilson stated, "I believe in democracy because it releases the energies of every human being."

Quipped Rutherford B. Hayes, "Fighting battles is like courting girls: those who make the most pretensions and are the boldest usually win."

A Hawaiian fish and an Oregon elk were named for Theodore Roosevelt.

Dwight Eisenhower observed, "The spirit of man is more important than mere physical strength, and the spiritual fiber of a nation than its wealth."

After hearing Warren Harding had been elected President, famed defense lawyer Clarence Darrow once remarked, "When I was a boy, I was told that anybody could become President. I'm beginning to believe it."

John Quincy Adams gave his last speech in 1843 at the Wesley Methodist Episcopal Chapel in Cincinnati.

Said Jefferson, "Error of opinion may be tolerated where reason is left free to combat it."

Prince Charles and Princess Diana were guests of honor at a glittering White House reception in 1985. President Reagan, committing another one of his gaffes, rose and proposed a toast to the royal British couple: "To Prince Charles and Princess David."

Said William Taft, "Too many people don't care what happens so long as it doesn't happen to them."

President Jimmy Carter visited widow Mamie Eisenhower at Gettysburg one day. Upon leaving, he kissed her. Remarked the surprised First Lady, "My Lord, I didn't know what to do. I hadn't been kissed by a man outside the family since Ike died."

Vice President George Bush was touring the Middle East and asked a guide, "How dead is the Dead Sea?" The answer came back, "Very."

In 1786 George Washington went fox hunting fifty times.

While dealing with the vast problems of the Civil War, President Lincoln wrote, "I shall do nothing in malice. What I deal with is too vast for malicious dealing."

After a knee injury at West Point ended his football-playing days, Dwight Eisenhower revealed, "Life seemed to have no meaning. A need to excel was almost gone." His grades plummeted, but he still graduated in the top half of his class, while working as an assistant football coach.

Thomas Jefferson warned, "Beware of too much confidence in any man."

FDR pointed out, "People die, but books never die."

Prior to his Gettysburg speech in November of 1863, a war-weary Abraham Lincoln told a friend, "I have endured a great deal of ridicule without much malice; and have received a great deal of kindness, not quite free from ridicule."

In a speech to our northern neighbors, John F. Kennedy remarked, "Geography made us neighbors…. History made us friends…. Economics made us partners." Canadians agreed.

Ronald Reagan offered this advice: "Never start arguments with a woman when she is tired, or when she is rested."

During World War II the only hamburger stand in the South Pacific was the one run by Richard Nixon. Called "Nixon's Snack Shack," he served free hamburgers and Australian beer to flight crews.

To combat his suffering of Addison's Disease, doctors implanted a pellet in John Kennedy's thigh. Four times a year a compound of synthetic cortisone was slowly absorbed, giving him some relief.

As Chief Justice of the U.S. Supreme Court, William Howard Taft walked the six miles to the Court and back nearly every day. He needed the exercise and managed to keep his weight down to about three hundred pounds. At one time he weighed 355 pounds.

William Henry Harrison was nicknamed the "Eagle of the West."

President Gerald Ford declared the inflation was "Public Enemy Number One."

Martin Van Buren sounded like Thomas Jefferson when he observed, "The less government interferes, the better for general prosperity."

Warren G. Harding's last words were in the form of a question: "What did the [Cincinnati] Reds do?"

President Millard Fillmore found the summer heat and stagnant air so oppressive at the White House, he moved out one evening just to sleep in Georgetown.

John Adams reflected a few years after his single term, ended, "Had I been chosen President again, I am certain I could not have lived another year."

Lincoln once pointed out, "If slavery is not wrong, nothing is wrong."

John Quincy Adams was rather unkind to Martin Van Buren when he said of the New York Democrat, "His principles are all subordinate to his ambitions."

David and Ida Eisenhower had six sons. Dwight's mother once told a friend, "I spend all of my time keeping the boys out of other peoples' yards."

Herbert Hoover's proposal of marriage was sent by way of a cablegram from a mining camp in Australia.

How does one succeed? Harry Truman advised, "Make no little plans. Make the biggest one you can think of and spend the rest of your life carrying it out."

Franklin Roosevelt's mother, Sara, was somewhat overprotective. It wasn't until Franklin was nearly nine years old before he took a bath by himself.

John Tyler had no ambitions to become President. He said, "Such an idea never entered my mind. Nor is it likely to enter the head of any sane person."

Millard Fillmore was opposed to Republican ideals. Nevertheless, in 1861, he hosted newly-elected Abraham Lincoln for several days in his Buffalo home.

Chester Arthur was the last President born in a log cabin. Prior to his first birthday his family moved into a frame house.

Grover Cleveland lived an exciting, tumultuous life in Buffalo, New York, for thirty years. After a mud-slinging campaign for the White House, he described the city as "the place I hate above all others."

At one point during his Presidency in 1865, Andrew Johnson's former home in Greenville, Tennessee, was used as a brothel while Union forces occupied the city.

In 1954 Vice President Richard Nixon remarked, "Politics is war."

President Grover Cleveland did his best to avoid publicity, commonly referring to the press reporters as "the dirty gang."

James A. Garfield refused to permit any uniformed guards at the White House. He didn't want the public thinking the military or uniformed police guarded him.

Ohioan Rutherford B. Hayes planted a buckeye tree on the White House lawn in 1878. By 1918, however, it was gone, destroyed by a storm.

Though Willie Lincoln had been dead for months, the President sometimes visited the temporary tomb of his son while on carriage rides. On occasion Lincoln even ordered the tomb unlocked, and he lifted the metallic lid so he could look upon the boy's sleeping, angelic face.

The first telegraph installed in the White House was in 1866 by Andrew Johnson.

According to White House steward Hugo Zieman, President Benjamin Harrison once dozed off holding a banana in his hand and while he slept, the rats "pulled the banana from his hand and scampered away."

Dwight Eisenhower was born in Denison, Texas, but considered Kansas his home state. After the war in Europe was over, he remarked to some friends, "The proudest thing I can claim is that I am from Abilene…."

Two of the first three Americans depicted on a U.S. postage stamp were Presidents – George Washington and Thomas Jefferson. Ben Franklin was the other one.

LBJ's favorite dog was "Yuki," a small light colored stray picked up by his daughter Luci.

Jefferson once observed, "I like the dreams of the future better than the history of the past."

Gerald Ford admitted he was no handyman around the house. He no doubt realized this when he managed to hang a screen door upside down.

Sam Johnson once advised his son, Lyndon, "If you can't go into a room and tell at once who is for you and who isn't, you should stay out of politics."

Grover Cleveland was nominated for President in 1884 on the slogan, "We love him for the enemies he has made."

Millard and Abigail Fillmore of Buffalo, New York, had a personal library of more than 4000 books. Later, many of these stocked the White House library.

Rebekah Johnson once said of her son, "That boy Lyndon is going to wind up in the penitentiary. Just mark my words."

Richard Nixon once reflected on his California childhood: "I was the biggest crybaby in Yorba Linda. My dad could hear me even with the tractor running."

Ex-President Dwight Eisenhower enjoyed having his grandchildren with him at the Gettysburg home. That is, most of the time. Grandson David did incur the wrath of Grandfather at least once when David's Arabian horse got loose and destroyed Ike's putting green.

Harry Truman once observed, "Fiction is romantic adventure. For honest and wise teaching, read history."

During Warren Harding's Front Porch Campaign for the U.S. Senate at his home in Marion, Ohio, the front porch collapsed under the weight of well-wishers. It was replaced and later accompanied many more people when he ran for President in 1920.

John Tyler's son, John Jr., had a serious drinking problem, and the former President was well aware of it. When John Jr. visited the Tyler estate after 1845, he found the wine closet securely locked.

As Chief Justice, William Howard Taft described President Herbert Hoover as a "dreamer" with "rather grandiose views… much under the Progressive influence."

The first circus held in the U.S. took place in Philadelphia in 1793. George Washington attended one of its first performances.

Rutherford B. Hayes was prepared for any task. He once explained, "I shall show a grit that will astonish those who predict weakness."

Gerald Ford liked being President. Said Ford, "I can't wait to get to the office. Some days I am more disappointed than others, but I enjoy every day."

Harry Truman collected *Bibles.* He had more than five hundred of them, including paperback editions and elaborate illustrated volumes.

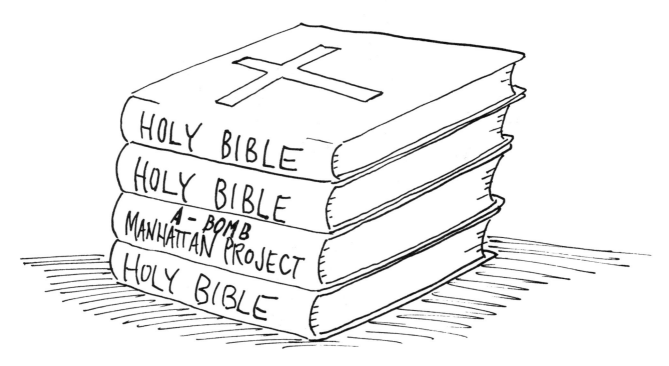

Abraham Lincoln was an avid reader of the *Bible.* Said Lincoln, "It is the best gift God has given to man. All the good the Saviour gave to the world was communicated through this book."

Woodrow Wilson once confided to a friend, "I feel sorry for those who disagree with me because I know they are wrong."

James Monroe was often criticized for his expensive formality because he complained that foreign diplomats constantly dropped in to the White House uninvited and expecting tea.

Calvin Coolidge's silence led to many stories, including a popular one about two men discussing the First Family. The first man pointed out that Grace Coolidge had taught the deaf to speak, and the second man inquired, "So why didn't she teach Cal?"

When Benjamin Harrison took office in 1889 the Republican Party controlled all three branches of the federal government. Being a weak President, and having a lot of haggling in Congress, the times were commonly referred to as "The Period of No Decisions."

In February of 1879 Rutherford B. Hayes signed a bill allowing women lawyers to argue cases before the U.S. Supreme Court.

President Tyler is not remembered for much, including his dedicating the Bunker Hill Monument in Boston on June 17, 1843!

To comfort the impending fear of conflict, President-elect Lincoln told a Cleveland crowd in 1861, "We North and South differ in opinion somewhat, but the crisis can't be argued up and it can't be argued down. Before long it will die of itself."

The first five Presidents had no middle names.

According to White House Chef Henry Haller, Ronald Reagan's favorite dish was macaroni and cheese.

As our ambassador to Russia in the early 1830s, James Buchanan observed Sundays as a holy day, even refusing to dance at the official court balls in St. Petersburg.

John Tyler's son, Alex, spent an unhappy seventeenth birthday. On April 9, 1865, he stood beside his confederate cannon at Appomattox where Lee surrendered to Grant.

Lincoln once observed that military glory "is the attractive rainbow that rises in showers of blood."

More than fifty color photographs were taken of John F. Kennedy's body during his autopsy. As of yet, only black and white pictures have been released to the public.

By the time he was fifteen years old, Chester Arthur had lived in eight different places. His father was a Baptist minister who lived in several parishes in Vermont and New York. Jack and Nell Reagan moved even more while their son Ronald was growing up.

John Tyler's Virginia estate, Sherwood Forest, had slaves, but Tyler forbid the use of chains or whips on his servants. He said, "My plan is to *encourage* my hands."

Zachary Taylor was born in Virginia but didn't remember it. He moved to Kentucky, near Louisville, when he was eight months old.

In 1855 ex-President Millard Fillmore visited England. Queen Victoria remarked that he was the most handsome man she had ever met.

Lincoln had two favorite tunes: "Battle Hymn of The Republic" and "Jimmy Crack Corn" (also known as "Blue Tail Fly").

The beauty of the outdoors is "too good for human beings," according to Grover Cleveland.

Growing up amidst poverty and hard work, James A. Garfield described his childhood years as "years of darkness."

After leaving the White House, Franklin Pierce was certain his administration had been "one of positive good or positive evil," but he wasn't sure which.

James Buchanan hated slavery, but believed it was protected by the Constitution. Several times he bought slaves in Washington and took them home to Pennsylvania where he set them free.

As a boy Lincoln had a pet pig. He taught it tricks and took him on trips with him. But when the day for slaughtering came, the boy cried over what he called "an awful tragedy."

Grant was seventeen-years-old when he arrived at West Point in 1839. He stood just 5'1" and weighed less than 120 pounds.

In 1901 Paul Dunbar, the celebrated, young Negro poet of Dayton, Ohio, was asked to ride in President McKinley's inaugural parade. Dunbar accepted the honor, but there was just one problem — he had never ridden a horse before.

All five copies of the Gettysburg Address which Lincoln personally wrote still exist. The fifth copy, considered the clearest and best, hangs in the Lincoln Room of the White House. It has been there since 1959.

The first President to ride in a helicopter was Dwight Eisenhower, in 1955.

Thomas Jefferson stated that banks were "more important than standing armies."

Harry Truman was a man of strong opinions, and had this to say about his successor: "The trouble with Eisenhower is he's just a coward. He hasn't got any backbone at all. Ike didn't know anything, and all the time he was in office he didn't learn a thing."

Grover Cleveland was not exactly an advocate of women's rights. He once told the *Ladies Home Journal*, "A good wife is a woman who loves her husband and her country with no desire to run either."

During the 1960 campaign, Harry Truman, in stumping for John Kennedy, told a crowd in San Antonio on October 11 that anyone who voted for Richard Nixon should go to hell.

FDR's bullet proof car had windows so thick that, when King George VI was riding to the White House on a warm afternoon, he didn't have the strength to roll them down. The king almost collapsed.

Jimmy Carter played college basketball. He was a starter at Georgia Southwestern Junior College.

George Bush flew fifty-eight combat missions as a naval pilot in World War II.

Andrew Jackson was perhaps destined for a life of confrontation and controversy. He was a fighter, and once remarked, "I was born for the storm. Calm does not suit me."

George Washington loathed slavery, but on rare occasion ordered the whip used on those who broke the rules. He cautioned overseers not to be extreme in administering punishment.

James Madison was the eldest of twelve children.

William Howard Taft was always big. His mother, Louise, noted, "He is very large for his age, and grows fat every day."

Woodrow Wilson told William McCombs in 1912, "God ordained that I should be the next President of the United States."

To prove he was physically fit, President Theodore Roosevelt once rode a horse 100 miles in one day.

Did John Kennedy possess the qualities needed to serve as President? He thought so. Kennedy once remarked, "Sure it's a big job. But I don't know anybody else who can do it any better than I can."

Both Lincoln and Jefferson Davis had the tune "Dixie" played at their inaugurations.

"True friendship is a plant of slow growth," said George Washington.

Harry Truman left us all with some good advice: "Men often mistake notoriety for fame, and would rather be rewarded for their vice and follies than not be noticed at all."

In 1940 the only delegate to the Democratic National Convention who refused to vote for FDR was Joseph Kennedy, JFK's father.

Richard Nixon said, "The true idealist pursues what his heart says is right in a way that his head says will work."

When a reporter asked Harry Truman what he did on his first day home after leaving the White House, he replied, "I took the suitcases up to the attic."

John F. Kennedy said, "The men who create power make an indispensable contribution to the nation's greatness. But the men who question power make a contribution just as indispensable – for they determine whether we use power or power uses us."

Dwight Eisenhower believed nominating conventions were a disgrace, saying they "resembled a rioting mob of juvenile delinquents." And Woodrow Wilson, remembering his 1912 victory at the Democratic convention after forty-six exhausting ballots, said, "There ought never to be another Presidential nominating convention…."

Feeling the increasing burden of the Watergate scandal, President Richard Nixon asked Nelson Rockefeller with sarcasm, "Can you imagine Jerry Ford sitting in this chair?" Ford confronted Nixon after he had heard this criticism, but the President denied making the remark.

As a boy Gerald Ford had a terrible stuttering problem. This severity of speech may have been related to his ambidexterity. Ford was left-handed while sitting down, and right-handed standing up. He would throw a ball with his right hand, and use a pen with his left.

Before moving from West Branch, Iowa, following his parents' death, Herbert Hoover's boyhood friends were Ironheels and Yellowrobe. These two boys were members of a nearby Indian tribe in 1880.

In his book *Leaders*, Richard Nixon noted, "I had learned long before never to ask a sick man how he feels, because he may tell you."

On Ronald Reagan's first date with Nancy Davis, he arrived on crutches. He had broken his leg in a charity baseball game.

Theodore Roosevelt once provided this insight concerning our republic: "Man can never escape being governed…I believe the majority of the plain people of the United States will, day in and day out, make fewer mistakes in governing themselves than any smaller class or body of men, no matter what their training, will make in trying to govern them."

Kennedy's christened name was John Fitzgerald *Francis* Kennedy.

Congressman Robert LaFollette explained that his colleague, William McKinley, was a magnetic speaker. When interrupted in a speech or debate, instead of lashing out at a person, McKinley would say, "Come now, let us put the personal element aside and consider the principle involved." Throughout his life McKinley rarely had a harsh word for anyone.

When President Harding died, his favorite dog, Laddie Boy, was given to a White House mail chief. Mrs. Harding gave the Airedale away on the condition it would never be bred. "His life must die with him," she instructed. But Laddie Boy got away, and may have had an opportunity to produce offspring.

Herbert Hoover's mother was a Quaker minister and preached often. She died when Herbert was nine.

Frank Pierce once denounced anti-slavery sympathizers as "reckless fanatics."

The first time he ran for elected office, James Madison lost. He sought a seat in the Virginia House of Delegates, but it was the only election he lost in forty years.

While fighting for the Union Army in 1862, James Garfield said of his commander-in-chief, Abraham Lincoln, "He is almost a child in the hands of his generals…. What a shameful humiliation when the President becomes a petitioner before one of his subordinates."

FDR was not always happy with his White House meals of chicken and sweetbread, served to him six times a week. In April of 1942 he wrote his wife, "I am getting to the point where my stomach positively rebels and this does not help my relations with foreign powers. I bit two of them yesterday."

In a controversial move JFK appointed his thirty-five-year-old brother as U.S. Attorney General. Cries of nepotism, and protests that Bobby Kennedy was too young, led the President to remark wryly, "I can't see that it's wrong to give him a little legal experience before he goes out to practice law."

After a seventh heart attack in 1968, Dwight Eisenhower was asked by a good friend if he still wanted to go ahead with plans to write articles. Replied the former President, "Yes, of course. Damn it, there are still some things I want to say to the American people."

By December of 1776 George Washington's Continental Army of 20,000 men had been reduced to a force of 3000. Outnumbered by the British, the commanding general faced terrible conditions of desertion, disease, lack of weapons and supplies, and battle casualties. After reviewing the condition of his army, he wrote his brother, "I am wearied almost to death."

In 1755 John Adams taught school in Worcester, Massachusetts, and found it rewarding, though at first he complained of "a large number of little runtlings just capable of lisping *A B C*, and troubling the master."

FDR said a "radical is a man with both feet firmly planted in the air."

John Adams once wrote of himself, "I have one head, four limbs and five senses like any other man, and nothing peculiar in any of them."

Calvin Coolidge had enough humor and common sense to escape that exaggeration of the ego which afflicted a good many of our Presidents. Awakening from a nap in the middle of a Presidential executive day, he opened his eyes, grinned, and asked a friend, "Is the country still here?"

Stated Lincoln, "Honest statesmanship is the wise employment of individual manners for the public good."

At the time of his promotion, James A. Garfield was the youngest brigadier general in the Union Army during the Civil War.

Despite a battle with breast cancer, Alice Roosevelt Longsworth (daughter of Theodore) lived a long life. At the age of ninety-three the Washington socialite informed friends that since she had two mastectomies, she was Washington's oldest topless woman.

During the Mexican War President Polk attended to every detail. Directing the war with great vigor, he planned troop movements and naval blockades, supervised the purchase of mules, settled quarrels among military surgeons, and negotiated treaties, even though he never left the White House.

In his duel with Charles Dickinson, Andrew Jackson was shot in the chest. He staggered, straightened himself, and shot Dickinson – in the groin. Dickinson died a slow, painful death while Jackson carried the bullet near his heart for the rest of his life.

William Henry Harrison was the first man elected President to garner more than a million votes – 1,275,017, in the 1840 election.

On the day he resigned from office (August 9, 1974), Richard Nixon told his cabinet and staff, "Always remember, others may hate you, but those who hate you don't win unless you hate them, and then you destroy yourself."

Raised in a log cabin, Millard Fillmore's baby crib was a maple sugar trough.

Both James K. Polk and William McKinley shared one thing in common: they had little interest in recreation or any sport. Both excluded outside interests in pursuing a career in politics and devoting a great deal of time to their wives.

While Chester Arthur was President, the price of a postage stamp fell from three cents to two cents.

When Dwight Eisenhower graduated from West Point in 1915, he received his diploma and handshake from President Woodrow Wilson.

John Tyler was born in 1790, but one of his daughters, Pearl, lived until 1947. When she was born in 1860, her father was sixty-nine-years-old, and her mother (Tyler's second wife) was thirty-nine.

Franklin Pierce was an Episcopalian and first expressed a deep faith in God at Bowdoin College. Every night he and his roommate, Zenos Caldwell, prayed on their knees before going to bed.

"Buffalo Bill" Cody referred to Theodore Roosevelt as "The American Cyclone."

When John Tyler died, his coffin was *not* draped with a U.S. flag. Instead, a Confederate flag covered his coffin. Tyler died in 1862 and is buried in Richmond, Virginia.

In 1887 President Cleveland ordered that all captured Confederate battle flags be returned to the southern states. This created a furor among Republicans in the North and West. Cleveland withdrew the order.

James Buchanan was the second of eleven children and learned math and bookkeeping while working at his father's store.

In 1839 Martin Van Buren became the first Chief Executive to grant an interview to a newsman.

Millard Fillmore was the first President to have a stepmother.

John Tyler was the first Chief Executive to have no Vice President during his entire term.

Nobody painted Presidents like James Reid Lambdin. Visiting the White House over a span of more than four decades, Lambdin painted portraits of every Chief Executive from John Quincy Adams to James A. Garfield.

When Jefferson was President in 1801, twenty percent of all Americans were slaves.

Regarding the ghosts stalking the White House, Harry Truman commented, "I'm sure they're here and I'm not half so alarmed at meeting up with any of them as I am at having to meet the live nuts I have to see every day."

Because of a remark by Lincoln to a U.S. Senator, the expression "lame duck" became part of American political lingo.

When U.S. Grant visited a centennial celebration in Concord, Massachusetts, he stopped at the Concord Inn and penned this note for the owner of the tavern: "You've got the best whiskey in town."

In more than thirty years of running his newspaper, *The Marion Star*, Warren G. Harding never once fired an employee. Harding dreaded hurting anyone's feelings or antagonizing people, and this proved to be his greatest weakness while serving in the White House.

Frank Pierce observed the Sabbath Day so strictly he refused to read any of his White House correspondence on Sundays.

Calvin Coolidge, in reflecting back on the career of Herbert Hoover, said, "That man has offered me unsolicited advice for the past six years, all of it bad."

William Henry Harrison said that John Quincy Adams was "a disgusting man to do business. Coarse, dirty, and clownish in his address and stiff and abstracted in his opinions, which are drawn from books exclusively."

In June of 1771, John Adams detailed in his diary a "recipe to make manure."

In 1986 Warren G. Harding's top hat was donated to the Smithsonian Institution where it has been stored away.

Thomas Jefferson once proposed that annual elections be held on February 29th – but he forgot that this date comes around only once every four years.

The first American political buttons were made for George Washington, celebrating his inauguration. Consisting of brass or copper, they were made to attach to clothing.

John Kennedy's first official act as President was issuing an executive order doubling food rations for four million poor Americans.

During his term as congressman, Lincoln wrote his wife and advised her: "Get weighed and write me how much you weigh." Lincoln was concerned about his wife's health and felt she needed to put on a few more pounds.

The first hideaway bed ever patented in the U.S. was invented by Thomas Jefferson.

Theodore Roosevelt carried six pairs of eye glasses during the Spanish-American War. T.R. felt this "six-pack" would come in handy in combat.

James A. Garfield once noted, "The sanctity of marriage and the family relation make the cornerstone of our American society and civilization."

In 1853 Franklin Pierce became the first President to have a personal bodyguard – an old army friend.

On the day Bill Clinton was sworn in as President, the moving van with all of the Clinton possessions couldn't get through the east gate of the White House. Eventually another entrance was used.

McKinley's last official act as President dealt with the evacuation of U.S. forces from Peking, China, following the Boxer Rebellion.

A Harvard classmate once told FDR, "Frank, if only you'd stuck to the newspaper game, you might have gotten somewhere." As a former editor of the Harvard *Crimson*, the President often recalled this comment with much humor.

When someone once criticized the Lincoln administration for plodding and stumbling along, the President responded, "It may be true, but please God, I think we are stumbling in the right direction."

Thomas Jefferson once noted, "When I see two doctors in conversation, I scan the sky for an approaching buzzard."

George Washington's last official act as President was on March 3, 1797, when he pardoned ten men convicted of treason in connection with the Whiskey Rebellion. He also canceled a fine imposed on a smuggler.

During the Mexican War, Frank Pierce missed out on the attack at Chapultepec. He was in bed with diarrhea.

Herbert Hoover once said, "If a man has not made a million dollars by the time he is forty, he is not worth much." Such thinking found disagreement among the millions of unemployed and hungry Americans during the Great Depression.

Presidents who have favored more government control and regulation can justify their position in the words of James Madison who stated, "A landed interest, a manufacturing interest, a moneyed interest, with many lesser interests, grow up of necessity in civilized nations and divide them into different classes, actuated by different sentiments and views. The regulation of the various and interfering interests form the principle task of modern legislation."

John Adams once said that Thomas Jefferson was consumed "with ambition, yet weak, confused, uninformed, and ignorant." But Jefferson likewise had a low opinion of his predecessor. He said Adams was "distrustful, obstinate, excessively vain, and takes no counsel from anyone."

Harry Truman once summed up Lyndon B. Johnson in two words – "No guts!"

Dwight Eisenhower was unimpressed with decisions made by his successor, John F. Kennedy. More than once Eisenhower cited the old observation, "You can always tell a Harvard man, but you can't tell him much."

Woodrow Wilson referred to our twenty-first President, Chester Arthur, as a "nonentity with sidewhiskers."

James K. Polk announced, "I prefer to supervise the whole operation of government myself." And he did.

George Washington referred to Princeton College (then called the University of New Jersey) as "that nest of Presbyterians."

Theodore Roosevelt's favorite White House pet was a kangaroo rat which ate food at the breakfast table.

U.S. Grant's philosophy of battle was not complicated: "The art of war is simple. Find out where the enemy is. Get at him as soon as you can. Strike at him as hard as you can and keep moving."

President John Tyler keenly observed, "The only people who seem to like me are my children."

John Adams began reading at the age of four. In 1745 at the age of just ten years, he became the Massachusetts state spelling champion.

One of Gerald Ford's favorite snacks was eating raw onions. Perhaps this is the reason he had only a few close friends!

At the battle of Paintsville, Kentucky, in 1862, James A. Garfield's men charged General Humphrey Marshall's confederate forces and routed them. A bullet struck Garfield's canteen and emptied it.

Considering whether he should retain J. Edgar Hoover as Director of the FBI, Lyndon Johnson supposedly remarked, "I'd rather have him inside the tent pissing out than outside pissing in…." Hoover stayed.

Carter's Secret Service code name was Deacon; Nixon was Searchlight.

Ronald Reagan was president of his high school senior class.

In his memoirs, Millard Fillmore admitted he "had a great passion for hunting and fishing," but his father kept him busy working on the family farm near Skaneateles, New York.

Jimmy Carter's mother, Lillian, insisted her children read at the dinner table *while eating*. The future President learned to read when he was four years old.

Thanks to both Theodore Roosevelt and Woodrow Wilson, the Grand Canyon was declared a national landmark.

Lincoln was not the only President who had nightmares and bad dreams. James A. Garfield, Woodrow Wilson, and Lyndon Johnson all had recurring dreams of impending doom, and they all had many sleepless nights.

For more than 100 years the White House employed stewards to visit the mansion to wind up all the clocks there.

During a trip to Europe, Herbert Hoover met with Adolf Hitler on March 8, 1938. He found the Fuhrer "highly intelligent," but with "trigger spots in his mind which… set him off like a man in furious anger."

For the first and only time in our history, a President and his Vice President came from the same county. The Whig candidates in 1840 were William Henry Harrison and John Tyler, both born in Charles City County in Virginia.

John Tyler, our tenth President, once said, "In the consciousness of my own honesty, I stand firm and erect. I worship alone at the shrine of truth and honor."

Lyndon Johnson enjoyed demonstrating the power of the Presidency. As President, he ordered all passenger seats in *Air Force One* reversed. Guests now would not only fly "backwards" but also be able to view LBJ's conference room and see him in action.

In the 1972 Presidential race, George McGovern and the Democrats spent $32 million – a hefty sum. Nixon and the Republicans, however, raised and spent $65 million.

Theodore Roosevelt was a prolific letter writer. And when he sat down to write in his Trophy Room at Sagamore Hill he dipped his pen into a rhinoceros-foot inkwell.

In seeking advice about politics, Richard Nixon observed, "You should consult a lawyer only if you want to know what risks *not* to take. Lawyers are experts on how not to do something. They play it safe."

After residing in Washington, D.C., for several years, President Harry Truman said, "If you want a friend in *this* town, buy a dog."

Mt. McGregor in Moreau, New York, was where U.S. Grant completed his memoirs and died. This historic site was closed in 1985 because visitors had to pass gun towers, heavy gates, and armed guards to get in. It was turned into Mt. McGregor Prison.

Upon assuming office, Franklin Pierce commented in a letter to Jefferson Davis, "How I shall be able to summon my manhood and gather up my energies for the duties before me, it is hard for me to see."

As editor of the Harvard *Crimson*, Franklin Roosevelt urged fans to cheer louder at football games.

While serving as a secretary to the American ambassador in Russia, teenager John Quincy Adams keenly observed, "There is nobody here but Slaves and Princes."

John F. Kennedy was a young U.S. Senator. He once boarded a Presidential train in Springfield, Massachusetts, and was thrown off by James J. Rawley, who later became chief of Kennedy's Secret Service!

Growing up near Louisville, Kentucky, Zachary Taylor was educated in a pioneer school by a teacher from Connecticut. Still, Taylor misspelled his letter of acceptance to an infantry commission: "I *doo* accept."

Both major political parties wanted Eisenhower as their candidate, but knew nothing of his politics. Republicans were quite happy when the general declared, "The path to America's future lies down the middle of the road." That fit in perfectly with the Republican platform.

As a clerk for a San Francisco mining tycoon, Herbert Hoover proved versatile. He could type, take dictation, inspect mines, and even supervise operations. Sent on a fact-finding mission in the Sierras to a particularly tough mine, Hoover kept the peace with a six shooter in his belt and a rifle in his saddle guard.

Though Lincoln was strong willed, and not easily dissuaded, he rarely argued. "Quarrel not at all," he said, and added, "No man resolved to make the most of himself can spare the time for personal contentions. Better to give your pants to a dog than be bitten by him."

George Washington was desperate for more men and supplies. He advised the Continental Congress, "If you can't send money, send tobacco."

During much of his term as the seventeenth President, Andrew Johnson suffered from kidney stones.

During the last weeks of Andrew Johnson's administration, a crazed woman was found wandering through the White House with the intention of killing him.

At the age of seventeen Zachary Taylor performed an amazing feat. In the spring of 1801 he swam the width of the Ohio River and back again.

As a youngster Harry Truman once slammed the cellar door on his left foot, severing the tip of his big toe. A doctor reattached it successfully.

Chester Arthur was a late night person. After an evening meal he often took a guest on a stroll through the streets of Washington at three or four o'clock in the morning.

Woodrow Wilson was the son of a minister, but that didn't stop him from being a boy. He skipped school one day and followed the circus elephant into Augusta, Georgia. On the way back home he stopped at a cotton warehouse and moved some bales outside.

In May of 1984 President Ronald Reagan remarked, "You'd be surprised how much being a good actor pays off."

Before the battle of Trenton, George Washington had only three words of advice to his troops: "Victory or death."

Woodrow Wilson once said, "In the Lord's Prayer, the first petition is for daily bread; no one can worship God or love his neighbor on an empty stomach."

"What I value more than all things is good humor." So said Thomas Jefferson.

William McKinley and his wife loved music. As occupants of the White House they had four pianos there (three grands and one upright), and they doubled the size of the Marine band.

Warren G. Harding was not a genius, and he knew it. He once quipped, "If I knew as much now as I thought I knew at nineteen, I'd be the greatest President this country ever had."

James A. Garfield once noted, "I am trying to do two things: dare to be a radical and not be a fool, which is a matter of no small difficulty."

William Howard Taft admitted, "The trouble with me is that I like to talk too much."

Calvin Coolidge once confessed, "Whenever I indulge my sense of humor, it gets me into trouble."

Neither of Andrew Jackson's parents were born in America. They were both born in Ireland and emigrated to America in 1765.

Rutherford B. Hayes once reflected, "I am not liked as a President by the politicians in office, in the press, or in Congress. But I am content to abide the judgment – the sober second thought – of the people."

Woodrow Wilson explained, "My mind is a one-track road and can only run one train of thought at a time."

Thomas Jefferson, himself a lawyer, observed, "It is the trade of lawyers to question everything, yield nothing, and to talk by the hour."

"Office seeking is a disease. It is even catching," said Grover Cleveland.

Herbert Hoover once said, "The things I enjoyed most as President were the visits of children. They don't want public office."

Harry Truman once observed, "The difficulty with businessmen entering politics after they had a successful business career is that they want to start at the top."

When asked what he would like to be remembered for, Calvin Coolidge said, "I should like to be known as a former President who minded his own business."

John Adams was only sixteen-years-old when he entered Harvard in 1751, and his first job after graduation was teaching school in Worcester, Massachusetts.

U.S. Grant was only three-years-old when one day a customer visited his father's tannery in Georgetown, Ohio. While the two men were inside, Ulysses was swinging on the tail of the horse which belonged to the visitor.

In 1756 John Adams was an ardent patriot – of Great Britain. He wrote in his diary, "I rejoice that I am an Englishman and glory in the name of Briton."

Dwight Eisenhower's last words were, "I always loved my wife...."

Ronald Reagan's definition of Presidential leadership was quite simple: "Surround yourself with the best people you can find, delegate authority, and don't interfere."

Our nineteenth President, Rutherford B. Hayes, once observed, "Mrs. Hayes may not have much influence on Congress, but she has great influence with me...."

Though conditions were extremely rough for George Washington and his army at Valley Forge, on March 18, 1778, he found time to grant a request from Miss Kitty Livingston, giving her a lock of his hair.

During the 1992 campaign, Bill Clinton noted, "Politicians are people, too."

Calvin Coolidge once said of his wife Grace that she "has kept me running for public office ever since I married her."

Thomas Jefferson lived at Monticello with his fourteen grandchildren.

Benjamin Harrison once noted, "It is quite as illogical to despise a man because he is rich as because he is poor."

Though he could be quite mischievous as a student, Franklin Pierce was also considerate and compassionate. He often spent his recess tutoring slow learners.

Woodrow Wilson once explained, "I used to be lawyer, but now I am a reformed character."

In July of 1790 President George Washington had a large tumor surgically removed.

Thomas Jefferson had his wife Martha's gravestone inscribed in Latin.

John F. Kennedy observed, "There are three things which are real: God, human folly, and laughter. The first two are beyond human comprehension. So we must do what we can with the third."

Martin Van Buren was nicknamed "The American Talleyrand" because of his crafty and shrewd political moves.

One U.S. Senator remarked after conversing with President Benjamin Harrison, "It's like talking to a hitching post."

Bill and Hillary Rodham Clinton met at Yale, fell in love, and graduated together in 1973.

Not many Presidents have a reptile named in their honor, but Thomas Jefferson does. The Jefferson salamander, nicknamed a tunnel mole, is common throughout the woodlands of the Midwest.

Speaking of Jefferson, John Adams said of our third President that Jefferson was a man "whose mind is warped by prejudice and so blinded by ignorance as to be unfit for the office he holds."

Dwight Eisenhower considered Lyndon B. Johnson "a small man." He further commented that Johnson, "hasn't got the depth of mind nor the breadth of vision to carry great responsibility...Johnson is superficial and opportunistic."

Martin Van Buren observed that William Henry Harrison was "as tickled with the Presidency as a young woman with a new bonnet."

In the 1932 Presidential election the country overwhelmingly voted for Franklin D. Roosevelt, who ran against the incumbent Herbert Hoover. A Democrat sent a telegram to the White House on the night of the election, and when Hoover opened it, the message read, "Vote for Roosevelt and make it unanimous."

Jefferson reminded all Americans when he observed, "Ignorance of the law is no excuse in our country…because it can always be pretended."

While he was back in Texas one late evening, President Lyndon Johnson made a phone call to Ohio Congressman Wayne Hays. The problem was, it was two hours later back in Ohio, and when Hays answered the phone in the wee hours of the morning LBJ asked, "Wayne, did I wake you?" Hays replied, "No Mr. President. I've been laying here waiting for you to call."

The first Presidential Library opened in 1916 in Fremont, Ohio, where Rutherford B. Hayes lived. No federal tax dollars were used, and it is run today with private funds and donations.

Harry Truman must have enjoyed visiting Key West, Florida. As President he made eleven trips to the Little White House there, beginning in March of 1946. In addition, he vacationed there five times after leaving the Presidency, the last time in 1969.

Calvin Coolidge's father knew his son was special. Mr. Coolidge reminisced, "Calvin could get more sap out of a maple tree than any of the other boys around here."

Only one President had a son married in the White House. In 1828 young John Adams, son of John Quincy, married his pretty cousin Mary Catherine Hellen.

Dwight Eisenhower received news that he had been appointed by FDR as the Supreme Allied Commander in Europe during World War II. When asked how he felt about his appointment, Eisenhower said, "This new title has a certain ring to it – like that of Sultan."

In 1941 Warner Brothers Studios announced that Ronald Reagan received more fan mail than any other male movie star, with the exception of Errol Flynn.

Thomas Jefferson introduced corn to the people of Paris. While serving as an ambassador to France, he grew corn and served it to his guests.

In the year 1900 George Washington's birthday was a legal holiday in forty-five states, with Mississippi the lone exception. Lincoln's birthday, on the other hand, was celebrated in only eight states – all of them in the North.

In 1948 Harry Truman quipped, "Do your duty and history will do you justice."

Being a bachelor might seem to be an advantage, but when James Buchanan ran for President in 1856, a banner paraded by a group of women declared, "Opposition to Old Bachelors."

One of the jobs U.S. Grant had after he left the Army was working as a clerk in his father's leather store in Galena, Illinois. Many customers thought he was incompetent because he often forgot the prices. A few years later the Civil War began, and Grant had a permanent job.

Jimmy Carter's mother, Lillian, once described her son as "a beautiful cat with sharp claws."

In January of 1993 George Bush was asked what life was like after leaving the Presidency. Bush responded, "Well, for one thing, I find that I no longer win every golf game."

Six consecutive Presidents, the twelfth through the seventeenth, had no middle names: Taylor, Fillmore, Pierce, Buchanan, Lincoln, and Johnson.

James K. Polk was the first Chief Executive who did not outlive his mother. Polk died in 1849, his mother in 1852.

In 1807 former Vice President Aaron Burr was arrested for treason and tried before Chief Justice John Marshall. President Jefferson was ordered by Marshall to appear before him and testify at Burr's trial. Jefferson refused, sending information he saw fit. This action established the precedent of executive privilege and reinforced the separation of powers.

Martin Van Buren once observed, "All communities are apt to look to government for too much…but this ought not to be."

During the entire term as governor of Ohio, and during his time as President, William McKinley wrote his mother a letter everyday he was away from her.

Martin Van Buren and Theodore Roosevelt, both of Dutch descent, were third cousins.

In September of 1986 Boston Red Sox pitcher Joe Sambito received Ronald Reagan's autograph on a baseball. Sambito told a sportswriter, "His penmanship left a lot to be desired."

Herbert Hoover personally wrote only seven letters while President. Thus, a handwritten letter by him during his term in office is rare and valuable.

Speaking of handwritten letters, one written by President George Washington, dated April 1, 1789, fetched a whopping $635,000 when it was auctioned off in 1993.

Between the ages of nineteen and twenty-four, Thomas Jefferson studied law under the tutelage of attorney George Wythe. During that entire period Jefferson spent sixteen hours a day studying.

In early July of 1826 John Quincy Adams left the White House due to his father's ill health. He didn't return until three and a half months later, amid much criticism from many newspapers.

William McKinley was so pressured and harassed to declare war on Spain that he had to resort to sleeping powders before going to bed.

George Washington was a bad speller, and so was Andrew Jackson. The seventh President wrote "logg" for log, "oragagon" for Oregon, "potant" for potent, and "paralel" for parallel.

FDR was the first President to win by a *popular* majority since Franklin Pierce in 1852.

In 1950 Harry Truman said, "I never have bad luck."

Theodore Roosevelt claimed that Woodrow Wilson was nothing but a "damned Presbyterian hypocrite."

Just before he died in early 1924, Woodrow Wilson said he was, "tired of swimming upstream."

Lyndon B. Johnson wasn't President very long when he told his staff members, "Now that I got the power, I aim to use it."

Thomas Jefferson so admired the geometric precision of Ohio's ancient Indian mounds that he had some constructed on his Poplar Forest estate.

In 1794 young John Quincy Adams learned he had been appointed Minister to Holland. He wrote, "My country is entitled to my services…."

In 1856 James A. Garfield spent two months preparing for his final exams. Night and day, he plugged away, and later wrote, "I worked off about twenty pounds of flesh in the last eight weeks, but now I shall regain it soon, I think." Garfield graduated near the top of his class at Williams College.

Bill Clinton's father was killed in a car wreck three months before Bill was born.

There are thirty-four bathrooms in the White House.

For a brief period in New Salem, Illinois, Abe Lincoln owned and operated a general store. He made his bed on the front counter.

Franklin Pierce ranked last in his college class after his sophomore year. Two years later, he graduated third in his class at Bowdoin College in Maine.

President John Tyler's mother-in-law was nine years *younger* than himself. And Juliana Gardiner's daughter, Julia, was thirty years younger than the President when they were married in New York City in 1844. Tyler was a widower, and the marriage ceremony was done in secrecy.

George Washington's favorite horse during the Revolutionary War was Nelson. Not long after the war's end Nelson was put out to pasture at Mount Vernon and never required to do any work.

Among the many activities Thomas Jefferson enjoyed was jogging. As a law student at the College of William and Mary he ran a couple of miles every day.

According to Franklin D. Roosevelt, his greatest achievement of his New Deal programs was the adoption of the Social Security Act which benefited millions of elderly and retired citizens.

The longest funeral procession for a President was the one for U.S. Grant. When Grant died in 1885 a line seven miles long accompanied the body to Riverside Drive in New York City.

President Franklin D. Roosevelt appeared in a 1943 movie, a comedy entitled *Princess O'Rourke.* In the film, featuring actress Olivia de Havilland, Roosevelt played himself.

Theodore Roosevelt, being a staunch conservationist, banned live Christmas trees from the White House. During his Presidency, however, his children smuggled them into their bedrooms.

In 1995 Bill Clinton remarked, "Being President is like running a cemetery. Everybody is under you but nobody is listening."

William McKinley was the first candidate to use the telephone in a Presidential campaign. In 1896 he personally phoned all thirty-eight managers in the same number of states.

Gerald Ford observed, "The things that are good about football coincide with the things that are good about America."

Franklin Roosevelt once presented a bust of Benjamin Franklin to his wife, who was always traveling. He urged her to take it, remarking, "You can always say, 'I have Franklin with me.'"

Warren Harding's actual given name was Warren Gamaliel Bancroft Winnipeg Harding.

Lincoln loved animals, and he understood human nature as well. Perhaps these thoughts were on his mind when, during the Civil War, he observed, "No matter how much cats fight, there always seem to be plenty of kittens."

Most of the love letters Woodrow Wilson wrote to his wife Ellen have been saved. They totaled 3100, but 300 of these were destroyed by Wilson's daughter, Eleanor, because she considered them too intimate to ever be read or reprinted.

Franklin Roosevelt collected miniature pigs – ones made of glass or china.

James Madison's mother, Nelly, said her son was a good boy, especially in his teenage years. She remarked to a friend about James that, "never once did he commit an indiscreet act."

Like his father before him, Thomas Jefferson was also elected as a member of the Virginia House of Burgesses.

As a young man, Thomas Jefferson entered a contest and submitted architectural plans for the design of both the White House and Capitol Building. He lost both times.

FDR had a small false tooth, or budge, made to eliminate a slight whistling sound made by a gap in his lower front teeth. He used it when he spoke on the radio.

100X was the code name of the 1961 Ford Lincoln Continental used by Presidents Kennedy and Johnson.

Herbert Hoover received an average of 400 letters a day while President. This compares to FDR who, throughout World War II, received more than 4,000 per day.

While publishing the *Marion Star*, editor Warren G. Harding once advised an employee, "Select your boss; don't let him select you."

FDR's body was never brought to lay in state at the Rotunda of the Capitol. Evidence suggests he was cremated. His casket, and whatever remains were inside, were taken to Hyde Park, New York, for burial.

FDR once described his political decision-making: "I am like a cat. I make a quick stroke and then I relax."

No Presidents between McKinley and Kennedy had served in the House of Representatives.

The four greatest leaders in history, according to Franklin D. Roosevelt, were Benjamin Franklin, Thomas Jefferson, Theodore Roosevelt, and the Earl of Orrery, a confidential advisor of Oliver Cromwell.

When President Franklin Roosevelt received phone calls at his Hyde Park, New York, home, he could not always be certain of privacy. His mother, Sara, would listen in on his calls. A relative once heard Roosevelt say, "Mama, will you *please* get off the line. I can hear you breathing. Come on, now!"

During his 1880 Front Porch campaign in Mentor, Ohio, candidate James A. Garfield was serenaded by the Jubilee Singers, an all-black chorus from Fisk University. Their songs reminded him of the slaves he helped free when he was a general fighting in the Civil War. At the end of the program a deeply moved Garfield told his guests, "And I tell you now in the closing days of this campaign, that I would rather be with you and defeated than against you and victorious."

Though he was a quartermaster general in the Union army, Chester Arthur and his wife had divided loyalties during the conflict of the Civil War. His wife Ellen, a Virginian, had a brother serving in the Confederate government, plus several nephews fighting in the rebel army. One nephew was taken prisoner at Gettysburg and Arthur secured his release and allowed him to stay at their home in New York.

Charles Guiteau, the assassin of President Garfield, was a deadbeat who left a trail of bills and unpaid debts for years. He regularly abused his wife, and often they left a hotel or boardinghouse in the middle of the night to avoid paying for their stay. Guiteau announced at his trial, "The world owes me a living."

Abraham Lincoln was distantly related to Daniel Boone.

In explaining later why some evidence was destroyed concerning the Watergate scandal, Richard Nixon said, "I was under medication when I made the decision to burn the tapes."

While campaigning for re-election in 1992, President George Bush delighted Democratic opponents when he told a Ridgewood, New Jersey, crowd, "I don't want to run the risk of ruining what is a lovely recession." Bush meant to say *reception.*

When Lincoln was a boy growing up in Pigeon Creek, Kentucky, he was nearly killed by a horse. The mare kicked him in the forehead and he fell bleeding and unconscious. Abe's father found him and thought he was dead. Though he could not speak for several hours, the boy recovered with no permanent damage.

John Kennedy thought it was unfair for historians to judge Presidents. As Chief Executive, Kennedy once told a newsman, "No one has a right to grade a President – not even poor James Buchanan – who has not sat in his chair, examined the mail and information that came across his desk, and learned why he made his decisions."

James A. Garfield once observed, "Assassination can no more be guarded against than death by lightning; and it is best not to worry about either."

George Bush once told a crowd, "I have opinions of my own, strong opinions, but I don't always agree with them."

When Calvin Coolidge was twelve years old, he lost his sister, Abby, when she died from appendicitis.

In the early 1830s Zachary and Margaret Taylor, and their five daughters and one son, moved to a sugar plantation on the Mississippi River near Baton Rouge, Louisiana. After spending most of his adult life in the army Taylor became a successful businessman when his plantation turned a profit.

During one year in which he worked as postmaster of New Salem, Illinois, Abraham Lincoln earned $55.70.

U.S. Grant was the first President to paint. Armed with canvas, brushes and an easel, Grant found comfort in painting, especially horses.

Warren Harding died heavily in debt. In 1923, the year of his death, he owed his stockbroker an estimated $200,000.

Future President Rutherford B. Hayes met Abraham Lincoln for the first time in Indianapolis in 1861. Hayes remarked, "Homely as L. is, if you can get a good view of him by day light when he is talking he is by no means ill looking."

Before it was known as the birthplace of Bill Clinton, the town of Hope, Arkansas, was known for its watermelons.

President George Bush once left some listeners confused when he announced, "I believe in unions and I believe in non-unions."

On more than one occasion President Calvin Coolidge summoned his advisor Frank Stearns to the Oval Office. Stearns and Coolidge sat there in a haze of cigar smoke for an hour or more in total silence.

William Howard Taft was directly related to poet Ralph Waldo Emerson.

When Vice President Chester Arthur was informed of President James A. Garfield's death, he remarked, "I hope — my God, I do hope it is a mistake."

Though the family denied it, ancestors of Theodore and Franklin Roosevelt made part of their fortune in the African slave trade when Dutch sea captains brought their human cargo to America.

When George Washington campaigned for election to the Virginia House of Burgesses prior to the American Revolution, he offered voters 160 gallons of rum, beer and hard cider.

In 1930 William Howard Taft's funeral was the first one broadcast on radio.

Though John Adams served as Washington's Vice President, he may have been a bit unfair when he said that Washington was "too illiterate, unlearned, unread for his station and reputation."

George Washington knew that being President would be a difficult task, saying that his election was "the event which I have long dreaded," and further remarking about "the ten thousand embarrassments, perplexities and troubles to which I must again be exposed."

At age 32, Bill Clinton became the youngest governor of Arkansas when he was elected in 1978. He established another precedent by being elected five times.

Lyndon Johnson had politics in his blood. His father and grandfather were members of the Texas legislature. His Scottish ancestors on his mother's side were members of British parliament.

During the Spanish-American War in 1898, Theodore Roosevelt recruited several of his Rough Riders from the bar at the Menger Hotel in San Antonio, Texas.

In June of 1773 George Washington's step-daughter, sixteen-year-old Patsy Custis, died from epileptic seizures. Though crushed with grief, George and Martha kept busy at Mt. Vernon while the threat of war with England loomed on the horizon.

John F. Kennedy was the first Boy Scout to become President.

Herbert Hoover was the first President to have an asteroid named for him.

James A. Garfield juggled heavy wooden clubs to build up his biceps.

Woodrow Wilson was the first President to hold a press conference.

Bill Clinton was the first Rhodes Scholar to become President.

Theodore Roosevelt was thirteen years old when he discovered he couldn't read a distant billboard. He soon had his first pair of glasses, remarking, "I had no idea how beautiful the world was."

President Thomas Jefferson thought it was undignified to use the wooden outhouse when he had to go to the bathroom. He ordered two indoor water closets installed in the White House.

Calvin Coolidge was a firm believer in big business curing the ills of society. He once remarked, "The man who builds a factory builds a temple."

At the battle of Buena Vista a bullet tore through Zachary Taylor's sleeve and another ripped his coat. Very casually, he ordered his artillery to "double-shot your guns and give 'em hell."

Woodrow Wilson's pet ram, Old Ike, loved to chew tobacco, especially cigar stubs.

Richard Nixon once observed, "My first win for Congress was the victory I remember most."

Jimmy Carter said, "A simple and proper function of government is just to make it easy for us to do good and difficult for us to do wrong."

Throughout the Civil War U.S. Grant was often seen taking out a small knife and whittling pieces of wood.

While George Washington was earning an annual salary of $25,000, his Vice president, John Adams, was paid $5,000.

General "Mad" Anthony Wayne was an ancestor of Richard Nixon.

In 1994 President Bill Clinton and German Chancellor Helmut Kohl co-hosted a NATO summit in Brussels, Belgium. Clinton inadvertently paid a compliment to Kohl when he told the hefty chancellor, "I was thinking of you last night while I was watching sumo wrestlers on television."

Andrew Jackson's favorite horse was Sandpatch, which he kept in his stables at his 1100-acre plantation The Hermitage.

Shortly after he took office following John Kennedy's death, LBJ invited half a dozen magazine editors to a White House luncheon. After greeting each one he announced, "Now you all sit down and let me tell you how this government's going to work."

When Grover Cleveland entered the White House he measured the hay in the stables and sent a check to ex-President Arthur for it.

The tradition of signing congressional bills with several pens, then giving them away as souvenirs, was begun by FDR.

Eleven-year-old Charlie Taft was not too excited about his father's inauguration in 1909. He carried a copy of *Treasure Island* to the ceremony and told his sister Helen, "This affair is going to be pretty dry and I want something to read."

Although Calvin Coolidge knew how to drive, he never drove a car while President. He furthermore instructed his chauffeur not to exceed 16 miles per hour.

The Wakarusa War took place during Franklin Pierce's administration when violence erupted in the Kansas-Nebraska territory over the issue of slavery.

Back in 1916 when Harry Truman was a young farmer, he wrote his future wife, Bess, "There's no one [who] wants to win half so badly as I do."

From July to October of 1792, President George Washington paid seven dollars a day for the use of a carriage, horses and driver on a trip back to Mt. Vernon. In all, he rented them for 22 days.

After Richard Nixon resigned from the Presidency in 1974, he accepted no money for any speeches or appearances. He also declined to serve on any corporate boards. His only source of income was from the sale of the seven books he had written.

Chester Arthur wore black for the first six months of his administration. He did this to mourn the death of his predecessor James A. Garfield. Arthur also declined all invitations, and gave no White House dinners during that time.

FDR worked an average of 14 hours each day as President. He once told Governor James Cox of Ohio, "I never get tired."

Two days before he lapsed into a coma and died, Woodrow Wilson at age sixty-seven told his wife, "I'm a broken piece of machinery."

The first shower installed at the White House was during Andrew Jackson's second term, but he was so feeble he seldom used it.

George W. Bush said if he could go back in time, the one person he would like to talk with would be Abraham Lincoln.

George Washington's will was written in his own handwriting. It was forty-two pages long and written five months before his death. He left an estate worth $500,000.

President Frank Pierce's favorite method of relaxation was riding his horse through the streets of Washington late at night.

Webb Hayes, son of Rutherford and Lucy, learned to ride a bicycle at age 20. He practiced in the East Room of the White House.

William Henry Harrison had a pet goat during his brief term as President. Its name was His Whiskers.

Harry Truman never lacked opinions. When judging the various Presidents, Truman observed, "I tend to pair up Benjamin Harrison and Dwight Eisenhower because they're the two Presidents I can think of who most preferred laziness to labor. They didn't work at all."

Initially Franklin D. Roosevelt intended to serve just two terms. In fact, he even signed a contract to become chief editor of *Collier's* magazine, but events leading up to World War II changed his mind.

After leaving office, Grover Cleveland worked for the Prudential Insurance Company, then became one of the directors of Princeton University.

The fountain on the North Lawn of the White House was installed during U.S. Grant's second term.

William Howard Taft turned the White House stables into a garage, replacing most of the horses with automobiles.

After World War II President Truman passed through a shattered Berlin. Viewing the mass destruction he no doubt was thinking of German dictator Adolf Hitler when, he said, "That's what happens when man overreaches himself."

In August of 1800 John Adams had a stable built at the White House. The building was damaged by fire, set by the British in 1814. By 1821 it had been remodeled and used as a school.

Captain Archie Butt served as a military aide to both Theodore Roosevelt and William Howard Taft. Butt described Taft: "I have found out three things he does well. He dances well, he curses well, and he laughs well."

Lyndon Johnson observed, "No one arrives at the White House with an agenda all his own. He finds the blackboard already covered with the unfinished work of others."

During a time period when photography was still in its infancy, Abraham Lincoln had his picture taken 140 times.

Three U.S. Presidents have their statues in London – George Washington, Abraham Lincoln, and Franklin D. Roosevelt.

Harry Truman said that viewing modern art put him "in almost the same frame of mind as after I have had a nightmare."

Jimmy and Rosalynn Carter's third son, Donnel Jeffrey, was born in 1952 on Rosalynn's birthday – August 18.

James A. Garfield believed a President should always keep close contact with the people. It was a basic requirement of the job and Garfield quoted from Lincoln when he said Presidents should "take a bath in public opinion."

In 1979 pianist Vladimir Horowitz performed for the Carters at the White House. The last time he had played there previous to this was fifty years earlier for Herbert Hoover.

Ronald Reagan once said, "I'm not smart enough to lie."

Warren G. Harding once said of his corrupt secretary of the interior, "If Albert Fall isn't an honest man, I'm not fit to be President." Fall later went to prison.

Jimmy Carter's son, Jack, followed in his father's footsteps and joined the Navy. He served in Vietnam aboard a buoy tender.

Calvin Coolidge was once defeated in an election running for the school board in Northampton, Massachusetts.

Martin Van Buren was thrifty. Realizing he would need money after his retirement, he collected his four years of salary, a total of $100,000, at the completion of his term of office.

On May 23, 1828, President John Quincy Adams injured his neck when he was thrown from a pony.

Rutherford B. Hayes agreed to serve just one term even before he took his oath of office in 1877, believing he could "do more good...if untrampled by the belief I was fixing things for my election to a second term."

Rupert Hughes wrote a critical book discrediting the character of George Washington. When this was reported to President Calvin Coolidge, he looked out the White House window and said, "Well, his monument is still there."

On Andrew Jackson's deathbed, the former President could hear his relatives and servants sobbing. He gathered them together and softly told them, "Please don't cry. Be good children, and I hope to see you all in heaven, both white and black."

Though paralyzed by a stroke for several months, President Woodrow Wilson got a private showing of newly released films in the East Room. Movie producers sent more than 400 films.

A group of Whigs from Baltimore presented William Henry Harrison with an expensive coach for his inaugural ride, but Harrison refused the gift and rode his white horse instead.

Theodore Roosevelt had many horses in the White House stables. Among them were Rosewell, Georgia, Audrey, Yagenka, Jacko Root, Renown, Bleistein, Wyoming, Rusty, Grey Dawn, and a pony named Algonquin. And he rode a different horse everyday.

Although James K. Polk was completely exhausted when he left office, his stop in New Orleans no doubt precipitated his death. There was an outbreak of cholera there and he contracted the disease. He died at his Tennessee home on June 15, 1849.

After leaving the White House, Gerald Ford observed, "Once a man has been President he becomes an object of curiosity."

During the Lincoln-Douglas debates in 1858, Lincoln was asked to summarize his education. He simply answered, "Defective."

On August 6, 1914, the same day his wife Ellen died, President Woodrow Wilson issued a formal proclamation of neutrality to keep the U.S. out of Word War I.

When Lyndon Johnson was President he asked the Marine Band to play shorter and faster songs.

Bill Clinton earned good grades even in elementary school, except for a couple of Ds he got in Conduct.

George Bush exhibited signs of leadership and achievement in his high school days. As a student at Phillips Academy in Andover, Massachusetts, he was captain of the baseball, basketball and soccer teams.

Harry Truman once observed, "People over 50 years of age will not change."

At the time President Theodore Roosevelt was holding a press conference to reduce violence and the death rate in college football games, his son Ted was playing on the freshman team at Harvard.

When Thomas Jefferson died on July 4, 1826 (the same day on which John Adams died), he left his family in debt for $107,274. Jefferson's daughter Patsy had to sell Monticello and all of its furnishings.

During his inaugural parade in 1961, John Kennedy enjoyed the long review held in his honor. But in watching the U.S. Coast Guard Academy from the reviewing stand, he noticed there was not one black face in the ranks. One of his first official acts was issuing an order correcting this situation.

As a state legislator in Tennessee, James K. Polk sponsored a law to prohibit dueling.

A rainstorm drowned out the words of Benjamin Harrison at his 1889 inauguration. The outgoing President, Grover Cleveland, kindly held an umbrella over Harrison's bare head.

Herbert Hoover worked many jobs to help pay his way through Stanford University. One of them was delivering laundry.

Calvin Coolidge felt it was best just to ignore critical newspaper accounts and reporters who printed inaccuracies. He noted, "Don't argue with skunks."

Bill and Hillary Rodham Clinton both ran for president of their high school class (Bill in Hope, Arkansas and Hillary in Oak Park, Illinois). Both lost.

When Ronald Reagan entered the White House he ordered Calvin Coolidge's portrait brought out from storage to hang in the Cabinet Room.

John Quincy Adams made only one public speech while President.

James Buchanan was related to composer Stephen Foster.

Martin Van Buren and his wife Hannah spoke Dutch in their home.

At age 60, Harry Truman was the oldest Vice President to become President.

While serving as governor of Massachusetts, Calvin Coolidge was once punched in the eye by the mayor of Boston.

"Genius is the child of toil." So observed John Quincy Adams.

Herbert Hoover's last name was originally spelled Huber, before his German name was Americanized.

George Bush was the first President born in the month of June.

Lyndon Johnson was the first incumbent President to visit a pope.

John Tyler and his children span much of U.S. history. Tyler had fifteen children to two different wives. Tyler was born during George Washington's administration and his youngest child died during Harry Truman's term of office.

Bill Clinton's high school jazz trio wore sunglasses when performing. The boys were known as "The Three Blind Mice."

Eisenhower was a skilled chef. His specialties were vegetable soup, steaks and cornmeal pancakes.

February 29, 1968, occurred on Leap Year, and that day proved to be unlucky for Lyndon Johnson. The President had to visit the Pentagon where he was conducting a farewell ceremony for his Secretary of Defense Robert McNamara. Johnson and his entourage were several minutes late after they got stuck in an elevator for twelve minutes.

President Kennedy kept a coconut shell on his White House desk. The shell came from Nauro Island in the Solomons from his World War II days. It was carved with the SOS message that he sent from Nauro with a native messenger after the survivors from Kennedy's wrecked PT-109 were stranded on that island in 1943. The message read, "Native knows posit He can pilot 11 alive Need small boat Kennedy"

John F. Kennedy complained about the six gardeners on the payroll at the White House. He told his aide, Ken O'Donnell, "I've got one man up at Hyannis Port who could take care of this whole place. And he would have it looking better, too."

During the Civil War General U. S. Grant had a teamster tied to a tree for six hours because of mistreating a horse.

Dr. William W. Kean's 56-year-old patient, President Grover Cleveland, once told him, "Those officeseekers! Those officeseekers! They haunt me even in my dreams!"

In the fall of 1946 President Harry Truman took a vacation to Key West, Florida, and horrified the Secret Service by boarding a captured World War II German submarine and diving to a depth of 440 feet.

John Adams was the great-great-grandson of John and Priscilla Alden who were among the first Pilgrims who landed at Plymouth Rock in 1620.

Zachary Taylor and his running mate Millard Fillmore never met until after both men were elected.

Chester Arthur, our twenty-first Chief Executive, was nicknamed "Elegant Arthur" for his high style of living. While in the White House he owned more than 80 pairs of trousers.

James Monroe was the first President to ride on a steamboat.

James K. Polk was the great-grandnephew of John Knox, the founder of Scottish Presbyterianism.

Frank Pierce was the first elected President who failed to gain his party's nomination for a second term.

President Calvin Coolidge forbid his wife to shorten her skirts, cut her hair, or ride a horse because he felt such actions were undignified for a First Lady.

Harry Truman noted, "If you can't convince them, confuse them."

Herbert Hoover proposed to his future wife while he was in Australia and she was in California. She cabled back, "Yes," and their wedding took place in California on February 10, 1899.

Zachary and Margaret (Peggy) Taylor lost three daughters in three years.

Millard Fillmore was the second President whose father was alive when he was inaugurated – John Quincy Adams being the first.

When John Tyler wedded his second wife on June 26, 1844, his bride was younger than Tyler's three daughters.

Martin Van Buren lived, to see eight Presidents succeed him, and they were each from a different state.

Though born in Virginia, Zachary Taylor was the first President elected from a state west of the Mississippi River. He was a resident of Louisiana.

When Grover Cleveland was inaugurated on March 4, 1893, he noticed on the congressional roster that there were eight congressmen with the first and middle names of George Washington, three of them from Ohio.

FDR and JFK were the only Democratic Presidents to die in office.

Calvin Coolidge observed, "There is no dignity quite so impressive, and no independence quite so important, as living within your means."

George Washington's stepson was Jack Custis (Martha Washington's son to her previous marriage). He served as an aide to Washington during the Revolutionary War and died of dysentery before the war ended.

Following the Republican Convention of 1864, Andrew Johnson was reminded that he, a former tailor, had been nominated on the same ticket with Abraham Lincoln, a former laborer and rail splitter. Reportedly, Johnson replied, "What will the aristocrats do?"

FDR observed, "The only limit to our realization of tomorrow will be our doubts of today."

James Buchanan was the second of nine children, and out lived all of them except his brother Edward who died in 1895.

Eight vice presidents were born in the state of New York; the youngest and oldest vice presidents (Breckenridge and Barkley), were born in Kentucky.

During the 1960 campaign John F. Kennedy told his aides (with a twinkle in his eye), "O.K., if I win this election, I will have won it myself, but if I lose, you fellas will have lost it."

The Roosevelt family motto is "He who has planted will preserve."

At the age of 54, George Washington told William Triplett that he had never gone back on his word and never "broke a promise made to anyone."

Jimmy Carter was a speed-reader and read over 2000 words a minute with 95 percent comprehension. He devoured three or four books a week, occasionally sipping some Scotch and smoking a cigar.

Thomas Jefferson observed, "When the press is free and every man can read, all is safe."

Bill Clinton was the youngest Chief Executive to wear a hearing aid.

U. S. Grant had the first swimming pool installed at the White House.

On the therapy of horseback riding, Ronald Reagan observed, "Nothing is as good for the inside of a man as the outside of a horse."

Jimmy Carter explained at a political rally why there was such a vast age difference between his three sons and his youngest child, Amy: "My wife and I had an argument for fourteen years...which I finally won."

Visitors to the White House were constantly taking matches as souvenirs. FDR resolved this by imprinting on all matchbooks, "Stolen from the White House."

Herbert Hoover's niece once asked her uncle what to do about dinner speakers who talk to long. The former President told her, "You just pass up a little note saying, 'Your fly is open' and he'll sit down right away."

Press Secretary Pierre Salinger faced the media one afternoon just after Caroline Kennedy's pet hamster escaped in the White House. He announced, "Our security is very tight, but these were extremely intelligent hamsters."

William Henry Harrison's wife Anna outlived her husband and nine of her ten children.

Ronald Reagan observed, "Government doesn't solve problems. it subsidizes them." He later added that government doesn't solve problems, "It only rearranges them."

Warren G. Harding was a born talker. His parents entered him into an oratorical contest at age four. When he was five years old, Harding heard bells ringing and told his family, "They're ringing for [George] Washington. Some day they will ring for me."

Benjamin Harrison had small feet. His shoe size was 6.

During his trips as Vice President, Richard Nixon got stuck in an elevator in Mexico City, called a "son of a dog" in Casablanca, and was nearly killed by a communist-led mob in Caracas, Venezuela.

After the death of his son, President Calvin Coolidge went into deep despair and lost his drive to work. He spent less than five hours a day working and grew distant from his family. And he became so much of a hypochondriac he often had an electrocardiogram taken twice in the same day.

William Henry Harrison collected mastodon teeth. He was also an expert on Indian mounds and wrote of his findings of them while he lived in southern Ohio and Indiana.

In 1862 Officer Ulysses Grant wrote his Illinois congressman "Notoriety has no charm for me...."

Benjamin Harrison was a bright child. Educated by private tutors, he entered college at age 14.

Before becoming President, William Howard Taft visited Japan three times.

Warren Harding's emotional and physical health was often a problem. He was a patient four different times at Dr. Kellogg's sanitarium in Battle Creek, Michigan.

James Monroe was the first U.S. Senator to be elected President.

Bill Clinton was the first incumbent President to attend an NHL hockey game. He watched the Washington Capitals play on May 24, 1998.

Washington, Lincoln and Theodore Roosevelt all snored loudly when they slept.

Ronald Reagan was the first President to address a session of British Parliament.

As William McKinley lay dying at the Milburn House in Buffalo, New York, a nurse walked in the room to close the window shade. McKinley stopped her, saying, "Let me see the trees. They are so beautiful."

A reporter asked Quentin Roosevelt, the ornery son of Theodore, how the President relaxed. The boy replied, "I see him sometimes. But I know nothing of his family life."

Jimmy Carter once flew blimps for the U.S. Navy.

In the late 1920s Richard Nixon worked as a barker for the wheel of chance at the "Slippery Gulch Rodeo" in Prescott, Arizona. He did a fine job, earning one dollar an hour, which was good pay for a fourteen year old. When he worked there in 1929, during the Great Depression, he was paid only 50¢.

In 1814 President Madison stationed 100 soldiers on the White House grounds but the troops made a quick exit as 4500 British redcoats marched toward the city.

Dwight Eisenhower's eighteen-car campaign train in 1952 was dubbed the "Look Ahead, Neighbor" Special.

One of Richard Nixon's forefathers crossed the Delaware River with George Washington and fought at Trenton and a dozen other battles during the Revolutionary War. Another was buried at the battlefield at Gettysburg in 1863.

Harry Truman observed, "I hope some day someone will take time to evaluate the true role of the wife of a President, and to assess the many burdens she has to bear and the contributions she makes."

John Adams desperately wanted a second term as President, but the country decided instead on his political opponent (and former friend) Thomas Jefferson. When Jefferson arrived at the White House Adams roared, "You have put me out! You have put me out!"

Theodore Roosevelt had one boss while living in the White House – his wife. Whenever he worked too long in his upstairs study, Edith would tap her foot on her bedroom floor and yell "Theodore!" Immediately he abandoned his desk.

President Grover Cleveland wanted privacy after marrying his young bride. He startled White House staff members by purchasing a house near the Potomac River where he and Francis lived most of the time. The home was named "Red Top."

Many historians believe Thomas Jefferson started the American wine industry. He planted the first European grapevines at Monticello in 1773.

In the 1856 Presidential race Republican candidate John C. Fremont used this slogan to defeat Democrat James Buchanan: "The White House – no place for an old bachelor!" Most voters disagreed and elected Buchanan.

Andrew Jackson was the founder of the first Masonic lodge in Tennessee.

In 1902 William Howard Taft, at the urging of his wife, refused an appointment to the U.S. Supreme Court by an insistent Theodore Roosevelt. Taft remained governor of the Philippines.

On the eve of the Civil War, former President Millard Fillmore noted, "Let us remember that revolutions do not always establish freedom."

Theodore Roosevelt's favorite author was Joel Chandler Harris (Uncle Remus). The President visited Atlanta for a brief stop and insisted on meeting the shy writer. Later, Harris was invited to the White House to the delight of the Roosevelt children.

General William Henry Harrison's constant talking and nervous energy agitated many people. Among those who complained was John Quincy Adams.

During the Mexican War, captain U.S. Grant regularly visited with leaders of volunteers. One of the officers he often confided in was Franklin Pierce, later our 14th President.

In the late 1880s, former President Rutherford B. Hayes told a group of Civil War veterans, "As we grow older, and our army stories grow larger, we thank God we are able to believe them."

In his inaugural address, James A. Garfield remarked, "The elevation of the Negro race from slavery to full rights of citizenship is the most important change we have known since the adoption of the Constitution…."

In March of 1886, Senator (and future President) Benjamin Harrison wrote his friend John Norris, and offered this observation: "There is no better school for the cure of modesty than Washington."

One promise William Howard Taft did not keep was made in March of 1904: "I would never run for President if you guaranteed the office. It is awful to be made afraid of one's shadow."

Dr. George Harding was the first President's father to outlive his son. President Harding died suddenly in 1923. Papa Harding, incidentally, was a drummer boy in the Civil War.

On the eve of World War II, FDR was showing off his Scottish terrier, Fala, to a group of reporters. After Fala performed a couple of tricks, the President announced, "The more I hear about the Nazis, the more I love my dog."

John Adams had this to say about public officials: "Rulers are no more than attorneys, agents and trustees for the people; and if the cause, the interest and trust is insidiously betrayed, or wantonly trifled away, the people have a right to revoke the authority that they themselves have deputed."

In March of 1880 Senator Benjamin Harrison observed, "While the Republican Party may not always have been right, it has been nearer right than any other party that existed…."

When William McKinley wed Ida Saxton, his father-in-law said to him, "You are the only man of all that have sought her that I would have given her to." (Author's note: The McKinleys were married at what is now Christ Presbyterian Church in Canton, Ohio, the home church of the author.)

Attorney Rutherford B. Hayes studied German so he could better represent the German-speaking citizens of Columbus, Ohio.

Long before White House occupants Jimmy Carter, George Bush and Bill Clinton made jogging popular, Teddy Roosevelt sneaked out of his office to jog around the Washington Monument.

Herbert Hoover collected more than 20,000 cartoons of himself, keeping them stored at the White House. He referred to this collection as his "Chamber of Horrors."

James Buchanan briefly boxed as a prizefighter.

FDR collected small statues of donkeys (as well as pigs).

Fifteen Presidents have been elected without getting 50% of the popular vote, but they did get more than half of the electoral votes.

Woodrow Wilson remarked, "Consult your grandmother when in doubt."

During a canoe trip near Plains, Georgia, President Jimmy Carter was attacked by a rabbit.

Andrew Johnson's last words were, "Oh, do not cry. Be good children and we shall all meet in heaven."

Nine U.S. Presidents have owned slaves. Zachary Taylor had hundreds. Grant briefly owned a couple.

Both Vice Presidents under James Madison died in office.

Calvin Coolidge announced at the White House, "Any man who doesn't like dogs and want them about shouldn't be President."

When questioned about criticism from the press, President Bill Clinton observed, "In medieval times it was the rack. Today, it's the media."

When James K. Polk was elected in 1844, future President Millard Fillmore complained, "May God save the country, for it is evident the people will not."

Theodore Roosevelt's portrait is on the $10,000 U.S. Savings Bond.

After Gerald Ford was appointed Vice President, comedian Bob Hope declared, "Any man who has spent 20 years in Congress deserves a rest."

In July of 1989 actor and former President Ronald Reagan was inducted into the Cowboy Hall of Fame.

In his homespun philosophy, Lyndon Johnson observed, "You ain't learnin' nothin' while you're talking."

In his 1817 inaugural address, James Monroe reminded his listeners, "National honor is National property of the highest value."

When critics cited Ronald Reagan for taking too many vacations and not putting in enough hours at the White House, he brushed off such criticism by stating, "No one ever died from hard work, but why take the chance."

In a proclamation to the people of Louisiana in 1814, General Andrew Jackson stated, "The individual who refuses to defend his rights when called by his Government, deserves to be a slave, and must be punished as an enemy of his country and friend to her foe."

In a 1920 speech Calvin Coolidge announced, "Civilization and profits go hand in hand."

Because of the approaching of the Civil War, James Buchanan actually believed he would be the last President of the U.S.

James Madison thought he knew the main reason for discontent in America. As a leading member of the Constitutional Convention in 1787, he wrote in his *Federalist Papers,* "...the most common and durable source of faction has been the various and unequal distribution of property."

James A. Garfield defined a brave man as one who "dares to look the devil in the face and tell him he is a devil."

Millard Fillmore recognized that, though slavery was legal, it was also immoral. He stated, "God knows I detest slavery, but it is an existing evil, for which we are not responsible, and we must endure it...."

Historian and novelist Gore Vidal was not impressed with Ronald Reagan's election as President. In 1981 he described Reagan as "a triumph of the embalmer's art."

Because he joined the Confederacy during the Civil War, John Tyler's full citizenship wasn't restored until 1927.

John Quincy Adams felt the U.S. should not get involved in European affairs. In 1821 he stated, "America does not go forth in search of monsters to destroy."

Ten Presidents have been defeated in re-election.

Alfred Jackson, Andrew Jackson's loyal black servant, outlived his master. Alfred was buried next to the former President.

Martin Van Buren's farm at Kinderhook, New York, covered more than 200 acres. The farm's most successful crop was potatoes.

One Republican leader noted that meeting President Benjamin Harrison was like shaking hands "with a wilted petunia."

Warren G. Harding's favorite breakfast consisted of waffles smothered with chipped ham and gravy.

Chester Arthur observed that the only thing left for an ex-President to do was to "move to the country and raise big pumpkins."

Theodore Roosevelt could speak German, French and Dutch.

The parents of James Buchanan operated a trading post in Mercersburg, Pennsylvania, in the 1790s.

At any given time John Tyler owned between 60 and 90 slaves. He raised tobacco, wheat, corn and potatoes and found time to make wine.

After James A. Garfield's horse Billy was wounded at Chickamauga he wrote his wife that he loved the animal even more.

Television star and Screen Actors' Guild president Ed Asner spoke out against Ronald Reagan's foreign policy. The press enjoyed a hearty laugh when President Reagan asked, "What does an actor know about politics?"

The Mohawk word for President of the United States literally meant "burner of villages."

James Garfield's first case as an attorney was in the U.S. Supreme Court. This rare event involved the case of ex parte Milligan of 1866. As a junior partner with Jeremiah Black, the future President won the case and gained a reputation overnight as a constitutional lawyer.

After Lee's surrender to Grant at Appomattox in 1865, the victorious general met his cousin Charles Grant, a Confederate soldier. General Grant remarked that "the fight had been a bad business." He then loaned Charlie some money.

Lyndon Johnson was a pretty good judge of others. He observed that the most important thing a man is telling you is what he's not telling you.

President George Bush once remarked, "If this country ever loses its interest in fishing, we got real trouble."

William McKinley's favorite activity as a boy was playing "old sow," a game where one used a stick to hit a wood cube into a hole.

Prior to his impeachment, President Bill Clinton was called to testify before the grand jury. In responding to one of the many questions, he stated, "It depends on what the meaning of 'is' is."

In 1890 Woodrow Wilson said, "The art of compromise is the art of government." This was something Wilson found difficult to do during his second term as President.

Harry Truman observed, "Most of the problems a President has to face have their roots in the past."

While Ronald Reagan was a college student, he went to a fortune teller in Eureka, Illinois. He was told he would someday become President of the United States.

Jimmy Carter served the second longest military career of any 20th century President. Eisenhower served longer.

In 1862 U.S. Grant issued orders banning Jews from serving in his army. He said later he regretted that decision.

Theodore Roosevelt volunteered to help elect William McKinley as President in 1900. In a June 27 letter to Mark Hanna, he wrote, "I am as strong as a bull moose and you can use me to the limit."

One of Andrew Jackson's last requests was that no dirt be thrown on his casket. His wish was granted.

Six Presidents have also served as Secretary of State.

When the Prince of Wales, visited President James Buchanan in 1860, they renewed their old friendship. Among the places they visited were George Washington's home at Mount Vernon.

A total of 20 states have been the birthplace of Presidents.

Charles Dickens visited the White House in 1842 and found John Tyler to be a fine gentleman and a nice "contrast to the large group of tobacco spitters" who made up the House of Representatives.

When Chester Alan Arthur entered Union College at Schenectady, New York, in 1845 his tuition was $28.

Harry Truman's first full day as President began on Friday the 13th.

Grover Cleveland said that if he had not spent most of his time in public service he would have been fishing.

In referring to his qualities as an officer in the Civil War, Benjamin Harrison explained he was just a simple Hoosier from Indiana. He wrote, "I'm not a Julius Caesar or a Napoleon."

Following the Civil War Chester and Ellen Arthur's home in New York housed twenty-seven people. Among these were in-laws, grand children, servants and eleven student boarders.

When Lincoln learned in 1860 that he might be nominated by the Republicans for the Presidency, he told Illinois governor Lyman Trumbull, "I will be entirely frank. The taste *is* in my mouth."

Commenting on Rutherford B. Hayes becoming President, James A. Garfield said of him, "Hayes is so pristine no nickname can be pinned to him."

Calvin Coolidge took a rather dim and pessimistic view of the Presidency. In 1926 he lamented, "I suppose I am the most powerful man in the world, but great power does not mean much except great limitations. I cannot have any freedom to go and come. I am only in the clutch of forces that are greater than I am."

Grover Cleveland was described by many of his New York supporters as "ugly honest."

George Washington described his group of advisors as his "first characters." These four men became his cabinet.

John Adams was a bit frustrated when he assumed the Presidency, inheriting his predecessor's cabinet. He remarked, "Washington saddled me with three secretaries who seek to control me, but I shall soon see to that."

William Henry Harrison's inaugural speech was 48 pages.

Richard Nixon said, "There is no greater tribute we could pay to America's war dead than to find the road to peace."

During World War II General Dwight Eisenhower carried six lucky coins in his pocket. The money represented a coin from each of the six countries fighting for the allies in Europe – the U.S., Canada, Great Britain, New Zealand, South Africa and Australia.

Harry Truman's idea of heaven was sitting in a comfortable chair under a soft light and reading a good book.

Concerning his role as President during the turbulent 1960s, John Kennedy observed, "The possibilities for trouble are unlimited."

LBJ's Vice President, Hubert Humphrey, once told a reporter, "No sane person in the country likes the war in Vietnam, and neither does President Johnson."

Just prior to his secret surgery to remove part of a cancerous jaw, President Grover Cleveland observed, "I've learned just how weak the strongest man can be."

When allegations were made to the War Department that U.S. Grant continued to have a drinking problem, the general informed his superiors, "I am sober as a deacon, no matter what is said to the contrary."

On assuming his duties as the first Chief Executive, George Washington remarked, "I feel like a man condemned to death as the time of his execution draws near."

During most of his first year as President, John Adams handled government business from his farmhouse in Quincy, Massachusetts.

After two years in the White House, Warren G. Harding observed, "The Presidency is hell. There is no other word to describe it."

Shortly after his collapse in July of 1850, President Zachary Taylor told a friend, "In two days I shall be a dead man."

After serving a single term in the White House, Rutherford B. Hayes noted, "While I am not wealthy, I am happily independent."

As President, Calvin Coolidge requested that 21-gun salutes not be fired in his honor. The loud noise made his collie dog, Prudence Prim, howl. In addition, the thrifty Coolidge explained, "It costs money to fire so many guns. So I have the band play *The Star-Spangled Banner*.

Rutherford B. Hayes became the first "transcontinental" President when, while in office, he toured the west coast by train.

Lyndon B. Johnson was once a doorman at the U.S. Congress.

Ulysses S. Grant once said, "We believe we have a government and flag worth fighting for, and, if need be, dying for."

William McKinley told a crowd, "With Patriotism in our hearts and with the flag of our country in the hands of our children there is no danger of anarchy and there will be no danger to the Union."

James Monroe did not go to school until he was eleven years old, attending Campbelltown Academy in Virginia. He walked several miles each day, carrying a rifle with him to school. Often he would bring home a wild turkey or squirrel for dinner, along with his books.

After a three month siege, the city of Vicksburg, Mississippi, surrendered to U.S. Grant's federal forces. The date was July 4, 1863, and Vicksburg residents never celebrated Independence Day again until 1945.

President Hoover often amused himself at banquets and luncheons by clocking the interval between the time a speaker reached his conclusion and ought to have sat down and the moment when, having restated it several more times, he finally did.

In the 1876 Presidential race Mark Twain actively campaigned for Rutherford B. Hayes.

On the last day of his life, January 5, 1933, Calvin Coolidge sat down in his living room in Northampton, Massachusetts. He worked on a jigsaw puzzle of George Washington and chatted briefly with one of his hired men. The former President then went upstairs to shave before lunch. Just past the noon hour his wife Grace returned to find him dead.

James Monroe did not go to school until he was eleven years old, attending Campbelltown Academy in Virginia. He walked several miles each day, carrying a rifle with him to school. Often he would bring home a wild turkey or squirrel for dinner, along with his books.

After a three month siege, the city of Vicksburg, Mississippi, surrendered to U.S. Grant's federal forces. The date was July 4, 1863, and Vicksburg residents never celebrated Independence Day again until 1945.

President Hoover often amused himself at banquets and luncheons by clocking the interval between the time a speaker reached his conclusion and ought to have sat down, and the moment when, having restated it several more times, he finally did.

Millard Fillmore was the first Chief Executive to purchase a working stove for the White House kitchen. The cook didn't know how to operate it, so Fillmore went to the patent office to study the plans, then came back and taught her.

James K. Polk and his wife Sarah were the first President and First Lady to be photographed together in the White House.

Secretary of State James Buchanan rejected an appointment to the U.S. Supreme Court by President Polk. The President was happy to keep him in the cabinet. Buchanan informed Polk that he "did not desire to be President and never had..."

Grover Cleveland said of himself: "I have no style. I simply say what is in my mind and seems to be necessary at the time, and say it in my blundering way...."

Martin Van Buren kept political cartoons of himself on the wall in his library at his Lindenwold, New York, home. The ex-President had a sense of humor, and several of the cartoons were quite critical.

Abe Lincoln wrote a 22-page poem in 1848 called *The Bear Hunt.* This handwritten work was purchased by millionaire J. P. Morgan in 1910.

On Monday, October 19, 1896, President Polk had a large number of visitors. One was a lady from Fredericksburg, Virginia, who appeared as a beggar. Polk gave her a small sum and later remarked in his diary, "I doubt whether she was worthy of it."

William Howard Taft told his military aide and good friend, Archie Butt, "It is very hard to take all the slaps Roosevelt is handing me at the time." The President further noted that his friendship with his predecessor was "going to pieces like a rope of sand."

"If wrinkles must be written upon our brows, let them not be written upon the heart. The spirit should never grow old." So said James Garfield.

In 1970 George W. Bush applied to the University of Texas Law School, but was rejected. He then got a job working at an agricultural company where his job involved making chicken manure fertilizer.

Theodore Roosevelt quipped, "It is better to be faithful than famous."

James Buchanan was the only President who had fewer states in the Union at the end of his term than at the beginning. When he took office on March 4, 1857, there were 31 states. Four years later there were 24 when several southern states seceded.

Dwight Eisenhower refused the Medal of Honor. FDR wanted to give it to him after the D-Day invasion, but Eisenhower felt he didn't deserve it.

In the last words Elizabeth Jackson ever spoke to her son, Andrew, she cautioned him against sin. She also advised him not to rely upon the courts for or against libel and slander. She said, "Settle them cases yourself." And throughout his life Andrew Jackson did just that.

Commenting on earning degrees from both Yale and Harvard, George W. Bush said, "I'm proud I went there....The degrees don't define intellect. Just because you went to Yale and Harvard doesn't make you a smart person."

William Henry Harrison's son, Benjamin (not to be confused with his grandson of the same name), was wounded and taken prisoner by Mexican forces during the Texas war for independence in 1836.

Initially the Kennedys did not like to watch television and had all the sets removed from the White House. Later, however, they brought one set back so their daughter Caroline could watch "Lassie."

When President McKinley was shot, he had in his possession $46.80 ($4.80 of that in change), three lead pencils, three cigars, and a wallet with a number of business cards – but no identification of his own. In addition, there was a silver nugget he carried for good luck.

George Washington once remarked, "It is impossible to rightly govern the world without God and the *Bible*." Theodore Roosevelt added, "A thorough knowledge of the *Bible* is worth more than a college education."

When U.S. Grant learned his father was seeking an appointment for him at West Point, young Ulysses was not very happy. He said later, "A military life has no charms for me, and I had not the faintest idea of staying in the army even if I should be graduated, which I did not expect."

Herbert Hoover noted, "A good many things go around in the dark besides Santa Claus."

Thomas Jefferson was the first of our Presidents to have twins as siblings. His parents had ten children, among them Anna and Randolf who were born October 1, 1755.

When Andrew Johnson was informed he had been nominated on the same ticket as Abraham Lincoln, the former indentured servant asked, "What will the aristocrats do?"

Martin Van Buren's mother had the maiden name of Maria Goes Hoes Van Alen.

Eight Presidents were juniors, or bore the same given name as their fathers.

Following his retirement from public office, Benjamin Harrison was a professor of international law at Stanford University.

Gerald Ford observed, "In politics there is no such thing as an enemy — only someone who disagrees with you today and who might be with you on the next vote."

John Kennedy was on Harvard's swim team.

Jimmy Carter ran cross country at the Naval Academy.

In the 1860 Presidential election Lincoln voted for every Republican, except himself! He left the choice for President blank.

William Taft loved baseball. As governor of the Philippines he introduced the sport in 1900 to the Filipinos.

George Washington was defeated twice in his bid for election to Virginia's House of Burgesses. After finally winning in 1758 he never lost another election.

James Polk abstained from drinking alcoholic beverages. Opponents criticized him by saying he "drank too much water."

The 23rd Ohio Volunteer Infantry marched a lot in October of 1862. A young Civil War officer, William McKinley, told the story for many years that his army ate breakfast in Pennsylvania, had lunch in Maryland then ate supper in Virginia – all in one day.

While playing baseball during his college days, Rutherford B. Hayes sometimes bruised his fingers so badly he couldn't write. Ball players used no gloves in the mid-1800s.

Bill Clinton and his Vice President's wife, Tipper Gore, both celebrated their birthdays on the same day – August 19. Clinton was born two years earlier.

After working as a mining engineer in southern Australia, Herbert Hoover described the country as a place of "red dust, black flies and white heat."

When he was ten years old, Theodore Roosevelt cried when some men chopped down some trees near his house.

During and following his term as President, George Washington entertained hundreds of guests at Mount Vernon. He described his home as "a well resorted tavern." Incidentally, he ate steak for dinner every Thursday.

When actor Ronald Reagan was elected governor of California, he was asked by a reporter what kind of governor he thought he would be. Reagan quipped, "I don't know. I never played a governor before!"

There have been two sets of father and son to serve as President: John Adams and John Quincy Adams, and George Bush and George W. Bush.

As a Congressman, James Garfield established the Department of Education. This office was a non-cabinet creation and several years later it was abolished.

FDR didn't want the public to know he was crippled and confined to crutches, leg braces and a wheelchair. He said being seen in this condition "would inspire pity."

Lyndon Johnson said his Vice President, Hubert H. Humphrey, had "the greatest co-ordination of mind and tongue of anybody I know."

Reportedly, Zachary Taylor's last words before he died in the White House were, "My only regret is for the friends I leave behind me."

A knee injury in 1997 forced Bill Clinton to stop jogging. Consequently he regained most of the weight he lost, even though he continued to exercise indoors.

When he addressed crowds in Louisiana, Theodore Roosevelt spoke in French.

During his eight years as President, Dwight Eisenhower managed to golf more than 800 times, despite a couple of heart attacks.

Each President's portrait in the White House is selected by the President himself. He selects his own artist and must approve the painting. Most of the portraits are done while he is in office.

Frederick John Smith, a shoemaker in Canton, Ohio, continued to make shoes and boots for William McKinley when he went to the White House.

As a warning to a bickering Congress in 1881, James A. Garfield named his pet dog "Veto."

Our 43rd President, George W. Bush, narrowly defeated Vice President Al Gore. On December 13, 2000 he reminded Americans, "Common courtesy and common goals will keep America strong."

Lafayette Square, next to the White House, was also called The President's Square. At one time it was a graveyard.

The Marine Band has been performing in the White House since 1801.

John Adams once told his son, John Quincy, "You'll never be alone with a poet in your pocket." The second President was a great lover of books.

Civil War was approaching. During this turbulent time, President James Buchanan had many northerners and southerners in his administration. There were heated arguments at White House dinners and eventually Buchanan removed all black servants there.

The only original White House artifact which is still there is the Gilbert Stuart portrait of George Washington.

In 2001 George W. Bush appointed the first black Secretary of State — Colin Powell.

Anecdotes on the First Ladies

PROBLEMS

In 1933 Eleanor Roosevelt received more than 300,000 letters, and answered many of them personally. Many were from poor women who had been hit hard by the Depression. Some of these letters were passed on to her husband, while other requests were met with donations of her own. One woman wrote to tell her of her ailments – poor liver, a hernia, "female troubles," fallen arches, and hemorrhoids. Then the woman added, "Thank goodness, it doesn't all hurt at once."

AHEAD OF HER TIME

Abigail Adams was a strong voice for women's rights. While her husband served in the Continental Congress, she wrote him, "Whilst you are proclaiming peace and goodwill to men, emancipating all nations, you insist on retaining absolute power over wives." To which John responded, "I cannot but laugh, you are so saucy." But Adams always appreciated his wife's opinions on all matters, and advised her, "I want better communications. I want to hear you think and see your thoughts."

TAKE A PEEK

Following President Wilson's stroke in 1919, very few people saw him. His doctors and a few top aides were permitted to make brief appearances in his bedroom, as long as the matter was really important. Edith Wilson was very strict about limiting her husband's exposure to the burdens of the Presidency, and for seventeen months she, in effect, ran the executive branch. She also made some exceptions as to no visitors when King Albert and Queen Elizabeth of Belgium, and later the Prince of Wales, were allowed to look in on the President.

CLIMBING THE LADDER OF SUCCESS

Martha Washington was a real tomboy in her youth. She also loved riding her father's horse through fields, woodlands, and down to the plantation wharf to watch supply ships come in. Once, she rode the horse up the stairs onto the veranda of her Uncle William's house. When her stepmother tried to reprimand her, Martha's father intervened and said to leave her alone, "she's not harmed William's staircase. And, by heavens, how she can ride!"

TAKING NO CHANCES

At several sessions with a fortune teller, Mrs. Harding was told there were impending dangers and scandals facing her husband. Having heard rumors of Warren's affairs and corruption within his cabinet, Florence asked that a Secret Service agent be assigned to her – the first First Lady to do so. She kept him sitting in the hall outside her bedroom at night.

PROUD TO SERVE

During each winter while the War for Independence was being fought, Martha Washington visited her husband in camp. Her visits, however, were not merely spent in idleness or being with her husband. She organized volunteer nurses and tended to the sick and wounded. She had other women in camp patching clothes, knitting socks, repairing shoes, and making shirts for the destitute army. A female resident of Valley Forge recalled, "I never in my life knew a woman so busy from early morning until late at night as Lady Washington…."

NOT RESPONSIBLE

For five weeks following the assassination of her husband, Mary Lincoln remained in an upstairs room at the White House. Shuddering in her darkened room and screaming in torment, she could not bear to attend funeral services. While she was lying in bed, souvenir hunters descended on the unguarded White House. They tore off bits of expensive upholstery, carted away furniture and lamps, ripped down the curtains, and cut holes in the carpet. Mrs. Lincoln finally boarded a train, and when the damage was discovered, critics accused her of stealing taxpayers' property. Newspapers were particularly harsh on her, only adding to her woes.

Yuk!

Abigail Smith Adams was born in Weymouth, Massachusetts, in the midst of an epidemic (probably diphtheria or small-pox). When she developed a fever and sore throat, the infant was administered the standard concoction of the day – snail water. This liquid medication consisted of roasted garden snails, baked earthworms, and salt. In spite of this treatment, she survived.

Raising Questions with Raisa

Ronald Reagan and Soviet leader Mikhail Gorbachev met five times and each meeting went smoothly, except for some differences between the First Ladies, Nancy and Raisa. After receiving a lecture once from Raisa, Nancy Reagan reportedly remarked, "Who does that dame think she is?" Mrs. Reagan later told reporters they overstated their differences, but admitted they were "not on the same wave length." She furthermore told the media that "too much attention" was paid to the matter.

The Tribulations of Motherhood

Lucretia Garfield probably spoke for millions of American mothers when she wrote these words to her husband three years before he was elected President: "It is horrible to be a man, but the grinding misery of being a woman between the upper and nether millstone of household cares and training children is almost as bad. To be half civilized with some aspirations for enlightenment, and obliged to spend the largest part of time the victim of young barbarians keeps one in perpetual ferment."

French "Frank" Comments

While the Kennedys were visiting Paris in 1961, First Lady Jackie Kennedy charmed her hosts with her knowledge of French history, art, and her frank conversation. Seated with French Minister of Culture Andre Malraux at a state dinner, Jackie referred to German Chancellor Adenauer as "a little nutty." She also remarked how she despised Queen Frederica of Greece, and how pompous the Shah of Iran was. Then, being brutally frank, she turned to Malraux and asked, "Have you ever seen your wife throw up?" The French Minister found the question puzzling and amusing, and years later dedicated his book, *Anti-Memoirs*, to her.

LEAVE ME ALONE

First Lady Bess Truman, often referred to as "The Boss" by her husband, cherished her privacy. In 1945 she promptly informed the Secret Service agents assigned to her protection that, under no circumstances, would she tolerate anyone trailing her while shopping or visiting friends back home in Independence, Missouri. Reluctantly, agents honored her demand and her only escorts were her daughter Margaret or an aunt.

YOU CAN DEPEND ON ME

Rain or shine, sleet or hail, sick or healthy, conditions did not matter. Even on the verge of exhaustion, Pat Nixon always fulfilled her duties as First Lady be it campaigning for her husband, giving a speech, or dedicating a new building. Such devotion puzzled those who knew her. She was probably one of our most traveled First Lady, and she often said, "I do or die. I never cancel out."

MAMIE HAD A LITTLE LAMB...

Mamie Doud Eisenhower once accepted what she thought was a little lamb while living in Cedar Rapids, Iowa. Mother Doud was pleased at the affection her young daughter showed towards it. But the lamb turned out to be an infant ram. One day, all in the spirit of fun, the ram backed up about ten feet, lowered its horny bullet head, and charged Mamie. It scored a direct bullseye on Mamie's stomach, knocking her breathless to the ground. That was the last of the ram, and the Douds found another owner.

INQUISITIVE NATURE

In 1952 a young female journalist-photographer interviewed six-year-old Tricia Nixon, took her picture, then had it published in her *Washington Times Herald* column, "Inquiring Photographer." Tricia's father had just been elected Vice President, and the reporter asked, "What do you think of Senator Nixon now?" Little Tricia answered, "He's always away. If he's so famous why can't he stay home?" This same reporter later complained about the media invading *her* privacy, particularly when she became a mother while serving as First Lady. This reporter was no other than Jackie Kennedy.

Wandering Widow

It is not surprising that Mary Lincoln had emotional problems. By 1871 she had witnessed the death of her husband and two sons, Willie and Tad. She went into a deep depression, followed by temper tantrums and a persecution complex. She refused to eat for fear of being poisoned, and trembled in public thinking she would be attacked. Since her husband's violent death she suffered from severe headaches. Incurring large debts, she attempted to coerce officeholders into paying her bills. Her oldest son, Robert, tried to help her as best he could. One evening he found her wandering naked in the hallway of a cheap Chicago hotel, and when he forced her back into her room, she screamed, "You're trying to murder me!" Finally, Robert, along with a team of physicians and a Cook County judge, testified at a court hearing where she was judged insane. But just after four months in a private asylum, she petitioned for a release and was granted permission to live with her sister. Several months later a second hearing determined that she was "restored to reason," but her condition had not changed at all.

In Need

Abigail Adams was highly intelligent and very practical. While raising four children and tending the farm, she had to think about her family's safety when in 1775 the battlefield was located nearby. When war broke out between English and colonial forces, she noted, "Courage, I know we have in abundance; conduct, I hope we shall not want; but powder, where shall we get a sufficient supply?" She also met with George Washington in Boston, providing him with encouragement and advice. The British soon withdrew but difficult times lay ahead.

Make Way!

Eleanor Roosevelt had difficulty learning how to drive the family car. During her "trial runs" she drove into the back door of the Hyde Park house, knocked over a stone pillar flanking the driveway, backed into a ditch, and ran off the road several times. Eventually she got the hang of it.

Jackie Corrected

In 1968 Senator Robert Kennedy announced he was running for President. Lyndon Johnson had become very unpopular because of U.S. involvement in Vietnam, and Kennedy felt he could win the Democratic nomination. At the Kennedy home one evening the family gathered to discuss the campaign, all agreeing that Bobby could win. Former First Lady Jackie Kennedy, enthused, said, "Won't it be wonderful when we get back into the White House?" Bobby's wife, Ethel – who for years had resented the way her sister-in-law overshadowed her – gave her an icy look and remarked, "What do you mean *we*?"

Never Too Young

When Nancy Davis Reagan was a young actress in New York City, she was asked her age by a magazine writer. She refused to answer. Related the First Lady: "When the story was published the writer had guessed at my age and made me five years older than I was. I immediately wrote the magazine asking them to give me back five years because I had plans for them. They printed my letter but I learned a good lesson. When you're asked a question, it's better to give an answer, or someone will give one for you…."

Frightening Adventure

In her diary and unpublished autobiography entitled "Adventures of a Nobody," Louisa Adams told of her husband's insensitivity, and the numerous problems she encountered while her husband served as ambassador to Russia. An infant daughter died, and when Louisa became depressed, John Quincy bought her a gift–a book on "the diseases of the mind." She wanted to study astronomy but her austere husband objected. To meet John in France, she left St. Petersburg with three servants and their eight-year-old son. The journey was quite an ordeal, the carriage sinking several times in the mud, and traveling on a road where a Russian cutthroat had murdered a passenger the previous day. It was so cold her food and wine froze. Her servants were villainous men of the worst character and deserted her. She hid her money and seldom slept, fearing for her life. She was treated rudely by border guards and in Germany her carriage was surrounded by a mob shouting, "Kill them. They are Russians!" Showing her American passport saved their lives. After forty days she entered Paris just as a revolution was taking place. Though her health was never good, Louisa immediately renewed her schedule while her maid needed two months of bed rest to recover. Of all the early Presidential couples, the John Quincy Adamses were the most traveled.

More Important Things To Do

Lucretia Garfield played almost no part in her husband's political and social world during his years in Congress. Like most other married women with a family in the 1800s, she devoted her time to raising a family. Eight pregnancies from 1860 to 1874 kept her tied to the duties and miseries of motherhood.

No "Will"

A short time before Ida McKinley died in May of 1907, a friend paid her a visit in Canton. The former First Lady, still grieving over her husband Will's assassination in 1901, appeared frail, dressed in black, and her hair cut short and curled at the ends. During the visit, she moaned over and over to her guest, "Why would I linger? Please, God, if it is Thy will, let me go. I want to be with him. I am so tired."

Accepting Humility With "Grace"

Grace Coolidge once attended a reception at Continental Hall in Washington. A doorman stopped her, and an interesting conversation took place:

Doorman: "What is your name, please?"
Mrs. Coolidge: "I am Mrs. Coolidge."
Doorman: "What's your husband's first name?"
Mrs. Coolidge: "Calvin."
Doorman: "What's his business?"
Mrs. Coolidge: "He's the Vice President."
Doorman: "Vice President of what?"
Mrs. Coolidge: "Of the United States!"
A frustrated and humbled Grace Coolidge was given permission to enter.

Bitter Butter

Years before she met Ronald Reagan, Nancy Davis was a struggling young actress living in New York City. Male companions often took her to dinner at the Stork Club. In an effort to economize, she regularly sneaked a dinner roll or two into her purse to take home for breakfast. One evening, she was embarrassed and surprised when the restaurant owner, Sherman Billingley, sent a package of butter to her table with a note: "I thought you might enjoy some butter on my rolls."

Laying Down the Law

Following her husband's death, Lucretia Garfield and her family settled in at Lawnfield in Mentor, Ohio. Years later Crete set down some rules for her family and visitors. Nobody was allowed to play cards on Sunday, and reading comics in the newspaper was forbidden. The former First Lady didn't think it was proper reading for youngsters. In spite of these, and other regulations, the Garfield clan enjoyed happy, carefree times.

A Familiar Sound

In 1980 George Bush first ran for President, trying to defeat Ronald Reagan for the nomination (Reagan won but selected Bush as his Vice Presidential candidate). Barbara Bush campaigned hard for her husband. While driving through Iowa she was listening to a talk show on the car radio when a young man called in and said he was voting for Bush because he was the best candidate and had a great family. Barbara got excited, until she recognized the voice – it was their son, Marvin.

Presents for the Wrong Party

Washington newspaperwoman Sarah Booth Conroy told of a birthday party held for fellow reporter Helen Smith at Conroy's house. But due to illness, the guest of honor didn't show. After a brief delay First Lady Pat Nixon showed up and announced, "Helen Smith isn't here so I want all her presents!"

A Lucky Lady

After Lou Hoover died in 1944, the former President went through his wife's papers to settle her estate. He discovered tens of thousands of dollars in uncashed checks. These were from people whom she had helped over many years. These repayments of "loans" Lou turned into gifts by not depositing them in a bank. Then, Hoover found a sealed letter addressed to their sons. In it was written, "You have been lucky boys to have had such a father and I am a lucky woman to have had my life's trail alongside the path of three such men and boys."

How Do We Say That?

Ida Saxton (McKinley), her sister, Pina, and their female chaperon toured Europe in 1869. The three young ladies discovered, among other things, that their French needed improvement. Ida got a bit frustrated when, in August, they were touring France and Belgium. While dining at a hotel Ida asked a waiter for some matches, but he returned with a knife. Later, the girls ordered some table oil, and the male waiter returned with a cup of egg white!

Helper Harriet

Since James Buchanan was a bachelor, his niece Harriet Lane served as the official hostess of the White House. A woman of rare beauty and refinement, her role as First Lady in the late 1850s made her the most popular woman in America. Harriet was one of the first individuals to call attention to the plight of American Indians. She initiated programs to raise money and help educate Native Americans and constantly prodded her uncle to make certain western tribes were treated fairly. She became known as "the Great Mother" by many Indians, and tribes named their newborn daughters "Harriet" in her honor.

Mad Mary

Temperamental Mary Lincoln had few female friends. She was jealous when other women got too close to her husband, and she could be spiteful to other wives of politicians. While visiting Crown Point, Virginia, near the end of the Civil War, she was seated on a sofa engaged in conversation. Julia Grant, wife of the general, came to see her. When Mrs. Lincoln rose, Julia sat down on the sofa next to where the First Lady had been seated. Mary exclaimed, "How dare you be seated until I invite you!" An embarrassed Mrs. Grant immediately rose and sat in a nearby chair.

Meeting a Murderer

On April 26, 1881, First Lady Lucretia Garfield opened the White House to receive callers. One of her guests was a pesky office seeker named Charles Guiteau. This man later remarked how much he enjoyed talking to Mrs. Garfield, saying she was "chatty and companionable." Nine weeks later Guiteau shot President Garfield in the back. Garfield died eighty days later from the mortal wound.

A Snub or Compliment?

The Kennedys made their ill-fated trip to Texas on November 21, 1963. While visiting Houston they stayed at the Rice Hotel. When they entered the building, the manager ignored the President, looked at Jackie and shouted, "Good evening, Mrs. President!"

May I Vote Please

In 1988 George and Barbara Bush voted in Houston, Texas. A large crowd naturally gathered to witness the event. After casting his ballot Bush stopped to chat with reporters when suddenly a loud voice boomed, "Hey Fella, I've been waiting in this line for a long time. Move along!" It was his wife.

Not a Jailbird

Eleanor Roosevelt was always on the go and even her husband didn't know where she was. One evening the First Lady left the White House to inspect a New York penitentiary. FDR, unaware of her leaving, asked Tommy Thompson of her whereabouts. "In prison," said Thompson. The President replied, "I'm not surprised. What's she in for?"

Off Limits – Maybe

First Lady Lou Hoover gave a private tour to incoming hostess Eleanor Roosevelt in March of 1933. After showing her the various rooms, Mrs. Hoover was asked by Mrs. Roosevelt to take her to the White House kitchen. As both ladies neared it, Lou stopped and turned to Eleanor and explained that in four years she never entered that territory. "I'm sorry," she explained, "but the housekeeper will have to show you the kitchen. I never enter the kitchen." The first room Eleanor Roosevelt entered as First Lady was the kitchen where she oversaw meals prepared for the new President and his guests.

Personal Letter

While serving as governor of California, Ronald Reagan received a very interesting letter from a woman who, due to many other commitments, was regretfully quitting her unsalaried position on the California Arts Commission. The letter ended, "I am sure that you can appreciate my reasons for resigning. I really don't see enough of my husband as it is." It was signed, "Affectionately yours, Nancy." And underneath the sender's name, lest the governor have any doubts, was typed, "Mrs. Ronald Reagan."

It May Have Cost Some Votes, But...

When First Lady Lou Hoover invited Mrs. Oscar De Priest to the White House, she had little idea it would generate such controversy. Mrs. De Priest was black, the wife of an Illinois black Republican. After the event on June 12, 1930, southern newspapers bitterly attacked her. The *Mobile Press* was typical of editorial responses when it stated that Mrs. Hoover "offered to the South and to the nation an arrogant insult yesterday when she entertained a Negro woman at a White House tea. She harmed Mr. Hoover to a serious extent."

Barbara Battles Bowl

Barbara Bush will always remember what she did the first day after her husband was elected President. She spent part of the morning pulling toilet paper out of the commode. Her twin granddaughters stuffed it, and the future First Lady was up to her elbows reaching in the toilet to clean it.

A House to Build a Dream On

In 1971 the Nixons invited Jackie Kennedy to the White House. Richard and Pat Nixon gave her a personal tour. At one point, Jackie turned towards President Nixon and remarked, "I always lived in a dream world."

Smokers Beware!

In the 1992 campaign Bill Clinton was asked if he ever smoked marijuana. His clumsy admission that he did only once but "didn't inhale" was followed by the same question to his wife Hillary. The future First Lady responded, "No, I don't like smoke, cigarettes, or anything." In one of her first actions after moving into the White House, she declared the building a "No Smoking" zone. This may have caused a slight problem for her husband, who occasionally enjoyed smoking a cigar.

Trouble with a Fly

Barbara Bush always liked to look her best. During the 1992 campaign she decided to get her hair done while campaigning for her husband. She walked into Peggy Swift's room (Peggy was one of the campaign coordinators) where there was a middle aged male hairdresser and his wife waiting. Unfortunately, the man had forgotten to zip up the fly in his pants. Everyone seemed to notice but the hairdresser. When the man had finished the First Lady's hair, he asked if he and his wife could pose with Barbara for a picture. Very diplomatically, Barbara asked them to wait a minute while she put on her pearls and some lipstick. To the relief of everyone, when she returned, the man had zipped up his pants.

Nightmares for Nancy

Nancy Reagan would like to forget at least some of the events which took place during her term as First Lady. In one twenty-four hour period she was put to the test. It began one night when she lost a filling after going to bed. A dentist was summoned to the White House and replaced it. Later that morning she was meeting with a woman and after they were finished, Nancy got up from her chair and lost her skirt, standing in front of her guest in her pantyhose and blouse. She then got on a plane that same evening. When she went to the bathroom she forgot to lock the door. The pilot opened it and stood in terror as the First Lady seated on the toilet.

Backward Ways

Though not generally known for her humor, Jackie Kennedy enjoyed playing pranks. Even as a youngster she demonstrated this trait. In the early 1950s she and her step-sister Nina disembarked from a train with their hats and coats on backward to see how many people would notice.

Oh, You Beautiful Doll

Dolley Madison, like many other refined ladies in the early 1800s, used cosmetics. But it should be pointed out that she did not *overuse* makeup like many of her contemporaries. Dolley emphasized her naturally long eyelashes by daubing them with a mixture of grease and soot, an early form of mascara.

Dying Wish

Rachel Jackson lived to see her husband elected President but died before his inauguration. Political opponents accused her of adultery and other indiscretions, and the strain of a dirty campaign brought her much grief. Prior to her death in December of 1828, she said of her husband's election, "For my own part, I never wished it."

Curses

Teddy Roosevelt's daughter was not fond of Mrs. Nellie Taft. Both women were headstrong, ambitious and highly opinionated. Prior to the Tafts moving in to the Executive Mansion in 1909, Alice put a curse on the new First Family by burying a voodoo doll on the White House lawn and calling upon the gods to rain woe and sadness on the new occupants.

Seeing Red

First Lady Pat Nixon, in the spirit of Jackie Kennedy, wanted to decorate the White House with Americana. When the White House curator Clement Conger acquired a portrait of Dolley Madison from The Pennsylvania Academy of Fine Arts, and learned it had once hung in the Red Room, Pat decided to hang it there again and had the room painted in the exact shade of the velvet draperies in the portrait.

All Dolled Up

One day Mamie Eisenhower arrived late for a formal dinner. Her husband, always punctual, felt she deserved a reprimand. "Do you realize you've kept the President of the United States waiting?" Mamie responded, "Why no; I've been busy making myself pretty for my husband."

Lack of Privacy

Not long after arriving at the Executive Mansion on Cherry Street in New York City, Martha Washington realized her days of privacy were nearing an end. In a letter to a niece she complained of feeling like a "state prisoner" and added, "I have not had one half hour to myself since the day of my arrival."

FOLDING CHAIR

When Lou Hoover moved into the White House in 1929 she described the place as "bleak as a New England barn." After much effort, she went about restoring various parts of it, particularly after her husband sat in a chair (which once belonged to Dolley Madison) and it collapsed.

DECISION MAKER

Mamie Eisenhower was a take charge lady. As a wife of a much traveled military leader she learned early on how to organize and maintain a household. One day White House usher J. B. West showed her a luncheon menu she had not seen before. "What's this?" Mamie demanded. West explained the President had approved it several days ago. Mamie retorted, "I run everything in my house. In the future all menus are to be approved by me and no one else."

NOTORIOUS ABSENTEE

Jackie Kennedy was not fond of entertaining groups in the White House. When organizations such as the Girl Scouts, American Heart Association or the March of Dimes were scheduled to show up, Jackie often did not. Her phrase "Give them to Lady Bird" kept Vice President Lyndon Johnson's wife quite busy. Jackie even refused to appear at a reception in her honor. The President was furious, yelling, "Jackie! You can't do this!" JFK went in her place, offering the crowd an excuse for her absence.

PROPHET OF DOOM

Ellen Wilson suffered from Bright's disease, an incurable kidney ailment at the time. A little more than a year after her husband was President, she knew the end was near. In the spring of 1914 she was walking arm-in-arm with her nurse in the White House garden. The gardener was working on a design Ellen had created. "It will be so lovely, Charlie," she said. "But I'll never live to see it finished." She died a short time later.

BELATED TRIBUTE

Perhaps the one First Lady whose accomplishments have been largely ignored by historians is Florence Harding, who established a precedent for those who followed her. Among the problems she publicly attacked were women's rights, discrimination against blacks and Native Americans, ill treatment of the mentally disturbed, suffering war veterans and abuse of animals. She expanded the Red Cross, improved orphanages and, at her insistence, demanded that women be given positions of authority within state and federal agencies. With boldness and tenacity she instituted changes, despite the protests of many groups and political leaders. She also made cutbacks in spending of many wasteful government projects and programs. Some of her protests fell on deaf ears at her husband's cabinet meetings. Nor did she put much faith in President Harding's promises to include more women in his administration. Mrs. Harding felt that women should no longer serve a subordinate role in business and government. Her experience as a single-divorced mother, a newspaper publisher and campaign organizer gave her great insight to many problems. The scandals of her husband's term and his sudden death in office, however, overshadowed her achievements. Though she had her faults and perhaps lacked physical beauty, Florence was immensely popular and deserves a higher place in history.

LET THERE BE LIGHT

In 1848 workmen installed gas lights at the White House. This would make it cheaper, brighter and safer than using candles, but Sarah Polk found it inconvenient at least once when the gas company unexpectedly cut off the flow of gas during a reception. The flames in the chandeliers flickered and died, throwing the entire room into darkness. The First Lady ushered everyone into the smaller Blue Room where she continued to entertain guests in the glow of dozens of candles.

GIFTS FROM GALT

Edith Galt was familiar with the tastes of First Ladies. She and her husband Norman owned and operated a Washington shop which sold expensive jewelry, picture frames, and vases. Among their regular customers were First Ladies Frances Cleveland, Caroline Harrison, Ida McKinley, and Edith Roosevelt. When Norman died, Edith ran the shop herself. When she was invited to the White House for tea, she met Woodrow Wilson, whose wife had recently died. Wilson fell "head over heels" in love. Mrs. Galt became the second Mrs. Wilson.

A Bad Break

Bess Truman absolutely hated publicity but realized part of a First Lady's duties was to show up at important ceremonies. She was asked to christen two hospital planes and reluctantly consented. She swung a champagne bottle eight times against the fuselage of the airplane, but it didn't break. A military aide stepped in, and it took him five more swings to break it. On the second plane, the bottle was scored (cut on the surface) to make it easier. Bess took a mighty swing, and the bottle showered champagne all over her. Newsreel cameras recorded the embarrassing moment. Her daughter Margaret thought this was very amusing, and when they returned to the White House, the President teased his wife about the incident and made several jokes about it. The First Lady was not in good humor and replied that she would have had a better time had she cracked the bottle over Harry's head.

A Feeling of Emptiness

Following World War I Herbert Hoover was busy trying to feed the war-ravaged starving masses overseas. His wife Lou spent her time back in the states arranging special banquets to raise money for European relief. She charged $1000 a plate dinners for the cause, serving plain food with tin utensils. And at each banquet there was always an empty chair for the Invisible Guest – a hungry child.

Louisa's Lament

Louisa Adams, wife of John Quincy, found living in her native America rather drab and coarse. Having grown up in England and France, she settled in Boston with her new husband. Yankee customs, the condition of roads, and even the clothing appalled her. She remarked, "Had I stepped into Noah's ark I do not think I could have been more astonished." More than a decade later, she would serve as First Lady of the Executive Mansion.

Chastised by Julia

When widow Julia Grant visited the Chicago World's Fair in 1893 she met a woman sculptor, Enid Yandell. The former First Lady did not approve of women working outside the home and explained to the young sculptress that it was nothing personal but, "I don't disapprove of *you*, Mrs. Yandell, but I think every woman is better off at home taking care of husband and children. The battle with the world hardens a woman and makes her unwomanly." Miss Yandell asked, "And if one has no husband?" Mrs. Grant replied, "Get one."

Spinach Not So Special

When Rosalynn Carter was six years old she and her mother visited the White House where they had lunch with President and Mrs. Hoover. Years later, when she was First Lady, Rosalynn recalled another incident involving the Hoovers: "Mr. Hoover kindly wrote my ten-year-old brother, whose school friends were insisting that no one could possibly have had spinach for lunch at the White House." In the letter, Hoover wrote, "We indeed had spinach at the White House and I don't like it either. Mrs. Hoover makes me eat it."

Caught with Their Pants Down

In 1943 First Lady Eleanor Roosevelt visited American troops in New Zealand. During one impromptu visit she toured a Red Cross club, accompanied by several generals and admirals. When she entered the building two army privates were standing by an electric heater in their underpants. While onlookers gasped, Eleanor coolly chatted with the two young men. Though they were paralyzed with fear, the privates were thrilled that the First Lady took time to talk with them.

Oops

Nancy Reagan's anti-drug campaign continued even after leaving the White House. While she was attending a "Just Say No" rally a reporter asked her a political question. The former First Lady probably wasn't thinking clearly when she responded, "I didn't intend for this to take on a political tone. I'm just here for the drugs."

A Sight for Sore Eyes

Though only in her early twenties, First Lady Frances Cleveland was very popular with White House guests of all ages. Her charm and wit were her greatest assets. She once kept a group of distinguished guests roaring with laughter as she described a carefully planned political event where people came to look at her and listen to her husband speak. When the couple was introduced, she appeared with a bandaged eye, and the President had a sore throat.

SURE SHOT SHIRLEY

Little Shirley Temple was Hollywood's biggest star. At age ten she and her parents, who were strict Republicans, were invited to the White House by President Franklin Roosevelt. The President enjoyed Shirley's company, and the Temples were asked to visit the Roosevelts at their Hyde Park home. When she was not under the watchful eye of her mother, Shirley could be mischievous. As Shirley recalled, "Mrs. Roosevelt was bending over an outdoor grill cooking some hamburgers for us. I was in my little dress with the puffed sleeves and white shoes and had this very feminine lace purse – which contained the slingshot I always carried with me. When I saw Mrs. Roosevelt bending over, I couldn't resist. I hit her with a pebble from my slingshot. She jumped quite smartly, and the Secret Service men assigned to her were extremely upset for a while. But no one saw me do it except my mother, and she didn't blow the whistle on me until we got back to the hotel. Then she let me have it in the same area I'd attacked the First Lady."

PRETTY IN PINK

Mamie Eisenhower was aware of the importance of color in regard to fashion. Pink was her favorite color because it highlighted her blue eyes and her soft milky complexion. She hated to wear blue dresses, however, though she had to wear that color as a child. As she once explained, "You have to use the gifts you have. I know I have beautiful eyes and I use them."

MOM WAS NOT AMUSED

During his last year in the White House, President Rutherford B. Hayes took his family on a tour of the West. At every train stop the First Family was besieged by autograph-seekers. The President gladly signed, but Lucy Hayes grew weary and at a couple of stops tried to keep out of sight by remaining in her seat. But as soon as the crowd spotted her, people began to pass cards and autograph books through the window for her to sign. She was soon on the verge of collapse from signing so many times. Finally, the train started, and her twenty-two-year-old son, Rutherford, came running into the Presidential car and handed his mother an autograph album he had been passing through the window to her. The mischievous Cornell graduate had obtained her autograph fifty-six times!

211

NOBODY IS IMMUNE

Even the First Family is not exempt from invasions of privacy. The FBI once had Eleanor Roosevelt's Chicago hotel room bugged while she entertained Joseph Lash, a young friend who later became her biographer. FBI Director J. Edgar Hoover suspected Lash of having communist ties, but the First Lady discovered the activity and complained to her husband. The bugging stopped.

REVENGE

In June of 1910, while Calvin Coolidge was mayor of Northampton, Massachusetts, his wife took a group of high school girls on a sight-seeing tour of Washington, D.C., which included a tour of the White House. When the group entered the East Room, Grace Coolidge was captivated by the large gilded piano there left by Theodore Roosevelt. She stepped over to touch it and was roughly pushed away by one of the guides. She later announced to the girls, "Someday I'll come back here, open that piano and play it, and he won't order me out!" Years later, as First Lady, she recalled the episode and got in the habit of giving the piano a little kick.

TEMPER, TEMPER

Hillary Clinton seemed well aware of her husband's nocturnal excursions and alleged affairs even while he was governor of Arkansas. Thinking that Hillary had gone to bed, Bill borrowed a car from a friend one evening to meet "a friend." When he returned to the Governor's Mansion his wife was waiting — and furious. A shouting match ensued in the kitchen. A cupboard door was broken off its hinges. Food, broken glass and pots and pans were scattered on the floor. It took more than two hours to clean the mess. Then, in February of 1994, First Lady Hillary got into a shouting match with the President, and smashed a lamp in the White House living quarters. The *Chicago Tribune* and *Newsweek* reported the incident and the Clintons blamed the Secret Service detail for leaking the story to the media. A short time later several White House agents were reassigned and the size of the contingent was reduced to allow the Clintons more privacy.

HILLARY TAKES THE PLUNGE

After her commencement speech at Wellesley College, Hillary Rodham Clinton indulged in one last act of ritual rebellion as a student. She stripped to a bathing suit she had worn under her dress and graduation gown and plunged into Lake Waban. Swimming in the lake was strictly forbidden, and while she was frolicking in the water, a campus security guard took her robe, dress and glasses. Having poor eyesight, Hillary had to feel her way back to the dorm.

DOG DAYS

In 1984 Barbara Bush wrote a book entitled *C. Fred's Story: A Dog's Life*, about a golden cocker spaniel which lived in the residence of the Vice President. All proceeds went to two national organizations to fight illiteracy. Five years later, as First Lady, she wrote another canine story, *Millie's Book*. This book sold very well, and once again all profits were donated to the literacy cause.

THE PARK RIDGE PRIZE FIGHTER

Hillary Rodham Clinton learned early to be strong and independent. As an elementary school pupil, she came home one day from school in Park Ridge, Illinois, having been roughed up by an older, bigger girl. Her mother scolded her and advised, "There's no room in this house for cowards. You're going to have to stand up to her. The next time she hits you, I want you to hit her back." Hillary followed her mother's instructions and was aptly rewarded.

ELEANOR AND IKE SOCK IT TO 'EM

While First Lady Eleanor Roosevelt was visiting wounded GIs in London during World War II, she asked if they needed anything. Among their complaints was the fact that they lacked warm woolen socks. With only thin cotton socks, their feet were constantly blistered. Eleanor promised to speak to General Eisenhower the next day. The general checked with his quartermaster and discovered there were two and a half million pairs of woolen socks waiting in warehouses. The socks were promptly distributed and the First Lady was overjoyed.

FIRST LADY PRANK

Betty Ford once "put a charge" into her daughter and a friend. Susan Ford and her girlfriend decided to stay in the Lincoln Bedroom overnight to test the White House rumors that Lincoln's ghost still roamed. Susan explained, "Mother came in at the crack of dawn to wake us up, with a sheet over her head and going 'Oooh-oooh' in her best ghostly voice." The startled girls let out a scream as the First Lady laughed.

Facts on the First Ladies

Only a few First Ladies could converse with the ambassador corps in fluent French. Among them were Elizabeth Monroe, Mary Lincoln and Jackie Kennedy.

First Lady Lou Hoover was known as "Buffalo." This was the name given her by the Girl Scouts while she served as their national president.

Martha Washington was attacked by the press for having too many white horses draw her carriage and for serving spoiled cream.

In a 1987 poll, history professors gave Jackie Kennedy high marks, but rated her last in the category of integrity among twentieth century First Ladies.

Louisa Adams, wife of John Quincy Adams, wished to be addressed as "her majesty" by White House servants.

The first First Lady to die in the White House was Letitia Tyler in 1842.

Lady Bird Johnson observed, "Children are likely to live up to what you believe of them."

Eliza Johnson, wife of our 17th President, appeared in public only twice: once at a dinner, where she left coughing, and once at a children's party.

Before she died, Martha Washington threw all of her love letters from George into the fireplace.

Mrs. McKinley once remarked to a young couple who was visiting her at the White House that her husband "was the only honest man who ever was President."

In 1957 Mamie Eisenhower underwent a hysterectomy. The White House would not use this medical term in its news release, describing the procedure as "an operation similar to those that many women undergo in middle age."

Only three women married men who were already President.

When Jacqueline Bouvier Kennedy graduated from prep school, her yearbook profile noted: "Ambition — not to be a housewife."

On Inauguration Day in 1909 William Howard Taft waggled his index finger at his ambitious wife and scolded, "Well, I'm now in the White House; I'm not going to be pushed any more."

At a White House New Year's reception Florence Harding shook hands for four hours, greeting nearly 6800 people. Her hand was so swollen the next several days she couldn't use it.

Dolley Madison received the highest honor accorded to any former First Lady when Congress voted her a lifetime seat on the floor of the House of Representatives.

Mary Todd Lincoln's mother and father had the same great-grandfather, John Todd.

In a 1934 speech, Adolph Hitler ranted, "Eleanor Roosevelt is America's real ruler."

One of Bess Truman's favorite activities was fishing. Her husband hated it. During their courtship, young Harry took her fishing, preferring to read a book while Bess tried to catch dinner.

Dolley Madison wore a gold locket around her neck. In it were intermingled locks of hair from her and her husband.

Grace Coolidge attended so many concerts that the President remarked, "I don't see why you have to go out to get your music. There are four pianos in the White House."

Speaking of music, only two First Ladies were professional musicians — Florence Harding and Caroline Harrison. Both taught music: Mrs. Harding gave lessons in Marion, Ohio, and Mrs. Harrison at Miami University in Oxford, Ohio.

In order to beautify America and maintain its natural environment, Lady Bird Johnson founded the National Wildflower Research Center in 1982. It is headquartered near Austin, Texas.

Eleanor Roosevelt probably worked the longest hours of any First Lady. Possessing a high energy level, she slept an average of five hours, often retiring at 3:00 A.M. and rising at 8:00.

Julia Grant became the first First Lady to go down into a mine, followed later by Lucy Hayes and Eleanor Roosevelt. Mrs. Grant and Mrs. Hayes visited the same Nevada silver mine, while Mrs. Roosevelt inspected a coal mine.

In 1841 Anna Harrison claimed she could not assume her duties as First Lady because of poor health. She was sixty-five years old at the time of her husband's election.

In 1844 Sarah Polk informed friends, "If I get to the White House, I expect to live on $25,000 a year and I will neither keep house or make butter."

In the late 1870s advertisers used the picture of First Lady Lucy Hayes for their products, and they did so without her permission.

The first widow to participate in her husband's funeral service in office was Lucretia Garfield. And a year after James Garfield's death, rumors reached the newspapers that Lucretia Garfield was planning to remarry. She expressed "humiliation that anyone could believe me capable of ever forgetting that I am the wife of General Garfield."

At a White House tea one afternoon a well known woman of Washington society rushed up to First Lady Grace Coolidge and proudly announced, "I'm so delighted I am going to have the honor of sitting beside your husband at dinner tomorrow evening…." Mrs. Coolidge replied, "I'm sorry for you. You'll have to do all the talking yourself."

The first female divorceé to become First Lady was Florence Kling Harding. In 1880 she eloped with her next door neighbor Henry DeWolfe. Four years later after a disastrous marriage, she got a divorce and gave her four-year-old son to her parents to raise.

Helen Taft and her husband took a honeymoon trip to Europe in 1886. They toured the continent 100 days at a total cost of $1000.

An optimist at heart, Eleanor Roosevelt once stated, "This I know. This I believe with all my heart. If we want a free and peaceful world, if we want to make deserts bloom…We can do it!"

Mrs. McKinley did a lot of crocheting. She made wool slippers for hospital patients and orphans. She once told a friend, "Would you believe it? I have kept count, and I find that I have made no less than four thousand pairs of slippers."

Said Nancy Reagan a year after she left the White House, "Nothing, nothing, prepares you for being First Lady."

Pat Nixon once told author Jessamyn West, "I am never afraid."

Said Lady Bird Johnson, "Perhaps no place in any community is so totally democratic as the town library. The only entrance requirement is interest."

Jackie Kennedy, like her husband, also possessed quick wit. During the 1960 Presidential campaign some Republicans accused her of spending $30,000 a year on clothes. Replied Jackie, "I couldn't spend that much unless I wore sable underwear."

During an interview with Barbara Walters, former First Lady Mamie Eisenhower said that she loved to sleep in, and that "no one should get up before noon."

Abigail Smith once told her future husband, John Adams, that compliments were "a commodity that you seldom deal in."

Always open and frank, Betty Ford urged women to get regular checkups for breast cancer. Following her mastectomy, the First Lady tried to calm the fears of patients. "For those who have gone through it, I don't see anything so great about it. All you need is a little foam rubber."

When Dolley Madison purchased a $40 imported mirror to hang in the Executive Mansion, the Senate was infuriated and launched an investigation. The investigation cost $2000. Such an incident is a reflection of today's politics.

Mary Lincoln was once committed to an insane asylum by her son Robert. She once explained, "Robert says I'm crazy, but he is crazy too. He was bit by a mad dog when he was a boy." She also accused him of stealing her jewelry and silverware.

When somebody asked Eleanor Roosevelt, "What have women done with the vote?," she had a quick reply, "I wonder why men are not asked the same question."

Following JFK's assassination at age forty-six, Jacqueline Kennedy dolefully remarked, "So now he is a legend, when he would have preferred to be a man."

Mrs. Zachary Taylor declined to sit for an oil painting and offered to send her daughter, Mary Elizabeth Bliss.

Eleanor Roosevelt once flew with Amelia Earhart. *Good Housekeeping* dubbed her "our flying First Lady" because of her extensive travels by plane.

Florence Harding did not want to be photographed beside a cigarette-smoking friend, Evelyn Walsh McClean, and once knocked the offending article from her mouth. Wishing to maintain a positive image, Mrs. Harding had her own ideas about morals.

Voiced Eleanor Roosevelt, "I think, at a child's birth, if a mother could ask a fairy godmother to endow it with the most useful gift, that gift would be curiosity."

The first First Lady to write her memoirs for publication was Helen Taft, in 1914.

Dolley Madison once served a Christmas feast on a huge mirror which held turkey, chicken, duck, pudding, and other desserts.

Eleanor Roosevelt had some misgivings on entering the White House. In 1932 she told a close friend, "I never wanted to be a President's wife and I don't want it now."

Caroline Harrison was the first wife of a Chief Executive to begin a collection of state and family chinaware used by Presidents.

During the bloody Boxer Rebellion in China in 1900 foreigners were being murdered. In Tientsin many foreigners and Chinese nationalists barricaded themselves for protection. Among these were Herbert and Lou Hoover. With only two doctors to tend the wounded, Lou volunteered to help, and she rode a bicycle to and from a makeshift hospital, dodging bullets on every trip.

When Florence Kling Harding assisted her husband in publishing the *Marion Star* newspaper, she took control. The strong-willed woman even spanked newsboys upon receiving complaints from irate customers.

Mamie Eisenhower spent a lot of time in bed while in the White House. Even after being served a breakfast tray in bed at 8:30 she remained there to go over her daily schedule with assistants. One maid dubbed her "Sleeping Beauty."

Soon after her birth in 1912, Claudia Alta Taylor's nursemaid stated that the child was a "pretty as a ladybird." Thus, Lady Bird Johnson received a name which stuck.

When Betty Ford learned of her husband's ascendancy to the vice-presidency, someone asked her what she planned to do. She answered, "Just wind me up and point me in the right direction and I'll be there."

John Quincy Adams grew mulberry trees. They proved very practical because his wife, Louisa, spun silk which came from the silkworms in the trees.

One evening John Adams found his future bride, Abigail Smith, reading John Locke's book *Human Understanding*. Adams remarked pompously, "A big book for such a little head." Abby retorted, "You may think so. Even a little head, Mr. Adams, may possess a longing for knowledge, or at least for understanding." Vivacious, beautiful, and independent, Abigail continued to advocate women's rights throughout her fifty-four years of marriage.

Nancy Reagan and Barbara Bush both attended Smith College, but did not know each other while students there.

Unlike her husband, Ida McKinley was not often in good humor and was known to snap at people. One guest at the White House was amazed when Ida pointed a finger at a startled cabinet member's wife and exclaimed, "There's somebody who would like to be in my place and I know who it is!"

Caroline Harrison agreed to help raise funds for the newly-founded John Hopkins Medical School in 1890 on the condition women be admitted. Thus, one of America's major medical colleges became coeducational.

The oldest woman to assume the role of First Lady was Florence Harding. Though she was sixty-one at the time, she used makeup to create a youthful appearance and would not allow her grandchildren to visit the White House.

Grace Coolidge remarked after moving into the White House, "Being the wife to a government worker is very confining."

Grover Cleveland bought his wife's first baby carriage — when *she* was a baby. Frances Folsom was the daughter of Cleveland's law partner. The future President, twenty-eight years older than she, was Frances' guardian.

Though three sons and a husband preceded her in death, Mary Lincoln never attended funeral services for any member of her family.

At John F. Kennedy's 1961 inauguration four First Ladies, past, present, and future, stood together in the front row of the Inaugural stand behind Kennedy. A photograph shows Pat Nixon, Mamie Eisenhower, Lady Bird Johnson, and Jackie Kennedy all side by side. Edith Wilson was also there.

When her husband suffered a bleeding cut one day, First Lady Edith Roosevelt scolded Theodore, "I wish you'd do your bleeding in the bathroom. You are spoiling every rug in the house!"

The first First Lady to attend an inaugural ball without her husband was Eleanor Roosevelt.

What did Lady Bird Johnson think of her husband's alleged womanizing? She told an interviewer, "My husband loved people. All people. And half the people in the world were women. You don't think I could have kept my husband away from half the people?"

Florence Harding was five years older than her husband, Warren.

Lou Henry Hoover always kept a $1000 bill on her dresser at the White House, and that was during the Great Depression.

Eleanor Roosevelt once said of the Russians, "You can't understand them. You just have to outlive them."

Anna Symmes Harrison always referred to her husband William Henry as "General."

Edith Bolling Wilson went to the White House basement to take lessons on riding a bicycle.

Mary Todd Lincoln had fifteen brothers and sisters.

Eight First Ladies have been born in the state of New York.

News of William Henry Harrison's election as President was received with mixed feelings at his home in North Bend, Ohio. Mrs. Harrison lamented, "I said that my husband's friends had left him where he is happy and contented in retirement."

Jackie Kennedy did not like the title "First Lady." She preferred not to be called that, explaining it sounded too much "like a race horse."

At the age of seventeen, Helen Herron visited the White House and vowed, "I shall marry only a man who can take me to the White House." Eight years later she married William Howard Taft, our twenty-seventh President.

Jane Pierce spent much of her time in the White House in an upstairs bedroom writing letters to her three dead sons.

Mamie Eisenhower was called "Puddin" by her father.

Barbara Bush observed, "As you get older, I think you need to put your arms around each other more."

Jackie Kennedy's first visit to the White House was when she was eleven-years-old. It was during FDR's term, and she was accompanied by her mother.

Will Rogers, the great cowboy philosopher-comedian, once visited the White House and was greeted by the First Lady Eleanor Roosevelt. "Where is the President?" Rogers asked. Mrs. Roosevelt replied, "Wherever you hear the laughter."

Eleanor Roosevelt once told her daughter Anna, "Sex is an ordeal to be borne."

"George is right. He is always right." So said Martha Washington.

In 1987 Lloyd Shearer conducted a poll of twentieth century First Ladies, ranking them on ten different categories. Eleanor Roosevelt topped the list, with Lady Bird Johnson and Rosalynn Carter finishing second and third. Rated last were Ida McKinley and Florence Harding.

The press chastised Nancy Reagan for her elaborate wardrobe, and one columnist declared she made her husband look like a "a wimp." Even the President's chief of staff referred to her as "a dragon." He was later replaced.

Though their marriage lasted fifty years, the John Quincy Adamses were not always happy. His wife wrote a friend, "My husband seems to have no sympathy or tenderness for me."

The first woman to see her husband's swearing in was Dolley Madison.

Lou Hoover used a series of hand signals during White House parties to notify employees what to do. Dropping a handkerchief or raising a finger might tell a servant to replenish the punch or move guests more quickly through a reception line.

Barbara Bush told a journalist, "I married the first man I ever kissed."

Eleanor Roosevelt visited wounded GI's in the South Pacific in 1943, setting a grueling pace which amazed reporters and military personnel. After a five week visit, she was not only exhausted, but lost thirty pounds.

Lady Bird Johnson was the first wife of a President to hold the *Bible* for her husband's swearing in.

Louisa Adams, wife of our sixth President, read the *Dialogues of Plato* to their sons in the original Greek.

First Lady Frances Cleveland attributed her beautiful complexion to taking arsenic — in very small doses, of course.

Florence Harding had an extensive collection of ceramic and glass elephant statuettes.

Though Julia Grant wrote her memoirs in 1891 (the first First Lady to do so), no publisher could be found. The book was finally published, but not until nearly eighty years later.

Ellen Wilson did not like Gilbert Stuart's portrait of George Washington, writing that his false teeth looked as if they "were about to leap out of his mouth."

Grace Coolidge wanted to make the Easter-egg roll at the White House even more festive. She dressed her pet dogs in Easter bonnets!

Protection of First Ladies began with Mary Lincoln. An officer of the Washington Metropolitan Police accompanied her in plainclothes and carried a pistol.

Abigail Adams urged her husband to give women the right to vote and hold office, way back in 1787. She further reminded him that American women "will not hold ourselves bound by any laws in which we have no voice or representation."

In September of 1957 Soviet Premier Nikita Khrushchev had a talk with Eleanor Roosevelt. When asked by reporters how the interview went, Khrushchev replied, "At least we didn't shoot each other."

Jackie Kennedy once remarked, "I don't think there are any men who are faithful to their wives. Men are such a combination of good and evil."

Mamie Eisenhower recalled she and her husband lived at seven different Army posts in one year.

Julia Tyler introduced both the polka and the waltz to the White House. Years before becoming President, John Tyler saw the polka performed and remarked, "It is rather vulgar, I think." But when his young wife did it as First Lady, it was fine.

Barbara Bush told a reporter that she and her husband had moved twenty-nine times prior to taking up residency in the White House.

Though eighty years old and nearly destitute, Dolley Madison was a welcomed guest at the Polk White House. First Lady Sarah Polk enjoyed her company so much that she even gave Dolley her seat next to the President during dinners.

Mrs. Abraham Lincoln was a big Boston Red Sox fan, and attended a few games when the Washington Senators played Boston. This was NOT the President's wife, incidentally. Mrs. Lincoln was John F. Kennedy's private secretary!

John Kennedy defended his wife's ambitions to decorate and refurbish the Executive Mansion. He said, "Everything in the White House must have a reason for being there. Restoration is a question of scholarship. The White House is part of our national heritage and should give a sense of history to all who visit it."

Martha Washington, like her husband, also had false teeth. She wore upper and lower lead-alloy plates which weighed four times what modern dentures weigh. And, like George, she had many dental problems.

Mrs. William Borah, wife of a distinguished U.S. Senator, used to say she would read Eleanor Roosevelt's schedule for the day in the morning newspaper, and promptly go back to bed, exhausted!

When Nancy Reagan, wife of California Governor Ronald Reagan, was asked by a reporter why she traveled to Los Angeles on the weekends, she replied, "No one in Sacramento can do hair."

On her honeymoon, Jane Pierce wrote her father-in-law, "We have both generally been very well, and not very unhappy." The future First Lady even then demonstrated her shy, reclusive, and pessimistic nature. The Pierces, incidentally, spent their honeymoon in a Washington, D.C. boardinghouse.

Some people accused Nancy Reagan of having great influence on her husband's decision-making. She responded, "For eight years I was sleeping with the President, and if that doesn't give you special access, I don't know what does."

It is quite amazing, but in September of 1947 there were six Presidential widows alive: Mary Dimmick Harrison, Frances Cleveland, Edith Roosevelt, Edith Wilson, Grace Coolidge, and Eleanor Roosevelt.

"Sahara Sarah" was one of the nicknames accorded to Sarah Polk because of her "dry" stand in not serving alcoholic beverages in the White House.

First Lady Julia Tyler's pet canary "Johnny Ty" died soon after her husband took office. She grieved for weeks until her imported greyhound pooch arrived from Italy.

Julia Grant was the first First Lady to grant interviews to the press.

Mary Lincoln stayed in the White House for nearly two months after her husband was killed. President Andrew Johnson meanwhile resided in a hotel.

Caroline Harrison was determined to clean out every White House storage room. An attendant later recalled how she screamed in the dim attic every time he shot a rat with his pistol.

Jackie Kennedy once observed, "If you bungle raising your children, I don't think anything else you do amounts to very much."

Julia Tyler's last word was "Tea." This was in response to a suggestion by one of her bedside doctors that she be given a sip of liquor. She died on July 10, 1889, at the age of 69.

First Lady Betty Ford held a reception for the National Foundation of Republican Women a month after she moved into the White House. Someone asked her opinion of the food there, and Betty replied, "It's excellent. That's partly because I don't help prepare it."

There was one White House reception James and Dolley Madison never forgot. Elizabeth Patterson Bonaparte, Napoleon's sister-in-law, appeared in a transparent Grecian gown — with nothing on underneath!

After her husband's first heart attack, Mamie Eisenhower personally signed every letter of acknowledgement and thanks for the 11,000 get-well messages!

Because of her dark features and black dresses, Sarah Polk was dubbed by the newspapers as the "Spanish Donna."

Hillary Clinton and Nancy Reagan shared at least one thing in common. They both wore the same nail polish. According to *Glamour Magazine*, both women used Jessica's #129, a pinkish beige polish.

Andrew Johnson was paying tribute to his wife when he said, "God's best gift to a man — a noble woman."

After years of childbearing, and more years of separation from her husband, Louisa Catherine Adams once complained that matrimony and death were almost the same. She wrote John Quincy Adams that "hanging and marriage were strongly assimilated."

While Jackie Kennedy was overseeing funeral arrangements for her husband, she conducted a White House birthday party for her three-year-old son John, Jr.

Mamie Eisenhower practiced playing the organ almost daily. She also enjoyed playing canasta and bridge.

Julia Dent Grant described life in the White House as a "feast of cleverness and wit."

Lyndon Johnson's daughter, Lynda Bird, sneaked away from mom and dad once and joined in a public tour of the White House. No one recognized her because she wore a trench coat.

While taping a segment of television's *Sesame Street* in October of 1993, the guest, First Lady Hillary Clinton, remarked "hardly anybody likes peas." In trying to get children to eat healthier foods, this comment brought forth an outcry from some vegetable growers.

Mrs. John Quincy Adams played the harp, wrote poetry in French, and raised silkworms at the White House.

Because of her tireless efforts, First Lady Eleanor Roosevelt was dubbed "Public Energy Number One." Native American Indians gave her the name "Princess of Many Trails."

During her senior year at Chicago's Girls Latin, Nancy Davis Reagan played the title role in the school play *The First Lady*.

In 1975 First Lady Betty Ford described Nancy Reagan as "a cold fish."

Eleanor Roosevelt shocked White House servants when she helped serve food at the inaugural buffet lunch in 1933.

One of the first guests Ida McKinley invited to the White House was former First Lady Lucretia Garfield.

Ida McKinley worshiped her husband and often had harsh words to say to anyone who criticized him in any way. At a White House dinner party one evening, an English woman told her that she loved the United States but preferred living back home in England. Mrs. McKinley scowled at her and asked, "Do you mean to say that you would prefer England to a country ruled over by *my husband?*"

Helen Taft was a strong-willed woman. One day she and the President argued over an appointment which Mrs. Taft disapproved. Taft told her, "I usually have my way in the long run." The First Lady retorted, "No you don't. You think you do, but you don't."

Julia Tyler was a Catholic, but not while she was First Lady. In 1872, thirty years after first entertaining at the White House, she converted to Catholicism amidst cries of protests from her children and other relatives.

Before becoming First Lady, Hillary Clinton did not have a passion for fashion. In fact, she bought her wedding dress the *night before* her marriage to Bill.

For her service during the Revolutionary War, Martha Washington was presented a coach which once belonged to William Penn. The gift came from the Pennsylvania Assembly.

By September of 1793 Dolley Madison, while living in Philadelphia during the yellow fever epidemic, had witnessed the death of her infant son, her first husband (John Todd), her mother-in-law, and her father-in-law.

Abigail Adams set high standards for her children. She once instructed her husband to "not teach them what to think, but how to think, and they will learn how to act."

Nancy Reagan spent much time on the phone as First Lady. She once said, "When I die, I'm going to have a phone in one hand and my phone book in the other."

As a child Dolley Madison ran through the woods and lost an emerald secretly given to her by her non-Quaker grandmother.

Though she was in good health on her birthday in 1852, First Lady Abigail Fillmore remarked, "Perhaps ere another anniversary, I shall be numbered with the dead...." She died in March of 1853.

First Lady Jane Pierce conducted a White House séance to try and communicate with her dead son Benny who, at the age of twelve, was killed in a train accident before her husband's inauguration in 1853.

The first Presidential candidate's wife to appear on a campaign poster was Lucretia Garfield in the 1880 race.

While Bill Clinton earned $35,000 as Governor of Arkansas in 1987, his wife Hillary was making three times that amount working in the Rose Law Firm and doing occasional honoraria.

Due to spending many hours in the sun, First Lady Nancy Reagan developed lip cancer. It was successfully treated.

Mamie Eisenhower once said of her successor Jackie Kennedy that she "had no respect for money at all."

Jackie Kennedy once said, "I am happiest when I am alone."

Grace Coolidge loved meeting people, and referred to herself as the "National Hugger."

Edith Wilson was the first wife of a President to speak at a national party convention. The widow of Woodrow Wilson, she addressed the Democratic Convention in 1927 amid thunderous applause.

Edith Roosevelt referred to picture-taking reporters as "camera fiends."

The only incumbent First Lady to give birth to a child in the twentieth century was Jackie Kennedy. Her baby, Patrick, was born in 1961 and died two days after birth.

Fashion designer Coco Chanel proclaimed Jackie Kennedy "the worst dresser on any continent."

In 1993 Hillary Clinton had a newly-developed tulip named in her honor.

When Rosalynn Carter remarked that she disliked "all that violence and bloodshed" in movies, her President-husband dryly added, "But you like Democratic party politics."

Pat Nixon rarely wore black because her husband hated that color on women.

Edith Wilson and Rosalynn Carter both brought their sewing machines to the White House.

Shortly before her death, Mamie Eisenhower was asked in a television interview how she would like to be remembered. She paused and said, "Just a good friend."

Lady Bird Johnson's efforts to beautify America earned her the nickname "Secretary of the Exterior."

Following John Kennedy's assassination, Jackie Kennedy was sent hundreds of thousands of telegrams and letters from mourners. Congress voted to give the former First Lady $50,000 for a staff and office to handle the mail.

First Lady Jackie Kennedy guarded her privacy. When a Secret Service agent followed her on a stroll along a beach, she turned and told him, "You keep doing that, and you'll drive the First Lady into an asylum."

Nancy Reagan once observed, "A woman is like a tea bag. You don't know her strength until she's in hot water."

Hillary Clinton was criticized as taking too active a role as First Lady. She explained, "I've done the best I can to lead my life. I suppose I could have stayed home and baked cookies, and had teas…." This comment did not endear her to housewives.

Dolley Madison had no enemies, and perhaps it was her love for people and indifference for politics. She once explained, "Politics is the business of men. I don't care what office they may hold, or who supports them. I care only about *people."*

When Dolley Payne Todd married James Madison in 1794, she gave up many of her Quaker habits. For that she was ex-communicated from the Society of Friends Church.

Florence Kling Harding was an expert equestrian. Her daring exploits on horseback became the envy of many men.

Frances Cleveland established a record of sorts when, as First Lady, she shook hands with more than 9000 guests at a reception in the Blue Room. Afterwards her sore and swollen arm had to be massaged.

Two of the four children Martha Washington had to her first husband died in infancy.

Barbara Bush was swimming in the White House pool when a large rat swam right in front of her. She screamed and made a quick exit. The President caught the rat in a net and did him in.

In 1923 Florence Harding heard that the Pennsylvania owner of Clover, the oldest horse in the world, was in dire need. She sent Reverend Uriah Myers of Cattawissa some money to ensure that neither the horse nor owner suffer in their declining years. Clover, incidentally, lived another year and a half, dying at age 53.

When she wasn't puffing on black cigars at the Hermitage, Rachel Jackson smoked a corn-cob pipe.

Eleanor Roosevelt said, "You must do the thing you think you cannot do."

Helen Taft's background had presidential overtones years before she became First Lady. Her father had been a college classmate of Benjamin Harrison's and a law partner of Rutherford B. Hayes. As a young lady she visited the White House several times.

Louisa Adams was admittedly addicted to chocolate. The wife of our sixth President was a "chocoholic" and consumed it in great quantities. She wrote friends that chocolate had medicinal and healing powers.

Sarah Polk hosted the first annual Thanksgiving dinner at the White House.

There are 132 rooms in the White House and 412 doors.

Barbara Bush observed, "The darn trouble with cleaning the house is it gets dirty the next day anyway, so skip a week if you have to. The children are the most important thing."

The only faults Abigail Smith Adams had, according to her future husband John, was her shyness and timidity, her inability to sing (which she freely admitted), and her pigeon-toed walk.

Hillary Clinton's professors at Wellesley College recognized she was a gifted student. When she applied to Yale Law School her advisor wrote in a recommendation, "She has the intellectual ability, personality, and character to make a remarkable contribution to American society."

Shortly after John F. Kennedy's death, First Lady Ladybird Johnson wanted to change the name of the White House Rose Garden to the Jacqueline Kennedy Garden. But Jackie felt it was inappropriate. She did, however, allow Ladybird to name a smaller flower garden after her.

Eleanor Roosevelt once stated, "Most of the good work in the world is done by people who weren't feeling all that well the day they did it."

The children of Jane and Franklin Pierce all died before they had reached their teens. The grief stricken First Lady was seldom seen in public. Abby Means, the wife of her uncle, served as the White House hostess.

As First Lady, Martha Washington made certain that guests did not overstay their welcome at the Executive Mansion in New York City. She reminded them, "The General always retires at nine, and I usually precede him."

As a child, Julia Dent dreamed of someday becoming a queen. After her husband was sworn in as the 18th President, U.S. Grant turned to his wife, took her hand and said, "And now my dear, I hope you are satisfied."

Julia Gardiner Tyler was the first incumbent First Lady to be photographed. In 1844 she posed for a daguerreotype.

Crete Garfield died of pneumonia on March 13, 1918, in South Pasadena, California. She survived her husband by thirty-six years.

Abigail Powers Fillmore was the first First Lady to hold a job outside the home. She taught school in Moravia and Aurora, New York. She was also the only First Lady born on St. Patrick's Day — March 17, 1798.

Nellie Taft learned to ride a surfboard off Hawaii's Waikiki Beach thus becoming the first First Lady to learn this skill. This was during the time her husband had been appointed as governor of the Philippines.

On her second trip to Europe, former First Lady Mary Lincoln stayed four years.

Edith Wilson was the first incumbent First Lady to accompany her husband overseas when she went with the President to Europe in 1918.

Sarah Polk explained why she forbid dancing at the White House: "To dance in these rooms would be undignified."

Bess Truman was a paid staff member in her husband's office while Harry was a U.S. Senator.

Grace Coolidge was asked why she, a happy outgoing woman, married a man who was dour and taciturn. She explained, "Well, I thought I would get him to enjoy life and have fun, but he was not easy to instruct."

Florence Harding was a plain-looking, folksy woman in her early sixties when she told newspaper photographers at the White House, "Alright boys, I always take a frightful picture and I hate this. But I know you've got to do it."

When Lady Bird Johnson was five years old, her mother fell and hurt herself so badly that she died a few days later. Her father, a Texas cotton grower, needed a helping hand, so Lady Bird's aunt Effie moved in to raise the child.

When James Polk asked Sarah Childress to marry him, she said yes, if he won election to the Tennessee legislature. Polk won the seat, and the couple was married January 1, 1824.

Margaret Taylor, for some unknown reason, said she would never have her picture taken or sit for a portrait painting.

John and Letitia Tyler were married on March 29, 1813. That date was also John Tyler's 23rd birthday.

In 1868 widow Mary Lincoln remarked, "General Grant…I think he had better let well enough alone. He makes a good general, but I think a very poor President.

Florence Harding once offered some valuable advice to future First Ladies: "Never let a husband travel alone."

Eleanor Roosevelt suggested that Susan B. Anthony's face be carved on Mount Rushmore.

Dolley Madison enjoyed playing cards for money.

In 1998 former First Lady Barbara Bush was asked to comment on the Bill Clinton–Monica Lewinsky sex scandal at the White House. She joked, "It's very disappointing and hurtful. How come nobody thought I had an affair with anyone?"

When Nancy Reagan visited an elementary school, a pupil asked her how she liked being married to a President. She responded, "Fine, as long as the President is Ronald Reagan."

The comedy team of Allen and Rossi asked Vice President Hubert Humphrey how it felt to be second-in-command of his country. Humphrey responded, "I don't know; ask Lady Bird!"

Abigail Adams once warned, "If particular attention is not paid to the ladies, we are determined to foment a rebellion, and will not hold ourselves by any law in which we have no voice or representation."

Nancy Reagan observed, "With faith as my crutch I've found peace, one of the few things I have left which is strictly my own."

Florence and Warren Harding were married at their home in Marion, Ohio, in 1891. The future First Lady never wore a wedding ring. A progressive thinker, she explained she insisted "on having a personality" of her own.

Rosalynn Carter attempted to eradicate measles in the U.S. More than 90% of American children were immunized through her efforts. By the time she left the White House the disease had been virtually eliminated.

We all know that George Washington was a poor speller. So was his wife Martha. In 1758 she wrote a friend in London, "I have sent a night gound to be dide of a fashanob Coler fitt for me to ware and beg you would have it dide better that I sent Las year that was very badly don this gound is of a good Lenght for me."

During the winter of 1885 Helen Herron and William Howard Taft exchanged their first kiss. It came in a play sponsored by some young couples in Cincinnati. The two appeared in a skit of *Sleeping Beauty*.

John Tyler did not permit his daughters to dance at White House parties. In spite of this, his second wife Julia, young and independent, danced the polka with several ambassadors. Her jealous husband simply looked the other way, and the polka soon became the national rage in 1843.

During the time her husband was Vice President, Pat Nixon remarked that politicians "are the most vicious people in the world."

In December of 1828 Rachel Jackson went shopping in Nashville to purchase clothing for her husband's inauguration. She collapsed, and died just a few weeks later.

While campaigning for her husband in 1976, Rosalynn Carter was asked if she ever committed adultery. She replied, "If I had I wouldn't tell you."

The Rose Bowl parade and the subsequent football game began in 1902. One of the first grand marshals of the festivity was former First Lady Lucretia Garfield who had moved to Pasadena, California, years after her husband's death.

Abigail Adams referred to her future daughter-in-law as a "half-blood." Louisa Adams, though an American citizen, was born in London. By the time she was First Lady, she and Abigail had become close.

Edith Roosevelt gave her husband an allowance of $20 each day, putting the money in his pocket. Theodore didn't concern himself with personal finances and often could not remember how he spent his money.

Ida McKinley owned a gold mine, located near Ely, Nevada.

Abigail Adams noted, "Learning is not attained by chance; it must be sought for with ardor and attended to with diligence."

Caroline Harrison was a fine painter. Her artistic subject was mainly flowers, in particular orchids.

As a child, Julia Dent Grant was raised in the slave state of Missouri. She grew emotionally close to her father's slaves and often sneaked them money so they could buy tobacco.

On March 31, 1882, Congress voted to provide widowed First Ladies an annual pension of $5000.

The beautiful Ellen Arthur never lived to see her husband as the twenty-first President. When Arthur assumed his duties in 1881, he still mourned her death and said, "Honors to me now are not what they once were."

In 1893 an eager tourist had to be restrained in the White House corridor. He was prevented from snipping a lock of baby Ruth Cleveland's hair as the child was being held in her nurse's arms.

When asked about her favorite reading, First Lady Grace Coolidge said, "People are my books."

Grace Coolidge was the first First Lady to try smoking cigarettes. She smoked only occasionally.

Bess Truman decided she would not be the kind of well-traveled First Lady her predecessor Eleanor Roosevelt was. She declared, "I am not going down any coal mine!"

Ellen Wilson was described by one White House servant as a "day dreamer." She had said, "I am a most unambitious woman."

Nearly everyone likes Girl Scout cookies. Thanks go to Lou Hoover who served as the organization's president.

Lucy Hayes had a beautiful singing voice and among the instruments she played were the guitar and piano.

Speaking of "Lemonade" Lucy Hayes, she owned the first Siamese cat in America. The First Lady received it as a gift from the U.S. Consul-General in Bangkok.

Martha Washington wanted her husband buried in the Capitol Building. Arrangements were made and a crypt was made (it is still there). But when Martha died her family wanted her entombed next to her husband at Mount Vernon.

During her husband's scandals, First Lady Hillary Clinton told her friend Sara Ehrman," I'd like to stay in bed, pull the covers over my head, and have a nervous breakdown, but I really don't have time."

The first First Lady to fly in an airplane was Florence Harding.

Susan Ford got a real treat in high school. Her prom was held at the White House.

During the 2000 campaign Laura Bush was often asked, "As First Lady, would you be more like Hillary Clinton or Barbara Bush (her mother-in-law)?" She answered, "I think I'll just be Laura Bush."

In 1958 Laura Welch and George W. Bush both attended the same school, San Jacinto Junior High, while they were in the seventh grade. The future First Lady and President, however, did not know each other then.

Jackie Kennedy observed, "Anyone who seeks the Presidency must have a fundamental flaw in his character."

Questions About the Presidents
(answers beginning on page 239)

1. To which event was Richard Nixon referring when he described it as "the greatest week in the history of the world since the creation"?

2. Which President was sworn in, dressed entirely in black?

3. According to John F. Kennedy, who was his "finest ambassador?"

4. Which President's costly haircut caused minor air traffic congestion at an international airport for a short while?

5. Which President gave away electric toothbrushes so he would be remembered?

6. Which top female film star once sat on FDR's lap, and the First Lady never complained?

7. Who was President when the following events took place: the construction of the first oil well, the laying of Atlantic cable, the establishment of the Pony Express, the development of the theory of evolution, and the granting of statehood to Oregon, Kansas, and Minnesota?

8. Which U.S. President ridded the nation of its outhouses?

9. Which President appointed the *second* woman to the U.S. Supreme Court?

10. Which President christened a town with watermelon juice?

11. Which President was nicknamed "The Enduring Common Man"?

12. During which President's term was there the largest turnover of Congressional seats?

13. Name the only President who was the son of a doctor.

14. Who used Hammersmith Farm as a summer White House?

15. What do Maine's Lincoln, Lincolnville, and Lincoln County have in common?

16. Which President vetoed two bills admitting two extra states into the Union?

17. Which President dedicated the Washington Monument?

18. Which one of the following Presidents never served in a military unit?
    A) Buchanan; B) Tyler; C) Harding; D) Lincoln; E) Nixon.

19. Which President attended Davidson College?

20. What is the longest period of time the U.S. has gone without a President since George Washington took office?

21. Who wrote the national best-seller *The Ordeal of Woodrow Wilson*?

22. Which Presidential couple had three sons graduate from Harvard?

23. Which President vetoed bills preventing Colorado and Nebraska from becoming states?

24. Which Chief Executive made the following appointments to his cabinet: Homer Cummings (Attorney-General), Cordell Hull (State), William Woodin (Treasury), George Dern (War), Dan Roper (Commerce), and Lewis Douglas (Director of the Budget)?

25. In 1985, 2000 American journalists covered the Reagan-Gorbachev summit talks in Geneva, Switzerland. But what event a couple months later attracted 2400 reporters?

26. Why were flags flown at half mast on FDR's inauguration, March 4, 1932?

27. This twenty-one-year-old future President attended seances to communicate with his father who had been dead for two decades. Name him.

28. Who served the longest as Commander-in-Chief of American military forces?

29. Just prior to the War of 1812, General William Henry Harrison attacked and defeated the Indians at Tippecanoe Creek, Indiana. Under his command was a young man who became the grandfather of a U.S. President. Who was the President?

30. Which future President defended a client whose ear had been bitten off in a brawl?

31. Which President introduced a new version of spelling, changing words like "dropped" to "dropt" and "chassed" to "chast"?

32. Who was President when the American flag first flew over foreign soil?

33. What do doctors Charles Leale, Smith Townshend, George Hall, and Charles Carrico share in common in regard to Presidents?

34. Which future President helped operate a ferry on the Ohio River?

35. Which President was born in the tiny hamlet of Stony Batter?

36. Which film was being shown when assassin Lee Harvey Oswald was captured inside a Dallas movie theater on November 22, 1963?

37. Which American Presidents were veterans of the Mexican War?

38. Who was the first father of a President to visit his son in the White House?

39. Which future President accompanied his dying brother on a Caribbean expedition, and nearly died himself from smallpox?

40. Which President flunked physical education in college?

41. Which President's mansion was named "Lindenwald?"

42. Which President's son was promoted for bravery in the Mexican War?

43. Which President asked major league baseball teams to travel as little as possible?

44. Who was the first President born in a city?

45. Which President's favorite horse was "Billy"?

46. Who was the first President to use taxing powers (i.e. the IRS)?

47. Rutherford B. Hayes tried to join the army and fight in the Mexican War, but didn't. Why?

48. Which President's father built a tennis court for his son?

49. Which President's grandfather was a hero at the battle of Bunker Hill?

50. Which Chief Executive as a boy picked potato bugs to earn money?

51. As a Congressman, this President voted against all of the following measures: building roads, establishment of the Smithsonian Institution, aid to famine-stricken Ireland, construction of railroads, and funds to expand the patent office. Name him.

52. As governor, which Chief Executive banned the sale of liquor to the Indians and ordered them inoculated against smallpox?

53. While serving as an ambassador, this President was removed because he insulted Simon Bolivar. Name him.

54. Which President's father warned him "none but knaves should ever enter the political arena"?

55. Which President as a young adult paid a man 50 cents to read for him?

56. In one of his last speeches, which President apologized to the American people for his mistakes, remarking, "... I may have committed many errors"?

57. On his last full day in office, which President signed a bill admitting Florida into the Union?

58. Who was the first President inviting a foreign power to co-sponsor a canal across Central America?

59. Who was President during the "Era of Sectionalism," when northern, southern, and western states planted the seeds of disunity?

60. Which future President was once a cheerleader and nicknamed "Lips" and "Tweed"?

61. Which President dispatched 2500 troops to subdue rebellious Mormons in Utah?

62. To whom was George Washington referring when he praised this man as "the most valuable public character we have abroad"?

63. Which Chief Executive, while serving as Vice President, secretly wrote resolutions for a southern state claiming the right to nullify federal law?

64. In early 1901 President McKinley ordered flags flown at half mast due to the death of a foreigner. Whose death precipitated this rare event?

65. Which President was a habitual user of cocaine?

66. It is well known among historians that Ronald Reagan and William Henry Harrison were the two oldest men ever elected President. Who was the next oldest?

67. Which Chief Executive earned degrees at Yale and Harvard and later co-owned a major league baseball team?

68. What is the average age at which America's Presidents have taken office?

69. Which President was popularly known as "The Ohio Plowman"?

70. Which U.S. President had an electric horse installed in his White House bedroom, riding it almost daily?

71. Which American President told a large gathering of supporters, "All we want is to be left alone"?

72. Which U.S. President was First Lady Barbara Bush's great-great-great uncle?

73. Which President, after leaving office, argued two major cases before the U.S. Supreme Court?

74. To whom was Harry Truman referring when he often used the name "squirrel-head"?

75. Which President attended a university when he was only thirteen-years-old?

76. Who was our first ambassador to Great Britain?

77. In the summer of 1799, where was the President's office and the seat of the federal government located?

78. Which Vice President did the most voting to break ties in the U.S. Senate?

79. Who created the U.S. Navy?

80. Which President served aboard the *USS Monterey*, an aircraft carrier?

81. According to President John Adams, what was the proudest act of his life?

82. Whose classmates at Yale included the distinguished Americans Cyrus Vance, Potter Stewart, and Sargent Shriver?

83. As governor, this future President built a mansion for himself and his successors known as "Taj Mahal." Name him.

84. Whose autobiography was entitled *Why Not The Best*?

85. Who was the last incumbent President to be denied his party's nomination?

86. Can you name the first President to receive a baseball team at the White House to congratulate them on a championship season?

87. In 1978, President Jimmy Carter, the Shah of Iran and their guests, openly wept at a ceremony on the White House lawn. Why?

88. Which future President was dropped from his high school choir because his voice changed?

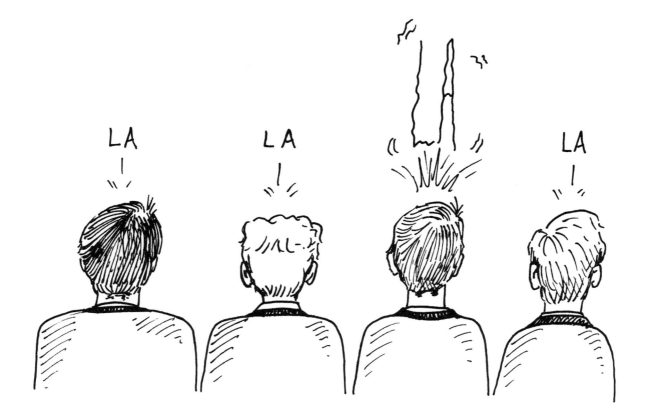

89. Did any of our Presidents lose a son in the Civil War?

90. Which college trustee president clashed with university president Woodrow Wilson over school policy?

91. Whose rifle was dubbed "Death and Destruction"?

92. Who was the first incumbent President to be involved in televised debates?

93. Lincoln's Emancipation Proclamation freed all Negro slaves in every U. S. state except one. Name it.

94. Which President had smoked four packs of cigarettes a day before he "kicked the habit"?

95. As a college student, this President dumped the school bell in a canal. Name him.

96. Who were the only two clean-shaven Presidents between Lincoln and Taft?

97. Where does the President's oath of office come from?

98. Who, according to Woodrow Wilson, was the greatest statesman who ever lived?

99. Which President once served as the Postmaster of Grandview?

100. Name the U.S. President Charles Dickens was describing when, after meeting him, remarked he had "one of the most remarkable faces I have ever seen…very powerful in its firmness, strength of will, and steadiness of purpose."

101. How many Presidents had sons named after them (as Juniors)?

102. Which future President's home was destroyed by Benedict Arnold?

103. This future President was afforded a unique opportunity when he was invited to stand on Lenin's Tomb in Moscow's Red Square. Name him.

104. Which President was known to his military buddies as "Shafty"?

105. Which President had a notorious reputation for losing buttons?

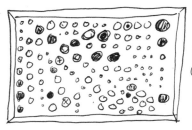

BUTTON COLLECTION

WASTED SHIRTS

106. Only one President between Andrew Jackson and Woodrow Wilson served two full consecutive terms. Name him.

107. Which President's mother was married five times?

108. Where is the body of assassin John Wilkes Booth buried?

109. Whose Vice President was called "the Smiler"?

110. Which man was elected President on his birthday?

111. Who was the first President to have a live press conference televised from the White House?

112. Can you name the man, related to Franklin D. Roosevelt, who slept in the same bed Lincoln died on at the Peterson House across from Ford's Theater?

113. Who was the first Chief Executive to have bowling lanes installed at the White House?

114. Here is a tough one: What did Presidents Taft, Polk, Kennedy, and William Henry Harrison have in common?

115. Without looking, can you tell me if Lincoln's bow tie can be seen on the penny?

116. Which President discovered a new animal, and had it named after him?

117. Which future President delighted in eating clam chowder to celebrate "Birthington's Washday"?

118. Who was the first President to order our flag to fly over the White House and all other federal government buildings?

119. Who was the only President to have been a prisoner of war?

120. Which President, along with *three* brothers, served in the same war?

121. Which 20th century President, along with *two* brothers, served in the same war?

122. What was the subject concerning FDR's "green light" letter in 1942?

123. Speaking of baseball, name the only President ever offered a contract to play major league baseball.

124. Can you name the southern President whose brother was expelled from Yale?

125. Which President's brother became deaf as a result of gunfire during the Civil War?

126. Why did President Benjamin Harrison once kill a pig while he was hunting?

127. Which President had a South American river named in his honor?

128. Which Presidential couple is buried in the "Place of Meditation"?

129. Which President was sworn into office by a Secretary of State?

130. Which future President, along with his mother, was shot at by a drunken stepfather?

131. To whom was President McKinley referring when he summoned his "sweet sunbeam"?

132. Which President once owned a baseball team in Ohio?

133. Which President threw out the most Opening Day pitches?

134. How many rooms in the White House are named for colors?

135. Which President's Chief of Staff resigned after he was arrested for homosexual activities in a Washington, D.C. YMCA pay toilet?

136. Which early President resigned as governor?

137. Who rode the horse Black Jack in John F. Kennedy's funeral cortege?

138. When Theodore Roosevelt led a large safari into Africa in 1909, what was it that escorted the head of the large column of men?

139. Which President first kissed his wife on stage when, as young adults, they appeared together in a comedy version of "Sleeping Beauty"?

140. During Harding's term as President, six Congressional Medals of Honor were presented – but no one received them. Why?

141. Two Presidents were married in London. John Quincy Adams was one. Who was the other?

142. In April of 1793 George Washington attended the country's first circus in Philadelphia and was paid $150. What was this money for?

143. Why did both Democrat Grover Cleveland and incumbent Benjamin Harrison quit campaigning two weeks before the 1892 Presidential election?

144. Who did FDR defeat for President in 1944?

145. Which President changed his wife's diapers and often rocked her to sleep?

146. How many jet planes flew over John F. Kennedy's grave at Arlington Cemetery during his funeral?

147. Which Presidential couple's son was voted "The Sexiest Man Alive?"

148. How many states joined the Union during George Washington's eight years as President?

149. Which President had four sons serve in the Civil War?

150. Franklin D. Roosevelt considered Louisiana Governor Huey Long as one of the two most dangerous men in America. Who was the other man FDR considered equally dangerous?

Answers to Questions about the Presidents

1. The Apollo 11 moon landing on July 20, 1969. Nixon made the comment four days later.

2. James Madison, in 1809.

3. His wife, Jackie.

4. Bill Clinton, whose $200 haircut aboard a grounded Air Force One backed up waiting air traffic in Los Angeles in May of 1993. The barber, Cristophe of Hollywood, also styled Hillary's hair.

5. Lyndon Johnson, who explained, "Then I know that from now until the end of their days, they will think of me the first thing in the morning and the last at night!"

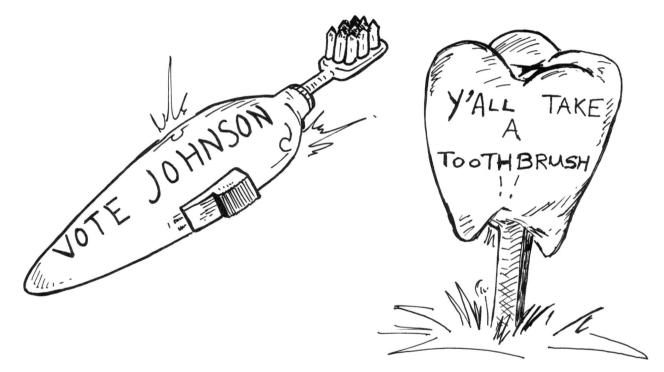

6. Six-year-old Shirley Temple.

7. James Buchanan.

8. FDR. In 1935 he established the Works Progress Administration which began a war against outhouses. WPA workers replaced them with buildings approved by the U.S. Public Health Service. In addition, many communities installed sanitary sewers.

9. Bill Clinton, when he chose Ruth Ginsburg in June of 1993.

10. Abe Lincoln, christening the community of Lincoln, Illinois.

11. Harry Truman.

12. In the congressional elections of 1894, during Grover Cleveland's unpopular second term, the opposing Republicans gained 117 members! The Republicans dominated the House for the next generation.

13. Warren Harding, whose papa was Dr. George Tryon Harding.

14. John Kennedy. Located on Narragansett Bay in Newport, Rhode Island, the Kennedys vacationed there. It is no ordinary farm; it's a mansion with twenty-eight rooms and spacious land.

15. None were named after the sixteenth President.

16. William Howard Taft, who refused to allow New Mexico and Arizona to become states because of their constitutional provisions for the recall of judges. After the clauses were removed, he signed the resolutions.

17. Chester A. Arthur, on Washington's birthday in 1885, just two weeks before he left office.

18. C – Harding. Buchanan, Tyler, and Lincoln all served brief stints in their state militia.

19. Woodrow Wilson, when he was sixteen. He became sick and had to spend one and a one-half years recuperating, then transferred to Princeton in 1875.

20. Fifty-three hours, in between William Henry Harrison's death and John Tyler's oath to succeed him in April of 1841.

21. His friend and former advisor Herbert Hoover. The book was published in 1958.

22. John and Abigail Adams' sons John Quincy, Charles, and Thomas.

23. Andrew Johnson. He believed the two territories did not have enough population and opposed their constitutions which granted voting rights to all blacks.

24. Franklin D. Roosevelt, in 1932.

25. Super Bowl XX in New Orleans.

26. Because of the death of Montana Senator Thomas Walsh. The popular Democratic leader had been designated as Roosevelt's Attorney-General.

27. James Garfield.

28. It was not FDR. George Washington, who served two terms as President, previously served for eight and one-half years as commander during the Revolutionary War, giving him a total of almost seventeen years.

29. William McKinley, whose grandfather, James, served gallantly in the Revolutionary War as well. McKinley's maternal grandfather also fought in the War of 1812 under Harrison.

30. Andrew Jackson. The young lawyer won this case, and the court awarded him and his client $4.00 in damages.

31. Theodore Roosevelt, who also wanted a federal divorce law. He abandoned both these ideas.

32. Thomas Jefferson, in 1804 when the Navy and Marines stormed the fort of Barbary pirates at Tripoli, Libya.

33. Each of these physicians were the first to administer aid to our assassinated Presidents. Leale to Lincoln, Townshend to Garfield, Hall to McKinley, and Carrico to Kennedy.

34. Abraham Lincoln.

35. James Buchanan of Pennsylvania. The village is located four miles west of Mercersburg, but the original log cabin in which Buchanan was born was relocated to Chambersburg, a few miles away.

36. *War is Hell.* Oswald ran into the theater without buying a ticket.

37. Zachary Taylor, Franklin Pierce, and U.S. Grant. Jefferson Davis, who was also a president, served in that war.

38. Nathaniel Fillmore, who lived to be ninety-two-years-old.

39. George Washington, whose brother, Lawrence, died in 1752.

40. LBJ.

41. Martin Van Buren of Kinderhook, NY. He lived in this thirty room brick home until his death in 1862.

42. Martin Van Buren, whose son, Abraham, was an aide to General Zachary Taylor.

43. FDR, in 1943. This was due to a fuel and energy shortage during World War II. Many teams stayed indoors up north for their spring training.

44. Theodore Roosevelt, born in New York City.

45. James A. Garfield, who rode him during the Civil War. Another mount he used was named "Harry."

46. FDR, who in 1942, asked for investigations of suspected communists and Nazi sympathizers. In addition, a couple of newspaper columnists became targets.

47. He was sick with pneumonia for several months.

48. Jimmy Carter, whose father Earl, could beat Jimmy on the courts even when the boy became an adult.

49. U.S. Grant, whose grandfather, Noah Grant, later settled in Pennsylvania. Incidentally, Noah's son, Jesse (Grant's father), lived for a time with the fiery abolitionist John Brown in a two-story red brick building in Deerfield, Ohio.

50. Herbert Hoover, who received a penny for every 100 bugs killed.

51. Andrew Johnson of Tennessee. He believed Congress did not have the right to spend federal money for such purposes. It is interesting to note that, unlike the other Congressmen, Johnson contributed $50 of his own money to help the impoverished Irish.

52. William Henry Harrison, while serving as territorial governor of Indiana in 1800.

53. William Henry Harrison, who was recalled from Colombia by Andrew Jackson.

54. Benjamin Harrison, whose papa was once a U.S. Congressman.

55. Andrew Johnson, in his tailor shop in Greenville, Tennessee.

56. George Washington.

57. John Tyler in 1845.

58. Zachary Taylor, in the 1850 Clayton-Bulwer Treaty with Great Britain.

59. John Quincy Adams.

60. George W. Bush, our 43rd Chief Executive. He was fifteen years old and attending Phillips Exeter Academy in Massachusetts.

61. James Buchanan. Before the soldiers reached Utah, Buchanan's emissary had negotiated a peaceful settlement whereby Brigham Young and his followers agreed to abide by federal laws.

62. John Quincy Adams, then serving as our ambassador to Holland.

63. Thomas Jefferson, when he penned the defiant Kentucky Resolutions of 1798. His activities caused considerable difficulties for his President, John Adams.

64. Queen Victoria of England.

65. U.S. Grant, whose doctor regularly prescribed it for the suffering ex-President. Grant had cancer of the throat and found relief by using cocaine. Its addictive powers were unknown at the time, but Grant wrote that it was difficult to limit its use, even though he tried.

66. James Buchanan, age sixty-six when elected in 1856.

67. Former Governor George W. Bush, who bought and later sold the Texas Rangers.

68. Fifty-four years of age.

69. William Henry Harrison.

70. Calvin Coolidge.

71. Jefferson Davis! Davis was referring to the Confederacy in 1861.

72. Franklin Pierce. Barbara's maiden name is Pierce.

73. Richard Nixon, while practicing law in New York.

74. Richard Nixon.

75. John Quincy Adams. The gifted son of our second President, he was enrolled in Leyden, Holland, in 1780 while John Sr. was the Dutch Ambassador. Father, incidentally, was admitted to Harvard in 1751 when he was only fifteen.

76. John Adams, who was accompanied by his sixteen year-old son, John Quincy. By the time Adams returned home, he had not seen his wife, Abigail, in four and a half years.

77. In Trenton, New Jersey. It was moved there temporarily due to the epidemic of yellow fever in Philadelphia.

78. John Adams, during Washington's two terms as President. Adams voted twenty-nine times.

79. John Adams, as a delegate to Congress.

80. Gerald Ford, during World War II where he saw plenty of action.

81. The appointment of John Marshall as Chief Justice of the Supreme Court.

82. Gerald Ford, while attending law school there.

83. Ronald Reagan of California.

84. Jimmy Carter.

85. Chester Arthur in 1884 when he lost the Republican bid to James G. Blaine.

86. U.S. Grant, back in June of 1869. Members of the Cincinnati Red Stockings, the first professional team, were invited to the White House. They were undefeated the first year in nearly 70 games, not losing until June 14, 1870, when they were defeated 8-7 in extra innings by the Brooklyn Atlantics.

87. Tear gas. Protesters gathered in Washington to demonstrate against the Shah's arrival, and police dispersed the crowds when disorder began. Reporters and dignitaries alike at the White House coughed and wiped their eyes.

88. FDR, at Groton in 1897.

89. Yes. Andrew Johnson; his oldest son, Charles, a doctor in the Tennessee Union Infantry, was killed when he was thrown from his horse in 1863.

90. Former President Grover Cleveland at Princeton.

91. Grover Cleveland, who used it while hunting in the Adirondacks.

92. Gerald Ford, when he debated challenger Jimmy Carter in 1976.

93. Tennessee. Its governor was Unionist Andrew Johnson, who convinced him that such a move would antagonize Union supporters in a confederate state.

94. Eisenhower, who gave up smoking in 1949.

95. Chester Arthur, as a student at Union College in Schenectady, New York.

96. Andrew Johnson and William McKinley.

97. In Article II, Section I of the Constitution.

98. William Gladstone, the great Prime Minister of England.

99. Harry Truman, in the small Missouri town during 1914-15.

100. Andrew Johnson.

101. Fifteen! They were Andrew Jackson (an adopted son), Van Buren, William Henry Harrison, Tyler, Pierce (a son which died in infancy), Andrew Johnson, Grant, Arthur, Theodore Roosevelt, Coolidge, Hoover, Franklin D. Roosevelt, Kennedy, Reagan and Bush.

102. William Henry Harrison. In 1781 Arnold led Hessians and American Tories in an attack at Berkeley, Virginia.

103. Dwight Eisenhower. After the allied victory over Nazi Germany in 1945, Stalin allowed the general to view a large sports parade from atop the shrine.

104. John F. Kennedy, whose PT-boat skippers said he frequently complained, "I've been shafted."

105. Abe Lincoln, who kept his seamstress-wife busy all his married life.

106. Ulysses Grant.

107. Bill Clinton, whose mother, Virginia, died of breast cancer in January of 1994.

108. At an unmarked grave in the Booth family plot in Baltimore. In 1865 Booth's body was secretly buried beneath the floor of the ammunition room of the Old Penitentiary in Washington, D.C. Four years later it was removed by relatives to Baltimore.

109. Abraham Lincoln's first V.P., Schyler Colfax.

110. Warren G. Harding, on November 2, 1920. Harding turned fifty-five-years-old.

111. John F. Kennedy.

112. John Wilkes Booth, who occupied the same room just a couple of weeks before he shot the President.

113. Harry Truman.

114. They all had brothers who served in the U.S. Congress, either in the Senate or the House of Representatives. All of these men were also elected only once as President.

115. Yes!

116. Theodore Roosevelt. After retiring from office, TR went on several adventures. While on a safari in British East Africa in 1910, he discovered a small carnivorous fox. The Smithsonian Institution announced the animal would be labeled "Vergatus Otocyon Rooseveltus."

117. FDR, while vacationing in the early 1920s.

118. Benjamin Harrison.

119. Andrew Jackson, who at thirteen years old served as a messenger to continental forces in 1780. He and his brother were taken as prisoners by the British the following year, spending two weeks in captivity. Incidentally, both of Jackson's brothers, Hugh and Robert, along with their mother, all died during the war.

120. Zachary Taylor, during the War of 1812. One other brother who served as an artillery officer, was killed in battle by Indians in 1808 in Tennessee.

121. John Kennedy, during World War II. Brother Joe flew a bomber in Europe and was killed when his plane exploded in mid-air. Bobby served on a destroyer in the Caribbean.

122. In this letter the President urged major league players to continuing playing, even though World War II raged. He felt it would be good for morale.

123. William Howard Taft, on a verbal offer with the Cincinnati Reds.

124. James K. Polk, whose brother, Samuel, was dismissed from Yale for taking part in a student riot.

125. Chester Arthur, whose brother William was wounded at the battle of Ream's Station. Chester, incidentally, served as a quartermaster and brigadier general during the war, but saw no battlefield action.

126. He thought it was a raccoon.

127. Theodore Roosevelt, who explored the jungles of Brazil and chartered an unknown river which was called the River of Doubt, also known as the Rio Tedo.

128. The Eisenhowers. That is the name of their burial plot at the twenty-one acre Eisenhower Library in Abilene, Kansas.

129. Thomas Jefferson, whose cousin and political opponent, John Marshall, was also Chief Justice at the time. Jefferson had appointed James Madison as Secretary of State, but he was not in Washington. Jefferson asked Marshall to remain as Secretary of State for one day.

130. Bill Clinton, when he was four years old.

131. His niece, Mabel McKinley, who later became a singer and songwriter.

132. Warren G. Harding, who owned the Marion ball club in the Ohio State League.

133. FDR, who attended eight Openers, from 1933 to 1941. The Washington Senators won four of the eight games. Eisenhower, incidentally, threw out the first pitch at seven opening Day games.

134. Technically, four. The Green Room, Blue Room, Red Room, and the Yellow Oval Room.

135. Lyndon B. Johnson's. Walter Jenkins' indiscretion caused the President much anguish and he remarked, "I had a heart attack and he had another kind of attack."

136. Thomas Jefferson, on June 1, 1781. He felt his term of office as Governor of Virginia was up. George W. Bush also resigned as Governor of Texas after his election as President in 2000.

137. No one.

138. The American flag, carried by a native porter.

139. William H. Taft in 1885.

140. Harding, along with Congress, presented the medals to Unknown Soldiers from Britain, France, United States, Italy, Belgium, and Rumania.

141. Theodore Roosevelt, who married Edith Carow (his second wife) in 1886.

142. To allow Jack, Washington's white horse he rode during the Revolutionary War, to be put on exhibit.

143. Out of respect for President Harrison's wife, who died on October 25.

144. New York Governor Thomas Dewey, who lost to Truman four years later.

145. Grover Cleveland, who raised Francis Folsom. As one of her legal guardians, he was twenty-eight years her senior and married her when she was twenty-one.

146. Fifty-one. There were fifty fighter planes (one for each state) and Air Force One.

147. The Kennedys, whose son, John Jr., was selected by *People* magazine in 1988. He died in a plane crash off the coast of Massachusetts in 1999, along with his wife and sister-in-law.

148. Only three – Kentucky, Tennessee, and Vermont.

149. John Tyler, whose four sons all joined the Confederacy. A fifth son worked in the southern Treasury for Jefferson Davis.

150. General Douglas MacArthur.

Questions about the First Ladies

(answers beginning on page 249)

1. Which 20th century First Lady was only thirty-one-years-old when she assumed her duties in the White House?

2. As a child, this First Lady was so sick she was never sent to school by her parents. Name her.

3. Which First Lady was the daughter of a Scottish shoemaker?

4. This future First Lady opened her home as a refuge for wounded and sick soldiers, and spent two winters as a volunteer nurse in a camp hospital near battlefields. Name her.

5. Name the First Lady who complained to a reporter, that "there are only five sleeping rooms and there is no feeling of privacy (in the White House)."

6. Which First Lady, prior to her term in the White House, underwent a blepharoplast – a procedure to correct drooping eyelids?

7. Which First Lady began Spanish classes at the White House, much to the delight of Latin Americans?

8. Who bore four children before she met her future husband/President?

9. Which First Lady dragged Congressmen through the slums of Washington, D.C. during her crusade to clean them up?

10. Which First Lady suffered from acrophobia, claustrophobia, and Méniére's Disease, a rare inner-ear syndrome causing dizziness?

11. Which First Lady's first name was Anna?

12. Which First Lady was always called "Frank" by her husband?

13. Who began the National Wildlife Research Center?

14. Which First Lady died on her husband's birthday?

15. Which First Lady's father went to Penn State University on an athletic scholarship and starred as a football player?

16. Which First Lady's father was Phi Beta Kappa and earned nine varsity letters at Miami University in Oxford, Ohio?

17. Who was first officially addressed as "First Lady"?

18. Which President's wife was formally addressed as "Your Majesty"?

19. As a college student, this future First Lady majored in interior decorating. Name her.

20. Which First Lady once taught deaf students?

21. A portrait by which artist hung above Mamie Eisenhower's White House bed?

22. Which President's wife assumed her duties as First Lady when she was 22 years old?

23. Name the First Lady who was a descendent of Pocahontas.

24. Which First Lady, christened Thelma Ryan, was born in Nevada?

25. Who was the first wife of a President to live in the White House?

26. Which First Lady was born overseas?

27. Who was born Elizabeth Bloomer and later became a dancer and model?

28. This President's wife also served as her husband's personal secretary. Name her.

29. Whose pet German shepherd dog once bit the Prime Minister of Canada?

30. Mary McElroy served as the official White House hostess for which President?

31. True or False: Both Pat Nixon and Jackie Kennedy were heavy smokers (cigarettes).

32. This future First Lady worked in a bank, taught Sunday school, cut her hair very short, and had a brother murdered by a jealous woman. Name her.

33. Which twentieth century First Lady discontinued the New Year's Day White House receptions, a tradition begun by Abigail Adams in 1801?

34. Which First Lady taught school and worked as a librarian in Texas?

35. She was the orphaned daughter of a Maryland planter, and made few appearances at the White House. Name her.

Answers to Questions about First Ladies

1. Jackie Kennedy

2. Abigail Smith Adams. She was tutored by her grandmother.

3. Eliza McCardle Johnson, wife of our seventeenth President.

4. Lucy Webb Hayes, wife of the 19th President, during the Civil War.

5. Mrs. Caroline Harrison, wife of our 23rd President.

6. Rosalynn Carter.

7. Bess Truman.

8. Martha Parke Custis. Two of her children died in infancy, and when the wealthy widow remarried, George Washington adopted the remaining two.

9. Ellen Wilson, Woodrow's first wife. As the First Lady lay dying, Congress passed her slum clearance bill. She died on August 6, 1914.

10. Mamie Eisenhower.

11. Eleanor Roosevelt.

12. Frances Cleveland.

13. Lady Bird Johnson, in December of 1985, at age 70.

14. Mrs. Edith Wilson. A widow, she died on December 28, 1961, at the age of 89.

15. Hillary Rodham Clinton, whose father Hughe Rodham played for the Nittany Lions.

16. Barbara Pierce Bush. Her father, Marvin, was the first person selected for Miami's "M" Club for his outstanding achievement.

17. Lucy Hayes, wife of our 19th President.

18. Martha Washington, who held receptions in New York City and Philadelphia.

19. Rosalynn Carter.

20. Grace Coolidge.

21. Her husband, Dwight D. Eisenhower.

22. Frances Folsom Cleveland.

23. Edith Wilson, the President's second wife.

24. Pat Nixon.

25. Abigail Adams.

26. Louisa Catherine Adams, born as an American citizen in London in 1775.

27. Betty Ford.

28. Sarah Polk.

29. Eleanor Roosevelt.

30. Chester Arthur, whose wife Ellen, died before he became President. Mary was his sister.

31. True.

32. Ida McKinley.

33. Lou Hoover

34. Laura Bush, wife of our 43rd President.

35. Margaret Mackall Smith Taylor, whose daughter Mary assumed the duties as hostess from 1849-50.

Lists and Matching Wits

Who were our most intellectual Presidents? Here is a list of Chief Executives who, in my opinion, rate among the top scholars, based on their scholastic achievement, originality, creativity, pursuit of knowledge, and published writings:

1. Thomas Jefferson
2. James A. Garfield
3. John Quincy Adams
4. Theodore Roosevelt
5. Woodrow Wilson
6. John F. Kennedy
7. Herbert Hoover
8. James Madison
9. Franklin D. Roosevelt
10. Bill Clinton
11. Chester A. Arthur
12. Harry Truman
13. James Buchanan
14. John Adams
15. Abraham Lincoln
16. Rutherford B. Hayes

THE 10 GREATEST PRESIDENTS
1. Abraham Lincoln
2. George Washington
3. Franklin D. Roosevelt
4. Thomas Jefferson
5. Woodrow Wilson
6. Theodore Roosevelt
7. Harry Truman
8. James Polk
9. Grover Cleveland
10. Andrew Jackson
    William McKinley

THE 10 GREATEST FIRST LADIES
1. Eleanor Roosevelt
2. Dolley Madison
3. Martha Washington
4. Harriet Lane (Buchanan)
5. Edith Wilson
6. Abigail Adams
7. Barbara Bush
8. Lou Hoover
9. Lucy Hayes
10. Lady Bird Johnson
    Hillary Clinton

THE 10 LEAST EFFECTIVE PRESIDENTS
1. Warren Harding
2. Ulysses Grant
3. Franklin Pierce
4. James Buchanan
5. Millard Fillmore
6. John Tyler
7. Benjamin Harrison
8. Andrew Johnson
9. Richard Nixon
10. James Madison

Match the Quotation with the President Who Made It

A. Lyndon B. Johnson

B. Theodore Roosevelt

C. Andrew Jackson

D. John F. Kennedy

E. Thomas Jefferson

F. Harry Truman

G. Dwight D. Eisenhower

1. "There is much vice and misery in the world, I know; but more virtue and happiness, I believe."

2. "Keep clear of two besetting sins — hardness of the heart and softness of the heart."

3. "The world has narrowed to a neighborhood before it has broadened to a brotherhood."

4. "Conformity is the jailer of freedom and the enemy of growth."

5. "The potential for the disastrous rise of misplaced power exists and will persist."

6. "The best way to give advice to your children is to find out what they want then advise them to do it."

7. "It's a damn poor mind that can think of only one way to spell a word."

Answers are on page 255

252

Match The Doodles

Presidents like to doodle, making sketches or drawings on note pads or stationery during a meeting. Listed below are seven examples of doodling. Match the respective drawings with the "artist."

1.   John F. Kennedy

2.   Abraham Lincoln

3.   Ronald Reagan

4.   Herbert Hoover

5.   Theodore Roosevelt

6.   Dwight Eisenhower

7.   George Bush

A.

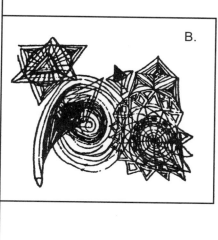

B.

F.

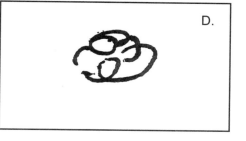

G.

D.

E.

C.

Answers to "Match Doodles" on page 255

More Lists and Matching

MATCH THE FOLLOWING PRESIDENTS WITH THEIR NICKNAMES

1. Petticoat Pet
2. Minority President
3. Old Granny
4. Teacher President
5. Great Peacemaker
6. Last of the Cocked Hats
7. Backwoodsman

A. Benjamin Harrison
B. James Monroe
C. William Henry Harrison
D. Ulysses S. Grant
E. Martin Van Buren
F. James A. Garfield
G. Abraham Lincoln

Answers to "Match the Presidents with Their Nicknames" on page 255

The 10 Presidents with the Greatest Wit and Sense of Humor (in order)

1. John F. Kennedy
2. Ronald Reagan
3. Abraham Lincoln
4. Gerald Ford
5. Franklin D. Roosevelt
6. Lyndon B. Johnson
7. William Howard Taft
8. Warren G. Harding
9. James A. Garfield
10. William McKinley
    Bill Clinton

The 10 Most Humorless Presidents

1. James K. Polk
2. Benjamin Harrison
3. John Adams
4. Richard Nixon
5. George Washington
6. Woodrow Wilson
7. Franklin Pierce
8. Herbert Hoover
9. Grover Cleveland
10. Jimmy Carter
    Rutherford B. Hayes

Match the Presidential Home with the Chief Executive

1. Lindenwald
2. The Beeches
3. Montpelier
4. Cyprus Grove
5. Spiegel Grove
6. Oak Hill
7. Westland
8. Wheatland

A. Calvin Coolidge
B. Zachary Taylor
C. James Buchanan
D. Martin Van Buren
E. Grover Cleveland
F. James Monroe
G. Rutherford B. Hayes
H. James Madison

Answers to "Match the Presidential Home with the Chief Executive" on page 255

Answers

Answers to the matching items on page 252

    1-E
    2-B
    3-A
    4-D
    5-G
    6-F
    7-C

Answers to "Match the Doodles" on page 253

    1-C
    2-D
    3-A
    4-B
    5-E
    6-F
    7-G

Answers to "Match Presidents and Their Nicknames"

    1-E
    2-A
    3-C
    4-F
    5-D
    6-B
    7-G

Answers to "Match the Presidential Home with the Chief Executive"

    1-D
    2-A
    3-H
    4-B
    5-G
    6-F
    7-E
    8-C

American Presidents III – Bibliography

Alden, John R. *George Washington: A Biography*. Wings Books, New York and Avenel, New Jersey, 1995.

Alsop, Joseph. *FDR 1882-1945: A Centenary Remembrance*. Thorndike Press, Thorndike, Maine, 1982.

Ambrose, Stephen E. *Eisenhower – Soldier and President*. Simon and Schuster, New York, 1990.

Anderson, Judith Icke. *William Howard Taft*. W. W. Norton & Company, New York, 1981.

Angelo, Bonnie. *First Mothers: The Women Who Shaped the Presidents*. William Morrow, New York, 2000.

Anthony, Carl Sferrazza. *First Ladies: The Saga of the Presidents' Wives and Their Power 1789-1961*. William Morrow and Company, Inc., New York, 1990.

Armstrong, William H. *William McKinley and Civil War*. Kent State University Press, Canton, Ohio, 2000.

Aurandt, Paul. *More of Paul Harvey's The Rest of the Story*. William Morrow and Company, Inc., New York, 1980.

Baker, James A. III. *The Politics of Diplomacy: Revolution, War, and Peace*. G. P. Putnam's Sons, New York, 1995.

Baker, Leonard. *John Marshall: A Life in Law*. MacMillan Publishing Company, New York, 1974.

Bassett, Margaret. *Profiles and Portraits of American Presidents*. The Bond Wheelwright Company, Freeport, Maine, 1964.

Bauer, Stephen M. *At Ease in The White House*. A Birch Lane Press Book, New York, 1991.

Beard, Charles A. and Mary R. *A Basic History of the United States*. Doubleday, Doran, and Company, New York, 1944.

Belden, Henry III. *Grand Tour of Ida Saxton McKinley and Sister Mary Saxton Barber, 1869*. The Reserve Printing Company, Canton, Ohio, 1985.

Bennett, William J. *The Death of Outrage*. The Free Press, New York, 1998.

Berg, A. Scott. *Lindbergh*. G. P. Putnams' Sons, New York, 1998.

Bergere, Richard and Thea. *Houses of the Presidents*. Dodd, Mead, and Company, New York, 1962.

Bishop, Jim. *FDR's Last Year*. William Morrow and Company, New York, 1974.

Blodgett, Bonnie and Tice, D. J. *At Home with the Presidents*. The Overlook Press, Woodstock, New York, 1988.

Bloom, Vera. *There's No Place Like Washington*. G. P. Putnam, New York, 1944.

Boller, Paul F. Jr. *Presidential Wives*. Oxford University Press, New York and Oxford, 1988.

Boller, Paul F. Jr. *Presidential Campaigns*. Oxford University Press, New York and Oxford, 1996.

Brinkley, David. *David Brinkley: A Memoir*. Alfred A. Knopf, New York, 1995.

Brodie, Fawn M. *Thomas Jefferson–An Intimate History*. W. W. Norton and Company, Inc., New York, 1974.

Brooks, Stewart M. *Our Assassinated Presidents: The True Medical Stories*. Bell Publishing Company, New York, 1985.

Brown, Edmund G. and Brown, Bill. *Reagan – The Political Chameleon*. Praeger Publishers, New York, 1976.

Buchman, Dian Dincin. *Our 41st President – George Bush*. Scholastic, Inc., New York, 1989.

Burns, George. *Gracie: A Love Story*. G. P. Putnam's Sons, New York, 1988.

Bush, Barbara. *A Memoir*. Charles Scribner's Sons, New York, 1994.

Bush, George. *Looking Forward*. Doubleday, New York, 1987.

Butcher, Harry C. *My Three Years with Eisenhower*. Simon and Schuster, New York, 1946.

Canfield, Cass. *The Iron Will of Jefferson Davis*. Fairfax Press, New York, 1978.

Caro, Robert A. *The Years of Lyndon Johnson: Means of Ascent*. Alfred A. Knopf, New York, 1990.

Caroli, Betty Boyd. *First Ladies: An Intimate Look at How 36 Women Handled What May Be the Most Demanding, Unpaid, Unelected Job in America*. Oxford University Press, 1987.

Carr, William H. *JFK: A Complete Biography 1917-1963*. Lance Books, New York, 1963.

Carter, Jimmy and Rosalynn. *Everything to Gain*. Random House, New York, 1987.

Carter, Jimmy. *The Virtues of Aging*. The Ballentine Publishing Group, New York, 1998.

Cash, James B. *Unsung Heroes–Ohioans in the White House: A Modern Appraisal*. Orange Frazer Press, Wilmington, Ohio, 1998.

Catton, Bruce. *U.S. Grant and the American Military Tradition*. Little, Brown, and Company, Boston, 1954.

Celsi, Teresa. *John C. Calhoun And The Roots of War*. Silver Burdett Press, Englewood Cliffs, New Jersey, 1991.

Chellis, Marcia. *Living With the Kennedys: The Joan Kennedy Story*. A Jove Book/Simon and Schuster, New York 1986.

Chidsey, Donald Barr. *And Tyler Too*. Thomas Nelson Inc., Publishers, New York and Nashville, 1978.

Clifford, Clark. *Counsel To The President: A Memoir*. Random House, New York, 1991.

Collins, Herbert Ridgeway. *Presidents on Wheels*. Acropolis Books, Ltd., Washington, D.C., 1971.

Condon, Dianne Russell. *Jackie's Treasures: The Fabled Objects from the Auction of the Century*. Cader Books, Clarkson Potter Publishers, New York, 1996.

Dole, Bob. *Great Political Wit*. Nan A. Talese–Doubleday, New York, 1998.

Donaldson, Sam. *Hold On, Mr. President!* Random House, New York, 1987.

Edwards, Anne. *Early Reagan: The Rise to Power*. William Morrow and Company, Inc., New York, 1987.

Edwards, Anne. *Shirley Temple: America's Princess*. William Morrow and Company, Inc., New York, 1988.

Eisenhower, Dwight D. *Crusade in Europe*. Doubleday and Company, Inc., Garden City, New York, 1948.

Eisenhower, Julie Nixon. *Special People.* Simon and Schuster, New York, 1977.

Fay, Paul B. Jr. *The Pleasure of His Company*. Harper & Row, New York, 1966.

Felsenthal, Carol. *Alice Roosevelt Longsworth*. G. P. Putnam's Sons, New York, 1988.

Ferling, John. *John Adams – A Life*. Owl Books, Henry Holt and Company, New York, 1996.

Ferrell, Robert H. *Truman – A Centenary Remembrance*. Viking Press, New York, 1984.

Ferrell, Robert H., ed. *Dear Bess – The Letters from Harry to Bess Truman*. W. W. Norton and Company, New York, 1983.

Flood, Robert, ed. *America – God Shed His Grace On Thee*. Moody Press, Chicago, 1975.

Ford, Gerald. *A Time To Heal*. Berkley Books, New York, 1979.

Frost, Elizabeth, ed. *The Bully Pulpit: Quotations from America's Presidents*. Facts On File Publications, New York, 1988.

Gallen, Dave. *Bill Clinton As They Knew Him*. First Gallen Publishing Group, New York, 1994.

Gardner, Gerald. *All The Presidents' Wits*. Beech Tree Books, William Morrow, New York, 1986.

Garraty, John A. *1,001 Things Everyone Should Know About American History*. Doubleday, New York, 1989.

Garrison, Webb. *A Treasury of White House Tales*. Rutledge Hill Press, Nashville, Tennessee, 1989.

Gerson, Noel B. *The Velvet Glove: A Life of Dolly Madison*. Thomas Nelson Inc., Nashville, Tennessee, 1975.

Goldhurst, Richard. *Many Are The Hearts: The Agony and Triumph of Ulysses S. Grant*. Reader's Digest Press, New York, 1975.

Gould, Lewis L. *The Presidency of William McKinley*. The Regents Press of Kansas, Lawrence, 1980.

Goustad, Edwin S. *Faith of Our Fathers*. Harper & Row, Publishers, San Francisco, 1987.

Green, Mark and MacColl, Gail. *Reagan's Reign of Error*. Pantheon Books, New York, 1987.

Hagedorn, Hermann. *The Roosevelt Family of Sagamore Hill*. The MacMillan Company, New York, 1954.

Haig, Alexander M. Jr. *Inner Circles*. Warner Books, New York, 1992.

Harwood, Richard and Johnson, Haynes. *Lyndon*. Praeger Publishers, New York, 1973.

Hatch, Alden. *Red Carpet for Mamie*. Henry Holt and Company, New York, 1954.

Hay, Peter. *All the President's Ladies*. Viking Penguin Inc., New York, 1988.

Herbert, David Donald. *Lincoln*. Simon & Schuster, New York, 1995.

Hinckley, Jack and Joann. *Breaking Points*. Chosen Books, Grand Rapids, Michigan, 1985.

Hope, Bob. *Bob Hope's Confessions of a Hooker: My Lifelong Love Affair with Golf*. Doubleday & Company, Garden City, New York, 1985.

Hope, Bob. *Don't Shoot, It's Only Me*. G. P. Putnam's Sons, New York, 1990.

Hornby, George. *The Great Americana Scrap Book*. Crown Publishers, Inc., New York, 1985.

Hoyt, Edwin P. *Andrew Johnson*. Reilly and Company, Chicago, 1965.

Johnson, Gerald W. *The Cabinet*. William Morrow and Company, New York, 1966.

Johnson, Gerald W. *Woodrow Wilson*. Harper & Brothers, Publishers, New York, 1944.

Johnson, Rossiter. *Campfires And Battlefields*. The Civil War Press, New York, 1967.

Kessler, Ronald. *Inside Congress*. Pocket Books, New York, 1997.

Kirk, Elise K. *Music at The White House*. University of Illinois Press, Urbana and Chicago, 1986.

Knepper, George W. *An Ohio Portrait*. Ohio Historical Society, Columbus, Ohio, 1976.

Koch, Freda Postle. *Colonel Coggeshall – The Man Who Saved Lincoln*. PoKo Press, Columbus, Ohio, 1985.

Koenig, Louis W. *The Chief Executive*. Harcourt, Brace and World, Inc., New York, 1968.

Kohlsaat, H. H. *From McKinley to Harding: Personal Recollections of Our Presidents*. Charles Scribner's Sons, New York, 1923.

Kunhardt, Philip, Jr., ed. *Life in Camelot – The Kennedy Years*. Little, Brown and Company, Boston, 1988.

Kutler, Stanley I. *Abuse of Power: The New Nixon Tapes*. The Free Press, New York, 1997.

Leggett, Carol. *Reba McEntire: The Queen of Country*. A Fireside Book, New York, 1992.

Les Benedict, Michael. *The Impeachment and Trial of Andrew Johnson*. W. W. Norton & Company, Inc., New York, 1973.

Levin, Phyllis Lee. *Abigail Adams*. St. Martin's Press, New York, 1987.

Linton, Calvin D. *The Bicentennial Almanac*. Thomas Nelson, Inc., New York and Nashville, 1975.

Lynch, Denis Tilden. *An Epoch And a Man: Martin Van Buren and His Times*. Kennikat Press, Port Washington, New York, 1971.

Lyons, Eugene. *Herbert Hoover – A Biography*. Doubleday and Company, Inc., Garden City, New York, 1964.

Magill, Frank N. and Loos, John L. *The American Presidents: The Office and the Men*. Salem Press, Pasadena, California, 1986.

Mazo, Earl. *Richard Nixon*. Avon Book Division, New York, 1960.

McClendon, Sarah. *Mr. President! Mr. President!: My 50 years of Covering the White House*. General Publishing Group, Los Angeles, 1996.

McCullough, David Willis, ed. *American Childhoods: An Anthology*. Little, Brown and Company, Boston and Toronto, 1987.

McElroy, Richard L. *American Presidents: Fascinating Facts, Stories & Questions of Our Chief Executives and Their Families*. Daring Books, Canton, Ohio, 1984.

McElroy, Richard L. *James A. Garfield, His Life and Times – A Pictorial History*. Daring Books, Canton, Ohio, 1986.

McElroy, Richard L. *William McKinley and Our America: A Pictorial History*. Stark County Historical Society, Canton, Ohio, 1996.

McReynolds, B. S. *Presidential Blips: Dips, Flips, Lip, Pips, Quips, Slips, Tips and Zips*. B. S. Book Publishing, University City, California, 1998.

Mead, William B. and Dickson, Paul. *Baseball – The Presidents' Game*. Farragut Publishing Company, Washington, D.C., 1993.

Means, Marianne. *The Woman in the White House*. Random House, New York, 1963.

Meredith, Roy, ed. *Mr. Lincoln's General – U.S. Grant: An Illustrated Autobiography*. Bonanza Books, New York, 1981.

Moody, Sid. *Pearl Harbor: 50th Anniversary Special Edition*. Longmeadow Press, Stamford, Connecticut, 1991.

Morgan, H. Wayne. *William McKinley and His America*. Syracuse University Press, Syracuse, New York, 1963.

Morgan, James. *Theodore Roosevelt: The Boy and the Man*. Grosset & Dunlap, New York, 1919.

Morris, Roger. *Partners in Power: The Clintons and Their America*. A John Macrae Book. Henry Holt and Company, New York, 1996.

Morris, Sylvia Jukes. *Rage for Fame: The Ascent of Clare Booth Luce*. Random House, New York, 1997.

Moses, John B., M.D. and Cross, Wilbur. *Presidential Courage*. W. W. Norton & Company, New York, 1980.

Myers, Elisabeth P. *William Howard Taft*. Reilly & Lee, Chicago, 1970.

Nash, Bruce and Zullo, Allan. *The Baseball Hall of Shame #3*. Pocket Books, New York, 1987.

Nelson, Rex. *The Hillary Factor*. Gallen Publishing Group, New York, 1993.

Nisenson, Samuel and Gollings, Franklin. *Great Moments in American History*. The Lion Press, Inc., New York, 1967.

Niven, John. *Martin Van Buren*. Oxford University Press, Oxford and New York, 1983.

O'Neill, Thomas P. *Man of the House*. Random House, New York, 1987.

Osbeck, Kenneth W. *101 Hymn Stories*. Kregel Publications, Grand Rapids, Michigan, 1982.

Parks, Arva Moore. *Harry Truman and the Little White House in Key West*. Centennial Press, Miami, Florida, 1991.

Peare, Catherine Owens. *The FDR Story*. Thomas Y. Crowell Company, New York, 1962.

Pierpoint, Robert. *At the White House*. G. P. Putnam's Sons, New York, 1981.

Piersall, Jimmy. *The Truth Hurts*. Contemporary Books, Inc., Chicago, 1984.

Powell, Colin L. *My American Journey*. Random House, New York, 1995.

Quayle, Dan. *Standing Firm–A Vice Presidential Memoir*. Harper Collins Publishers, New York, 1994.

Reagan, Nancy. *My Turn: The Memoirs of Nancy Reagan*. Random House, New York, 1989.

Reagan, Nancy. *Nancy*. Berkley Books, New York, 1980.

Ring, Malvin E., DDS. *Dentistry – An Illustrated History*. Harry N. Abrams, Inc., New York, 1985.

Roosevelt, James. *My Parents: A Differing View*. A Playboy Press Book, Chicago, 1976.

Rutland, Robert A. *James Madison: The Founding Father*. MacMillan Publishing Company, New York, 1987.

Sandburg, Carl. *Lincoln Collector: The Story of Oliver Barrett's Great Private Collection*. Bonanza Books, New York, 1960.

Schafer, Kermit. *The Bedside Book of Celebrity Bloopers*. Price Paperbacks–Crown Publishers, Inc., New York, 1984.

Scharf, Lois. *Eleanor Roosevelt, First Lady of American Liberalism*. Twayne Publishers. Boston, 1987.

Schlesinger, Arthur M. *The Imperial Presidency*. Houghton Mifflin Company, Boston, 1973.

Schroeder, Pat, Congresswoman. *Champion of the Great American Family*. Random House, New York, 1989.

Seager, Robert II. *And Tyler Too*. McGraw Hill Book Company, Inc., New York, 1963.

Seale, William. *The President's House: A History*. White House Historical Association, Washington, D.C., 1986.

Sharp & Dunnigan Publications. *The Congressional Medal of Honor*. Sharp & Dunnigan, Forest Ranch, California, 1984.

Shaw, Maud. *White House Nanny: My Years with Caroline and John Kennedy, Jr.* The New American Library, New York, 1966.

Shorto, Russell. *David Farragut and The Great Naval Blockade*. Silver Burdett Press, Englewood Cliffs, New Jersey, 1991.

Shultz, Gladys Denny. *Jenny Lind, The Swedish Nightingale*. J. B. Lippincott Company, Philadelphia and New York, 1962.

Sievers, Harry J. *Benjamin Harrison: Hoosier President (The White House Years and After, 1889-1901)*. The Bobbs Merrill Company, Indianapolis, 1968.

Smith, Don. *Peculiarities of the Presidents*. Wilkinson Printing Company, Van Wert, Ohio, 1938.

Smith, Gene. *When The Cheering Stopped*. William Morrow and Company, Inc., New York, 1964.

Smith, Paige. *Trial By Fire: A People's History of the Civil War and Reconstruction*. McGraw Hill Book Company, New York, 1982.

Smithsonian Institution. *Every Four Years*. Smithsonian Books, Washington, D.C., 1984.

Soberg, Carl. *Hubert Humphrey–A Biography.* W. W. Norton and Company, New York, 1984.

Spada, James. *Peter Lawford: The Man Who Kept The Secrets*. Bantam Books, New York, 1991.

Spencer, Cornelia. *Straight Furrow: The Biography of Harry S. Truman for Young People*. The John Day Company, New York, 1949.

Spielman, William Carl. *William McKinley: Stalwart Republican*. Exposition Press, New York, 1954.

Sterling, Bryan B. *The Will Rogers Scrapbook*. Bonanza Books, New York, 1976.

Stewart, James B. *Blood Sport*. Simon & Schuster, New York, 1996.

Strouse, Jean. *Morgan: American Financier.* Random House, New York, 1999.

Tharp, Louise Hall. *The Peabody Sisters of Salem*. McIntosh and Otis, Inc., New York, 1997.

Trefousse, Hans L. *Andrew Johnson – A Biography*. W. W. Norton and Company, New York, 1989.

Truman, Harry (edited by Margaret Truman). *Where The Buck Stops.* Warner Books, New York, 1989.

Truman, Margaret. *Bess W. Truman*. Jove Books, New York, 1986.

Truman, Margaret. *First Ladies*. Random House, New York, 1995.

Welsh, Douglas. *The Complete Military History of The Civil War*. Dorset Press, Greenwich, Connecticut, 1990.

White, Theodore. *Breach of Faith*. Atheneum Publishers, Reader's Digest Press, New York, 1975.

Williams, John Hoyt. *Sam Houston*. Promontory Press, New York, 1993.

Wilmerding, Lucius Jr. *James Monroe: Public Claimant*. Rutgers University Press, New Brunswick, New Jersey, 1960.

Witcover, Jules. *Marathon: The Pursuit of the Presidency 1972-1976*. Viking Press, New York, 1977.

Young, Hugo. *The Iron Lady: A Biography of Margaret Thatcher*. Farras Straus Giroux, New York, 1989.

Newspapers and Magazines

Akron Beacon Journal
Arizona Daily Star
Buckeye Flyer
Canton Repository
Cleveland Plain Dealer
Columbus Dispatch
Echoes (Ohio Historical Society)
National Geographic
Newsweek
Parade
Presidential History
Presidential Studies Quarterly
Profiles in History
Reader's Digest
Theodore Roosevelt Association Journal
Time
USA Today
Washington Post